About the Au

As a magazine writer in Boston, Barbara Carlson feasted on raw oysters; as a reporter on the *Louisville Times,* she savored country ham and, on visits to the racetrack, mint juleps and burgoo; reporting for the *Hartford Courant,* she often sustained herself with pizza or spinach bread, both invented in Connecticut. Newspaper assignments overseas took her from Iceland to Egypt to Vietnam and countries in between, enabling her to continue eating and also providing the opportunity to study the foods of other cultures: Caviar for breakfast, lunch, and dinner in Russia. Turkey stew eaten with the fingers in a thatch-roofed mud hut in Uganda. Reindeer meat in Finland.

She began her gastronomical explorations at Wellesley College, where she threw codfish cakes at trees. Career high points since then have included covering the Gilroy Garlic Festival in California to wolf down garlic-flavored ice cream and alligator tail, and being a Christmas tree in a three-ring circus, proving that she is not obsessed with food.

She and her husband live a stone's throw from clam flats in Branford, Connecticut.

Let Visible Ink Press
Help Satisfy Your Wanderlust

Music Festivals From Bach to Blues: A Traveler's Guide

"A unique listener's guide to all genres of tuneful revelry across North America." —*Time International*

Music Festivals takes you coast to coast, exploring the full spectrum of North American music festivals, including the Chicago Gospel Festival, New York's Lake George Opera Festival, and the South by Southwest Music and Media Conference in Austin, Texas.

Tom Clynes ⊛ ISBN 0-7876-0823-8 ⊛ 582 pages

Pop Culture Landmarks: A Traveler's Guide

"Celebrates the grand and the goofy." —*Washington Post*

On your weekend getaways, cross-country treks, or armchair expeditions, *Pop Culture Landmarks* will help you explore some 300 shrines to modern Americana, from the Rod Serling Exhibit in Binghampton, New York, to the National Cowgirl Hall of Fame in Hereford, Texas, to the Drive-In Movie Motel in Monte Vista, Colorado.

George Cantor ⊛ ISBN 0-8103-9899-0 ⊛ 401 pages

Wild Planet! 1,001 Extraordinary Events for the Inspired Traveler

"An extensive and exhilarating guide to the world's festivals, celebrations, and other amazing moments." —*Outside Magazine*

With *Wild Planet*, you can access the world's most extraordinary events, enabling you to participate in the culture of the places you visit, rather than just watching from a tour bus.

Tom Clynes ⊛ ISBN 0-7876-0203-5 ⊛ 669 pages

Historic Festivals: A Traveler's Guide

"Takes travelers on an entertaining coast-to-coast tour celebrating the richness of America's cultural heritage." —*Time International*

Journey across the U.S. with *Historic Festivals*, celebrating the nation's history with visits to such events as Florida's Gasparilla Pirate Invasion, Iowa's Steamboat Days, and the Boston Tea Party Reenactment in Massachusetts.

George Cantor ⊛ ISBN 0-7876-0824-6 ⊛ 392 pages

Food Festivals

Food Festivals

Eating Your Way from Coast to Coast

Barbara
Carlson

VISIBLE
INK
PRESS

DETROIT • NEW YORK • TORONTO • LONDON

Food Festivals
Eating Your Way from Coast to Coast

Published by Visible Ink Press ®
a division of Gale Research
835 Penobscot Building
Detroit, MI 48226-4094
Visible Ink Press is a trademark of Gale Research.

Most Visible Ink Press books are available at special quantity discounts when purchased in bulk by corporations, organizations, or groups. Customized printings, special imprints, messages, and excerpts can be produced to meet your needs. For more information, contact Special Markets Manager, Gale Research, 835 Penobscot Bldg., Detroit, MI 48226. Or call 1-800-776-6265.

Art Director: Pamela A. E. Galbreath
Typesetting: The Graphix Group

Library of Congress Cataloging-in-Publication Data

Carlson, Barbara W.
    Food festivals: eating your way from coast to coast / Barbara W. Carlson.
        p. cm.
    Includes bibliographical references and index.
    ISBN 1-57859-003-5
    1. Festivals—United States—Guidebooks. 2. Cookery—United States—Guidebooks. 3. United States—Social life and customs—1971—Guidebooks. I. Title.
GT4803.C37   1997
394.26973—dc21   97-971
                                                    CIP

For Helen M. Ahles
A true princess

SRA   XOXO
     CockBook
Food Festivals

     $ 3.00

Contents

Northeast

Southeast

Great Lakes & Ohio Valley

Great Plains

West & Pacific

Introduction

No matter how much you've studied and prepared for a long journey, there will always be surprises around that bend in the road, in that hamlet beyond the next hill.

Writing this book was a journey, alternately exciting, fun, arduous, comical, instructive, and, above all, surprising. The biggest surprise was that the more I learned of the festivals and foods of America, the more I began to visualize the United States as one huge festive table, stretching from the Atlantic out into the Pacific.

Picture this table as I do: A brimming buffet of foods—bright mounds of oranges and papayas and guavas in one sunlit corner, and across from that lush corner, scarlet boiled lobsters and pitchers of maple syrup clinking against plates stacked with blueberry buckwheat pancakes. Move along the table to sonkers and sorghum and Pennsylvania Dutch dumplings, and, where there's steel tableware, look for kielbasa and kolaches. The center of the table sags with heavy stews and *saucisebroodjes*. Peanut brittle is in a dish next to a platter of sizzling fried catfish; and then in a bounteous welter there are stuffed chiles and strawberries and baked salmon and apple pies and geoduck stew and fermented whale and—ah, relief—steaming cups of Kona coffee to sip and savor.

Enough.

The vision is fanciful. But it is not as absurd as it might at first seem. America is the greatest exporter of foods in the world, and among the greatest producers. We are the number-one grower of corn, the second largest producer of pigs, chickens, tomatoes, and apples (China is first in all those categories). We rank third in the production of cattle and wheat (India and Brazil surpass us in cattle production, China and India in wheat).

The agriculture of California alone is one of the most diversified in the world. The state produces more than 250 crop and livestock commodities, ranging from dates, originally imported from Egypt, to practically all the almonds, artichokes, figs, prunes, and raisins grown in the United States. Florida grows 32 percent of the world's grapefruit, and only Brazil grows more oranges than the Sunshine State. The United States and Canada produce virtually all the world's supply of maple syrup, cranberries, and tiny lowbush blueberries.

Some of our vegetables and fruits are native; more have come, now or in the past, from around the world. The migration of crops is a wondrous thing: Consider the tomato, which was first known in South America, went to Europe, came back to America, but was regarded suspiciously for quite a while. First people thought it was poisonous, and then they worried that it was an aphrodisiac.

What we have done with these wandering crops is to cultivate and hybridize them, and transform them with the recipes from every land. Some argue that America has no national cuisine. I don't agree. We retain ethnic foods—Norwegian *lefses,* Italian lasagnas, German bratwurst—but we have synergized them into a marvelous whole. We eat food every day that might come from a dozen lands.

This insight, that the diversity of our cuisine is what makes it a distinctive national cuisine, was another surprise—and it shouldn't have been. As a child in Connecticut, I ate steamers and lobsters and succotash, all introduced to early settlers by Native Americans; my bred-in-the-bone Yankee mother served up baked beans and fried shad roe and pumpkin pie; my Swedish aunt treated us to *inlagd sill* and lutefisk. Visits to my grandparents in Florida gave us tastes of the tropics; my grandfather grew mangoes and papayas out back and had a grapefruit tree in the front yard. I was an American child eating American food.

There is nothing new about the importation and cross-pollination of foods. In the tangled history of pasta, Marco Polo is credited with bringing noodles back to Italy from China, but Arabs or Indians might have slipped noodles into Italy earlier. Thomas Jefferson, a passionate farmer and gourmet, collected recipes when he lived in Paris. One recipe was for noodles. At home in Virginia, he mixed them with parmesan, and today macaroni and cheese is rarely absent from a potluck supper.

The festivals in this book have been chosen to illustrate the great abundance of American foods and the diversity of our heritage as it's mirrored in the American cuisine. The festivals, lively affairs, also show the pride of Americans in their heritage, their towns, and the fruit of their fields or rivers or oceans.

You see this pride in the contests for biggest tomato or best apple pie, and in a water tower painted like a pumpkin, or a big concrete strawberry in front of the firehouse. You see it in Dutch street-washing ceremonies, Basque contests of strength, and Cajun two-step dancing to accordion music.

There were several criteria for selecting a festival. The most important were that the festival honor a crop grown or harvested in the region, and important to the region, or at one time grown in the region (like Lenexa, Kansas, now a suburb but once the place where a Belgian farmer topped spinach-growing records); or that it reflect the ethnic history of a region; or that it feature an unusual regional food or crop (like grape pie in Naples, New York, ramp in Waynesville, North Carolina, alligator in Anahuac, Texas).

There was a final reason for choosing any festival: it struck my fancy. I like a festival that has the world's biggest bowl of guacamole, or a hollering contest, or a parade with people dressed like vegetables.

This, then, is a somewhat arbitrary listing, and it is by no means a listing of every food festival in the United States. There could be a book the size of this on nothing but Oktoberfests and other German festivals, and another only slightly thinner book on every strawberry and watermelon festival. Two rattlesnake festivals are listed; there are countless more.

I hope you will use this book both as a guide and an inspiration to find other festivals and to learn more about the bounty and heritage of our country. Above all, I hope it will lead you to an understanding of how much our crops and cookery owe to both the natives of our land and America's waves of immigrants. They have given us—and continue to give us—the rich culinary traditions, the foodways, that are as much a part of our culture as jazz and blues and baseball and Georgia O'Keeffe paintings and Carl Sandburg poetry.

How to Use Food Festivals

Food Festivals is a guide to more than 400 noteworthy or unusual food festivals in the United States and to the histories and life cycles of the foods. It has been arranged and indexed to help you find festivals in the region you want to visit, at the time you'll be there, featuring the foods you would enjoy eating.

To find festivals in a particular region or state, consult the **Table of Contents.** States are arranged alphabetically within regional sections; cities where festivals are held are arranged alphabetically within the state; festivals are arranged chronologically within cities. The heading for each festival entry gives the date on which it is held. If the date says "weekend" it means Saturday and Sunday, unless other days are specified.

Each festival description concludes with **Location** and **Contact** information. Sometimes museums, landmarks, and the like are cited as points of interest that you may want to look into **While You're There.** Under **See Also,** you are referred to festivals covered elsewhere in the book that are related or that give additional information about the festival food.

To give you the flavor of some of the festivals and a hint of what's to come, several **recipes,** many of them winning cook-off entries, are included.

If you like cooking and competing, look in the **Cook-offs and Recipe Contests Index.** If you have a specific time frame in mind, consult the **Date Index.** If you have a hankering for a certain food, check out the **Food Type Index,** where you'll find listings for specific foods as well as general ethnic food categories, like Italian, Polish, or German.

For everything else—festival names; agricultural data, such as the chief crop-producing regions; historical figures; food characteristics (e.g., aphrodisiacs); best-known contests (like oyster-shucking); activities such as bagpipe playing or Swedish folk dancing—peruse the **General Index.** It has everything but the kitchen sink.

If you're not sure what burgoo or lefses or quahogs are, consult the **Glossary,** which defines a number of regional foods and dishes that might not be universally known. It does not attempt to be all-encompassing; *Food Festivals* assumes the reader has some familiarity with food.

For those inspired to further exploration of food genealogies, the **Selected Bibliography** can serve as a jumping-off point.

A word of caution: The information for every festival was meticulously checked, but festivals do come and go. A festival could be rescheduled or canceled in the time it takes to load paper onto the press. Take advantage of the contact information provided at the end of each entry to confirm dates, times, and locations.

Bon appetit.

Acknowledgments

Literally thousands of people had a hand in this book. Festival organizers gave their cooperation unstintingly. People with expertise on such varied subjects as the mating habits of oysters and the history of spiedies willingly shared arcane facts. The writers of books and articles provided information and leads; most are listed in the bibliography.

Above all, I am thankful for the imaginative and invaluable assistance of friends. Helen Ahles was there at the beginning and the end, operating the Research Capital of the World (slogan: "We know everything") out of Riverton, Connecticut. She extracted data and lore from people all over the country, brought to light some truly curious food celebrations, and came up with histories of foods and regions from her eerily eclectic personal library. She also kept me from going batty with her off-the-wall humor. Carolyn J. Rodis established the ad hoc Hotrod Research and Editing Center in Baltimore, from whence she persistently chased elusive experts and wandering small-town festival volunteers, discovered offbeat festivals, caught and reconstructed clumsy clauses, and e-mailed encouragement. Lisa Felber in Takoma Park, Maryland, mined and polished festival diamonds from Massachusetts and the Southern mountains, some of them rare gems indeed. Constance A. Neyer of Bloomfield, Connecticut, tracked down the histories of a number of regional celebrations. Marian Darling, Patricia Kelly-White, Aimee Lykes, and Audrey Nelson all pitched in on sundry jobs. And my husband, Lawrence Rasie, was on the field, playing any position, when the home team needed him. The book wouldn't exist without these good friends.

I am further indebted to the kindness of strangers: festival directors and volunteers, agricultural agents, and the staffs of Chambers of Commerce, visitors centers, museums, libraries, churches, growers' associations, food processors, state departments of tourism and agriculture, the U.S. Department of Agriculture, and the National Agricultural Library in Beltsville, Maryland. They not only supplied me with information but helped me understand it.

Finally, I thank Ed Knappman, my always supportive agent; Judy Galens, my editor at Visible Ink Press, who conscientiously and creatively put the book in shape; and the Visible Ink Press and Gale Research staffers and freelancers who helped her guide *Food Festivals* to its final published form: Dean D. Dauphinais, Rebecca Nelson, Marlene Hurst, Maria Franklin, Michele Lonoconus, Pam Hayes, Robert Duncan, Kathy Dauphinais, and Brigham Narins.

My profound thanks to all. I toast you with garlic wine.

Food Festivals

Northeast

Connecticut

Delaware

Maine

Maryland

Massachusetts

New Hampshire

New Jersey

New York

Pennsylvania

Rhode Island

Vermont

Connecticut

Clinton Bluefish Festival

Third weekend in August (Friday through Sunday) The bluefish is a ferocious creature: when schools of them go after bunker fish, the water boils with the fury. People tell stories about these fish—with their big mouths and razor-sharp teeth—doing grievous harm to humans, especially to children playing in shallow water when the blues come racing in like hungry pit bulls. Commercial fishermen, however, pooh-pooh such stories, admitting only to the occasional nip.

Despite the reputation of its resident fish, Clinton, once a major ship-building and commercial fishing center, has proudly called itself the Bluefish Capital of the World since it began the festival in 1970.

The festival features bluefish dinners—fillets wrapped in foil and cooked on grills— but also offers lobster, clam chowder, scallops on skewers with bacon, as well as non-seafood items.

There are games of chance, music, magic acts, children's activities, and a "dunk-a-cop" booth. On Sunday there's the blessing of the fleet, with lavishly decorated fishing and pleasure boats escorted by a Coast Guard cutter.

Blues start running in late summer, migrating south after spawning in more norther-ly waters. The young ones are sweeter and are called snappers; the bigger ones, known as choppers, can weigh in at 30 pounds. Blues are rich in omega-3 fatty acids, which some studies have indicated can stave off heart attacks.

Location: Town docks at Clinton, about 20 miles east of New Haven, off I-95 at exit 63. **Contact:** Clinton Chamber of Commerce, 50 E. Main St., Clinton, CT 06413; Tel: (860)669-3889.

Essex

Essex Rotary Shad Bake

First Saturday in May ☼ Shad can be cooked in various ways. Some bake shad fillets with cream and poach or sauté the roe with bacon or mushrooms. At the Essex bake, however, you get "planked" shad. The Rotarians nail salt pork and each end of the fish (boned fillets, because shad is very bony) to an oak board, marinate with lemon juice and butter, tilt the boards toward a fire, bake, and serve with salads and apple pie for dessert. Entertainment is provided by a jazz band and chantey singers.

Essex began the bake in 1960; tickets are now limited to 1,000. It's a modest but very Yankee feast in a small, picturesque town near the mouth of the Connecticut River.

Location: The Essex Elementary School near exit 3 off Connecticut 9, about 35 miles south of Hartford. ☼ **Contact:** Essex Rotary Club, Box 484, Essex, CT 06426; Tel: Essex Town Hall, (860)767-4340.

Fairfield

Garlicfest

First weekend in May (Friday through Sunday) ☼ "Garlicks, tho' ufed by the French, are better adapted to the ufes of medicine than cookery."

That was what Amelia Simmons thought about garlic. Her *American Cookery,* published in Hartford, Connecticut, in 1796, is considered the first American cookbook written by an American.

And now in the state where her book was published, they are flouting her words. The principal of Fairfield's Notre Dame High School, the Reverend Bill Sangiovanni, started the garlicfest in 1992 as a modest scholarship fund-raiser; now it's held in a huge tent and some 20,000 people attend, contributing about $30,000 a year toward scholarships.

Tables are placed in the middle of the tent, providing a café-like ambience for devouring garlic foods of many ethnic designs: Italian, Middle Eastern, Tex-Mex, Greek, Oriental. Desserts, except for garlic-flavored ice cream, are the only garlic-free foods served.

Vendors sell garlic knickknacks and food products—mayonnaise, cooking wines, jellies, dog biscuits (garlic helps repel fleas). One vendor from Vermont brings bottled barbecue sauce made of maple syrup and garlic.

There are entertainers and an information area. (Did you know that garlic, if rubbed on the bottom of your feet, will be on your breath in a matter of minutes? Something to think about if you're planning to rub garlic on your feet.)

Location: Notre Dame High School in Fairfield, just off the Merritt Parkway (Connecticut 15) at exit 47. ☼ **Contact:** Garlicfest, Notre Dame High School, 220 Jefferson St., Fairfield, CT 06431; Tel: (203)372-6521, Fax: (203)374-0387.

Lobsterfest

Memorial Day weekend (Saturday through Monday) Lobster in the rough is served during Lobsterfest at the Mystic Seaport, the "Museum of America and the Sea." held on Memorial Day weekend. "Decoration Day"—Memorial Day as it was known in the 1800s—is re-enacted with a wreath placed on a cannon to honor Army veterans. A second wreath is carried by rowboat into the Mystic River and left floating there to honor Navy heroes.

The Seaport, a popular tourist attraction, is a re-created nineteenth-century coastal village on the banks of the Mystic River, with tall ships and shops where early-American trades like barrel-making are demonstrated.

There is an admission fee to the museum and additional charges for the food.

Location: Mystic Seaport, one mile south of I-95 at exit 90.   **Contact:** Mystic Seaport, 75 Greenmanville Ave., P.O. Box 6000, Mystic, CT 06355; Tel: (860)572-5315.

A Taste of History

First week in August (Sunday through Tuesday) The Seaport stages A Taste of History in August to let visitors sample foods of the nineteenth century: fish chowder; corn soup; smoked ham sandwiches; *scouse,* a meat and vegetable stew that was popular on long sailing voyages; and traditional desserts, like blueberry pudding.

Chowderfest

Columbus Day weekend (Saturday through Monday) Soup bubbling in cauldrons over wood fires, with tall ships and the Mystic River in the background: that's Chowderfest at Mystic Seaport. Local community groups raise money as visitors sample all varieties of chowder, from Maine to Manhattan clam, fish, corn, whatever, plus apple fritters, apple cider, and other New England favorites.

Concerts of sea chanteys and folk music are presented while people eat at picnic tables on the riverbank. There's also a full schedule of gallery exhibitions, children's activities, and demonstrations, which include chowder making, lobster trapping, and other salty tasks. Attendance is about 10,000.

Main Street USA

Second Saturday in June Historians are amazed by the ethnic diversity of this medium-sized city. For, while New Britain is landlocked, it has all the melting-pot qualities of major port cities. What brought people from all over the world was industry; from 1850 on, New Britain clanged with the sounds of manufacturing and by 1900 the city was legitimately the Hardware Capital of the World.

The town's wonderful hodgepodge of languages and customs is celebrated with Main Street USA, a festival that began in 1976 as a bicentennial event and kept going. Crowds are estimated at 50,000.

Entertainment ranges from a strolling bagpiper to Polish dancers in native costume to an Irish balladeer.

Churches and ethnic clubs run food booths that offer moveable multiethnic feasts. You might start with French pea soup, move on to African American barbecued-rib sandwiches, go from there to Spanish paella brimming with shrimp and served from a huge eight-foot pan, top that off with Polish sauerkraut pierogis, and wind up with Italian ice for dessert. Or you might opt for a light repast of Puerto Rican stew and Scottish scones. . . .

The British settled in New Britain in the early 1700s, and Irish immigrants began arriving in the mid-1800s. They were followed by Germans, Swedes, Greeks, Lithuanians, Italians, Slovaks, Poles, and in more recent days, Asians and Hispanics.

Location: Main Street, in the Central Park/City Hall area. Take exit 35 off I-84, about 8 miles southwest of Hartford.   **Contact:** Main Street USA, P.O. Box 517, New Britain, CT 06050; Tel: (860)223-3586.

Dozynki

Fourth Saturday in August   In Polish, Dozynki means harvest festival. It's believed that the festival's roots go back more than a thousand years to the time of the feudal system, when the lord of the manor would invite workers to share in the harvest's bounty.

New Britain Poles began celebrating Dozynki in the 1930s, let it lapse with the onset of World War II, and revived it in 1982. About 5,000 turn out for food, music, and dancing—all traditionally Polish. Polish immigrants at one time made up 40 to 50 percent of New Britain's population. The Polish community is now about 20,000 strong, in a total population of 75,000.

The day begins with a traditional harvest mass in which bread is blessed and then shared among the congregation, signifying the culmination of the harvest and the giving of thanks.

Then the eating begins. Among the foods are pierogis and kielbasa; *nalesniki,* stuffed crepes, like blintzes; *bigos,* hunter's stew, with cabbage and carrots and various meats; *golabki,* stuffed cabbage; *paczki,* filled donuts; and *placki,* potato pancakes, which sell like hot cakes.

Daytime attractions include folk dancing and vendors selling Polish crafts; in the evening, Polish bands play for dancing. On Sunday, the festival winds up with a picnic.

Location: Falcon Field in New Britain, on Farmington Ave., off I-84 at the Finneman Rd. exit (which becomes Farmington Ave.).   **Contact:** Polish-American Council of New Britain, P.O. Box 32, New Britain, CT 06050; Tel: (860)225-4385.

Festival-goers in New Haven take a break from the Italian fare to pay tribute to a statue of Maria Maddalena, patron saint of Atrani, Italy. (Barbara W. Carlson)

Feast of Santa Maria Maddalena

Third weekend in July (Thursday through Sunday) ⬝ Dating from the 1920s, this feast is among the oldest of the several Italian festivals in New Haven. Maria Maddalena is the patron saint of Atrani, Italy, and the Society of Santa Maria Maddalena was incorporated as a mutual-aid society in 1898 by immigrants from that town. Italians came in great waves to New Haven beginning in the 1880s because of poverty and a repressive government at home. In 1880, there were 102 Italians in New Haven, in 1900, 5,262, and more than double that amount ten years later.

In the old days of the festival, opera singers came from New York to perform. Today, while the talent is local, the festival is probably not much changed: lots of food, singing of old Italian songs, a variety of Italian entertainers, carnival rides, and the procession of the saint through the historic streets of Wooster Square, a largely Italian enclave.

The food is traditional. That means peaches in red wine, fried dough, espresso with a dollop of anisette in it, sausages and peppers in an Italian roll, *sfogliatella,* and sometimes *suffrito,* a combination of calf hearts, onions, tomatoes, and peppers.

Sfogliatella, a specialty of Naples, is a flaky pastry filled with sweet ricotta cheese and orange rind. Atrani is on the Amalfi coast, just south of Naples, so sfogliatella is very traditional. And very good.

About 20,000 people attend the festival, which winds up on Sunday with the procession of a statue of the saint carried through the streets, accompanied by a band, to St. Michael's Church facing the Wooster Square park. The band plays the Star Spangled Banner and a mass is conducted. Then it's back to the sausage and sfogliatella.

Location: Chapel St., a block east of Wooster Square, near downtown New Haven. **Contact:** Feast of Santa Maria Maddalena, P.O. Box 8938, New Haven, CT 06532; Tel: (203)239-2902.

While You're There: New Haven claims to have invented pizza, and the many pizzerias in town back the claim. Take a walk over to Wooster Street, a block south of the festival, and visit Pepe's. It was there in 1925 that Frank Pepe decided to make tomato pies, or pizzas. Today, they're still made there, on 12-foot peels in coal-burning ovens, but you can get much more than plain tomato toppings now.

Norwalk

Norwalk Oyster Festival

Weekend after Labor Day Norwalk, on Long Island Sound, was once a major seaport, and the festival was started in 1978 as a celebration of the city's seafaring past. It remains a sea-oriented festival, with tall ships to visit, an oyster-shucking contest, and educational displays about the oystering industry, which waned but is now coming back. In fact, Connecticut now produces more oysters than Chesapeake Bay and ships them all over the world.

There are numerous food booths, among which you can find oysters on the half shell and fried oysters. But this is not primarily an oyster-*eating* festival. About 100,000 attend for a fun time on Long Island Sound, children's entertainment at Kids' Cove, and carnival rides.

Location: Norwalk Harbor; exit 14 off I-95.   **Contact:** Norwalk Seaport Assn., 132 Water St., Norwalk, CT 06854; Tel: (203)838-9444, or toll-free, (888)701-7785.

Orange

Odyssey: A Greek Festival

Labor Day weekend (Friday through Monday) *Opa!* That's an exclamation of delight and is heard quite often at Odyssey, probably the state's biggest Greek festival.

Food, most of it cooked right at St. Barbara Greek Orthodox Church, is available all day every day. A sample: a *meze* platter that includes Greek meatballs, stuffed grape leaves, Greek sausage, feta cheese, olives, tomatoes, cucumber, *spanakopita* (spinach pie), and *tiropita* (cheese pie).

That's just the *meze*. There are also dinners of *souvlaki*, skewers of marinated meat; *moussaka*, eggplant layered with ground beef and topped with a cream sauce; roast lamb, and whole lamb roasted on open pits. For something sweet, try the familiar baklava; *galaktoboureko*, a flaky pastry filled with custard and covered with honey; *kourabiedes*, sugared butter cookies; or *loukoumades*, hot honey puffs. Okay, there are hot dogs and hamburgers, too. For a mere snack, the Kafenio offers Greek or American coffee, pastry, and *tsoureki*, sweet breads.

Entertainment includes clowning, Greek dance and music, Greek cooking demonstrations, games in the kids' tent, and tours of the church. Shoppers may browse in the Byzantine Book Store, the flea market, and a boutique where there are gifts imported from Greece.

The festival began in 1981 and attracts about 15,000 people.

Location: St. Barbara Greek Orthodox Church in Orange, about 7 miles from New Haven. Take exit 41 off I-95, go right at end of ramp; at third traffic light, go right on U.S. 1 to first traffic light, then left onto Race Brook Road. **Contact:** Odyssey, c/o St. Barbara Greek Orthodox Church, 480 Race Brook Rd., Orange, CT 06477; Tel: (203)795-1348.

Southington

Apple Harvest Festival

First two weekends of October (Usually first weekend Saturday and Sunday; second, Thursday through Sunday) Begun in 1969, this two-weekend apple celebration has been on the American Bus Association list of top 100 events and draws some 200,000 people to town. Events include a parade, line dancing, gymnastics exhibitions, dance bands, and a crafts show featuring apple motifs.

Southington is known for both hardware manufacturing and apple orchards; but, not to worry, only the apples find their way into the hugely popular apple fritters. Other apple dishes include hot apple sundaes, apple pies, caramel apples, and apple-cider doughnuts. You'll also find German, Italian, Mexican, and Cajun food.

Of course, there are fresh apples, too, in several varieties, including Idareds, Red Delicious, McIntosh, and, in greatest abundance, the Macoun, a McIntosh cross that came into being in 1923. The McIntosh—a Connecticut favorite and the most widely planted apple in the northeastern United States—was developed in Ontario in 1811 on the farm of John McIntosh, the son of Scottish immigrants. Macs possess a pleasing balance of sweetness and tartness.

Location: Town green of Southington, about 15 miles south of Hartford, off I-84 at exit 32. ☼ Contact: Greater Southington Chamber of Commerce, 51 N. Main St., Southington, CT 06489; Tel: (860)628-8036.

Stonington

Blessing of the Fleet

Last weekend in July ☼ Stonington is a fishing port on Long Island Sound. At one time, most of the fishermen there were of Portuguese descent, some of them having come over at the time of the American Civil War. The blessing, while it memorializes all fishermen, has a distinctly Portuguese flavor, and the food available on Sunday combines the sea's bounty and traditional Portuguese cuisine. There is always Portuguese sweet bread; linguiça; and Portuguese soup, a brothy melange of beef stock, kale, cabbage, potatoes, and linguiça. From the sea are lobster rolls, fish, scallops.

The celebration begins on Saturday evening with dancing, music, a lobster bake, and beer.

The following morning a mass is said at St. Mary's Catholic Church, followed by a two-hour parade. The statue of St. Peter, the patron saint of fishermen, is taken from St. Mary's Church and carried in the procession to the dock, where the bishop boards the flagship fishing boat to bless the boats.

The flagship sails to the breakwater where the widow of the most recently deceased fisherman drops a broken-anchor wreath into the water, commemorating all deceased fishermen but especially those lost at sea. A wreath is also laid at a memorial on land. And then the eating begins!

The festival began in 1955 and attracts from 5,000 to 7,000 people every year.

Location: The harbor at Stonington, near the Rhode Island border off I-95 at exit 91. ☼ Contact: Blessing of the Fleet, 236 Water St., Stonington, CT 06378; Tel: (860)535-3150.

Holy Ghost Feast

Labor Day weekend (Saturday and Sunday) ☼ Feeding the masses is the soul of this festival, which has been held in Stonington since 1911. It affirms the people's faith in the Holy Ghost and the Portuguese tradition of generosity. The feast also commemorates Santa Isabel de Portugal, who was known as Queen Elizabeth.

According to legend, during floods that destroyed the spring crops, the queen prayed to the Holy Ghost for relief, promising that she would sell her crown and scepter to feed the people (or, according to another story, give her crown to the first poor person she saw). The floods receded and the famine ended.

The Portuguese Holy Ghost Society in Stonington plans this feast a year in advance by raising a bull that will be slaughtered before the celebration. The bull is then used for a soup served over bread and for a roast-beef dinner. All comers are welcome, and 400 to 500 line up at the society building for the dinner. Outside, vendors sell Portuguese sweet breads (made in varying ways, sometimes with potato, candied fruit, or grated lemon peel), boiled fava beans, linguiça, lobsters, and crabs.

The festival begins Saturday night with music and food. Sunday's agenda includes the celebration of a mass, a procession, the "feeding," and more music. The final event is a raffle that determines which family will keep Isabel's crown in its home during the coming year.

Location: Stonington harbor (see above). **Contact:** Portuguese Holy Ghost Society, 26 Main St., Stonington, CT 06378; Tel: (860)535-3855.

Windsor

Shad Derby Festival

Third Saturday in May In 1954, the Windsor Rod and Gun Club held a one-day shad-fishing contest, aimed at showing the importance of cleaning up the Connecticut River to protect its resources. The event has ballooned into a month of activities, starting about the time the shad run begins, and winding up on festival day. About 20,000 jam the town green for an arts and crafts exhibit, entertainment, music, a parade with a shad queen, and lots of food.

Usually, the Lions sponsor a dinner that includes baked shad with corn on the cob and cole slaw. Sometimes circumstances prevent the Lions from giving their dinner. If you want to be sure the shad dinner's on, it would be best to call first.

During the 10-day shad-fishing tournament, swarms of fishermen cover the banks of the Connecticut and Farmington Rivers, which meet in Windsor, to try to get the biggest shad on the end of their lines. Fact: The world record shad, weighing eighteen pounds, was taken in the Connecticut River. Shad usually range from one to ten pounds.

Location: Windsor Town Green, 1½ miles off I-91 at exit 37, about 6 miles north of Hartford. **Contact:** Windsor Chamber of Commerce, 261 Broad St., P.O. Box 9, Windsor, CT 06095; Tel: (860)688-5165.

See Also: Shad Festival (Lambertville, NJ).

Delaware

Delmarva Chicken Festival

Usually mid-June (Friday and Saturday) ☼ This festival, a big chicken fry, celebrates the Birthplace of the Broiler Industry. Broilers—unlike chickens kept to lay eggs—are young birds raised for their meat, and, oddly enough, they weren't common until a woman from Delaware hatched the idea, so to speak. Now broilers are the backbone of the Delmarva economy.

Delmarva, by the way, is a 200-mile-long strip of land between the Chesapeake and Delaware Bays, consisting of the entire state of Delaware and the 11 Eastern Shore counties of Maryland and Virginia. The states share in the broiler business, so the festival, which began in 1948, moves from state to state, attracting about 35,000 people. In 1997, Milford, Delaware, hosts the festival; in 1998, it moves to Millsboro, Delaware.

There's no fooling around with other meats at this festival. From 8,000 to 10,000 pieces of chicken are fried during the weekend, and you can also have chicken frankfurters, chicken sandwiches, barbecued chicken, and chicken in different ethnic styles. But don't even *think* of a beef hamburger.

The chicken pieces are fried in a 10-foot-diameter fry pan, 8 inches deep, with an 8-foot handle; it can cook 800 chicken quarters at one time. The pan currently in use is the festival's second, but it's the same size as the first one which was the world's largest when it was built in 1950. Presently, Pittsfield, Maine, has a bigger one, used for cooking eggs; and London, Kentucky, also has a bigger one, which is used for cooking chicken.

On even-numbered years, 20 finalists take a flutter in the chicken-recipe contests. Among recent winners: Jamaican jerk chicken with papaya salsa, and chicken in pearadise (chicken cooked in a blend of pears, orange juice, marmalade, garlic, ginger, and allspice).

Other events include rooster-crowing and cackling-hen contests, an egg toss, and a spoon race. There's also a chicken scratch, in which kids dive into a mound of corn meal (that's chicken feed, son) and scratch around for money hidden in it. They can keep the money they find, as a kind of nest egg.

Jamaican Jerk Chicken with Papaya Salsa

4 broiler-fryer chicken leg quarters
2 tablespoons hot pepper sauce
1 teaspoon spicy seasoned salt
½ teaspoon cinnamon

½ teaspoon allspice
Papaya Salsa (recipe follows)
cooked rice

In a shallow container, place hot pepper sauce. Add chicken, one piece at a time, turning to coat. Sprinkle salt, cinnamon, and allspice over chicken. Place chicken, skin side up, in single layer in large shallow baking dish. Bake in 400-degree oven, basting twice with pan juices, 45 minutes or until chicken is fork tender. Arrange rice and chicken on platter. Spoon papaya salsa over chicken. Makes 4 servings.

For papaya salsa: In a bowl, make salsa by mixing together 1½ cups diced papaya, ¼ cup minced red onion, 2 tablespoons sugar, 2 tablespoons minced red pepper, 2 tablespoons hot pepper jelly, and 2 tablespoons chopped cilantro. Makes about 2 cups.

Gloria E. Pleasants, Williamsburg, VA;
from Chicken Cookery, published by the Delmarva Poultry Industry

The person behind all this was Mrs. Wilmer Steele of Ocean View, Delaware. In 1923 she started a brood of 500 chicks with her laying flock, and then sold them when they reached about two pounds. These young chickens could be fried, broiled, or roasted instead of stewed, the normal fate of old hens. Soon hatcheries sprang up to fill orders for baby chicks, and then feed mills moved in, and then large processing plants.

Today, Delmarva produces about 10 percent of all broilers grown in the United States, and is the fourth largest broiler producer after Arkansas, Georgia, and Alabama. Sussex County, Delaware, is the top broiler-producing *county* in the United States, having an annual production of more than 200 million birds.

That's something to crow about.

Location: Varying communities on the Delmarva Peninsula. **Contact:** Delmarva Poultry Industry, Inc., R.D. 6, Box 47, Georgetown, DE 19947-9622; Tel: (302)856-9037, Fax: (302)856-1845.

Wilmington

Italian Festival

Eight days including June 13 (Sunday through Sunday)
St. Anthony of Padua Roman Catholic Church began holding street fairs in 1925, stopped

them during World War II, and resumed them in 1975. Now 250,000 to 300,000 people come to celebrate.

The festival raises funds for the church school with all kinds of music, a midway, thrill acts, children's rides, a string band from Philadelphia, and food, glorious food. Homemade spaghetti dinners are served in two dining rooms, and there are six outdoor cafes, each with its specialties.

You'll find *spezzato,* veal cubes with mushrooms, peppers, and onions in a sandwich or over rice; *pizza frita,* fried dough; spinach bread; mozzarella sticks; porkette smothered in garlic; cannolis. The Caffe Nona Strada is famous for its *muffuletta*—round Italian bread, split and filled with provolone, salami, and ham topped with an olive salad marinated in oil-and-vinegar dressing. The olive salad includes green olives and garlic and is what makes this heroic sandwich different from a hero, say, or a hoagie. The muffuletta originated in New Orleans in 1906, according to food scholar Sharon Tyler Herbst.

The Feast Day religious celebration is held on the last Sunday, with a mass in honor of St. Anthony, followed by a procession of saints through the parish streets. A fireworks show gives the fair a spectacular finale.

Location: DuPont St., in the area of St. Anthony's Church, Wilmington. Take the Delaware Ave. exit off I-95, go west 8 blocks on Pennsylvania Ave. **Contact:** St. Anthony's Italian Festival, 901 DuPont St., Wilmington, DE 19805; Tel: (302)421-3790.

Wilmington

Old-Fashioned Ice Cream Festival

Second full weekend in July I scream, you scream, we all scream for ice cream! That old-fashioned saying is right in vogue at this ice-cream social that evokes the birthday parties for young Edward Bringhurst III in the late 1800s. Held on the grounds of the Rockwood Museum, a 72-acre estate with an 1851 Rural Gothic manor house, the festival re-creates those Victorian celebrations. It was first held in 1983, and now about 12,000 attend.

Edward Bringhurst III was the grand-nephew of Joseph Shipley, who had lived in England and returned to Wilmington to build Rockwood in 1851 in the style of English country houses. Edward III was born on July 4, and his family moved into Rockwood in 1892, when he was eight. The lavish parties held on his birthday led him to believe, naturally enough, that the entire country was celebrating with him.

The celebration today features 28 flavors of ice cream made by a local dairy. A special ice cream, Rockwood strawberries and cream, made with local berries and sweet cream, is created exclusively for the festival and is available nowhere else. There's also homemade lemonade. Some non-Victorian foods, like hamburgers, creep in, too.

The Victorian atmosphere is enhanced by calliopes and hand-cranked organs, bands whomping out Sousa, demonstrations of ladies' side-saddle riding and high-wheel bicycle riding, and a Victorian fashion show. There are also hot-air balloons and an old-time travel-

Eating ice cream is serious business during this contest at the Old-Fashioned Ice Cream Festival in Wilmington. (Photo by Carson Zullinger, courtesy of Rockwood Museum)

ing carnival that might include a stilt-walker and a fire-eater. Especially for kids: a dunking booth and an ice-cream-eating contest.

Location: Rockwood Museum, off I-95 at exit 9, on the northern outskirts of Wilmington. **Contact:** Rockwood Museum, 610 Shipley Rd., Wilmington, DE 19809; Tel: (302)761-4340, Fax: (302)764-4570.

Maine

Maine Potato Blossom Festival

Usually third week in July (eight days) Maine is the only state in the country where children are dismissed from school each fall to help harvest potatoes. Potatoes are the state's number-one row crop, and about 95 percent of them are grown in Aroostook County, known as "The County." It's the northernmost part of Maine, the biggest county east of the Mississippi, bigger than Connecticut and Rhode Island combined.

Scotch-Irish settlers brought potatoes to the state around 1750. Joseph Houlton is supposed to have planted the first potatoes—-a variety called Early Blue or Blue Nose—in The County in 1807. At first, potatoes were grown for family and livestock consumption, but soon dozens of starch factories were built and about a fifth of the potato crop went into starch.

As rail lines were extended into Aroostook, more potatoes were grown and exported, and Maine became the nation's biggest potato grower. That was before French fries and potato chips got so popular. In 1958, Maine slumped to number three in the potato race, behind Idaho and Washington, where they grow the perfect French-fry potato, the Russet Burbank; Maine is now ranked about eighth. Maine grows many varieties but largely the "round white," which is supposed to be the best for mashing.

Fort Fairfield has celebrated potatoes with a festival since 1948. Attendance is about 20,000. The food includes a bean-hole supper (baked beans), a chicken barbecue, and baked potatoes with such varied stuffings as broccoli and cheese; sour cream, bacon and chives; and chili.

Entries in a potato recipe contest run the gamut from soup to casseroles to bread to fudge. For entertainment there are sports, a pet show, the Little Miss Potato Blossom Pageant, the Maine Potato Queen Pageant, a parade, a kiddie carnival, music, and a fireworks finale.

Houlton, Aroostook's county seat, has a smaller festival, Potato Feast Days, on the last full weekend of August, Friday through Sunday. It features a booth of baked potatoes with four or five toppings, and a church supper with potatoes scalloped, mashed, and every which way. Contact Greater Houlton Chamber of Commerce, (207) 532-4216.

Location: Fort Fairfield is on U.S. 1A, 47 miles north of Houlton, which is the northern terminus of I-95. ⁂ **Contact:** Fort Fairfield Chamber of Commerce, P.O. Box 607, Fort Fairfield, ME 04742; Tel: (207) 472-3802.

See Also: Idaho Spud Day (Shelley, ID).

Lisbon Falls

Moxie Festival

Second weekend in July (Friday through Sunday) ⁂ There's something irresistible about a festival honoring a soft drink that was originally advertised as a "nerve food" and is now almost extinct but the name of which has come to mean vigor or pep or nerve.

That's Moxie. About 20,000 people come here in July to drink Moxie, a dark brown bittersweet carbonated drink, and to eat Moxie-flavored ice cream. The festival has pancakes for breakfast and barbecued chicken, and a firemen's muster and parade, but Moxie is the draw. Anyone with vanity Moxie license plates can drive in the parade, and that brings people from as far away as Florida.

Moxie was invented in 1876 by Augustin Thompson, a pharmacist, in Union, Maine, and was first carbonated in 1884. Dr. Thompson advertised the tonic as a remedy for just about everything, including locomotor ataxia, mental imbecility, and loss of manhood. He claimed the drink was made from a sugarcane-like plant found by a Lt. Moxie near the equator. Actually, there was no Lt. Moxie, and the main ingredient was the bitter juice of gentian roots.

Moxie is the oldest carbonated beverage continuously on the market, and, in its heyday in the early decades of the 1900s, was sold in 38 states and three Canadian provinces. Now it can be found only in New England and a couple of towns in Pennsylvania.

But its fans are ardent. Frank Anicetti, who was responsible for starting the Moxie Festival, claims to drink a half gallon a day, says it calms nerves. He owns the Kennebec Fruit Company in Lisbon Falls, which has a soda fountain, and during a festival he'll dip over 600 Moxie ice-cream cones, until his arm is numb.

The festival began in 1982 as an autograph-signing party for Frank Potter, author of *The Moxie Mystique.* It just kept growing.

Location: Lisbon Falls, about 30 miles north of Portland, is at the intersection of Maine 125 and 196, about five miles west of I-95. ⁂ **Contact:** Androscoggin County Chamber of Commerce, P.O. Box 59, Lewiston, ME 04243; Tel: (207)783-2249, or Kennebec Fruit Co., Lisbon Falls, ME 04252; Tel: (207)353-8173.

Machias

Blueberry Festival

Weekend of third Saturday in August (Friday and Saturday) ☼ The Machias festival began in 1976 as a thanksgiving for the blueberry harvest. Now between 10,000 and 18,000 people come, but it's still a down-homey, no-frills affair. On Friday night, there's a Down East fish fry with wild blueberry pie for dessert, and Saturday brings an all-you-can-eat wild-blueberry pancake breakfast, a wild-blueberry dessert bar in the Centre Street Congregational Church vestry, and chowder and lobster.

Events include a pie-eating contest, a wild-blueberry bake contest, and the presentation of an original musical, "Red, White and Blueberry." The story line is updated each year, but the title song remains the same. The chorus goes:

Blueberry, blueberry, blueberry blues
Blueberry, blueberry, blueberry blues
Oh you rake all day; you rake all night;
You rake, rake, rake 'til they're out of sight.

Location: Machias is 75 miles northeast of Bar Harbor off U.S. 1A. ☼ **Contact:** Machias Bay Area Chamber of Commerce, P.O. Box 602, Machias, ME 04654; Tel: (207)255-4402.

See Also: State of Maine Wild Blueberry Festival (Union, ME).

Madawaska

Acadian Festival

June 28 and varying days around that date ☼ Madawaska, the most northeasterly town in the United States, separated from Canada only by the St. John River, is the birthplace of the Acadian culture in Maine. Acadians living in New Brunswick traveled by canoe upriver in 1785 and settled on the river's south shore at what's now Madawaska after they were forced to flee from New Brunswick.

Their ancestors had migrated from southeastern France to Nova Scotia in the 1600s but were expelled by the English in 1755. Many found new homes elsewhere in Canada and in the United States, especially in Louisiana.

The festival was started in 1978 to preserve the Acadian culture. It's open to all and about 10,000 attend.

The Acadian Supper is a festival highlight, featuring *pot-en-pot* (a spicy meat casserole), *ployes* (buckwheat pancakes eaten with meals, instead of rolls), *creton* (a pork spread often eaten with ployes), *fougère* (fiddlehead ferns), *pâté chinois* (a dish like shepherd's pie made of hamburger, corn, and mashed potato). Also available are chicken stew and a bean-hole supper, baked beans cooked in a pot in a pit over hot coals.

Other events include a talent review, an Acadian mass, an arts and crafts fair, a parade, and a reenactment of the original Acadian landing.

At the same time as the festival, a different Acadian family each year holds a private reunion. Traditional events include planting a tree at the Acadian Monument, which is a marble cross on the banks of the St. John honoring the original 16 Acadian families who settled here. Some years, thousands come to the reunion from all over the country.

Location: Madawaska is on United States 1, about 30 miles north of Presque Isle. **Contact:** Greater Madawaska Chamber of Commerce, 378 Main St., Madawaska, ME 04756; Tel: (207)728-7000, Fax: (207)728-4696.

See Also: Festivals Acadiens (Lafayette, LA).

Pittsfield

Central Maine Egg Festival

Fourth Saturday of July This is one zany *egg*stravaganza of a festival. It began in 1973, about 25,000 attend, and the puns get worse every year.

One of the festival's distinctions is the aluminum fry pan that's 12 feet and one inch in diameter. It's used to cook a farmer's breakfast of ham and eggs, home fries, baked beans. Most of the food for sale doesn't include eggs because they're so perishable, but there *are* pickled eggs, the kind saloons used to have on their bars, and there's a chicken barbecue (which came first . . .). There's also a cooking contest for quiches and cheesecakes.

The festival trademark is the contest for the biggest chicken egg, which can be white or brown. A poultry expert makes sure there are no ringers, like goose eggs, and the eggs are measured by water displacement. Contestants have come from all over the world. The big eggs are not normal, not "necessarily something a chicken would be very proud of," according to the Brown Egg Council of New England.

Other happenings are a parade, the hatching of baby chicks every two hours, numerous egg games and *egg*shibits, and a crafts fair. Politicians are allowed on the grounds, but they are not allowed to stump.

Maine has five million laying hens and they all lay brown eggs, which are barely known outside of New England. Eggs are Maine's single largest commodity shipped abroad, mostly to Hong Kong. The Chinese have always had brown eggs, because white to them is the color of death. But Hong Kong is so crowded there's no room for chickens, and a smart Maine entrepreneur discovered this in about 1970.

Brown eggs came to New England in the China-trade days. The clipper-ship captains stocked up on chickens in China so there would be fresh eggs on board, and this led to the establishment of the first commercial poultry farm in Little Compton, Rhode Island. These pioneer layers got to be known as Rhode Island Reds, and they're the forerunners of all the chickens that produce brown eggs.

As the sign says, the Maine Lobster Festival in Rockland claims theirs is the World's Largest Lobster Cooker. (©Lunt Studio/Paula Jean Lunt))

Except for some chickens in parts of Connecticut and Vermont, all New England chickens lay brown eggs. The white eggs that *are* produced are for New Yorkers. Truth to tell, brown eggs and white eggs taste just the same. The color is determined by the breed.

Location: Pittsfield is off I-95, about 20 miles north of Augusta. ⊚ **Contact:** Central Maine Egg Festival, 14 School St., Pittsfield, ME 04967; Tel: (207)487-5282.

Rockland

Maine Lobster Festival

First weekend of August (Thursday through Sunday) ⊚ Maine lobster, *Homarus americanus,* with a mottled greenish-brownish shell that turns, well, lobster-red when cooked, is a totally different animal from the crawfish of the South or the dark blue *Homarus gammarus* found along the European coast. And in Maine, it's not only considered far superior to those other crawlers but is also a cause for celebration and no-holds-barred eating.

At the Rockland festival, more than five tons of lobster are cooked in the World's Largest Lobster Cooker, which can steam up to 400 pounds of lobster every 15 minutes. For a nominal price, people buy a 1¼-pound lobster, with drawn butter, a roll, and potato chips.

The festival also offers fried shrimp, clam chowder, lobster-salad rolls, other seafood dishes, corn on the cob, and blueberry (another big Maine crop) pancakes for breakfast.

Rockland is the county seat of Knox County, which is the richest lobster-harvesting area of Maine and the Lobster Capital of the World. The county ships about 8 million pounds of the state's annual total of 20 to 30 million pounds.

The Penobscot Indians of Maine were eating lobster when the first European settlers arrived, and they were also using it for fertilizer because it was so plentiful that it piled up on beaches after storms. Lobsters averaged five to six pounds then, and often weighed as much as twenty-five pounds. They're smaller now because they're caught when they're younger, but they're still good and sweet because of the cold north Atlantic waters, Mainiacs say. Catching them hasn't changed much in 100 years. Lobsters are caught in lobster "pots" that are slatted wooden (or, now, metal) boxes, baited with fish, and attached to buoys.

Festival events include a coronation pageant for the Maine Sea Goddess; a parade; a Great Crate Race, in which contestants try to run across lobster crates tied in a row from pier to pier without winding up in the icy sea (which, however, they usually do); boat, train, and helicopter rides; and a blindfolded rowboat race.

There are seafood-cooking contests, in which contestants must use seafood caught in Maine waters, and lobster-eating contests.

The festival began in 1948 and now draws about 60,000 people, which is a lot of people in Maine.

Also of interest is the Winter Harbor Lobster Festival, a more small-town event that cooks up about 1,500 lobsters and features lobster-boat races, kids' games, and local crafts. It's held the second Saturday in August. Contact Winter Harbor Chamber of Commerce, (800)231-3008.

Location: Harbor Park, just off U.S. 1, in Rockland, 81 miles north of Portland. **Contact:** Maine Lobster Festival, P.O. Box 552, Rockland, ME 04841; Tel: (800)LOB-CLAW, or (207)596-0376.

South China

Maine Maple Sunday

Fourth Sunday in March Maple Sunday is one of Maine's most popular events, when more than 60 sugar makers in South China and elsewhere in Maine hold "open sugarhouse" to let people taste syrup and see how it's made.

Like other sugarhouses, Wagner's Maple Sugar House in South China gives visitors free ice cream with warm maple syrup and takes them on a hike to the sugarbush—the grove of maples that produce the sap. Wagner's also sells popcorn with maple-syrup coating, chocolate-covered maple-cream candy, maple fudge, and maple lollipops. Some sugarhouses also have pickles and doughnuts, a traditional accompaniment to "sugar on snow." And some invite visitors to pet barn animals and take horse-drawn wagon rides.

While syrup production varies, Maine generally taps between 150,000 and 160,000 gallons of syrup a year, about 15 percent of the total U.S. production, behind New York, 19 percent, and Vermont, which is number one with 33 percent.

Location: Wagner's Sugar House is on Maine 32, 2 miles west of the intersection with Maine 3, in South China, 14 miles north of Augusta. **Contact:** R.R. 2, Box 1620, South China, ME 04358; Tel: (207)445-2214. For information on all sugar houses: Maine Department of Agriculture, Division of Market Development, 28 State House Station, Augusta, ME 04333; Tel: (207)287-3491, Fax: (207)287-7548.

See Also: Vermont Maple Festival (St. Albans, VT).

Union

State of Maine Wild Blueberry Festival

Friday of the last full week of August It's *wild* blueberry. Mainers are adamant about calling their blueberries wild blueberries, which are not the same as cultivated blueberries (called "tame" blueberries by the United States Department of Agriculture). Maine wild blueberries are "lowbush," as opposed to the cultivated highbush (which, it turns out, also grow wild), and grow only 6 to 18 inches high. The lowbush berries are smaller and sweeter than the highbush, with a more intense flavor, and are less likely to burst when baking because they have firmer skins than the squooshy highbush berries. So say the Mainers.

Blueberries are one of North America's few native berries and the lowbush ones grow in thick mats on sandy barrens, primarily in the coastal regions of Maine and Canada. Maine produces about 72 million pounds, about half the crop of wild blueberries, and the other half comes from Canada.

You'll learn all this at the blueberry festival, which began in 1960 and is part of the Union Fair, which has been held since 1869. (They start something here, they stick with it.)

The fair runs Sunday through Saturday, the last week in August, and while the official blueberry day is Friday, events are scattered throughout the week. The blueberry-coffee-cake contest is Tuesday, the blueberry-pie-baking contest Wednesday. The Blueberry Hut is open all week selling blueberry coffeecakes, doughnuts, fudge, pies, muffins, breads, ice cream (a best-seller, made on the premises). There are also blueberry jam, candy, popcorn, and juice. And blueberry shirts, hats, postcards, and crafts.

Special events make Friday different: a wild-blueberry-pancake breakfast, 3,500 little pies (cooked with 600 pounds of blueberries) given away, a blueberry-pie-eating contest, the coronation of the State of Maine Wild Blueberry Queen. And four big blueberries running around the grounds greeting people and passing out blueberry balloons.

The Union Fair is a standard old-time agricultural fair, with livestock shows, harness racing, horse and oxen pulls, and such. Crowds run to about 35,000 for the entire week, and are biggest—the blueberry people say—on blueberry day.

The wild blueberry has a rich history. On top of each wild blueberry is the base of its earlier flower, a calyx in the shape of a five-pointed star. American natives believed the Great Spirit sent these "star berries" from the night of heaven during a time of famine to relieve the hunger of children.

When settlers arrived, Native Americans taught them many uses for the wild blueberry. Indians smoked wild blueberries to preserve them as a seasoning for soups and stews in the winter. They also made a strong tea from the root that they used as a relaxant during childbirth, and they used blueberry juice as a cough medicine.

Although the berries grow wild, human help improves the yield. The barrens are usually burned or mowed after each crop to prune weeds, and growers import hives with billions of bees to increase pollination. (Bees, like migrant workers, start in the South pollinating citrus crops, are taken gradually north to help out with cranberries and then blueberries.) The berries are still largely hand-harvested with a steel rake invented in 1883 that looks like a dustpan with teeth.

Commercial harvesting began at the time of the Civil War when berries were canned for the Union Army. Freezing began in 1928, and now about 99 percent of the berries are frozen and shipped throughout the United States, Canada, western Europe, and Japan. They're crazy about them in Japan.

Not to worry. You can still go to Maine and buy them fresh at roadside stands.

Location: The Union fairgrounds are just off Maine 17, 14 miles northwest of Rockland. ☼ **Contact:** Maine Wild Blueberry Festival, P.O. Box 426, Union, ME 04862; Tel: (207)785-4173.

See Also: Whitesbog Blueberry Festival (Whitesbog, NJ).

Yarmouth

Yarmouth Clam Festival

Usually third weekend of July (Friday through Sunday) ☼
This is "a clambake that got out of hand," the locals say, semi-jokingly. The original clambake in 1965 was a neighborhood affair; now more than 50,000 people flock to small coastal Yarmouth during the festival and go through 1,200 lobsters, 1½ tons of French-fried Maine potatoes, and 60 bushels of steamers.

That's just the clambake food. Food booths, all operated by nonprofits, also offer a bounty of seafood and regional specialties: oysters and clams on the half shell; shrimp cocktail and fried shrimp; fried scallops and fried battered clams; clam cakes and stuffed clams; lobster rolls, crabmeat rolls, and scallop rolls; clam chowder and lobster stew; corn on the cob. Still hungry? For dessert, there are homemade pies, strawberry shortcake, peach shortcake, strawberry cheesecake. There are pancake breakfasts Saturday and Sunday, and other non-seafood items.

There's entertainment, too: concerts, line dancing, an old-fashioned hymn-sing, humorists, jazz, rock, symphonic music, carnival rides, a crafts show, fireworks. And there's serious stuff: the Maine State Clam Shucking Contest (cash and clam prizes), and the Great Royal River Canoe Race.

Location: Yarmouth is 10 miles north of Portland on I-95, at exit 16 or 17. ⊛
Contact: Yarmouth Chamber of Commerce, 16 U.S. Rt. 1, Yarmouth, ME 04096; Tel: (207)846-3984, Fax: (207)846-5419.

Maryland

Ice Cream Festival

Second weekend in July (Friday through Sunday) ❀ They raise dairy cattle in Maryland, and ice cream doesn't exist without dairy cattle, so there's some logic behind 45,000 people converging on Baltimore's famed Lexington Market in July. That's where the ice cream is. About 2,500 pounds of ice cream are consumed each day of the festival. There are cones, plain and covered with sprinkles or dipped in chocolate sauces; root-beer floats; sundaes with bananas and cherries and lots of whipped cream. Vendors from major ice-cream makers are on hand, usually with new flavors for people to test-taste. Special events include a gooey sundae-eating contest, music, and entertainment. Proceeds go to a city-wide reading program.

Baltimore is known for its city markets, and the Lexington Market is one of the oldest, founded in 1782; it's also the largest of the six city-operated indoor markets. These markets are crowded with stalls where vendors sell everything from seafood to baked goods. Lexington has a contemporary addition called the Arcade, which has two restaurants, a stage for entertainment and community events, and more food vendors.

Location: Lexington and Eutaw Sts., eight blocks from the Inner Harbor. ❀ **Contact:** Lexington Market, 400 W. Lexington St., Baltimore, MD 21201; Tel: (410)685-6169, Fax: (410)547-1864.

Old Bay Crab Soup Stakes

First or second Wednesday in October ❀ This midday two-hour contest has been held since 1988, and the reason it attracts several thousand people is the soup's mystique: crab soup is a Baltimore tradition, something to be venerated, saluted, celebrated.

Entrants are local restaurants that submit either a cream-of-crab soup or a vegetable-crab soup. Attendees line up, get a taste of each soup, vote for their favorite in each category. The soups are also judged by a panel of assorted food experts, including representatives of McCormick & Company, which manufactures Old Bay seasoning in Baltimore.

The real point of the event is to promote Chesapeake Bay and McCormick. It's required that Old Bay be used in the soup recipes. The seasoning is a combination of spices, among them mustard, red and black pepper, cloves, ginger, and paprika, and it is always, make that *always,* used in steaming hard crabs. It's also used in soup and in preparing shrimp. It's a Baltimore tradition that borders on sacred.

Since the entries are judged on presentation as well as taste, they get quite elaborate, some with ice sculptures. One year, a restaurant featured what appeared to be an enormous bouquet of flowers, but was actually a bouquet of finely carved vegetables.

Location: Harborplace Amphitheatre, at the Inner Harbor in Baltimore. **Contact:** Harborplace Management Co., 200 E. Pratt Street, Baltimore, MD 21201; Tel: (410)332-4191.

While You're There: The restaurants and stalls of Harborplace are a delight to visit, and Little Italy, a residential area with bountiful Italian restaurants and greengrocers, is just east of the harbor.

Lexington Market Chocolate Festival

Third week in October (Thursday through Saturday)
This may seem like the epitome of decadence: chocolate chocolate chocolate. But the proceeds of this chocoholic's dream benefit the Ronald McDonald House, making it almost incumbent to indulge, and about 25,000 do. The festival began in 1983 to celebrate the opening of the market's Arcade, and it was such a hit it just kept going.

The sweets available are from all over Maryland. Some of the more imaginative are from Rheb's Candy, which offers what look like chocolate mice on cheese. The mice are fudge, with licorice tails, and the cheese is yellow chocolate. Rheb's also has chocolate lollipops in the shape of witches, skulls, pumpkin heads, and ghosts.

Konstant Candies, a tenant of the market since the late 1890s, makes fudge-covered apples. It takes a week to complete the process of dipping, rotating, cooling. Konstant also has chocolate-covered pretzels.

Harbor City Bakery comes up with black-bottomed strawberry shortcake (double chocolate cakes with cream cheese).

A jazz band sets the musical tone, and events include chocolate-pie-eating contests, with prizes donated by area merchants, contests to guess the filling in chocolate candy, and demonstrations of cake and candy decorating.

Location and contact: See Ice Cream Festival in Baltimore (above).

National Hard Crab Derby and Fair

Labor Day weekend (Friday through Sunday) ⊛ Crisfield, the Crab Capital of America, is on an inlet of Chesapeake Bay, and it's supposedly built entirely on oyster shells. True or not, it's certainly a shellfish town, where watermen oyster in the winter and crab in the summer.

The crab harvest is celebrated with piles of fresh soft-shell crabs (crabs that have molted their hard shells) sizzling from the fryer, and hard-shells, generally steamed in a peppery, vinegary vapor. The hard-shell crabs are eaten with a mallet and knife, on a newspaper tablecloth spread out on a picnic table.

For those who don't want to work so hard, there are crab cakes, rich with crab, Maryland delicacies. There's also stuff that doesn't come out of the bay, like chicken, pizza, sausages—but why even mention it?

The derby part of the fair is the Governor's Cup Race on Saturday, a crab version of a horse race, except that the racetrack is a sloping platform. Governors from more than 30 states enter crabs, most of them Maryland crabs. The race began in 1948 when a newspaper editor dumped some crabs in a circle on Main Street and called it a derby.

Other contests include the crab relay races, where racers hand off crabs rather than batons; a plastic-container-boat regatta; and a crab-picking contest in which contestants vie to pick the most crab meat out of a pile of crabs in 15 minutes. Most of the pickers work at the town's processing plants; they're *fast*. There are also fireworks, band concerts, professional entertainment, and a chance to admire Miss Crustacean, a 16-year-old crowned Thursday before the fair, and Mr. and Mrs. Crustacean, 4- and 5-year-old tots.

Blue crabs, called sooks if they're females and jimmies if they're males, are found along the Atlantic coast and in the Gulf of Mexico. Sooks and jimmies have baby crabs through an interesting process. A couple of days before the female is ready to molt, the jimmy grabs her, turns her so she's stomach up, and carries her off to a patch of eelgrass. When she starts to molt, he couples with her for six to twelve hours, and then continues to cradle her for another two or three days while her new shell hardens. Then he goes off to find another playmate. The sook now has about a million eggs and is fertile for the rest of her life.

Scientifically speaking, crabs are *Callinectes sapidus*. *Calli* means beautiful, *nectes*, swimmer, and *sapidus*, savory or delicious. They are called blue crabs because they have some blue on their large claws.

Location: Somers Cove Marina in Crisfield, on Maryland 413, off 13. ⊛ **Contact:** National Hard Crab Derby and Fair, P.O. Box 215, Crisfield, MD 21817; Tel: (800)782-3913 or (410)968-2682.

While You're There: Tawes Museum has interesting displays of old-time crabbing methods, old boats, and photographs of crab shanties. The town has six crab-processing plants, and most are glad to give tours.

Leonardtown

St. Mary's County Oyster Festival

Third weekend in October ☼ Some people are squeamish about oysters, especially raw ones. William Makepeace Thackeray, on eating his first (and, presumably, last), said he felt as though he had just swallowed a baby. Jonathan Swift commented: "He was a bold man who first ate an oyster."

Such squeamishness is foreign to this festival, which started in 1967 and carries on a long-standing tradition of oyster mania. Around Chesapeake Bay, which has reputedly yielded more oysters and blue crabs than any other body of water in the world, settlers in the 1600s got the idea that oysters were good to eat when they saw the piles of shells left by Native Americans.

By the 1800s, people were going crazy over oysters shipped from Maryland. "The country was in the throes of an oyster cult," write Waverly Root and Richard de Rochemont in *Eating in America.* "Oysters were eaten raw, naked, fried, fricasseed, in soup, in pies, in stuffings, and riding triumphantly on top of grilled steaks." In Springfield, Illinois, Abraham Lincoln gave oyster parties.

Oysters remain big in St. Mary's County in southern Maryland. On festival weekend, oysters get fried, scalded, served on the half shell, and plopped in stews, and better than 20,000 people turn out to eat them. Folks becoming momentarily oyster sated can browse through a flea market, listen to music, including a barbershop choir (that's right, choir), visit educational exhibits, and hand off the kids to hay rides, pony rides, puppet shows, carnival games. Or they can brush up on their oyster skills: chefs demonstrate cooking their favorite oyster dishes, and expert shuckers give shucking lessons.

Two big-time competitions highlight the festival: the National Oyster Shucking Championship and the National Oyster Cook-off.

The shuck-off is a timed match, with contestants getting penalties for broken shells or cut oysters. The winner gets cash plus a trip to Galway Bay in Ireland to represent the United States in the International Oyster Shucking Contest. In the cook-off, 12 finalists compete, chosen from more than 200 recipes submitted from around the country. Winners get cash, and their recipes go in the cookbook published each year. After the judging, visitors who get there fast enough can "taste test" entries.

For eaters, here's the menu: Oysters in all manner of dishes. Soft-shell-crab sandwiches, crab cakes, steamers, shrimp, fried clams, catfish, seafood chowder. Barbecued pork, beef, chicken. Stuffed ham sandwiches—a St. Mary's County specialty. Ham shanks are stuffed with spicy country sausage and kale, and then thinly sliced.

One of the many good things about oysters is that they're high in calcium, niacin, and iron; another good (or at least interesting) thing is that they're supposed to be aphrodisiacs.

Speaking of which, an odd thing about oysters is how they reproduce. Most East Coast oysters begin life as males, and then, as they mature, turn into females that can produce up to 60 million eggs each season. The eggs just kind of drift around, but some of them meet up with the huge amounts of sperm the young males have sprayed, and those turn into larvae.

Location: County Fairgrounds in Leonardtown, 55 miles south of Washington D.C., on Maryland 234.   Contact: St. Mary's County Oyster Festival, P.O. Box 766, California, MD 20619; Tel: (301)863-5015.

Montgomery County Ethnic Heritage Festival

Usually the second weekend in June   Montgomery County, just north of Washington, D.C., boasts an extraordinarily diverse cultural population, and this festival showcases more than 80 different cultures through food, crafts, dance, and music. There are regional American foods (Cajun, soul, Hawaiian), as well as worldwide foods; you can sample German, French, African, West Indian, Colombian, Spanish, Israeli, Greek, Thai, Japanese, Chinese, and Australian treats. And more, too.

The Caribbean is especially well represented and some of the foods from that area include tropical ice creams—mango, papaya, coconut, pineapple, soursop (a tropical fruit with a somewhat pineapple-ish flavor); rotis; jerk chicken; and green coconut (you drink the milk with a straw and then eat the jellyish substance in the bottom).

From Trinidad, a man demonstrates chopping sugar cane with a machete, and then sells pieces to suck and chew.

Events include crafts exhibits, games from around the world for children, concerts, native-costumed dancers and musicians, an African "mystery" dancer on stilts, and, after the final concert, a blaze of fireworks.

The festival began in the 1980s and draws crowds of 30,000 to 40,000.

Location: The streets near the Armory in downtown Silver Spring, a suburb of Washington off I-95.   Contact: Montgomery County Recreation Dept., 12210 Bushey Drive, Silver Spring, MD 20902; Tel: (301)217-6798.

Cozy's Strawberry Festival

First weekend in June   Thurmont has nine strawberry farms right in the area, and you can pick your own, or you can visit the festival and, with less effort, get them fresh and every which way. There are standards like strawberry shortcake, but also strawberry milk shakes, sundaes, frozen drinks and pies, all made from local berries.

The strawberry-eating contest, open to all ages, is a messy highlight. Contestants build huge leaning towers of shortcake, strawberries, and whipped cream, and dig in, using spoons at first, but then only their mouths and fingers. The prize is a strawberry-covered trophy.

Other events are line dancing, folk music, crafts displays, and a teddy-bear parade for youngsters, who may bring their own bear or borrow one from a local woman who lends them out from her collection.

Location: Cozy Village, a small shopping center of a dozen specialty stores, in Thurmont, on U.S. 15, 52 miles northwest of Baltimore. **Contact:** Cozy Village, 103 Frederick Rd., Thurmont, MD 21788; Tel: (301)271-4301.

German Fest

Second full weekend in October Even though there's cordovax music, this is a festival that concentrates on eating, not fripperies like entertainment. The food is strictly *deutsche,* a nod of appreciation to Jacob Weller who stopped here with his family in 1751, stayed, and fathered and grandfathered lots more Wellers. They introduced so many industries that most of the people became mechanics and the town was called Mechanicstown for a while.

Here's a sample of the food: German potato salad, the kind with a vinegar base, served warm; pretzel bread sandwiches, made from pretzel dough, shaped like a pretzel and topped with ham and Swiss cheese; bratwurst steamed or fried with peppers and onions; side dishes of spicy red cabbage served hot with raisins. No hot dogs here—but plenty of knockwurst.

This being apple country, there are apple dumplings and apple strudel. And it wouldn't be a real German experience without German Black Forest cake.

All this to the tunes of a cordovax, an accordion-like instrument, played by a local resident.

Catoctin Mountain Park is two miles west of Thurmont and the Catoctin Colorfest is held at the same time as the German Fest. It celebrates the colorful fall foliage and has been drawing leaf-peepers since 1960. The town center of Thurmont is closed off for Colorfest's more than 1,000 vendors of crafts and food and 200,000 visitors. It's a huge yet small-townish party, where local kids set up lemonade stands on their lawns.

The presidential retreat Camp David is also in this region, and while it doesn't quite welcome tourists, it's interesting to think you might be eating knockwurst within hollering distance of powerful people planning world affairs.

Location and contact: See Cozy's Strawberry Festival in Thurmont (above).

Massachusetts

Lord's Acre Corn Festival

Sunday before Labor Day ☼ This festival, in a little town with one flashing yellow light, three churches, and a lot of apple trees, is sponsored by St. Francis Xavier Church.

The church is built in the shape of a corn crib—that is, trapezoidal, with the top bigger than the base—because corn, in a sense, built it. Parishioners had been worshiping in the next town over, and they learned that if they wanted their own church they would have to raise the money for it.

Thereupon a farmer named Harry Brazeau planted an acre of sweet corn that he said was for the Lord. When the corn ripened, a mass was said in the field, and to this day mass is said outside at 10 a.m. before the fair begins.

Mostly, the fair is eating. There's corn on the cob, of course, and also a barbecued chicken dinner (including corn), and various food booths. The small congregation—about 140 families—goes all out in the cooking department, and sells more than 100 homemade apple pies, freshly cooked doughnuts, and lots of pastries, homemade breads, chutney, jams, piccalilli, and herb vinegar. A vegetable stand sells locally grown produce.

An Irish-American band plays, and between sets a juggler plies his craft. It's estimated that about 4,000 to 5,000 attend. For many, it has simply become a tradition. The first festival of the Lord's Acre corn was in 1948.

Location: Derby Field, behind the elementary school, in Bolton, 27 miles west of Boston, and a mile from I-495 at exit 27. ☼ **Contact:** St. Francis Xavier Church, 808 Main St., Bolton, MA 01740; Tel: (508)779-2750.

At the BankBoston Scooper Bowl, visitors typically consume more than 12 tons of ice cream and frozen yogurt while raising over $100,000 for charity. (Ed MacKinnon/New England Dairy and Food Council)

Boston

BankBoston Scooper Bowl

First week in June (Tuesday through Thursday) ☼ Boston is known as the land of the bean and the cod. It should be bean, cod, and ice cream.

Some 50,000 Scooper Bowl visitors consume more than 12 tons of ice cream and frozen yogurt, sampling 36 flavors from nine or so different companies. Ice cream makers including Ben & Jerry's, Häagen-Dazs, and Breyers dish up everything from the dietetic to the decadent, from tried-and-true chocolate and vanilla to such exotic blends as cappuccino twist, dinosaur crunch, and chocolate blend-nutrageous yogurt. Visitors are among the first ever to taste new flavors that the makers are trying out; almost a third of the flavors are making their debut at the Scooper Bowl.

In the 13 years after the event began in 1982, 680,000 visitors consumed 131 tons of ice cream and frozen yogurt. They needn't feel guilty about ice cream excess, though. This is the largest charity ice-cream event in the country, averaging more than $100,000 in its three days for the Jimmy Fund, the fund-raising arm of the Dana-Farber Cancer Institute in Boston. The event was started by an ice-cream executive who was on the Jimmy Fund's board of directors.

New Englanders love their ice cream, eating an average 19 quarts per person annually versus the national average of 15 quarts.

Location: City Hall Plaza, Boston. By car: Mass Pike to Southeast Expressway; follow signs for Government Center. By subway: Green or Blue Line to Government Center; Orange Line to State Street. Take public transportation! Parking in Boston can be expensive and impossible to find. ※ **Contact:** The Jimmy Fund, 375 Longwood Ave., Boston, MA 02215; Tel: 617/632-3300.

Boston Harborfest

First week in July (six days) ※ This party for 1.5 million people packs about 170 events into six days. Among the highlights are a Jazzfest concert, Fourth of July fireworks over Boston Harbor choreographed to music, and a fleet of tall ships that includes the USS Constitution, America's oldest warship, sailing into Boston Harbor.

For foodies, the highlights are the long-popular Chowderfest held on the Sunday of Harborfest week, and a newer event, a Lobsterfest, a traditional New England clambake with lobster entrees. There is also a plethora of other seafood.

At the Chowderfest, major restaurants from the Greater Boston area and even a couple of Navy ships compete for the honor of best New England clam chowder, chosen by tourists who sample the chowders (for a small price) and vote.

The Chowderfest shows how snooty Boston can be when it comes to chowder. Woe betide any chowder chef who wants to enter some kind of brothy chowder wannabe, or the kind tarted up with tomatoes. New England clam chowder, say Bostonians, is the thick and creamy chowder made with quahogs, milk, onions, salt pork, and potatoes. Anybody leaving out the milk or trying exotic spices is not even remotely likely to win best-chowder honors. (While the ingredients don't vary that much, they are all top secret.)

Understand that this Boston chowder that Bostonians call New England chowder is not universally accepted throughout New England. In Maine, they make chowder with steamers, not quahogs. In Rhode Island, they make what they call red chowder with tomato sauce. In Connecticut, true chowder *is* the brothy kind, made the way the creamy kind is but with a water stock instead of milk. Manhattan clam chowder is made with cooked or canned tomatoes.

Old Yankees do not countenance tomato in chowder. In 1939, a Maine legislator named Seeder introduced a bill to make it illegal to add tomatoes to the pot. The facts on this are vague, but apparently civil rights won over culinary principles.

There *are* some facts shedding light on this chowder megillah: In the eighteenth century, chowder was made with a water-based broth, as is done today in Connecticut. In the nineteenth century, milk replaced the water, and that's what Bostonians think is the only chowder. Up north of Boston, milk is added to the water stock, making it milky but not creamy as in Boston. At some time in the nineteenth century, the juice of tomatoes replaced water or milk in New York (typical City Slicker gilding of the lily).

There are various theories about the introduction of tomatoes: The first tomato-based chowder was served at a stand in Coney Island, or the recipe for tomato chowder came from Delmonico's restaurant, or Italian immigrants added the tomatoes. Austin P. Winters, a

"Chowderheads" from the Chart House restaurant meet His Majesty's First Regiment of Foot Guards at the Boston Harborfest's Chowderfest. (Steven Senne, Boston Harborfest)

New Yorker, wrote in 1978 that his grandfather and great-uncle, who owned a fish store in lower Manhattan in the late 1800s, used tomatoes in chowder because milk was too expensive, and they called it Manhattan clam chowder, which is what it's called today.

In Maryland they add chicken and vegetables to chowder, but what do they know? They're crab people.

Clam chowder is an American original, although its name probably comes from the French *chaudière,* meaning a pot and also the fish stew cooked by Brittany fishing families in the pot. But New England chowder is not like French fish stew; it's too plain, and its plainness "is its hallmark and genius," notes food historian Raymond Sokolov.

Location: Events are held throughout the city but primarily on the waterfront. The Chowderfest is at City Hall Plaza and the Lobsterfest in East Boston, across the harbor from downtown Boston. 🌐 **Contact:** Boston Harborfest, 45 School St., Boston, MA 02108; Tel: (617)227-1528.

Caribbean Carnival

Second Sunday of August through following Saturday 🌐
Ever find your mouth watering for the exotic food of the islands? Then put Boston's Caribbean Carnival on your calender; it's the biggest Caribbean festival in New England,

getting crowds of 350,000 from all over the United States and Canada. No wonder. It's pungent with genuine island specialties.

Among them are Trinidadian *roti,* a fried knish-like treat of chicken, beef, goat, or shrimp wrapped in potato dough; knock-your-socks-off spicy Jamaican jerk chicken, and exotic fruits grown only in the Caribbean. To wash this down, there's *mauby,* a drink made from bark from Barbados, or a Jamaican concoction made of tree pods boiled with ginger and spices. (Sounds odd, but it's delicious.) All told, there are dishes from the Bahamas and most of the Caribbean Islands as well as from Ghana and Liberia.

And remember, this is a Carnival! Meaning floats, colorful costumes, steel drums, and marching bands of up to 200 members. Entrants are competing in various contests so they go all out to outdo each other in being the most spectacular and flamboyant. The big contest is for King and Queen of the Carnival. There's also a Kiddie Carnival, in which children aged two to thirteen dress in exotic island costumes to compete to be Kiddie King and Queen.

The festival is held at Franklin Park, where the area neighborhoods have a growing Caribbean community. The people decided in 1974 to remember their culture with a festival that felt like home. This is it.

Location: Take I-93 (Southeast Expressway) to Granite Ave. exit, go north to Gallivan Blvd., where you go left. At Massachusetts 28 (Blue Hill Ave.), go right. This leads to Franklin Park. **Contact:** Caribbean American Carnival Association, 26 Central Ave., Hyde Park, MA 02136; Tel: (617)282-2605.

St. Anthony's Feast

Last full weekend in August (Friday through Sunday)
Abbondanza! There's an abundance of everything—music, dancing, processions, fun, cheering, and especially Italian food—at St. Anthony's Feast. It seems like a neighborhood block party, only bigger, attended by 100,000 in the heart of Boston's North End.

Old grandmothers, little babies, and big families turn out to eat, visit, eat, dance in the streets, and eat.

Favorites with native Italians are tripe, calamari fried, stuffed, or in a savory salad, and ravioli stuffed with ricotta. The feast has the distinction of being Boston's only Italian festival that features *zeppole,* ball-shaped dough fried in hot oil and sprinkled with powdered sugar. If you don't want to experiment, you'll be happy with the sausage, peppers, and onion; spaghetti and meatballs; calzone; pizza; and fried mozzarella. Or loosen your belt for cannolis, ricotta pie, Italian pastries, or refreshing Italian ices, all polished off with an espresso or cappuccino.

While you eat, watch the theater of the vendors. They hit dramatic heights arguing about who has the best food, trying to entice customers away from each other. It's all in good fun.

Not to be missed is the procession during the weekend of the huge statue of St. Anthony. Eight burly men carry the statue through the neighborhood on a heavy wooden platform; the job is considered a special honor. The statue is festooned with 13 ribbons symbolizing St. Anthony's death on June 13, and, along the way, people pin money to the ribbons, confetti is thrown, and onlookers cheer. An outdoor mass in honor of St. Anthony is held at 5 p.m. on Saturday.

The nights ring with dancing and singing and music by Italian-American bands. Men with an itch to dance ask girls and grandmothers to join them under the stars. No introductions needed.

The festival was started in 1920 by Italian immigrants from Montefalcione in Avellino province in the mountains east of Naples. It was a re-creation of a traditional feast held each year for centuries in their small village.

Boston's North End is the heart of the city's Italian community. The biggest wave of Italians came in the years from 1909 to 1920 when Italy was economically depressed. Different villagers settled in different neighborhoods. The area around Endicott Street, for example, is home to the Avellino folks, while the waterfront was the destination for Sicilians.

Note: If you can't make it to St. Anthony's Feast, don't worry. Although St. Anthony's is the largest, there are seven other saints' feasts held in the North End during the summer.

Location: Endicott St. in Boston's North End. Take the subway to North Station, and then Causeway St. to Endicott. Warning! Parking in the North End can be an exercise in frustration. Take public transportation. **Contact:** St. Anthony's Society, 201-203 Endicott St., Boston, MA 02113. For information on all feast days, call the City of Boston's Cultural Affairs Office, (617)635-3911.

While You're There: A trip to the North End is like a mini-vacation to Italy. At greengrocers and cheese and butcher shops, most customers speak only Italian. Visit a cafe for cappuccino, or cool off with harbor breezes at the waterfront park and watch men playing bocci, the Italian bowling game.

Bourne

Bourne Scallop Fest

First weekend after Labor Day (Friday through Sunday)
The Bourne locals claim this is one of the largest seafood festivals on the East Coast; they dish up more than 4,200 pounds of fried scallops and play host to some 100,000 visitors.

Scallops are bivalve mollusks, and what's eaten in America is the abductor muscle that hinges the two shells. (In Europe, they also eat the coral or roe, and some gourmets say you can eat the whole thing). The scallop doesn't crawl or burrow like some mollusks. It swims, zapping through the water by vigorously opening and closing its valves, and this activity is what gives it a well-developed muscle.

There are about 300 species of scallops, but they're generally classified in two groups—bay scallops, found on the east coast, and sea scallops. The Buzzards Bay scallops at the festival are bay scallops, very small (the muscle can be about half an inch in diameter) and sweeter and more tender than the sea scallop. The muscles of sea scallops are about 1½ inches in diameter, and chewier. Along with other kinds of seafood, scallops have long been a major factor in the Cape Cod economy.

Most festival visitors opt for the fried scallop and cole slaw plate, but for non-scallop eaters, there are Italian sausages, burgers, hot dogs, and barbecued chicken.

The festival began in 1969 to raise money to keep two tourist information booths open. Proceeds now go toward a scholarship fund and a third information booth in a once-abandoned train station adjacent to the festival site.

Events include a parade on the Thursday afternoon before the festival, and during the weekend there's non-stop entertainment ranging from 1950s be-bop, blues, and big-name rock performers to the United States Navy Show Band, the Sweet Adelines, and dancers from the local dance academy. There are also 75 craftspeople and kiddie rides.

Location: Buzzards Bay Park in Buzzards Bay, a section of Bourne, on Main St. (U.S. 6). Buzzards Bay is on the mainland side of the Cape Cod Canal, which separates the mainland from the Cape.   **Contact:** Cape Cod Region Chamber of Commerce, 70 Main St., Buzzards Bay, MA 02532; Tel: (508)759-6000.

While You're There: Bike, jog, or walk on the 14 miles of newly paved paths alongside the Cape Cod Canal, the world's largest sea-level canal, and watch fishing boats, sailboats, and fancy yachts sailing by.

Essex ClamFest

Saturday after Labor Day (rain date is the next day)
Essex is an old New England fishing village on Cape Ann, where the folks like to brag about their clam heritage. It's some heritage: The fried clam was invented here in 1916 by the founders of Woodman's Restaurant.

Food aficionados Jane and Michael Stern have written, "To devotees of the fried clam, Cape Ann is Mecca."

You may rightly conclude from this that the Essex ClamFest is an occasion for fried-clam connoisseurs. But you will also find here clam fritters, clam cakes, and steamers (clams steamed in a small amount of water until the shells open). These all involve the clams known as steamers: soft-shell bivalves, with long rubbery necks, that live in tidal flats and are dug out at low tide. The famous Ipswich clam comes from beds ranging from sandy to mucky mud, and these flats are shared with neighbors Essex and Gloucester.

The clamfest also spotlights clam chowder, made with quahogs. Local restaurants compete to be named best chowdermaker, and visitors (for a small price) sample the chowders and vote. Most competitors stick with milky or creamy chowder; this is not tomato-based-Manhattan-chowder country. Perish the thought.

In Cape Ann, they favor a thinner chowder than the thick Boston or New England chowder, which has been known to be thickened with flour. "I don't put flour in chowder," Steve Woodman of Woodman's Restaurant says in tight-lipped fashion. Woodman's chowder is made of quahogs, onions, potatoes, water, milk plus a little half-and-half, and butter. It's soupy, not thick.

Back to fried clams: There are two kinds—whole steamers fried, and fried strip clams, which are quahogs, also known as round clams, cut in strips. Most often, restaurants serve the strip clams.

Well, on July 3, 1916, business was slow at the little stand in Essex that Lawrence (Chubby) and Bessie Woodman had opened two years earlier to sell fried potato chips, steamers, and raw clams. A fisherman suggested frying clams as well as potato chips. Big joke. How do you fry something in shells?

But Chubby and Bessie shucked some steamers, and threw them in hot lard. The fried clam was invented. Today Woodman's Restaurant, still run by Woodmans, dips Ipswich clams in milk, breads them lightly in a cornmeal mix, fries them, and gets written up all over as having the best fried clams anywhere. They do strip clams, too, but their fame rests on the fried Ipswich steamers.

P.S. For those who can tear themselves away from the clams, the fest has arts and crafts exhibits, Dixieland bands, pony rides, and children's entertainment.

Location: Essex is about 25 miles north of Boston, 5 miles west of Gloucester, on Massachusetts 133. The fest is in Memorial Park, just off 133.   **Contact:** Cape Ann Chamber of Commerce, 35 Commercial St., Gloucester, MA 01930; Tel: (508)283-1601.

Gloucester

New Fish Festival

Wednesday before last full weekend in June   What's a new fish? At this festival, a new fish is an old fish that is not a household name—like cusk, or pout, or ling.

Don't look for haddock or salmon; the exotic struts its stuff here. You can sample hake Vera Cruz, Cajun fried pout cakes, bluefish gumbo, baked stuffed cusk with dill sauce. Or California-style squid casserole, baked monkfish in saffron sauce, broiled Cape shark wrapped in bacon, char-grilled mackerel with tropical fruit.

For the relatively modest price of the ticket, you can sample as much fish as you want. The specialties are prepared by a dozen or more restaurant chefs, and about 300 pounds of fish are dished out in a couple of hours. The affair is a sell-out, limited to 200 to 250 people, so it's necessary to reserve tickets.

The festival began in 1986 to give a boost to the floundering fishing industry and to make people aware that using less expensive and less popular fish can be good business for both the consumer and the industry.

About the fish:

Cusk and pout are related to the cod. Shark has been looked down on in the United States, although it has been popular for eons in other parts of the world. Bluefish is known as the bulldog of the ocean, the most voracious fish of the Atlantic seaboard.

And monkfish, poor monkfish, is usually described as one of the ugliest fish in the ocean. It goes by other names—bellyfish, frogfish, goosefish, sea devil. To lure its prey, it lies partially buried on the sea floor and twitches a long filament that grows from its head and resembles a worm. This attracts smaller fish to the sea devil's huge mouth. For all its ugliness, the flavor of its tail (the only edible part) is compared to that of lobster.

Location: Gloucester House Restaurant, Seven Seas Wharf, 500 yards past St. Peter's Park in Gloucester, 17 miles north of Boston. Take Massachusetts 128N to first rotary, then right on Washington Street. The park is one mile from the rotary in the center of Gloucester. **Contact:** Cape Ann Chamber of Commerce, 33 Commercial St., Gloucester, MA 01930; Tel: (508)283-1601, Fax: (508)283-4740.

Gloucester Seafood Festival

Third weekend in September (Friday through Sunday)
This festival, which began in 1994, draws about 40,000 visitors who come for a truly nautical weekend. Arts and crafts are marine-related. Shellfish neophytes can watch demonstrations on how to eat lobster. Entertainers sing sea chanteys. Water events include blind-man dory races (the rower is blindfolded).

A huge pavilion tantalizes taste buds with seafood dishes: boiled lobster and lobster-salad rolls, calamari, fish and chips, chowder, seafood sausage, stir-fried seafood, steamers, seafood salads, fish kebabs, and sushi. And be sure to taste free samples from The Fishermen's Wives, a local group that demonstrates different ways to cook fish. For the non-fishy set, there are hot dogs, hamburgers, ice cream, and corn on the cob.

While you eat, you learn. There are demonstrations of lobster-pot building, net mending, clam shucking, and a simulated Coast Guard sea/air rescue. There's also an aquaculture display.

A trolley takes people to the Coast Guard station, the local historical society, and to the famous fisherman sculpture, *The Man at the Wheel*, erected on the shoreline in 1923 to commemorate the seaport's 300th anniversary. That's right—Gloucester was founded by the Plymouth pilgrims as their first fishing port in 1623, only three years after the Plymouth landing.

Today, Gloucester is the top port in the state for landing lobster and is one of the top seafood producers. The waterfront is crowded with Gloucester's fleet of 150 trawlers and lobster boats, and fish-processing plants dot the downtown.

Location: St. Peter's Park in Gloucester (see New Fish Festival, above).

While You're There: Gloucester is the self-proclaimed whale-watching capital of the world, so go whale-watching. Or visit nearby Rockport, once a rugged fishing village and now an art colony with many galleries. It's especially known for Motif #1, a barn-red harborside fishing shack that has been painted by countless artists.

Harwich

Harwich Cranberry Festival

Early in September (Saturday through following Sunday, nine days) ⊗ Between 160,000 and 200,000 people pack this Cape Cod town, population 11,000, for the "Biggest Small Town Celebration in the Country." Held before the harvest when the berries are still only yellow, it's more fair/carnival than a cranberry fest. Ah, well—you can still drink the secret-formula cranberry cooler, a cranberry and coconut drink. About 180 gallons are sold. And you can buy cranberry breads, muffins, jellies. Commercial cranberrying began in Dennis, which abuts Harwich, justification for the festival's name.

The Taste of Harwich, a festival adjunct, gives visitors a chance to taste and vote on the specialties of 30 restaurants.

The festival began in 1977, and is kicked off with Cape Cod's largest crafts fair, boasting 300 exhibitors. A two-and-a-half-mile parade provides the finale.

Location: Harwich is on the southeast coast of Cape Cod, just off U.S. 6, at exits 10 or 11. Most events are at the Harwich High School. ⊗ **Contact:** Harwich Cranberry Festival, P.O. Box 555, 24 Purity Plaza, Harwich Port, MA 02646; Tel: (508)430-2811, Fax: (508)430-2725.

Nantucket

Cranberry Harvest Weekend

Weekend after Columbus Day (Friday through Sunday) ⊗ Cranberry harvest time on this island off Cape Cod brings a bright blush to more than 200 acres, demonstrations of cranberry-wreath making and cranberry-candy making at the Cranberry Marketplace, cranberry cookbooks and cranberry specialties—candies, muffins, pizza, cakes, bread—for sale, and a Cranberry Cookery contest for both amateur and professional chefs. To complete the celebration, small planes and buses take visitors on bog tours.

Cranberries were first cultivated here in 1857. Before 1959, Nantucket had the largest contiguous natural cranberry bog in the world, 254 acres. But the bog was divided into smaller, more water-efficient units, and the "biggest" distinction was lost.

Location: Nantucket can be reached by plane from several points or by ferry from Hyannis year-round and in the summer from Hyannis and Harwich Port. Main festival events are at the Folger Hotel on Easton Street. ⊗ **Contact:** Nantucket Island Chamber of Commerce, 48 Main St., Nantucket, MA 02554; Tel: (508)228-1700, Fax: (508)325-4925.

While You're There: The African Meeting House, dating from 1827, used as a school and church, is the nation's second oldest structure still standing that was built by free African Americans for their own use. Slavery was abolished on Nantucket in 1770. Cape

Verdeans came here to work in the maritime and cranberry industries in the nineteenth and twentieth centuries. For information, call (508)228-4058.

The Standard Times Great New Bedford Summerfest

Three or four days including Fourth of July ⊛ New Bedford has a protected harbor that made it the world's busiest whaling port in the 1880s, and it's still one of the ten largest fishing ports in the country. So it's no surprise that it's the site of a huge seafood festival where more than 5,000 pounds of seafood—clam cakes, fried fish, and scallops fresh from the waters off New Bedford—are eaten in four days.

If fish isn't your thing, salads abound as well as burgers, dogs, and Portuguese linguiça. More than 20,000 meals are served.

For fish lovers who cook, there are cooking demonstrations (and tastings) of less well known varieties of fish: hake cooked Portuguese style, skate kebabs, sea catfish.

The festival began as the New Bedford Seafood Festival in 1990 to spotlight New Bedford's fishing industry. With more and more events, it became a Summerfest in 1993, visited by about 50,000, with nonstop activities on the waterfront and in the downtown historic district.

Activities include whaleboat races, a puppet theater with 10-foot-tall puppets, crafts, children's events, and live entertainment. Music runs the gamut—jazz, blues, Cajun, Portuguese, Latin, and Irish.

New Bedford, the state's fourth largest city, has a mixed ethnic heritage, with many Portuguese and Cape Verdeans, and the Cape Verdean National Day dance and celebration on July 5 is part of the Summerfest.

There are usually tall ships open to the public. The Ernestina is a tall ship must-see; she was given to New Bedford by the people of the Cape Verde Islands.

A festival highlight, held on Sunday, is the blessing of the fleet to insure safe and prosperous voyages. Tall ships, fishing vessels, and pleasure boats are all decorated for the blessing.

Location: New Bedford is 60 miles south of Boston, 33 miles north of Providence. From I-195, take the New Bedford downtown exit and watch for signs. ⊛ **Contact:** New Bedford Area Chamber of Commerce, 794 Purchase St., New Bedford, MA 02742; Tel: (508)999-5231.

While You're There: Take a walk through town to see the mansions once owned by whaling captains; they were built in the nineteenth-century heyday of tall ships and whaling. Around the dock, you'll see huge fishing trawlers.

Feast of the Blessed Sacrament

First weekend in August (Thursday through Sunday) ⊕

This feast began in 1915 as a religious thanksgiving for a safe ocean crossing by the people from the Portuguese island of Madeira, off the African coast. Madeirans began arriving here in the early 1900s; people from mainland Portugal arrived somewhat earlier. There are now about 25,000 people of Portuguese heritage in the New Bedford area. The Madeira hometown of many of the immigrants was Estreito da Calheta, and the New Bedford feast is a re-creation of that town's big feast day.

Attended by 100,000 to 200,000, it's considered the largest Portuguese festival in the world. Needless to say, some secularization has crept in.

While a solemn high mass is celebrated at Immaculate Conception Church on Sunday, the main events for the throngs are a two-hour parade, kids' activities, band music, singing of Portuguese songs, and eating. And drinking.

Typically, the New Bedfordites send to Madeira for 3,000 liters of Madeira wine, a forti-fied wine that was enjoyed by George Washington and Thomas Jefferson as a dessert drink. It's sold at the festival by the glass or bottle. There's beer, too.

Of the mounds of food sold, a favorite is *carne de espeto* (meat on a stick), which is beef that people grill themselves on a skewer over an open fire. About 7,000 pounds of the carne are devoured, and there are often as many as 100 people standing around the fire.

Other favorites are *bacalho*, salted codfish; *carne de vinho de alhos*, pork marinated in wine and garlic, cooked in a big pot and served in a sandwich or as a meal; rabbit stew; goat stew; tuna steaks; *linguiça*, pork sausage; and sweet Portuguese breads. It's possible to sam-ple a little of everything at a buffet, or to order full meals of one specialty.

Location: Take the Washburn St. exit off I-95 to Cape Cod; at the stop, follow Belleville Ave. right for about a mile to Madeira Ave. The festival covers three or four blocks in the vicinity of 50 Madeira Ave. ⊕ **Contact:** Club Madeirense S.S. Sacramento, 50 Madeira Ave., New Bedford, MA 02746; Tel: (508)992-6911.

North Adams

La Festa

Weekend after Father's Day, Friday through Sunday ⊕ It's

not really so strange that you can sample the cuisines of Greece, Poland, France, Thailand, and Mexico, not to mention New England, in rural New England.

The diverse food at this festival reflects the amazing cultural diversity of the area. In the late 1800s, German, French, Italian, and Polish immigrants came to this northwest cor-ner of Massachusetts to work in the textile mills, and to help build railroad tunnels.

The festival's 26 international food vendors offer everything from pad thai (Asians are more recent arrivals) to souvlaki. Most of the food is made by local clubs, including the Sons of Italy, the Irish Club, the Jewish League, and the Polish Ethnic Alliance.

Ethnic groups try to outdo each other with music as well as food. Every two hours the festival stage moves musically to a different country. You can sit and enjoy Italian crooning or a Greek love song or dancers doing an Irish jig. There are also games for kids, 50 to 75 crafts booths, and a baseball grudge match between a local team and a team from Boston.

The festival was started in 1981 as a community event to raise money for local schools. It's a real hometown family affair that has nonetheless attracted visitors from 45 states. Attendance is about 10,000.

Location: Noel Field Athletic Complex on State St. (Massachusetts 8) in North Adams, 5 miles east of Williamstown.   **Contact:** La Festa, P.O. Box 1704, North Adams, MA 02147; Tel: (413)66FESTA.

South Carver

Massachusetts Cranberry Harvest Festival

Columbus Day weekend (Saturday through Monday) As crops go, the cranberry crop is small, totaling about 30,000 acres in North America, the acreage some individual farmers have in corn alone. Furthermore, Massachusetts is losing ground (bog ground) to other areas, and in 1995, Wisconsin actually beat (gasp) Massachusetts in cranberry production. But Massachusetts is where it all started, cranberries remain the commonwealth's number-one agricultural product, and South Carver is the Cranberry Capital of the World (well, it was until those upstart Wisconsinites started growing so much). So celebrating the cranberry harvest is a Massachusetts tradition.

About 30,000 people visit the Edaville Cranberry Bog in Plymouth County at festival time, when they can see, on foot or by helicopter, the scarlet bogs and the actual harvesting.

There are also various cranberry drinks and dishes to try: chocolate-covered dried and sweetened berries, cranberry fudge, cookies, and salsa. In the "Make It Better with Cranberries Cooking Contest," contestants try everything—pies, cream cakes, rolls, mustard, catsup, trail mix, candies, cobbler. Other festival attractions are hay rides, a farmers' market, music, crafts, and historical exhibits.

Legend has it that the Indians brought cranberries to the first Thanksgiving in Plymouth in 1621, and the Pilgrims learned from the Indians that the bitter berries could be used as a dye, as a poultice to draw poison from wounds, and as a food, especially mixed in pemmican. Later, American ships carried barrels of cranberries, rich in vitamin C, to ward off scurvy. Cranberries were such a precious crop in the eighteenth century that in 1773 Provincetown, on Cape Cod, passed a law banning the picking of more than a quart before September 20. Disobeying brought a dollar fine and "the berys taken away."

Not long ago, cranberries were used chiefly in sauce, but now they are processed and blended and baked into various foods and beverages, and are also being studied for their possible use in treating urinary infections.

Five states—Wisconsin, Massachusetts, New Jersey, Oregon, and Washington—grow most of the North American cranberries, with British Columbia and other parts of Canada growing about 3,000 acres. Massachusetts has more than 13,200 acres of cranberry bogs, most of which are in Plymouth County, and in 1995 produced about 1,600,000 barrels (a barrel is 100 pounds) of cranberries; Wisconsin meanwhile came through with 1,725,000 barrels. Of course, as Massachusetts folks would be quick to say, production fluctuates, depending on the weather. It is expected, however, that ultimately Wisconsin will be number one in the cranberry rankings, because Massachusetts doesn't have the land to expand its crops that Wisconsin has.

The first recorded cranberry cultivation was in Dennis on Cape Cod in 1816 by Henry Hall; the methods haven't changed much since his time.

Cranberries grow in peat bogs, not in water, and growers flood the bogs in winter to prevent wind damage. Sand is sprinkled on the ice, and, as the ice melts, the sand helps control insects and stimulates the vines' propagation.

About 90 percent of cranberry harvesting is wet harvesting. (They wet harvest at the Edaville Bog.) To wet harvest, the beds are again flooded in the fall, and a water reel, or "egg beater," stirs the submerged vines; the buoyant berries rise to the surface and are corralled to the edge of the bog. In dry harvesting, mechanical pickers that look like big lawn mowers comb through vines and deposit the berries in bags.

In the spring, cranberries have a pink blossom that looks like the head and neck of the sand hill crane. Thus the name, crane berries.

Location: South Carver is about 3 miles off I-495 at exit 2. **Contact:** Cranberry World, 225 Water St., Plymouth, MA 02360; Tel: (508)747-2350.

While You're There: Cranberry World Visitors' Center, operated by Ocean Spray, the grower cooperative, has daily demonstrations of cranberry cookery, displays of antique and modern harvesting tools, and a scale-model cranberry farm. It's on the waterfront in Plymouth, about 14 miles north of South Carver.

Springfield

World's Largest Pancake Breakfast

Saturday closest to May 14 ☼ There's no waffling in Springfield when more than 60,000 people sit down for breakfast.

In three hours, from 8 to 11 a.m., they consume vast quantities of buttermilk pancakes, containing 600 pounds of eggs, and drink about 3,400 gallons of coffee. People eat at a 1,500-foot table stretching down the middle of Main Street, where they're entertained by local dance schools and, in a different way, by the 400 flapjack-flipping volunteers.

The breakfast began in 1986 to celebrate Springfield's 1636 founding and as a competition with Battle Creek for the World's Longest Breakfast Table. That battle was dropped when a dispute couldn't be resolved over whether the table had to extend in a single line, so both cities claimed the title. Then the cities competed to serve the most breakfasts, and from 1986 through 1995, Battle Creek, which puts on a big feed at its Cereal Festival, had lost only twice. But in 1996, Springfield served 67,997 breakfasts—that's 135,994 pancakes—and won. Battle Creek forfeited, said it wasn't competing any more, that its festival had gone beyond just being a cereal event. Oh, sure.

Location: Springfield is off I-91 about 10 miles north of the Connecticut border. **Contact:** Spirit of Springfield, 101 State St., Suite 220, Springfield, MA 01103-2006; Tel: (413)733-3800, Fax: (413)739-0276.

See Also: Cereal Festival (Battle Creek, MI).

New Hampshire

Hampton Beach Seafood Festival

Weekend after Labor Day ❄ This festival began in 1989 just to have a post-season seaside party at a summer resort at a pretty time of year. Now the American Bus Association has called the festival one of North America's top 100 events, and about 200,000 people come to stroll on the boardwalk and beach, listen to continuous entertainment on two stages, and enjoy the street performers, including mimes, a juried crafts show, and fireworks.

More than 50 restaurants and about a dozen nonprofit organizations offer food, and a judging panel of culinary experts gives awards to restaurant dishes. That means the restaurant chefs try hard, and they come up with several kinds of chowder, crabcakes, boiled lobsters, steamers, various seafood Newburgs, Cajun seafood, and desserts that usually include homemade pies and blueberries flambé.

Location: Hampton Beach is 45 minutes north of Boston, off I-95 at exit 2. ❄ **Contact:** Hampton Beach Chamber of Commerce, P.O. Box 790, Hampton, N.H. 03843; Tel: (603)926-8717, Fax: (603)964-7293.

Milford

Milford's Great Pumpkin Festival

Columbus Day weekend (Friday through Sunday) ❄ Glowing pumpkins and pumpkin pies set the theme for this festival, which raises close to $5,000 for charitable groups in town. A resident grows about 700 pumpkins just for the festival and donates them, and the rest are bought from nearby growers to be sold.

The festival is held in the center of town in what's called the oval, and on Saturday night a few hundred carved pumpkins are lit there. All the windows of the town hall also have lit pumpkins in them, and a huge fabricated pumpkin in a third-story window of the town hall is lit on opening night. A runner carries a torch to a volunteer fireman who climbs a ladder to light the pumpkin. People cheer and oooh and aaah.

There's a pumpkin-pie contest with separate categories for adults and children, and slices are sold after the judging. Some entries are a bit exotic, with liqueur, for example, in the filling, but the winners are generally those who bake a traditional pie.

Food vendors sell regular fair food and also pumpkin pie, muffins, and bread, and other New Hampshire dishes—fish chowder, apple crisp, apple pie.

Events include band concerts, an arts and crafts display, and pumpkin painting for children. The festival began in 1990 and is attended by a few thousand.

Location: Milford is 12 miles from Nashua on New Hampshire 101. **Contact:** Milford Town Hall, 1 Union Sq., Milford, NH 03055; Tel: (603)673-2257.

Portsmouth

Chowder Festival

Saturday in late May or early June Portsmouth is an ocean city, and chowder goes with salt spray. It's therefore axiomatic that Portsmouth dishes out a lot of chowder—more than 500 gallons, in fact—on festival day.

The chowder is all kinds: Manhattan and creamy clam, corn, fish, oyster, and potato. Some 20 restaurants along the seacoast offer their best chowders, and visitors buy a ticket to sample at their will. The festival begins at 11:30 in the morning and lasts till the chowder runs out, which is usually by mid-afternoon. Live music accompanies the slurps.

Location: Prescott Park, 105 Marcy St., across from Strawberry Banke, in downtown Portsmouth, 70 miles north of Boston off I-95. **Contact:** Prescott Park Arts Festival, P.O. Box 4370, Portsmouth, NH 03802; Tel: (603)436-2848.

While You're There: Portsmouth was originally called Strawberry Banke because settlers disembarking along the Piscataqua River in 1630 found the banks covered with strawberries. This site is now occupied by the Strawberry Banke Museum, 10 acres of more than 40 buildings from the late 1800s up through the 1950s. Period gardens can be viewed, and every day there are demonstrations of eighteenth-century cooking in the 1780 John Wheelwright House. The museum is bounded by Marcy, State, Washington, and Hancock Streets.

See Also: Boston Harborfest (Boston, MA).

New Jersey

New Jersey Seafood Festival

Second weekend in June ☼ It's called the "*offish*al" start of summer at this coastal resort, and that means Jersey seafood dishes of every variety: lobster, clam chowder, clams on the half shell, clams casino, tuna steaks, calamari rings, blue crabs, crab croquettes, oysters, fried shrimp, fish broiled and fried. And dipping into Cajun and Southern cuisines, the festival also offers seafood gumbo, shrimp jambalaya, alligator sausage, shark steak.

Since a purpose of the festival is to showcase Jersey seafood *and* agricultural products, there are wine tastings provided by the New Jersey Winegrowers, and a Jersey Fresh Corn Eating Contest and a Very Berry Blueberry Pie Eating Contest.

Demonstrations of recreational sports—for example, skimboarding and bodyboarding—are held at the beach, and there are special children's activities, juried arts and crafts, continuous live music, crab races, and an in-water model-boat competition. Started in 1987, the fair has an attendance of about 80,000.

Location: Silver Lake Park and Taylor Pavilion, Ocean Ave., Belmar; take the Garden State Parkway to exit 98. ☼ **Contact:** Belmar Tourism, Municipal Building, 601 Main St., Belmar, NJ 07719; Tel: (908)681-2900; Fax: (908)681-3434.

See Also: Massachusetts Cranberry Harvest Festival (South Carver, MA).

Chatsworth Cranberry Festival

Third weekend in October ☼ When the organizers of this festival said cranberry, they meant cranberry. Flower show arrangements must use cranberries. Quilt pieces and arts and crafts have cranberry motifs. There are contests for the best cranberry-decorated hat, the largest Jersey-grown cranberry, the most cranberry-colored classic car, the oldest vehicle used in the cranberry bogs.

There's a cranberry-recipe contest, and visitors can sample the entries—cakes, pies, cookies, candy, jams, jellies, relishes, sauces—after they're judged. There's a cranberry-pancake breakfast. The Cranberry Cafe offers cranberry preserves, chutney, pies, ice cream, salsa, cheesecakes, tarts, vinegar, honey, and bags of fresh cranberries.

Events include tours of the cranberry bogs, music (country, folk), a Pinelands photography display and contest, and historical exhibits that relate to the year's historical theme. One year it might be Blackbeard the Pirate, another the Blue Comet train.

Chatsworth is the "capital" of the New Jersey Pine Barrens, a national reserve of a thousand square miles of Pitch Pine forests, shallow lakes, and swamps, and beneath it an aquifer thought to hold 17 trillion gallons of pure water. The availability of water, the vast swampland, and the flat terrain all are good for growing cranberries, and commercial growing began at the time of the Civil War. The Chatsworth area has 3,200 acres of bogs.

The festival, attended by about 50,000, was started in 1984 to promote cranberries and benefit the restoration of the three-story White Horse Inn, the only surviving building of a resort complex visited by Astors, Vanderbilts, and their ilk until World War I.

Location: Chatsworth fairgrounds, east side of County 563, 8 miles south of New Jersey 72.   **Contact:** Chatsworth Club II, Box 331, Chatsworth, NJ 08019; Tel: (509)859-9701. Or contact Chatsworth Cranberry Assn., Barnegat Road, Chatsworth, NY 08019.

See Also: Massachusetts Cranberry Harvest Festival (South Carver, MA).

Lambertville

Shad Festival

Last full weekend in April   The Delaware River, the last major undammed, free-flowing river on the east coast, yielded 16 million pounds of shad in 1896. But by the 1940s the river was so filthy that shad couldn't migrate upriver to spawn. Finally people decided to take action, the river began to heal—and the shad came back.

This was cause for celebration, so in 1982, the Delaware Riverkeeper, a watchdog group, organized this shad feed. It attracts about 20,000 people who sample offerings from local restaurants in Shad Row: shad cakes, shad gumbo, shad on a stick, smoked shad, shad salad, you name it. There is also a riverside cookout dinner (the Chamber of Commerce sells about 1,000 tickets) of charcoal-broiled shad filet, baked potato, and cole slaw.

Other happenings are fish tales told by a story teller, and demonstrations of shad hauling using the seine technique taught to early settlers by the Indians. There are children's events, a poster auction, music (folk, rock, blues), an art show, the Shad Festival Boogie Dance. The Riverkeeper provides educational materials on conservation and the environment.

The American shad (*Alosa sapidissima,* meaning most delicious) is the largest of the herrings and is anadromous; that is, it lives in the ocean but migrates up coastal rivers to spawn. Shad are found along the east coast of North America from Florida to New Brunswick, but are most abundant between Connecticut and North Carolina.

Shad are group broadcast spawners; a group of three to five males surround an individual female, and they all swim in a circular pattern, spraying eggs and sperm into the water. A female produces from 100,000 to 600,000 eggs.

They do their spraying at night, and this is when commercial fishermen go out on the rivers with nets to catch them. Sports fishermen catch them on rods. They are best eaten at spawning time, because they get thin and tasteless after that.

Shad roe is considered a delicacy, the caviar of the eastern rivers, and the shad itself has a closely textured, rich-tasting flesh. The catch is that it's very bony, one of the most difficult fish to bone; most people eat the filets boned.

Fans of the shad like to remember that shad is a part of history: it's recorded that an unusually large and early run on the Schuylkill River filled the hungry stomachs of General George Washington's troops at Valley Forge in 1777–78.

Location: On the waterfront in Lambertville, 15 miles northwest of Trenton on New Jersey 29. **Contact:** Delaware Riverkeeper Network, P.O. Box 753, Lambertville, NJ 08530; Tel: (609)397-4410. Or contact Lambertville Chamber of Commerce, 4 S. Union St., Lambertville, NJ 08530-2110; Tel: (609)397-0055.

New Brunswick

Hungarian Festival

First Saturday in June Hungarians first arrived in New Brunswick in the 1880s, the men to work in foundries and factories, the women to roll cigars in cigar factories. They brought their cuisine, rich with sour cream and paprika, with them; it has been adopted nationwide.

Chicken paprikash, or *paprikas csirke,* was accepted by the Magyars as a national dish when it appeared on the menu of the parliamentary dining room in 1844. Platters of it are served at the festival. The dish is made with chicken and onions browned in bacon drippings, braised in chicken stock and paprika, and smothered in a sauce made from the braising liquid mixed with sour cream.

Also on the menu: stuffed cabbage; sausage; *pecsenye,* fried pork with rye bread and sauerkraut; *langos,* fried dough, like a small pizza, fried quickly in lard until it's golden and sprinkled with garlic salt or powdered sugar. And crepes, called *polescenta,* filled with cottage cheese, sugar and lemon, nuts and marmalade, or apple jam. Sometimes there's a pig roasted on a spit, served at day's end.

And there's always *gulyas,* a herdsman's soup, cooked over an open fire and made with the ingredients a herdsman would have at hand—pork, onions, potatoes, paprika, lard. This is *not* the same as goulash, with all sorts of things in it, although the word goulash clearly comes from gulyas. The great chef Auguste Escoffier tasted gulyas in Szeged and took the recipe back to Monte Carlo as *gulyas hongrois.*

Pastries and strudels are served at a Budapest-style coffee house along with espresso and *habos,* which means foam and is similar to cappuccino.

You can watch some of this food being made. You can also watch Hungarian folk dancing, listen to Hungarian folk music and children's choirs, browse the vendors' stalls for Hungarian art. For children, there are Hungarian games.

Half a mile of Somerset Street is closed off for the festival, which draws about 15,000 people. It began in 1975 as part of the revitalization of New Brunswick.

Location: Somerset St. in New Brunswick, exit 9 from the New Jersey Turnpike. **Contact:** Hungarian Civic Assn., 300 Somerset St., New Brunswick, NJ 08903; Tel: (908)846-5777.

Point Pleasant Beach

Festival of the Sea

Third weekend in September This oceanside town, once a boat-building center and today a vital fishing area, is one of the state's leading resorts, boasting a mile-long boardwalk and white-sand beaches.

It also boasts the Festival of the Sea, a multi-faceted affair that features seafood and a wacky ocean inner-tube race. The festival started in 1978 and draws more than 50,000 visitors. About 150 tubers generally enter the tube race on Sunday, which is preceded by a Tube Parade.

The seafood-festival part of the festival highlights local catches prepared by area restaurants—clam chowder, clams on the half shell, clams casino, boiled lobster, boiled jumbo shrimp. Landlubbers have choices of babyback ribs, chicken, pizza, sub sandwiches.

In the arts and crafts department, more than 200 artisans display, among other miscellany, paintings and photographs of local landscapes and wildlife. And on the stage there's anything from live music to clowns to Perky the Penguin. Saturday ends with fireworks on the beach.

Location: Point Pleasant Beach is about 7 miles east of Garden State Parkway at exits 98 South and 90 North. **Contact:** Point Pleasant Area Chamber of Commerce, 517A Arnold Ave., Point Pleasant Beach, NJ 08742; Tel: (908)899-2424.

Stone Harbor

Wings 'n Water Festival

Third weekend in September This is a salty festival to raise awareness of coastal wildlife and to benefit the Wetlands Institute. It's also a chance to pig out (flounder out?) on seafood.

At the Wings 'n Water Festival, you can learn about the coastal environment while sampling a variety of seafood dishes like this tray of goodies. (Wetlands Institute–Wings 'n Water Festival)

The Wetlands Institute, a nonprofit organization, promotes understanding of the coastal environment through education and research. Located on 6,000 acres of wetlands on a thin ribbon along the New Jersey coast, the institute center is in Stone Harbor, a noted nesting place for herons. The festival takes place there and in nearby Avalon and Middle Township. The region is ideal for viewing salt marshes, beaches, dunes, tidal creeks, and birds.

The salt air whets appetites, and satisfaction comes by the gallon for the 40,000 visitors. At the clam chowder cook-off held Saturday in Avalon, visitors sample chowders prepared by Seven Mile Beach restaurants and pick a winner.

In Stone Harbor, the popular shrimpwich is featured, plus crab-cake sandwiches, a raw bar, deviled crabs and clams, shrimp salad, and chicken and fries and other non-seafood items. Dinners of Jersey flounder and Jersey corn, tomatoes, and cole slaw are served Saturday at the Cape May Courthouse in Middle Township.

Activities include retriever demonstrations, dune walks, duck and goose calling, a salt marsh safari, folk music, a fly-casting seminar, displays of wildfowl carving.

Location: Stone Harbor is three miles southeast of the Garden State Parkway at exit 10. ⁂ **Contact:** Wetlands Institute, 1075 Stone Harbor Boulevard, Stone Harbor, NJ 08247-1424; Tel: (609)368-1211; Fax: (609)368-3871.

Dandelion Festival

First Saturday in April unless it conflicts with Easter weekend ☼ Vineland was declared the Dandelion Capital of the World in the early 1980s by Vineland's mayor, with good reason. The Vineland region is the largest commercial producer of dandelions in the United States. The dandelions are grown under plastic in January and February, and harvested in March, the first crop of the season.

The festival, held regularly since 1991, although it began in 1973, is a dandelion dinner attended by about 150 people. The menu offers dandelion salads and soups and dandelion-and-sausage ravioli (and some foods for those who aren't wild about dandelions). A family with Italian roots donates dandelion wine; dandelions are fairly commonly used by Italians in cookery and wine making.

Music and dancing and the crowning of Miss Dandelion Festival follow the dinner. Dandelion cookbooks are available.

Vineland is a 69-square-mile city, and in the mid-nineteenth century was planned as a wine-producing region, attracting numbers of Italian immigrants familiar with vineyards. However, the vineyards became diseased, and the wine industry was abandoned.

Location: DeThomasi's Five Points Inn, East Landis Ave., Vineland. ☼ **Contact:** Miss Vineland Scholarship Pageant, 1370 S. Main Rd., Suite 134, Vineland, N.J. 08360; Tel: (609)692-5816.

See Also: Dandelion Mayfest (Dover, OH).

West Cape May Lima Bean Festival

Saturday of Columbus Day weekend ☼ Acres and acres of lima beans are grown in West Cape May County, providing the fodder for the Only Lima Bean Festival in the World. About 10,000 people visit the festival to see what wonders have been wrought with the bean.

Visitors will find refrigerator magnets with legends such as "Dalai Lima." They'll find lima-bean ice cream, a popular treat sweetened with honey and sort of resembling pistachio ice cream.

Civic groups serve up thousands of pounds of limas in chilis, salads, quiches, soups, casseroles, and succotash, which is corn and limas cooked together (the word is derived from the Narragansett Indian word *msickquatash*). Half a dozen or so pigs are barbecued, and vendors also sell standards like hot dogs, fried chicken, lemonade, and funnel cakes.

In the Better Better Best lima-bean cooking contest, local restaurants submit entries in the categories of soup, succotash, and "most innovative." Festival-goers sample and vote for the tastiest entries.

A festival highlight is the crowning of the Lima Bean Queen, who is selected by lot. Names are placed in a basket, and when the name is drawn at 1 p.m., if you're there, you're the queen; you get a tiara and trophy to keep. If no one comes forward in 10 minutes, another name is drawn. Past queens have been a 6-year-old first grader and a 65-year-old woman.

Entertainment is varied. Politicians always attend and work the crowd, but, while the mayor of West Cape May is the master of ceremonies, politicians are barred from giving speeches. Crafts are sold, many with a lima-bean theme. There are also flea markets, country and western music, and a lima-bean pitch, where people get 15 limas to pitch into plastic pots 15 feet away. Competition is keen.

The festival was started in 1985 by Alys Dolmetsch as a borough fund raiser, and proceeds still benefit the community. Alys is known for having bought up all the googly eyes in the county one year to make googly-bean refrigerator magnets.

The original habitat of the lima bean is somewhat vague. The name comes from the city of Lima, Peru, because John Harris, a United States Navy officer, brought some pale, flat beans back from there in 1824 and planted them on his farm near Chester, New York. But limas were around before that; by the late 1700s, the beans were growing in North America, Europe, Africa, and India.

Location: West Cape May is south of the end of Garden State Parkway, which turns into Lafayette St. Bear right at Collier's Liquor Store. **Contact:** Cape May Chamber of Commerce, 732 Broadway, West Cape May, NJ 08204; Tel: (609)884-1005.

Whitesbog

Whitesbog Blueberry Festival

Last Saturday in June   You *could* call this festival the Birth of the Blues Festival. Whitesbog is where Dr. Frederick V. Coville, a botanist, and Elizabeth C. White crossbred the wild highbush blueberries in the New Jersey Pine Barrens to develop plants with big berries that would ripen at different times.

To celebrate this, you can stuff yourself with blueberry bagels, muffins, funnel cake, sundaes, pastries, pies, cheesecake with blueberry sauce, fresh blueberries—and non-blueberry food, too. Other activities include no-hands blueberry-pie eating contests, a blueberry balloon toss, foot-stomping Pinelands music, documentary videos, educational bus and walking tours, and a crafts fair where many crafters display duck decoys.

The festival was started in 1984 and draws about 5,000 visitors.

Blueberries grow all over the world, but are grown commercially only in the United States and Canada. Michigan is the leading producer of highbush berries, followed by New Jersey, Oregon, and North Carolina. Highbush plants grow to five feet, whereas the lowbush wild berries grown in Maine and Canada are only about 14 inches high.

Whitesbog was the largest cranberry plantation in New Jersey at the end of the nineteenth century, and here Elizabeth White grew up. She wanted to develop a companion crop, and the U.S. Department of Agriculture dispatched Frederick Coville to set up a research station here.

Because blueberries thrive on acidic soil, they flourish in the Pinelands, and because the residents, called Pineys, knew where the best ones were, White promised cash for the plants with the biggest berries. This got her a nice selection.

She had also said she would name favored berries for the picker. Rube Leek found a delicious berry, but neither of his names seemed right for a fruit, so the berry was called Rubel. As it turned out, it was smaller than what Miss White wanted, so it wasn't crossbred, but the Rubel is now produced in New Jersey and Michigan and is the only pure-strain highbush berry commercially grown. It's very small and very sweet.

There are now 15 or 16 varieties of highbush berries, which all stem from the work of Coville and White; five of the varieties are grown commercially.

Location: Whitesbog is in the Lebanon State Forest, 30 miles east of Philadelphia, about midway between Philadelphia and the Atlantic Ocean. **Contact:** Whitesbog Preservation Trust, 120-24A Whitesbog Rd., Browns Mills, NJ 08015; Tel: (609)893-4646.

See Also: State of Maine Wild Blueberry Festival (Union, ME).

New York

Italian Heritage & Food Festival

Mid-July (five days, Wednesday through Sunday) ☀ *Sfinge,* *bruschetta, gucidatti:* just a few of the foods you can try at this street festival celebrating Italian culture. It features 110 food booths and three stages for song and dance—jazz, ballet, country and western, cloggers, and traditional Italian. There's a full midway, gambling to benefit local charities, and kids' rides and games.

About one-and-a-half million attend the festival, which began officially in 1988 but has its roots in church street fairs of the 1930s. It's still a street fair, but now a secular, gastronomical event sponsored by three business groups.

The festival foods range from standards—like Italian sausages, calamari, calzones, manicotti, fettuccini Alfredo, cannolis, fried dough—to more unusual specialties: *gucidatti* (fig cookies), *sfinge* (cream puffs), *bruschetta* (toasted Italian bread made with herbs, spices, and tomatoes), *bistecca di soffione* (steak and dandelions), *caponatina* (eggplant with capers, onions, and tomatoes), and *dinulata* (honey balls).

And there are sure to be Buffalo chicken wings, which were invented in 1963 at Buffalo's Anchor Bar by Teressa Bellissimo. The story is that Teressa created the wings (fried, then tossed in a hot sauce, and served with blue cheese and celery) out of desperation, using what was on hand, to feed a hungry bar crowd.

Buffalo has a sizable Italian community. The first wave of Italians came here in the 1880s and 1890s, after the Erie Canal was built and the railroads had come in, making Buffalo a major shipping terminus with plentiful jobs.

Location: The northern Niagara section of Buffalo, on Hertel Ave. between Delaware and Colvin Aves. ☀ **Contact:** Italian Heritage & Food Festival, P.O. Box 526 Buffalo, NY 14213; Tel: (716)874-6133.

Garlic Day

Third Saturday in September ⊚ This celebration on a Long Island herb farm is small, deliberately limited to 500 people, but choice. Its centerpiece is the breathtaking buffet lunch, starting with appetizers of peasant breads with garlic spreads, and including such specialties as *pissaladière,* which translates to French garlic and onion pie (sort of a like a pizza, but with a filling of just garlic and onion); heirloom tomatoes with a garlic, basil, and olive oil sauce; roasted vegetables with, of course, garlic. Dessert is usually a break, like local peaches. No garlic.

The day includes workshops on growing garlic and garlic's health aspects, and a cooking demonstration. A garlic bazaar carries seeds, T-shirts, books, garlic jams, salsas, vinegars, pickles.

Location: Peconic River Herb Farm in Calverton, just west of Riverhead, off the Long Island Expressway at exit 71. ⊚ **Contact:** Peconic River Herb Farm, 310-C River Rd., Calverton, NY 11933; Tel: (516)369-0058.

See Also: Gilroy Garlic Festival (Gilroy, CA) and Hudson Valley Garlic Festival (Saugerties, NY).

French Festival

Weekend nearest Bastille Day, usually second weekend in July ⊚ Napoleon, in uniform with a red sash, mounted on a gray horse, leads the 50-unit parade that's the high point of this festival.

French missionaries settled here in 1655, and the French became large landholders in the area. In 1816, after Napoleon I met his Waterloo and was exiled to St. Helena, a group of his former officers built a house for the emperor (it later burned down), planning a refuge for him in Cape Vincent. When Napoleon died in 1821, still in exile, the officers' mission ended, and several returned to France. But most of the émigrés stayed on, and the French heritage was passed along. On the day of the festival, Napoleon rides again.

So does the pastry named for him. Saturday morning before the parade, a tractor-trailer unloads about 20,000 French pastries. There are Napoleons (thin layers of puff pastry spread with a cream filling), croissants, tarts, cream puffs, fruit boats, palmiers. Beaucoup. They start selling at 8 a.m., and the pastries are usually gone by noon.

French Festival Day was inaugurated in 1968 with a parade that lasted two minutes. Now, besides the grand parade, there are 250 crafters, the crowning of a queen, French exhibits, a puppet show, band concerts, horse-and-buggy tours with guides telling about the town's French history, a festival mass at St. Vincent, and fireworks on the waterfront. Attendance is about 15,000.

Location: Cape Vincent, at the point where the St. Lawrence flows from Lake Ontario, is about 25 miles west of Watertown on New York 12E. ❀ **Contact:** Cape Vincent Chamber of Commerce, P.O. Box 482, Cape Vincent, NY 13618; Tel: (315)654-2481.

Endicott

Spiedie Fest and Balloon Rally

Usually first weekend of August (Friday through Sunday)
❀ A spiedie cook-off highlights this fest, and if you haven't the slightest idea what a spiedie is, you're not alone. When you get 50 or 60 miles away from the tri-cities of Endicott, Binghamton, and Johnson City, nobody has heard of them.

Endicott is the home of the spiedie, pronounced speedy, the word derived from the Italian *spiedo,* meaning spit. Spiedies are cooked on a spit or skewer. The inventor was Augustino Iacovelli, who came to this country in 1929 from the Abruzzi region of Italy, and started grilling spiedies in 1939 at a restaurant he opened in Endicott.

Of course, that may be an apocryphal story. Most bars in the area have spiedies, but few spiedie chefs seem to know their origin. Speidies have just always been around the Tri-Cities.

The word about them may start spreading, because more than 100,000 come to the Spiedie Fest, which began in 1985.

The cook-off attracts 40 to 50 chefs, and is not without controversy. The original spiedie was lamb, but now people use lamb *and* beef, pork, veal, chicken, and sometimes venison. Some, if you can imagine, have even used fish and tofu.

The meat is cut in chunks and placed on skewers, and most cooks sizzle them over charcoal, but they have also been deep fried, broiled, or fried in about half an inch of butter. When they're done, said Shirley L. Coons, a native Binghamtonian, "the best way to eat them is to wrap a slice of Italian bread over the meat as you pull the meat off the skewer." In other words, the bread becomes an edible mitt.

What makes spiedies different from just any shish kebab, and from each other, is the marinade. The marinades all contain vinegar and oil, and most include garlic. But then anything goes. A festival cook-off winner one year added lemon juice and mint; another used tomato-based salsa. One contender regularly adds a spoonful of honey from his own beehives.

Festival vendors sell spiedies (of course) and other fair food. For entertainment, hot-air balloons are launched in the early morning and evening. There are also band concerts, children's activities, and shows of arts and crafts and antique cars.

Location: Tri-Cities Airport, Endicott, about five miles from Binghamton, 200 miles northwest of New York City. From New York 17W, take the Endicott Main St. exit. ❀ **Contact:** Catholic Charities, 232 Main St., Binghamton, NY 13905; Tel: (607)729-9166.

A highlight of Cape Vincent's French Festival is a 50-unit parade, led by Napoleon on horseback. (Cape Vincent Chamber of Commerce)

Apple Fest

Third or fourth weekend of September ☼ This festival has two bragging points: The apple julius was invented here by Mary Whitman, also the festival's chief organizer. And the festival claims to have the longest apple strudel in New York. It has never actually been measured, but it starts at about 75 feet and parts of it keep getting replaced. Lots of strudel. It's very rich, and sells out.

Apple julius is made with cider or apple juice that's blended with ice cubes, a little cream or half-and-half, and a little vanilla. They wear out blenders making enough.

Strudels are layers of thin dough spread with a filling, then baked. The original German word means whirlpool.

The festival started in 1987, and it features a bike and trike parade, with prizes for the best decorated, funniest, and cutest vehicles; strolling musicians; square and couple dancing; a crafts show; an apple-pie baking contest; and lots of apple and ethnic and miscellaneous dishes, including, naturally, spiedies (see the Endicott Spiedie Fest and Balloon Rally above). Attendance runs from 25,000 to 30,000.

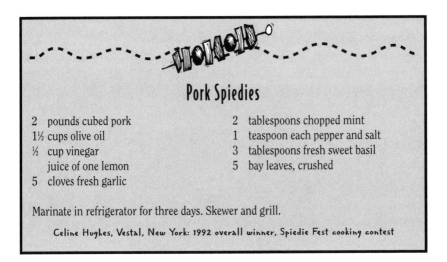

Pork Spiedies

2   pounds cubed pork
1½ cups olive oil
½   cup vinegar
    juice of one lemon
5   cloves fresh garlic

2   tablespoons chopped mint
1   teaspoon each pepper and salt
3   tablespoons fresh sweet basil
5   bay leaves, crushed

Marinate in refrigerator for three days. Skewer and grill.

Celine Hughes, Vestal, New York: 1992 overall winner, Spiedie Fest cooking contest

Location: Washington Ave., Endicott. **Contact:** Apple Fest, P.O. Box 0535, Endicott, NY 13761-0535; Tel: (607)785-4671.

Burgerfest

Third Saturday of July Hamburg's slogan is, "We're on a roll." Oh, groan. Well, you have to forgive a town known not only as the Birthplace of the Hamburger but also as The Town That Friendship Built.

The hamburger that Hamburg brags about was also first created at Seymour, Wisconsin; New Haven, Connecticut; and Athens, Texas. But Hamburg boosters boast, "We have *documentation.*"

The allegedly documented story is that the Menche brothers, Frank and Charles, concessionaires from Ohio, were at the Hamburg Fair (now the Erie County Fair) in 1885 to sell pork sandwiches. Their supplier ran out of pork, and suggested they try beef. The Menches formed beef patties, grilled them, tasted, and added a little brown sugar and salt and possibly coffee. (The recipe is secret.) They served the patties between bread, the customers liked them, asked what they were, and Frank, quite aware of where he was and no fool, said "Hamburgers."

Each year since the Burgerfest began in 1985 as a hamburger centennial, descendants of the Menches (who now own the Menches Brothers Restaurant near Akron, Ohio) have come to sell the original-recipe hamburgers. The Taste of Hamburg items also include regular fair food plus ice-cream cones (the Menches claim parenthood of the cones, too), hamburger doughnuts, watermelon cookies, and, of course, Buffalo chicken wings, since Hamburg is next door to Buffalo.

The fest has live musical entertainment, kids' events, a bed race, a farmers' market, and a meatball dance at day's end. Attendance is about 15,000.

Location: The Hamburg village. Hamburg is 15 minutes south of Buffalo on Lake Erie. **Contact:** Hamburg Chamber of Commerce, 8 S. Buffalo St., Hamburg, NY 14075; Tel: (716)649-7917, Fax (716)649-6362.

See Also: Burger Fest (Seymour, WI).

Hilton

Hilton Apple Fest

Weekend before Columbus Day Hilton is not only in the midst of apple country in one of the top apple-growing states in the union, it's also where an apple was developed. It was the Collamer, a red cooking apple, and while it's not as popular as some apples, it's still grown.

The town has another distinction, maybe. Legend has it that some Hilton folks baked the world's smallest apple pie . . . in a bottle cap.

Reasons enough for a fest. About 40,000 visitors come to this town near the shores of Lake Ontario for fun and various foods offered by two dozen nonprofit groups. A five-foot-diameter apple crisp is baked each day, and they also have apple pies, tarts, fritters, candied apples, fresh apples. There's a contest for apple desserts, and as many as 60 hopefuls enter each year. A farmers' market offers a selection of fruits and vegetables as well as homemade fudge and local honey.

Entertainment on two stages—the local high school band, country, and gospel music groups—is almost non-stop, and there are also hay rides, an antique car show, and crafts.

Location: Hilton is 15 miles northwest of Rochester, and 8 miles off I-390 on New York 104W. **Contact:** Hilton Chamber of Commerce, 1266 Hilton Parma Corners Rd., Hilton, NY 14468; Tel: (716)392-4433.

Lewiston

Peach Festival

Weekend after Labor Day (Friday through Sunday) The Kiwanis Club uses six to eight tons of peaches for the peach shortcakes it sells at this festival. Other events making this a peach of a festival are a peach dessert contest, which has seen peach pierogis and peach rugalach (crescent-shaped cookies with filling) among the submissions, a Peach Blossom and Peach Fuzz contest for kids aged five to seven, the crowning of a Peach Queen, a two-hour parade, and a cheerleaders' competition.

A great many of New York State's grapes, apples, cherries, pears, and peaches are grown in the fruit belt around Lewiston and can be found at the festival's farmers' market, along with assorted preserves and jams.

The festival is known for its Buffalo-area specialties as much as peaches. Vendors sell Buffalo chicken wings, now known all over the country—spicy fried wings served with blue-cheese dressing and celery—and beef on weck (pronounced wick), only found in western New York. Beef on weck is heaps of thinly sliced roast beef with horseradish on a kummelweck—caraway seed—roll. A staple.

The festival has been held since 1958 and has become an end-of-summer tradition, with an estimated 100,000 people attending.

Location: Academy Park on Main St. (New York Highway 104) in Lewiston, about 25 miles north of Buffalo. **Contact:** Peach Festival, Kiwanis Club of Lewiston, Lewiston, NY 14092; Tel: (716)297-0838.

Marathon

Central New York Maple Festival

Weekend in middle to late March The old custom of greeting the spring with sugar-making has grown into a weekend of big crowds—anywhere from 40,000 to 60,000—and marathon activities in Marathon. The first festival here was in 1971, and now it's the state's biggest maple celebration.

The Maple Museum is a focal point. There you buy maple syrup, lollipops, sugar, and sundaes; study displays of antique maple-processing equipment and farm tools; and watch crafters demonstrate their various skills (sometimes weaving, sometimes Ukrainian Easter-egg painting).

Festival highlights that are strictly maple include tours of a sugar shack and demonstrations of the syrup-making process (with free samples), and all-you-can-eat pancake-and-syrup meals. A Maple Festival Queen Pageant kicks off the event on Friday night, and weekend activities include bake sales, quilt shows, arts and crafts exhibits, chain-saw wood sculpture demonstrations, horse-drawn rides, helicopter rides, and entertainment in the high school by singers, morris dancers, and others.

New York ranks second behind Vermont in maple syrup production in the United States, and tapping the maples has been a tradition in Marathon's Cortland County from the days of American Indian culture.

Location: Marathon, 50 miles south of Syracuse, is just off I-81 at exit 9. **Contact:** Central New York Maple Festival, 10 E. Main St., Marathon, NY 13803; Tel: (607)849-3278.

See Also: Vermont Maple Festival (St. Albans, VT).

Naples

Naples Grape Festival

Third weekend in September ☼ Naples is famous for its grape pies; at grape harvesting time, people come from miles around to buy them. The town is in New York's Finger Lakes region, an area of vineyards. Many of the grapes grown are the blue-black Concords, the grapes that go into grape pies.

At the Grape Festival, attended by about 80,000, you can try grape pies; grape kuchens, a kind of coffee cake; Italian grape ice; grape bars, like fig bars; grapes by the bunch; and foods reflecting the area's ethnic melange.

There are also arts and crafts displays, music, and free tours and tastings at the local Widmer Wine Cellars. And there's the World's Greatest Grape Pie Contest. Pies have been entered with peanut butter for a sort of peanut-butter-and-jelly taste, with meringue, and with crumb topping.

Grape pies were invented in Naples. Irene Bouchard, who developed the recipe and at one time baked up to 7,000 grape pies a year, was still baking them in her late 70s. This is her story of the pies: The late Al Hodges, who owned the Redwood Restaurant across the street from the Bouchards, baked the first grape pies in the early 1960s. People wanted to buy them to take home, so, knowing that Mrs. Bouchard had started a small bake shop at home, Mr. Hodges asked if she would like to try grape pies. She said yes . . . and 30-odd years later, she was still making grape pies.

She used her own recipe, though: Take two cups of Concord grapes, slip the skins off, then boil the pulp until it liquefies. Strain the seeds out and pour the hot juice over the skins, mixing in a cup of sugar, and let the mixture sit over night. Mrs. Bouchard uses tapioca, not flour or cornstarch, as a thickener.

Concord grapes were discovered by Ephraim W. Bull in 1845 from "among our wildings" in Concord, Massachusetts. It is not a great grape for wine, but in the Northeast it is cherished as a grape for jellies and grape juice, and, in Naples, for grape pies.

Location: Naples is about 12 miles north of I-390 on New York 53. ☼ **Contact:** Naples Grape Festival, P.O. Box 70, Naples, NY 14512; Tel: (716)374-2240.

New York

Ninth Avenue International Food Festival

Third weekend in May ☼ The granddaddy of street festivals, this one's also known as the Ninth Avenue noshers' festival. Whatever you call it, this street festival, a tradition since 1973, transforms Ninth Avenue, from 37th Street to 57th Street (the old Hell's Kitchen neighborhood was in the vicinity of 39th Street), into a sea of a million or so grazing people and about 300 booths. A few of the stands sell T-shirts or plants, but most are devoted to food and are a real mirror of the 20 blocks of merchants—from old-time mom-and-pop stores to new ethnic restaurants and gourmet shops that are bringing back a lively multicultural atmosphere.

Highlights for the ethnic-food nosher: Sicilian seafood, Greek lamb souvlaki, Brazilian *bolhinho bacalhau* (a fried salt-cod casserole), Indonesian corn fritters flavored with shrimp, Thai peppery squid. There are American regional foods, too—bourbon-ham sandwiches, Cajun and Creole dishes, little-neck clams on the half shell, pork tostadas from the Southwest.

Few ethnic specialties are missing. There are also games and rides for the kids, and entertainers scattered along the 20 blocks. A Peruvian band, with flutes and guitars, is especially popular. On Sunday, there's ethnic music and dance on two stages from noon until 6 p.m.

Location: Ninth Avenue on the west side of Manhattan. **Contact:** Ninth Avenue Association of New York, 400 W. 50th St., New York, NY 10019; Tel: (212)581-7217.

West Indian-American Carnival

Labor Day weekend (Thursday through Monday) It's been called New York's biggest and brightest and noisiest festival; the police have to wear earplugs. It's full of bouncy band music, steel drums, singing, sashaying, shouting, and sounds of delight from two to three million people. They come from all over the United States and Canada, and some make a sort of festive pilgrimage from the islands to this island celebration in Brooklyn.

Countries from Bermuda to as far south as Guyana are represented, so there's variety everywhere you turn: all kinds of Caribbean food, calypso bands from the West Indies, reggae and French Caribbean music, glorious folk costumes.

The festival winds up on Monday with what may be the world's biggest parade. It's certainly the most delirious, with rainbow-colored floats and hundreds of thousands of dancers in feathers and spangles and beads, in butterfly wings, witches' hats, and hummingbird masks. *Mas* (pronounced mahs, short for masquerade) groups, led by their kings and queens, parade and compete for prizes for best costume, best band, best this, and best that. There's also a children's parade on Saturday.

Hundreds of vendors are spread along the street, selling everything from Bob Marley T-shirts to beaded necklaces to Puerto Rican flags.

Always wafting above and around the stalls and the dancers is the aroma of Caribbean food: rotis, which are crepes filled with chicken, beef, goat or conch, usually cooked with curry (warning: the chicken in Caribbean chicken rotis is not deboned). Patties that are baked like bread but filled with hot peppers and meat. Sugar-cane juice. Coconut bread. Curried goat. Peppery rice dishes with vegetables. Jerk chicken. Fish cakes.

And more: "bakes," 14-inch-diameter fried biscuits, often served with coconut. Smoked herring or salt fish (corned, soaked, and boiled, then cooked with onion and tomatoes and, maybe, hot peppers). Bakes and the fish are typically served as Caribbean breakfasts, but are available here all day long.

At the Ninth Avenue International Food Festival, foods from around the world are available from hundreds of vendors. (Ninth Avenue International Food Festival)

This mammoth party began as a quiet pre-Lenten parade and dance in a Harlem hall in the 1940s, organized by a Trinidad woman, Jesse Watle, to re-create the pre-Lenten carnivals of the islands. Since February can be a nasty time of year in New York, the affair was moved to September, and, in time, with the West Indian population growing in Brooklyn, the carnival moved there. In 1967, the carnival became a multi-day street festival. And that's where and how it is now, a noisy, merry carnival.

Location: Eastern Parkway, in the Crown Heights area of Brooklyn. **Contact:** West Indian-American Day Carnival Assn., 1028 St. John's Place, Brooklyn, NY 11213; Tel: (718)773-4052 or (718)774-8807, Fax: (718)773-3416.

Feast of San Gennaro

Mid September, 11 days including September 19 To most people elbowing their way through jampacked Little Italy during San Gennaro, the feast is a Brobdingnagian banquet of charcoal-broiled sausage-pepper-and-onion sandwiches. It is that.

It's also the biggest and oldest New York street fair, dating back to 1926, attended by about three million. It was started by the Neapolitans and Sicilians, or their children, who arrived in New York in the 1880s and 1890s, many to work on the Holland and Lincoln Tunnels.

A food/gambling/religious festival, it survived an upheaval in 1996 when city officials ordered a reorganization, charging financial corruption, and it continues to honor Gennaro, the patron saint of Naples who died a martyr in A.D. 305. Gennaro was arrested, tortured, and thrown headlong into a furnace, from which he emerged unscathed, only to be beheaded. An old man gathered up his body and head and wrapped them in cloth, and an old woman collected the blood in a vial.

The saint's body is preserved in Naples, where people pray to him for protection from fires, earthquakes, plagues, droughts, and the eruption of Mt. Vesuvius. His dried blood liquefies twice a year, on the first Sunday in May, the feast of the transfer of his relics, and on September 19, the anniversary of his martyrdom.

On that date in Naples, pilgrims pack the Duomo to pray for the semiannual miracle. In New York, a solemn high mass is celebrated at the Roman Catholic Church of Most Precious Blood, 113 Baxter St., a block west of Mulberry Street, the festival's aorta. The mass is followed by a procession with six men carrying the saint's bronze-and-silver statue through the streets, while the faithful pin dollar bills to it.

Through the years, the feast has had an exuberant Neapolitan character, with sparkling arches of light over Mulberry Street, strolling musicians playing Italian songs, bands continuously on the bandstand, and pungent smoke drifting from the food stalls.

Besides sausage, sausage, sausage, there's calzone and cannoli and *zeppole,* holeless doughnuts that eater-writer Calvin Trillin explains are "available almost exclusively at Italian feasts." New York being a melting pot and Chinatown being on the fringes of Little Italy, close to half the food booths now sell egg rolls and Filipino and other ethnic foods.

Location: Mulberry St., the feast's center, running north-south below Houston St., can be reached on the No. 6 subway, getting off at Canal Street or Spring Street, or by Broadway bus. **Contact:** Figlia di San Gennaro Inc., 109 Mulberry St., New York, NY 10013; Tel: (212)226-6427.

Oyster Bay

Oyster Festival

Weekend after Columbus day (usually third weekend in October) Moderation in all things is not the slogan of this festival. About 200,000 people converge on Oyster Bay, Theodore Roosevelt's favorite summer retreat, to eat 30,000 to 40,000 locally grown oysters raw on the half shell and thousands more fried, in fritters, or in stews or chowder.

Visitors also manage to consume quantities of shrimp, clam chowder, clam fritters, fried clams, and crab cakes as well as such gastronomic miscellany as Belgian waffles, fried chicken, and sweet-potato pie.

For contestants in the oyster-eating contest, moderation is not even a known word. Philip Michaels of Kings Park, New York, set an Oyster Bay record in 1992 when he downed

244 oysters in two minutes and forty seconds. Donna Kaye of Brooklyn became the first woman to win by chugging 120 in the same time period in 1996.

A less bloating event is the oyster-shucking contest, with the winner eligible to compete in the National Oyster Shucking Championship contest in Leonardtown, Maryland.

The oysters in Oyster Bay are provided by Frank M. Flower & Sons Inc., which markets oysters with the brand name Pine Island. The Flower company was founded in 1887, and family members are still associated with it. Like other east coast oysters, the Pine Islands are scientifically known as *Crassostrea virginica,* and, because Long Island Sound oysters are known as Bluepoints, they can also go by that name. The Pine Island oysters are a particularly salty variety, and are "domestic"—that is, they are hatched in a 5,000-square-foot hatchery and then planted in the bay.

The festival began in 1982 to call attention to the village and to the Sagamore Hill National Historic Site, TR's former home. Festival attractions other than oysters now include historic boat exhibits featuring restored oyster sloops and working oyster boats, harbor tours on a historic paddle boat, a display of oyster-farming techniques at the Flower company booth, a 5K run, arts and crafts, and all kinds of musical entertainment.

Location: Oyster Bay, on Long Island, is about 14 miles east of Manhattan. Take the Long Island Expressway to exit 41N, and New York 106N to Oyster Bay. **Contact:** Oyster Bay Chamber of Commerce, P.O. Box 21, Oyster Bay, NY 11771; Tel: (516)922-6464.

See Also: St. Mary's County Oyster Festival (Leonardtown, MD).

Penn Yan

Buckwheat Harvest Festival

Last full weekend in September (Friday through Sunday)
Buckwheat, which is not a grain but a fruit related to rhubarb, was one of the earliest crops grown in the United States, first planted along the Hudson River by the Dutch.

Today more than half of the total United States buckwheat production comes from New York, and the world's largest manufacturer of buckwheat products, the Burkett Mills, is in Penn Yan in the Finger Lakes district. And that's where about 30,000 people gather to watch a parade, listen to music (country and western, rock), and eat a lot of buckwheat.

The festival, which began in 1986, opens Friday afternoon, and the eating soon begins. There are dinners of buckwheat pancakes with whole-hog sausages, and barbecued chicken served with kasha pilaf and dinner rolls made with buckwheat flour. Vendors are required to use buckwheat in some form in their main product. This results in buckwheat rolls for hamburgers, buckwheat shortcake for strawberries, buckwheat burritos, buckwheat pretzels, Buckwheat Honey Praline ice cream, Kasha Cookie Krunch ice cream, Kasha Krunch candy bars, and beef on a buckwheat weck.

Applesauce-Kasha Cookies

1¾ cups all-purpose flour
1 teaspoon baking soda
½ teaspoon salt
1 teaspoon cinnamon
¼ teaspoon cloves
⅛ teaspoon nutmeg
½ cup butter or margarine

¾ cup brown sugar
1 egg
1 cup unsweetened applesauce
½ cup regular rolled oats
½ cup raisins or currants
½ cup medium kasha, uncooked

Sift together flour, soda, baking powder, salt, and spices; set aside. In large bowl, cream butter and brown sugar until light and fluffy, then beat in egg and applesauce. Slowly stir in flour mixture; mix well. Add oats, raisins, and kasha. Drop mixture by teaspoonful onto greased baking sheets. Bake at 375 degrees for 10 minutes or until golden brown. Makes about 4 dozen.

From Birkett Mills Buckwheat Cookbook

Festival activities include tours of the Burkett Mills, which was established in 1797, a tractor pull, a classic-car show, animal acts, a local talent show, games and comedy for kids, fireworks.

But the idea is to get people thinking and eating buckwheat, which was once a major crop in the United States and may be making a gradual comeback.

Here's what the National Buckwheat Institute says about it: Buckwheat is high in potassium and phosphorous, and has twice as much vitamin B as wheat. Each pound of buckwheat has as much protein as half a pound of beef, and, in fact, buckwheat is considered the best source of protein in the plant kingdom. There are possible medical applications, too; the immature plant has large amounts of rutin, which helps build up capillaries in the body, preventing hemorrhages.

The buckwheat seed is three-cornered, and the kernel inside the shell or hull is called a groat. Roasted groats are kasha, and are a staple in Russia and eastern Europe. Groats can be steamed, boiled, or baked; the unroasted kernels can be eaten as a cereal or side dish or ground for grits and flour. Russian blinis are made of buckwheat flour; and the ubiquitous Japanese *soba* are buckwheat noodles.

Buckwheat originated in Siberia and Manchuria, reached Europe in the Middle Ages, and is now cultivated throughout most of the world. It grows in poor soil and is cultivated without herbicides.

Location: Yates County Fairgrounds in Penn Yan, on New York 14A, 20 miles south of the New York Thruway at the Geneva exit. **Contact:** National Buckwheat Institute, P.O. Box 440, Penn Yan, NY 14527; Tel: (315)536-7434, Fax: (315)536-6740.

Phelps Sauerkraut Festival

First weekend in August (Thursday through Sunday) All it takes to make sauerkraut is cabbage, salt, and time. Cabbage is shredded, salt is added, and then it's put in a vat and covered so air can't get at it. If air gets in during the fermentation process, you get rotten cabbage, not sauerkraut.

Normally, sauerkraut (which means sour cabbage in German) is eaten as a vegetable or garnish with meats, especially hot dogs or sausages of some sort.

At the Phelps celebration, the sauerkraut is baked into a cake that weighs over 100 pounds. The Sauerkraut Prince and Princess then slice the cake and present it to the crowds, saying, we hope, "Let them eat sauercake."

The festival offers numerous other foods, most emphasizing sauerkraut, and entertainment includes live bands, Scottish bagpipers, rides, a parade, a car show, and fireworks. Attendance is about 10,000 each day. The festival began in 1967.

Phelps was once the Sauerkraut Capital of the World, and it used to have a Silver Floss sauerkraut plant, but the plant was bought out and moved away. However, considerable amounts of cabbage are still grown in Phelps and the surrounding area. Wisconsin, though, now grows more kraut cabbage than New York; the two states are the only ones that grow enough to have the U.S. Department of Agriculture keep statistics on the amount.

It's generally thought that sauerkraut originated in Germany, but Chinese laborers ate it as a staple when they built the Great Wall. They fermented it with rice wine, though, not salt.

Location: Firemen's Field in Phelps, on New York 96, a mile south of the New York State Thruway, 35 miles east of Rochester. **Contact:** Phelps Town Hall, Phelps, NY 14532; Tel: (315)548-5691.

Polish Town Street Fair and Polka Festival

Third weekend in August *Witamy!* Which is to say, in Polish, Welcome!

Since 1975, the Polish community of Riverhead on Long Island has been welcoming visitors who want to taste genuine Polish food, see the reenactment of a traditional Polish wedding, and polka the night away. About 150,000 accept the invitation.

Riverhead is the county seat of Suffolk County, and northern Suffolk County has some of the most productive farmland in New York. Poles came here in the 1800s to grow potatoes on this farmland, and they now call Riverhead Polish Town, U.S.A.

The street fair features 200 booths selling Polish imports, crafts, and food. It's old-country food: potato pancakes, pierogis with all kinds of fillings—cheese, potato, fruit,

Riverhead hosts the Polish Town Street Fair and Polka Festival, featuring traditional old-country food as well as a reenacted Polish wedding and plenty of dancing. (Polish Town Civic Association, Inc.)

sauerkraut; at least nine different kinds of kielbasa; *babka,* a sweet bread; *golabki,* stuffed cabbage. There are foods of other nations, too, as well as American standards.

A major attraction is the reenactment of an old-fashioned wedding, performed each day from St. Isidore's, the oldest and largest Polish Roman Catholic church on Long Island.

When the doors of the church swing open, the couple, wearing authentic Polish costumes, walk to a horse-driven carriage and are guided through the streets by girls carrying hoops entwined with flowers.

At the "wedding reception" on a street stage, the bread-and-wine ceremony is performed: A tray holding two glasses of wine, two pieces of bread, and a saltcellar is presented to the mothers of the bride and groom. They sprinkle salt on the bread and give it to their children, and then give them the wine. The salt represents the bitterness in life, the wine, the sweetness, and the bread the hope that the couple will never want.

After the ceremony, the bride's veil is removed, and her braid cut off, signifying that she is now a married woman, no longer a maiden. And finally, the bridal party dances to Chopin's Polonaise, a tradition at formal occasions.

Other events include dance performances, a corn-husking contest, and the introduction of Miss Polish Town, U.S.A. Polka dancing starts at 5 p.m. on Saturday and at 3 p.m. on Sunday.

Location: Rivertown is off the Long Island Expressway. At exit 73, go east for two miles, turn right at the second light onto Osborne Ave., which leads to the heart of Polish Town. **Contact:** Polish Town Civic Assn., Box 972, Riverhead, NY 11901; Tel: (516)369-1616.

Saugerties

Hudson Valley Garlic Festival

Last weekend in September In 1989, Patricia Reppert decided to promote her Saugerties farm herb shop by having a garlic festival. Her promotion worked; 125 people came, and she ran out of home-cooked garlic dishes.

The next year she planned for 200 and got 500 in her front yard. She was doing all the cooking, and everything had garlic in it, even the coffee and carrot cake and pumpkin cookies. After the third year, she turned the festival over to the local Kiwanis Club. Now about 45,000 come and Kiwanis members brag that Saugerties is the Stinky Breath Capital of the World.

Until the late 1980s, Reppert had tried growing garlic, with no success. Then she learned garlic was grown commercially in the Finger Lakes area of New York, and she started boning up.

Garlic is a member of the *Allium* family, which has two principal subspecies, *ophioscorodon* (hardneck) and *sativum* (softneck). Softneck, the more commonly grown of the two, is the major California garlic crop, but hardneck, called ophio by garlic cognoscenti, is hardier and can grow in colder climates. The ophios are sought after by chefs because all the cloves are large, and their flavor (said Reppert) is superior to that of softnecks. Note: Ophios are *not* elephant garlics, which actually are not true garlics.

Education was prominent at the first festival and still is, with lectures and chefs' demonstrations. It's fun, too. There are garlic-themed crafts, Mr. Garlic (a man dressed as a garlic) wandering around, and music by unusual groups (an all-woman Brazilian percussion group performed one year).

Farmers sell freshly harvested garlic by the pound or the braid, and food booths run the gamut: corn on the cob with garlic-spiced butter; spit-roasted pigs, with heads of garlic in their mouths instead of apples, served with a garlic barbecue sauce; soft-shell crab sandwiches with aioli (garlic mayonnaise); garlic ice cream.

There's a mystique to garlic that attracts people, said Reppert. "And garlic is funny," she said. "I don't know why."

Location: Cantine Field on the outskirts of Saugerties, about 80 miles north of New York City, off the New York Thruway (I-87) at exit 20. **Contact:** Hudson Valley Garlic Festival, P.O. Box 443, Saugerties, NY 12477; Tel: (914)246-5657.

See Also: Gilroy Garlic Festival (Gilroy, CA).

Pennsylvania

Arendtsville

National Apple Harvest Festival

First two weekends in October Adams County, where Arendtsville is located, is the biggest apple-growing area of the state, and they go apple-happy here at festival time. They've been holding the harvest festival since 1965, and between 80,000 and 90,000 turn out over the two weekends for fresh apples, all kinds of apple desserts, and 350 arts and crafts booths. Many of the craftspeople demonstrate such old-fashioned arts as yarn and moccasin making.

The Pancake Patio at the fair sells sausages and pancakes with apple syrup, and you can watch apple butter being boiled down and then sample it. Among the apple dishes available are apple pies, sundaes, turnovers, dumplings, and fritters. Beef sandwiches are cooked over an open pit fire, and this being Pennsylvania, there are Pennsylvania specialties like funnel cake and scrapple.

Location: South Mountain Fairgrounds in Arendtsville, 10 miles northwest of Gettysburg on Pennsylvania 234. **Contact:** National Apple Harvest Festival, P.O. Box 38, Biglerville, PA 17307; Tel: (717)677-9413, Fax: (717)677-4961.

While You're There: Learn all about apples! The National Apple Museum in nearby Biglerville has old farm machinery, a huge vinegar generator, an 1880s kitchen, and a honeybee display, showing how bees pollinate apple trees. Tel: (717)677-4556.

Doylestown

Polish-American Festival

Labor Day weekend (Saturday through Monday) and following weekend The National Shrine of Our Lady of Czestochowa in Doylestown was built by American Poles in 1966 to commemorate the 1,000th anniversary of Christianity in Poland. Earlier, on the same hilltop, a barn had been converted to a chapel and dedicated to Our Lady of Czestochowa, but the idea of a large shrine seemed fitting as the anniversary approached. The festival has been held here ever since, helping to support the shrine.

A Polish festival wouldn't be festive without polka music and pierogis, and this one has both. You'll also find kielbasa; *golabki,* stuffed cabbage; *bigos,* hunter's stew made with sauerkraut, tomatoes, and kielbasa or pork; *plaki,* potato pancakes; and *babka,* which literally means grandmother, but has come to mean sweet bread.

Entertainment showcases Polish culture with folk dance demonstrations, polka bands, Polish entertainers, Polish costumed "string bands" (known as Mummers) from Philadelphia. There are also rides and children's games.

The Shrine of Jasna Gora in Poland was built to hold the original painting of Our Lady of Czestochowa that legend says was painted by St. Luke the Evangelist. It was brought to Poland in 1382, and the painting in the altar area of the Doylestown shrine is a copy of it. When the shrine was dedicated, nearly 100,000 pilgrims were greeted by President Lyndon B. Johnson and Archbishop John Krol. It has since become a spiritual center for Americans of Polish descent. About 35,000 people come from throughout the United States for the festival.

Location: The shrine is on Ferry Rd., near the intersection with Pennsylvania 313, on the outskirts of Doylestown about 25 miles north of Philadelphia. **Contact:** Polish-American Festival, Shrine of Our Lady of Czestochowa, P.O. Box 2049, Doylestown, PA 18901; Tel: (215)345-0600.

Intercourse

Rhubarb Fest

Third Saturday in May Rhubarb, also known as pie plant because its stalks are widely used in pies and tarts, appears in early spring and is more welcome to pie lovers than spring's first robin.

When rhubarb is ready for picking in Lancaster County, Kitchen Kettle Village, a complex of 32 food and crafts shops in Intercourse, throws a rhubarb party for about 15,000 people. The first was in 1984.

On this day only, the village offers fresh rhubarb and made-in-the-village bluebarb, a blueberry and rhubarb jam that always sells out. Visitors can also enjoy strawberry-rhubarb and plain rhubarb pie, strawberry-rhubarb cookies, an almond-rhubarb pastry, and rhubarb-pecan muffins. A kettle-shaped soft pretzel (this is soft-pretzel country) is served with rhubarb dipping sauce.

At breakfast time, there's strawberry-rhubarb French toast, while lunch and dinner menus spotlight chilled strawberry-rhubarb soup, spiced rhubarb ham, rhubarb-pork-chop casserole, and rhubarb-glazed chicken kebabs and ham balls.

Kitchen Kettle founder Pat Burnley holds the fruit-like vegetable that is the star of the Rhubarb Festival. (©Tim Schoon Photo)

In case you've missed the point, Rupert Rhubarb walks around the grounds, and the World's Only Rhubarb Race Car Derby is run, with mini-dragsters made of rhubarb stalks. There's also a baking contest, with three categories, for the best rhubarb pie. And there's a rhubarb-pie throw; the throwee is usually a local celebrity volunteering for a worthy cause.

Rhubarb is one of the odder vegetables. The National Geographic has called it "rather unusual among our common vegetables," and indeed it is. Among other things, it can kill you.

Only the stalks are edible. The leaves have high levels of oxalic acid, which is poisonous. Deadly poisonous. The roots can cause "violent digestive disturbance," the Geographic tells us.

Rhubarb is treated in cookery like a fruit, but botanically it's a vegetable. It is supposed to have originated in Tibet. Ancient Greeks knew it and called it the vegetable of foreigners "beyond the Rha [Volga]." The history of how it came to North America is cloudy; one story is that a Maine gardener grew rhubarb in 1790, and another story is that it didn't reach western shores until after the Civil War. Rhubarb develops from an underground system of rhizomes, and is grown from divided crowns, since seeds don't produce true-to-type plants.

It now grows especially well in the northern states and in southern Canada. Washington is the major rhubarb-producing state.

Location: Kitchen Kettle Village, Intercourse, on Pennsylvania 340, 10 miles east of Lancaster. ❂ **Contact:** Kitchen Kettle Village, P.O. Box 380, Intercourse, PA 17534; Tel: (717)768-8261, or (800)732-3538.

Stuffed Mushrooms

2 pounds medium mushrooms	4 tablespoons mayonnaise
8 scallions, finely chopped	2 8 oz. packages of cream cheese
½ teaspoon salt	¼ teaspoon cayenne pepper
1 cup bread crumbs	1 cup grated Parmesan cheese

Salt mushroom caps. Mix cream cheese, scallions, mayonnaise, salt, and pepper together and fill mushrooms. Sprinkle with bread crumbs and Parmesan cheese. Broil 5 minutes and serve warm.

From Look What's Cooking, Pennsylvania Welcome Centers

Kennett Square

National Mushroom Festival

A weekend in early to mid September (Friday through Sunday) ⁑ Kennett Square claims the title Mushroom Capital of the World, and here's why: twenty-five percent of all *Agaricus* white mushrooms (the most common supermarket mushrooms) grown in the United States are grown within a 25-mile radius of Kennett Square, and the state as a whole grows about 350 million pounds, 47 percent of all *Agaricus* grown in the country.

It's not because of the soil or the climate, according to Jim Angelucci, general manager of Phillips Mushroom Farms in Kennett Square. It's because commercial mushroom growing got started here in the late 1800s and kept, well, mushrooming. The early growers were Quakers and Italians who came to work in the quarries, and then switched to mushrooms when the quarries closed down. Many of today's growers are the grandchildren of the first Italian mushroom farmers.

Highlights of the festival are a cook-off, a symposium and dinner, a parade, a street fair, and tours of mushroom farms. Vendors sell fried mushrooms and mushroom soup and standard festival foods.

The cook-off requires that mushrooms make up at least a quarter of all ingredients, and it has elicited a few off-the-wall dishes, like mushroom ice cream and mushroom cheesecake. Following the judging, a buffet of previous winning dishes is open to the public.

At the symposium (reservations required), a speaker discusses some aspect of mushrooms, and a noted chef provides a mushroom-motif dinner.

Exotic mushrooms have been growing in popularity, and Kennett Square is a center for these, too. Portobellos—large, dark brown mushrooms—have been taking off, partly because they're touted as meat substitutes, said grower Angelucci; they taste like beef but don't have the cholesterol. Others gaining in popularity are shiitakes, oyster mushrooms, and hen-of-the-woods mushrooms, which have a silky texture. Per capita consumption in the United States has increased, too, and now 36 states grow mushrooms commercially, California being second (a distant second) to Pennsylvania.

Mushrooms grow throughout the world. They were important in the diet of Australian aborigines, and the ancient Greeks and Romans are thought to have been the first to cultivate them. The Mexican Aztecs called certain hallucinogenic mushrooms "food of the gods."

Location: Kennett Square is just off U.S. 1 about 25 miles southwest of Philadelphia. **Contact:** So. Chester County Chamber of Commerce, P.O. Box 1000, Kennett Square, PA 19348; Tel: (800)932-6369, or (610)444-0774.

Kutztown

Kutztown Pennsylvania German Festival

End of June and early July for ten days including Fourth of July ☼ Kutztown, named for George Kutz, founder of the city in 1771, is in the heart of Pennsylvania Dutch country ("Dutch" is a corruption of the German word for German, *Deutsche.*) The culture here is actually a mix of the folkways of people who lived in Germany, Switzerland, Austria, and the long-disputed Alsace-Lorraine area, and who came here originally to work on farms. They became known for their arts, not the least of which was hearty food.

The festival's various crafts and folkways are displayed with as much authenticity as possible, since the goal is to showcase and preserve the culture. You'll find, therefore, an especially grand variety of regional foods.

Snacks: Funnel cakes—now *de rigueur* at festivals all over the country, they are a Pennsylvania Dutch specialty, made by pouring batter in spirals through a funnel into hot fat. Soft pretzels—they're made with kneaded yeast dough, the same as hard pretzels, but are cooked in a very hot oven for about 10 minutes, while hard pretzels are slow-baked for about two-and-a-half hours. Pennsylvanians usually squirt mustard on their soft pretzels. Hex waffles—thick waffles cooked on a waffle iron with the grid in the shape of a hex sign. *Schnitz un knepp*—pieces of dried apple and dough balls, or dumplings.

Main foods at sit-down meals: *Hinkel Bot Boi,* or chicken pot pie, ubiquitous in this area. It is *not* a pie, it is *not* baked, it is *not* prepared with a crust. It's made like a stew, and consists of chicken and vegetables boiled in a pot, with doughy egg-noodle squares added. Pork loin or pigs' knuckles with sauerkraut. Scrapple ("scraps" of pork mixed with cornmeal and cooked in a loaf), barbecued spare ribs, bratwurst. There's also an ox roast every day.

Various side dishes: Corn fritters and sweet-potato fries. "Potato filling," which begins as mashed potatoes but has bread crumbs and herbs added. Dried corn, which is dried kernels of corn soaked to reconstitute them and then cooked. Pepper cabbage, like cole slaw, but made with vinegar and sugar. Cottage cheese with apple butter on it. "Seven sweets and seven sours," a mix of flavors that tradition says each meal must have; the sweets might be

Great-Grandmom Moyer's Pennsylvania Dutch Chicken Pot Pie

For a moderate sized batch of egg noodles, mix together:

2 eggs, slightly beaten	¼ teaspoon salt
2 cups flour	

Add water by the tablespoon until the dough is soft enough to roll out on a floured surface. (For softer and richer noodles, to be used right away—not dried for later—add 2 tablespoons melted butter or margarine before adding water.) Roll out and cut into approximately 2½" x 2½" squares.

In a large pot (with a lid), start with about 8 cups of liquid (start with leftover gravy or stock and add water). If you have no gravy, mix chicken or beef bouillon according to directions to create stock.

Cut-up chicken (turkey or beef)	2 carrots
1 stalk celery, diced	3 medium potatoes (or add leftover
1 large onion	vegetables)

Place in a large pot with the liquid and bring to a boil. Reduce heat and simmer for 20 minutes. Bring mixture to rolling boil and gradually drop in pot pie squares, stirring occasionally. When all squares are in pot, reduce heat to a high simmer, cover for about 18 minutes. Remove lid and simmer for 15 minutes, stirring occasionally, until liquid partially thickens.

Kutztown Pennsylvania German Festival

apple butter, spiced peaches or cantaloupe, jam, and jelly, while the sours could include corn relish, pickled beets, mustard beans.

And, of course, there is shoo-fly pie, a rich pie made with molasses. To wash it down, try birch beer.

Need more to take home? A farmers' market sells sweets and sours, country meats, preserves, and pies.

Between meals, there are history and culture to absorb—authentic folk arts and crafts, including bread-dough creations, butter molds, corn-husk dolls, and tin work; a Quilt School (Deppich Schul) and the Amish Quilt Challenge, with more than 800 juried quilts auctioned off; and Mennonite a capella hymn-singing in the Mennonite meeting house. At the Heritage Center, visitors can inspect a nineteenth-century one-room schoolhouse and a summer kitchen to get a sense of how settlers learned and cooked; there are also demonstrations of eighteenth- and nineteenth-century farming techniques and a re-enactment of an Amish wedding.

The *Kinner Eck,* or Children's Corner, features story-telling, sing-alongs, jugglers, and a puppet show. Also for kids: pony and carousel rides.

In 1681, William Penn, a Quaker, obtained a land grant for what he called Pennsylvania and encouraged Quakers to settle there. Penn's "Holy Experiment" guaranteed freedom of conscience and attracted increasing numbers of Europeans, many of them Germans seeking relief from religious persecution. They represented a number of religions or sects; the largest religious groups were Lutheran and German Reformed, while the Mennonites, Bohemian Moravians, and Amish, known as the "plain people," made up only 10 percent of the settlers. The hex signs seen on barns were painted by "fancy" Pennsylvania Dutch, since the religion of the plain people forbids anything fancy or decorative.

The festival, named one of North America's 100 best festivals by the American Bus Association, was inaugurated in 1996 under the sponsorship of Kutztown University and the Kutztown Fair Association. About 100,000 attend.

Location: Kutztown Fairgrounds and Kutztown University, off U.S. 222, midway between Reading and Allentown. **Contact:** Kutztown Pennsylvania German Festival, P.O. Box 306, Kutztown, PA 19530; Tel: (800)963-8824 or (610)375-4085.

Lahaska

Strawberry Festival

First weekend in May Peddler's Village in Bucks County's Lahaska was opened in 1961 as a retail center of eighteenth-century-style buildings, brick paths, and flower gardens. There are eight restaurants, seventy specialty shops, and an inn here, and throughout the year, a number of festivals.

The Strawberry Festival gets the springtime juices flowing with strawberries in all forms sold at outdoor stands—fresh and plain, chocolate-dipped, in fritters, shortcakes, preserves, and smoothies. The restaurants also have special strawberry dishes on their menus.

Location: Peddler's Village on Pennsylvania 202 in Lahaska, 5 miles from New Hope. **Contact:** Peddler's Village, Box 218, Lahaska, PA 18931; Tel: (215)794-4000, Fax: (215)794-4001.

Apple Festival

First weekend in November Peddler's Village's Apple Festival in late fall features apple fritters, dumplings, cider made with an old press, chocolate-and-nut dipped apples, and fresh apples.

Like the Strawberry Festival, the Apple Festival is out-of-doors and provides quaint entertainment: an old-fashioned self-playing band organ churning out waltzes and marching music, sounding like an entire band, and puppets, jugglers, cloggers. Both festivals also have pie-eating contests and crafts shows, with demonstrations of craft-making. The festivals have been traditions since 1970.

Strawberries in all shapes, sizes, and forms are available in abundance at Lahaska's Peddler's Village during the Strawberry Festival. (Strawberry Festival, Peddler's Village, Lahaska, Bucks County, PA)

Lancaster

Turkey Hill Old-Fashioned Ice Cream Festival

Third Sunday of July ☼ The high point—literally—of this festival is the Great Ice Cream Stack-Up Contest. Twenty-five kids between the ages of 8 and 12 compete in stacking up as many ice-cream scoops on a cone as they can in one minute. The one who stacks the highest cone wins a half gallon of ice cream each week for a year, and also gets to be called Super Scooper. Runners-up also get prizes.

The festival, which draws up to 10,000 ice-cream lovers, has been held since 1983. It's sponsored by the local Turkey Hill Dairy, which got its start during the Depression when Armour Frey sold bottles of milk out of his touring sedan to his neighbors. Today the dairy is still run by the Frey family and sells ice cream and yogurt from Vermont to Virginia.

Ice cream is a logical festival theme here: Pennsylvania is a big cow state, second in the nation (behind California) in ice-cream production, turning out 71 million gallons of ice cream, and Lancaster County has by far more milk cows than any other county in the commonwealth.

So the festival sticks with ice cream and yogurt, and some 4-H youngsters display a cow, a heifer, and a calf in a penned area where kids can pet them. Booths have about two dozen varieties of ice cream, with intriguing names like Orange Swirl, Tin Roof Sundae, and White Chocolate Macadamia Crunch, which can be eaten in cones or slathered with rich sundae toppings, and nine or ten kinds of yogurt. The entrance ticket gives visitors all the ice cream they can eat. Turkey Hill donates the proceeds to the 17 public libraries in the Lancaster County system to buy books and equipment for children.

Entertainment runs the gamut—ethnic folk dancing and music, bluegrass, magicians, balloon animals, bubble blowing, pony rides.

Location: Lancaster Square in downtown Lancaster.   **Contact:** Lancaster County Library, 125 No. Duke St., Lancaster, PA 17602; Tel: (717)394-2651, Fax: (717)299-9645.

Lebanon

Lebanon Bologna Festival

First full weekend in September (Friday through Sunday)
Lebanon's origins go back to the Pennsylvania Dutch, people who believe in waste-not, want-not, and one way to waste not is to put left-over beef and hog scraps into bologna. So, starting back in the early 1900s, they did this, making some of the fattest bolognas in the United States, with a strong sweet flavor. There are now three factories in Lebanon County making bologna, but the generic name for all their products is Lebanon bologna, because of the taste and the size.

In 1989, the Kutztown Bologna Company won a place in the *Guiness Book of World Records* for the longest salami in the United States by creating one 61 feet, 3½ inches long, with a circumference of 2 feet, weighing 1,202 pounds and a few ounces. This is larger than what they usually make.

Anyway, the three Lebanon County factories, Weaver's, Seltzer's, and Kutztown, got together in 1984 to throw a bologna party. About 30,000 now attend, and the factories give out free samples and sell smoked bologna sandwiches. You can also get what are called "sweet" bologna sandwiches, and beef jerky sticks, and traditional Pennsylvania Dutch foods like chicken pot pie, corn soup, and funnel cake.

Entertainment is as lavish as the food: lots of carnival rides, a circus, a rodeo, motor-cycle thrill shows, and crafts, antique-car, and Corvette shows.

Bologna is named for the city of Bologna, Italy, where it originated, but it's now made everywhere, and in the United States it's almost always pronounced baloney.

Location: Lebanon County Fairgrounds, Lincoln Rd., Lebanon, 8 miles north of the Pennsylvania Turnpike at exit 20, on Pennsylvania 72.   **Contact:** Lebanon Bologna Festival, P.O. Box 758, Brownstown, PA 17508; Tel: (717)656-3559.

While You're There: Drive about 15 miles west on U.S. 422 and you'll be in the town with chocolate-kiss lampposts: Hershey, of course, the town that smells of chocolate. At the Hershey Museum, you can see how Milton S. Hershey developed his chocolate empire.

McClure Bean Soup Festival

Second Tuesday in September through Saturday ❁ The oldest festival in Pennsylvania began as a reunion for the veterans of a Civil War regiment, and then for their sons, their grandsons, and friends. . . . First organized by Snyder County Post 555 of the Grand Army of the Republic, it's now a major fair, but one thing hasn't changed; bean soup, made the way it was in 1891, is still served, and veterans in uniform still get a free bowl. One difference—it's served with oyster crackers instead of hardtack.

The soup is what Union troops ate during the war; it contains hamburger, Great Northern beans, suet, salt, and water. The soup is cooked for three hours in 35-gallon kettles, sometimes stirred by men in Civil War uniforms. Generally, 70 to 80 kettles are cooked, and altogether more than a ton each of hamburger and beans are used. Between 50,000 and 70,000 attend, and are able to stoke up on roast pork and standard fair food besides the soup.

Entertainment includes country-western music, a one-hour parade, 50 rides and dancing. On even years, a Civil War battle is re-enacted. Thursday is Rakestraw Ice Cream Day, when free ice cream cones are given to the first 200 customers who buy a bowl of soup after 4 p.m.

Location: Cold Springs Grove in McClure, 75 miles northwest of Harrisburg on U.S. 522. ❁ **Contact:** McClure Bean Soup Festival, P.O. Box 8, McClure, PA 17841; Tel: (717)658-8425, or (800)338-8389.

Peanut Butter Festival

Third weekend in September (Friday through Sunday) ❁ New Bethlehem's major employer is Smuckers, and Smuckers makes peanut butter here. So why not a peanut butter festival?

The first festival was in 1996, and it was full of *arachidbutyrophiles,* especially around the Smuckers booth. The booth, of course, is a *sine qua non* of the festival, selling peanut butter, peanut-butter ice cream, and peanut-butter rolls and pies. Food vendors dispense other types of food; the local Chamber of Commerce, as it has been doing since 1987, throws a pig roast on Saturday, and a fire company sets a fire for a chicken barbecue.

A baking contest, with several categories, requires that a main ingredient be peanut butter. Peanut-butter cheesecake has been a winner, and other entries have included peanut-butter balls (candy), pork with peanut-butter sauce, and peanut-butter cookies with a filling of peanut butter. Makes your mouth start feeling sticky.

Festival events include a teen dance, country line dancing, music by bluegrass bands, a mountain-bike race, magic acts, performances by the town barbershop quartet, a carnival, and crafts displays.

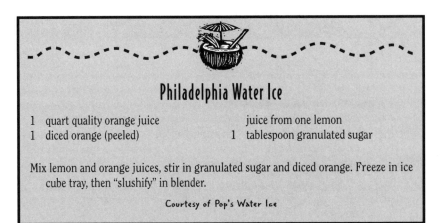

Philadelphia Water Ice

1   quart quality orange juice
1   diced orange (peeled)

juice from one lemon
1   tablespoon granulated sugar

Mix lemon and orange juices, stir in granulated sugar and diced orange. Freeze in ice cube tray, then "slushify" in blender.

Courtesy of Pop's Water Ice

About those *arachidbutyrophiles*. They are people who love peanut butter. If you're afraid of peanut butter (might stick to the roof of your mouth), you're an *arachidbutyrophobe*.

Location: Gumtown Park on Water St. in New Bethlehem, 17 miles south of I-80 at Pennsylvania 66 and 28. **Contact:** New Bethlehem Chamber of Commerce, 400 Broad St., New Bethlehem, PA 16242; Tel: (814)275-3929.

Philadelphia

Sunoco Welcome America!

Ten to 12 days surrounding the Fourth of July The United States was born in Philadelphia when the Declaration of Independence was signed there on July 4, 1776, so Philadelphia rates a really big birthday party.

There are four parades, nine concerts, four fireworks displays, six sporting events—and altogether more than 55 free events, cultural, inspirational, commercial, glitzy, and peculiar, but that's America, right?

Philadelphia is not only the birthplace of the nation, it is also the birthplace of the hoagie, the cheese steak, the ice cream cone (maybe), water ice, and probably some other dishes that have not exactly put Philadelphia up there with the top gourmet cities of the world.

This birthing syndrome lends itself nicely to a birthday party. WAWA Hoagie Day (WAWA owns a chain of convenience stores in the Northeast) combines a one-mile fun run with a novel project—building a one-mile hoagie. The builders compete to complete their portions the fastest. Pieces of the mile-long hoagie, built in a tent opposite the Liberty Bell pavilion, are free to frenzied feeders.

A hoagie, a.k.a. a submarine or grinder, is a long Italian roll filled with three or four types of Italian cold cuts, cheese, shredded lettuce, tomato, onions, and hot and sweet pep-

pers. One may swish the sandwich with mayonnaise or with oil and vinegar and Italian seasonings. A hoagie is not cut in half, making it a challenge to eat, because everything falls out when you put one end in your mouth. That's part of its mystique.

Legend says hoagies were eaten by Italian American workers at the Hog Island shipyard in Delaware County during World War I, and so got the name Hoggie, which later became hoagie.

Another story is that a Mrs. Ianelli, who operated Emil's in South Philadelphia, made the first hoagie in the 1930s for a policeman whose wife got mad at him and wouldn't make his lunch. Mrs. Ianelli made him a hoagie, and then started making them for the cop's buddies, and soon was turning out 1,000 hoagies a day for workers at the Naval Shipyard.

Another food thriller at Welcome America! is the contest for the Mayor's Cup (two cups, actually), sponsored by *Philadelphia* magazine. Two typical Philadelphia dishes are highlighted, and shops at Liberty Place Food Court prepare and offer them to the public, which tastes and votes for the best of each kind. One year, the dishes were cheese steaks and hoagies, another year soft pretzels and water ice. Soft pretzels are pretzels that aren't baked as long as hard pretzels. (See Kutztown Pennsylvania German Festival.)

A cheese steak is thinly sliced steak grilled with onions, dumped on a half loaf of Italian bread, and then drizzled with melted Cheez Whiz. You can add peppers or hot sauce. It was invented in 1930 at Pat's take-out stand by Pat Olivieri and his wife, and Pat's still exists near the Italian Market in South Philadelphia. Cheese steak is supposed to be an antidote for drunkenness.

Water ice is juice, diced fruit, and sugar mixed together and frozen, and then slushified in a blender. Water ice can be made of watermelon, kiwi, cantaloupe, blueberry, mango, the classic lemon and orange, or almost anything else. The drink was supposedly first sold out of a pushcart in South Philadelphia in 1931. Water ice, by the way, is both singular and plural; you drink one or six water ice.

Welcome America!

Location: Throughout Philadelphia.   **Contact:** Philadelphia Convention & Visitors Bureau, 1515 Market St., Ste. 2020, Philadelphia, PA 19102; Tel: (800)770-5883, or (215)636-3300; Fax: (215)636-3415.

Pittsburgh

Greek Food Festival

First full week in May (Sunday through Friday)   This is a food festival. There's bouzouki music and Greek dancing and a tour of St. Nicholas Greek Orthodox Cathedral to see the Byzantine icons and learn something of the history of the Greek Orthodox faith.

But food, which has special importance in Greek culture, is truly the heart of the festival. In classical Greece, food and dining "became an art form like drama, sculpture and art," Greek authority Marilyn Rouvelas has written. During the four-century subjugation of Greece by the Turkish Ottoman Empire, Greek cuisine was preserved by chefs who fled to Orthodox monasteries. They wore white hats to distinguish them from the priests in black hats—and it was there that the practice of chefs wearing high white toques began.

The festival began in 1962 when the Philoptochos (Women's Aid Society) of the cathedral held a small fund-raiser lunch and bake sale. It has ballooned into a festival that attracts 25,000 to 30,000 and is now emulated by many other Greek churches.

The cathedral's community center becomes a Greek taverna during the fest, and lunches, dinners, and take-out food are served. Some of the offerings: *souvlaki,* lamb shish kebab; *plaki,* haddock baked with tomatoes and onions; *souzoukakia,* meatballs simmered in a tomato and wine sauce; *dolmathes,* rice in marinated grape leaves. And there are always plenty of pastries, including *baklava; karithopeta,* walnut cake drenched with honey syrup; and *finikia,* cinnamon cookies dipped in syrup and sprinkled with ground walnuts. A clue to the abundance is a recent festival shopping list, which included 400 pounds of haddock, 1,960 pounds of cubed lamb, 1,690 pounds of spinach, 1,500 pounds of rice, and 482 pounds of walnuts.

Location: St. Nicholas Cathedral, 419 S. Dithridge St., across from Carnegie Museum. ⊛ **Contact:** St. Nicholas Greek Orthodox Cathedral, 419 S. Dithridge St., Pittsburgh, PA 15213; Tel: (412)682-3866.

Willow Street

Snitz Fest

First Saturday in October ⊛ *Schnitt:* the German word for a slice of food. In Pennsylvania Dutch, snitz, also spelled schnitz, means cut and dried apples.

Apples were staples for German settlers in colonial Pennsylvania; they were eaten fresh, dried, or cooked, and were used to make cider, vinegar, and brandy, and for livestock feed.

The historic role of the apple is celebrated at the Snitz Fest, which also provides a rare opportunity to try apples that you never find on shelves these days. The orchard of the Hans Herr House, a museum, is the festival's focal point. Visitors can tour the orchard in a Conestoga wagon and then taste and compare the apples, including the first American apple, the Roxbury Russet, developed in Roxbury, Massachusetts, in the 1640s.

Among others are the Albemarle Yellow Newton, one of Queen Victoria's favorites although it originated on Long Island, New York, in the early 1700s; the Doctor of Germantown, discovered by a physician in Germantown, Pennsylvania, sometime before 1817; the Duchess of Oldenburg, a Russian apple that bears fruit for over a century; the McIntosh, discovered by John McIntosh in Ontario in 1811; Sheepnose, named for its shape, originated in the late 1800s; and the Spitzenburg, a tart and crisp dessert apple and Thomas Jefferson's favorite. It originated in New York in the 1700s.

Harvest-time activities demonstrated are cider pressing, apple-butter making, apples being cut and dried, fodder shredding, flax processing, threshing, corn shucking.

Sausages, which may be sampled, are smoked over apple wood in the eighteenth-century smokehouse, and snitz pie and freshly made apple butter are sold to take home. There are eighteenth-century games for children.

About 1,500 attend the festival, a featured event at the Hans Herr House since 1985. The house, built in 1719, is a medieval-style Germanic stone house and the oldest documented Mennonite meeting house in America. It's considered one of the best examples of eighteenth-century German architecture in the United States and has been depicted in a number of paintings by Andrew Wyeth, a descendant of Hans Herr.

Location: Hans Herr House in Willow Street, about midway between Philadelphia and Baltimore, 5 miles south of Lancaster off U.S. 222. ⊛ **Contact:** Hans Herr House and Museum, 1849 Hans Herr Dr., Willow Street, PA 17584; Tel: (717)464-4438.

Rhode Island

Newport

Schweppes Great Chowder Cook-Off

First Saturday in June ⚙ "All the chowder you can eat for eight clams" is the cook-off's logo, and it means you can sample as much chowduh, as Rhodie clamdiggers say, as you want for your admission ticket, which is also your ballot to vote for the best chowduh. You can also get free Schweppes drinks and treats for the kids.

The chowders are judged in three categories—clam, seafood, and creative. Among the clam chowders, there are invariably creamy New England, tomato-based Manhattan, and both white and red Rhode Island varieties. More than two dozen restaurants from Rhode Island and Massachusetts participate, and the winner claims the title, first bestowed in 1982, "Best in New England."

Other events include cooking demonstrations; strolling entertainment by clowns, musicians, Larry the Lobster, Cathy the Crab, and Quentin the Quahog; band music; and children's rides and activities. Attendance is about 10,000.

Location: Newport Yachting Center at 4 Commercial Wharf. ⚙ **Contact:** Newport Yachting Center, P.O. Box 550, Newport, RI 02840; Tel: (401)846-1600, Fax: (401)847-7754.

While You're There: Tour some of the famous Newport estates, the summer cottages of the very rich, to get an idea of how America's royalty lived.

See Also: Boston Harborfest (Boston, MA).

Waterfront Seafood Festival

Third weekend in October ⚙ Seafood, sea chanteys, a lobster race, and a chance for kids to touch real live starfish, hermit crabs, and mussels are all part of this two-day eating marathon.

The seafood runs the gamut: chili (like regular chili, but with clams instead of meat), crabcakes, shrimp cocktail, steamed lobster, blackened sea bass, Cajun stuffed clams, clams stuffed with scallops, clams on the half shell, and Mexican and Italian seafood dishes.

Some non-seafood slips in, too. You can buy apple cider and apple pie from the Aquidneck Growers Market, and whole pumpkin pies or slices after the judging in the pumpkin-pie contest, a fund-raiser for the Seamen's Church Institute.

The festival also offers hayrides and pony rides for kids, clowns, bands, singers, demonstrations of such arts as totem-pole carving, and exhibits by marine environmental organizations, where people can not only touch strange sea creatures but also learn where a starfish's eyes are (end of the arms). About 10,000 people turn out for this end-of-summer wingding, which began in 1991.

Location: Bowen's Wharf on America's Cup Ave. **Contact:** Bowen's Wharf Co., Inc., P.O. Box 60, 13 Bowen's Wharf, Newport, RI 02840; Tel: (401)849-2120.

Warren

Warren Barrington Rotary Quahog Festival

Third weekend in July Quahogs, the hard-shell clams of the eastern seaboard, are clearly the stars of this festival.

So first, some background on the quahog (pronounced ko-hog): The name is an approximation of the Narragansett Indian word *poquauhocka,* meaning closed shell. When these clams are a year old and less than two inches across, they're called little necks; the medium-sized ones, at about two-and-a-half inches, are cherrystones, and when they're three inches or more, they're quahogs. The smaller clams are generally eaten raw on the half shell; quahogs are ground up to make chowder, or are baked with stuffing.

At the festival, you can eat stuffies, and you can sample red (tomato-based) and white (creamy) chowder made, of course, with quahogs. For something different, try the clam boil, a Rhode Island specialty. It consists of steamers (not quahogs), potatoes, onions, hot dogs, and various other bits and pieces, all put in a burlap onion sack and steamed in a pot. You'll also find lobster salad and steamed lobster and regular festival food and fresh produce at farm stands.

There are crab races (live crabs) and lobster races, interesting because lobsters don't exactly race, a mussel-eating contest, and a clam-shucking contest. Dozens of vendors sell all kinds of things.

The festival, started in 1983 and usually attended by 5,000 to 7,000 people, is held at the same time and same place as the Jay Barry Cultural Arts Festival, where local artists display and sell their works.

Location: Burr's Hill Park in Warren, about 10 miles south of Providence on Rhode Island 114 or 136. **Contact:** Warren Quahog Festival, Warren Rotary Club, P.O. Box 62, Warren, RI 02885-0062; Tel: (401)247-2188, Fax: (401)245-6270.

Vermont

Dummerston

Dummerston Congregational Church Apple Pie Festival

Sunday of Columbus Day weekend ☼ When it's apple time in Vermont, it's pie time, and church members spend a couple of weeks, morning to evening, making about 1,500 pies for the pie festival. The pies are sold by the slice or whole, and they usually sell out.

The festival began with the pies, but now the fire department adds to the fun with a breakfast of apple or blueberry pancakes at the firehouse, and the Grange Hall puts on a crafts fair. The Congregationalists sell cheddar cheese, cider, homemade ice cream, and doughnuts besides the pies.

The pies are made with Blessing cooking apples, also called "20-ounce" apples. They're donated to the church by Dwight Miller & Son Orchards, a local orchard that's been in business about 200 years. The 20-ounce is a huge green baking apple that "makes a nice pie," one of the orchard Millers said with typical Vermont understatement.

The church has been observing pie day since the 1970s.

Location: The town center in Dummerston, six miles west of I-91, immediately north of Brattleboro. ☼ **Contact:** Dummerston Congregational Church, R.D. 2, Putney, VT 05346; Tel: (802)254-9158 or 254-9111.

Enosburg Falls

Vermont Dairy Festival

First full weekend in June (Thursday through Sunday) ☼ At one time, Vermont had more cows than people. But then people started discovering the state, and in the mid-1970s the ratio shifted. Vermont now has about 550,000 people and

200,000 cows, and dairying accounts for 70 percent of the agricultural industry of the state. It helps that Ben and Jerry's ice-cream, a big dairy customer, is in Waterbury, Vermont.

This explains a dairy festival, where cartons of chocolate and white milk are given away, there's a lot of ice cream for sale, and there are raffles for five-pound slabs of Cabot cheddar cheese. Vermont's famous cheeses are produced by just six manufacturers, including Cabot Cheese, a cooperative with some 500 members.

The four-day festival has milking contests, a cooking contest, a cow-plop contest (you "buy" squares of land, and the winner is the one who owns the square that receives the most plop), and a Jake and Mabel raffle, Jake and Mabel being a bull and cow.

Between 20,000 and 40,000 people attend the fair, which has been going on since 1957, and also offers a carnival, crafts, a parade, dancing, and assorted fair food.

Location: Enosburg Falls is about eight miles from the Canadian border, at the junction of Vermont 108 and 105. ☼ **Contact:** Lions Club, P.O. Box 282, Enosburg Falls, VT 05450; Tel: (802)933-2513, or (802)933-4134.

St. Albans

Vermont Maple Festival

Third weekend in April (Friday through Sunday) ☼ St. Albans proclaims itself the Maple Capital of the World, which seems a tad presumptuous since close to 80 percent of the total world production of maple syrup comes from Canada (most of it from Quebec). Vermont does provide about 33 percent of all the U.S. syrup, and St. Albans is the county seat of Franklin County, which makes more syrup than any other county in the United States.

So there *is* a lot of syrup here, and the town celebrates it with a festival that began in 1968 as a town party, and now pulls in 55,000 people.

Visitors sniff sweet-smelling steam swirling around a demo sugarhouse, and eat hundreds of dozens of doughnuts with maple-cream icing, maple cotton candy, maple-sugar candies, taffy-like "sugar on snow," maple cupcakes, maple cheesecakes, and pancakes and waffles with maple syrup. There are contests for the best maple syrup and for the best apple pie made with maple syrup. There are arts and crafts exhibits, a talent show, a parade, and a maple supper where a king and queen are crowned and the menu includes maple-glazed ham.

Maple syrup comes chiefly from the sugar maple tree (*Acer saccharum*) and is made only in North America—in the northeastern United States (but as far west as Wisconsin) and in eastern Canada. The yield can fluctuate wildly from year to year, and anywhere from 3.5 million gallons to 5.7 million gallons (21.5 million liters) of maple syrup are produced each year.

The U.S. percentage of the total world production has been falling slightly, but is about 22 percent. Vermont's yield runs from about 300,000 gallons to 570,000 in a banner year. Of the top U.S. producers, Vermont is trailed by New York, Maine, Wisconsin, and with much smaller yields, Ohio, New Hampshire, and Michigan.

Native North Americans were tapping maple trees, using the syrup as a seasoning and often as money, when European settlers arrived. The Indians, who used clay pots to boil sap over wood fires under roofs of tree branches, taught the settlers the uses of maple. The settlers in turn added something to the sugaring process—iron kettles.

Maple producers tap the trees in early spring and drive a spile into the tap hole. Originally they gathered the sap from buckets hung from the trees and carried the buckets to the fires. Today, most commercial sugar makers use plastic tubing to transport the sap from trees to the evaporator in a sugarhouse.

Each tap yields about 10 gallons (about 38 liters) of sap a season, and that yields about one quart (a little less than a liter) of syrup. Syrup is made by boiling sap to 219 degrees, to evaporate water in it. Boiled a little longer to 234 degrees, the sap, when poured over snow, makes the sticky "sugar on snow." Increased boiling makes maple sugar.

Thomas Jefferson, that inveterate horticultural experimenter, visited Vermont to see how to make syrup and then tried to imitate the practice in Virginia but didn't have any luck. The weather wasn't right. Trees have to have cold nights and warm days, and once the trees bud, the sugaring is over because the sap gets a bitter flavor.

Location: St. Albans is halfway between the equator and the North Pole; U.S. 7 cuts through the town, and I-89 is on the outskirts. ❀ **Contact:** St. Albans Chamber of Commerce, P.O. Box 327, St. Albans, VT 05478; Tel: (802)524-2444, Fax: (802)527-2256.

Southeast

Alabama

Arkansas

Florida

Georgia

Kentucky

Louisiana

Mississippi

North Carolina

South Carolina

Tennessee

Virginia

Alabama

Blessing of the Fleet

Third Sunday in May Bayou La Batre, the Seafood Capital of Alabama, was founded by the French in 1787 as a little fishing village, where the "main street" is actually the bayou, a channel that twists two-and-a-half miles to the Gulf of Mexico. The village is no longer solely French; Vietnamese and Cambodians have found a haven here, and egg rolls are part of the fare.

However, the most popular food at the picnic following the blessing of the fleet continues to be seafood gumbo, made in 20-gallon batches. There are also dinners of boiled shrimp, stuffed crab or fried fish, and such tidbits as seafood-stuffed jalapeños, sharkburgers, and fried squid. For non-seafood lovers, hot dogs and sausage sandwiches are available, and, of course, hush puppies.

The tradition of the blessing began simply in 1950 with a priest offering the benediction, "God bless your going out and your coming in. . . . May He fill your nets." Today from 15,000 to 20,000 people are drawn to the blessing and its attendant events, especially the water parade of more than 50 runabouts, oyster boats, and big rigged shrimpers, with flags and pennants fluttering on every line and mast.

The day's events also include contests (shrimp heading, oyster shucking, crab picking), a street parade, games for youngsters, a pet show, arts and crafts, and the crowning of the Fleet Queen.

Bayou La Batre is the center of a major boat-building area, making trawlers and nets not only for Gulf use but for Central America and coastal African countries. Another Bayou claim to fame: Forrest Gump (the slow-witted movie hero of 1995) went into the shrimping business here, although the shrimping scenes were actually shot off North Carolina.

Location: Bayou La Batre, on Alabama 188, is 10 miles from the Mississippi border, and about the same distance south of I-10. **Contact:** St. Margaret Church, P.O. Box 365, Bayou La Batre, AL 36509; Tel: (334)824-2415.

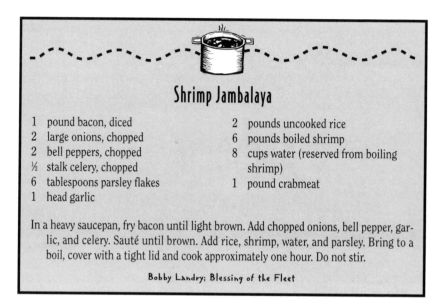

Shrimp Jambalaya

1   pound bacon, diced
2   large onions, chopped
2   bell peppers, chopped
½   stalk celery, chopped
6   tablespoons parsley flakes
1   head garlic

2   pounds uncooked rice
6   pounds boiled shrimp
8   cups water (reserved from boiling shrimp)
1   pound crabmeat

In a heavy saucepan, fry bacon until light brown. Add chopped onions, bell pepper, garlic, and celery. Sauté until brown. Add rice, shrimp, water, and parsley. Bring to a boil, cover with a tight lid and cook approximately one hour. Do not stir.

Bobby Landry; Blessing of the Fleet

While You're There: St. Margaret Church, the sponsor of the blessing, has stained-glass windows that memorialize the Daughters of Charity who escorted French women to the colony in 1704.

Brewton

Alabama Blueberry Festival

Third Saturday in June Brewton ships highbush Rabbiteye blueberries all over the Southeast, and is the only area in the state still shipping the berries commercially. This being a berry area, you can be sure you're getting local berries at the Brewton festival. They come in homemade ice cream, which sells out in no time—"they can't make enough of it," said a Brewtonian—and cobbler, which they also can't make enough of; and blueberry delight, a dessert; and waffles and cakes.

The festival began in 1981, and some 30,000 people now attend to eat and enjoy arts and crafts, an antique-car show, children's games and rides, tours of a local blueberry farm, a street dance on the Friday night before the festival, live entertainment, and usually a blueberry-recipe contest, in which contestants submit their blueberry dishes.

Location: Jefferson Davis Community College, Brewton, about 15 miles north of the Florida border, 17 miles south of I-65. **Contact:** Greater Brewton Area Chamber of Commerce, Box 19, Brewton, AL 36427; Tel: (334)867-3224.

See Also: Blueberry Festival (Alma, GA).

Peanut Butter Festival

Last Saturday in October ☼ Brundidge was a pioneer in the peanut-butter industry; in 1929, J. D. Johnston started one of the first peanut-butter mills in the Southeast. In the early 1930s, Grady Johnson opened another peanut-butter mill, and these two companies kept the town going during the Depression. Competition from huge food-processing companies eventually led them to close, however.

This peanut-butter history is honored by Brundidge, which got its second stop light in 1996, with festive things like an anything-goes Nutter Butter parade, goober-rolling contests (you roll a peanut with your nose), and a recipe contest in which each entry contains at least a cup of peanut butter. After the judging, festival-goers can sample entries, which have included peanut-butter tacos, soups, and pies.

Jane Treadwell, a local historian and daughter of a peanut-butter manufacturer, started the festival in 1992. Attendance is about 10,000.

The day starts with a 5K run, followed by a breakfast of toast with peanut butter and syrup. And then there's Alabama food all day—peanut-butter-and-banana sandwiches (a favorite here; banana-and-mayonnaise sandwiches are also a standard, and were Elvis Presley's favorite food); cracklin' bread, which is corn bread with bits of cracklings (the skin or fat of a hog fried until brittle and crisp); peanut-butter dip, soup, cakes, cookies, pies; boiled peanuts, and goober cocktails, which are Coca-Colas with peanuts poured into them.

The festival organizers also make Alabama's largest peanut-butter-and-jelly sandwich, usually about 55 feet long. Free slices are offered.

Also on the agenda are hog-calling and tobacco-spitting contests, arts and crafts, stilt walkers (the locals call them tom walkers), country music, line dancing, demonstrations of quilt making and basket making, and barnyard games for kids.

Peanuts are the biggest cash crop in the county, pulling in about $14 million annually, but the festival is just a small-town peanut-butter kind of day in the country.

Location: Downtown Brundidge, about 50 miles south of Montgomery, just off U.S. 231 on County Rt. 10. ☼ **Contact:** Peanut Butter Festival, 311 Gilmore Road, Brundidge, AL 36010; Tel: (334)735-3608.

While You're There: Clio is just 12 miles from Brundidge, and its Chitlin Jamboree is the same weekend. Follow your nose.

Alabama Chitlin Jamboree

Usually last Saturday in October ☼ As the Clio folks put it, the festival has other food, like steak sandwiches, "for those who haven't acquired a taste for those delicious delicacies." Those delicious delicacies are, of course, chitlins, and they cook up two tons of them, which means a lot of people do have a taste for them. You can have them cooked any way you want—boiled or fried, as a sandwich, or on a plate.

The festival, started in 1988, was patterned after the successful Chitlin Strut in Salley, South Carolina, and the idea of it was to promote pork products. It features a pork-cooking contest, where contestants bring along their prepared dishes with a copy of the recipe. Winners get cash prizes.

Other events include a parade, an antique-car show, gospel and country music, clog-dancing, and sometimes a pig chase, where children chase a young pig that becomes the property of the winner. Vendors sell T-shirts, hats, and aprons with a smiling-pig logo.

Clio (pronounced cly-o) has a population of only 1,200, but as many as 7,000 people come to the jamboree. Besides helping pork farmers, the jamboree raises money for philanthropic purposes. After expenses, proceeds go to people in the community who are in need, usually because of fire or sickness.

Location: Clio is 75 miles southeast of Montgomery, on Alabama 10. **Contact:** Ruritan Club, Box 64, Clio, AL 36017; Tel: (334)397-4518.

See Also: Chitlin Strut (Salley, SC).

Cullman

Oktoberfest

Last weekend in September through first weekend in October Cullman, founded by Bavarian immigrant John G. Cullmann (he spelled his name with a double "n," but the city's name is spelled with one), may have the only Oktoberfest anywhere with no beer or alcohol of any sort: Cullman County is dry. A dry Oktoberfest seems like an oxymoron, but this one, which began in 1982, is nonetheless a 10-day affair, with German foods served at various churches and restaurants. Attendance generally runs about 1,000. Some of the people wear lederhosen and there are games, polka dancing, fun runs, and the selection of a Miss Oktoberfest.

John G. Cullmann fled Bismarck's Germany for America, lived for a while in Cincinnati, and dreamed of establishing a colony of immigrant Germans on an expanse of land broken into small farms. He picked this central Alabama area on a railroad line and persuaded five German families from Cincinnati to come here in 1873, and they were followed by more immigrant families. Strawberries were once a major crop, but now poultry is the mainstay of the economy.

Location: Cullman is 25 miles south of Decatur, 2 miles east of I-65 at exit 308. **Contact:** Cullman Area Chamber of Commerce, P.O. Box 1104, Cullman, AL 35056; Tel: (205)734-0454.

Fantasy Cheesecake

1¾ cups graham cracker crumbs   ¼ cup sugar
⅓ cup melted butter   ½ cup chopped honey roasted peanuts

Crust: Combine ingredients in a bowl and press on bottom and side of a 9-inch spring-form pan. Set aside.

3 (8 oz.) packages softened cream   1 cup sour cream
    cheese   12 ounces chocolate morsels
2 teaspoons vanilla   1 cup chopped peanuts
1 cup sugar   3 ounces chocolate baking bar
3 eggs   ½ package caramel candies

Cheesecake: Beat cream cheese, vanilla, and sugar until creamy. Beat in eggs one at a time. Fold in sour cream. Fold in 6 ounces chocolate morsels. Bake at 350 degrees for approximately 60–70 minutes or until center is set. Turn off oven, leave door slightly open and cool for 1 hour in the oven. Chill for 4 hours. Remove side from pan, top with remaining chocolate morsels and peanuts. Melt caramel candy and chocolate baking bar over low heat, with ⅓ cup water. When melted, dribble candy and chocolate mixture over cheese cake with a spoon. Yield: 1 cake.

Martha Jones, Dothan, Alabama: Grand Prize Winner of Peanut Recipe Contest
sponsored by National Peanut Festival Association,
Alabama Peanut Producers Association, and Dothan Eagle.

Dothan

National Peanut Festival

Nine days in late October/early November (Friday through following Saturday) ⬡ This long-running peanut festival is a paean to the peanut and to all agriculture in Alabama's Wiregrass Region. At the first festival in 1938, the speaker was Dr. George Washington Carver, the man who made peanuts a major U.S. crop and gave farmers a substitute for cotton.

The festival was discontinued during World War II, resumed in 1947, and is now going strong, with attendance about 136,000 over the first eight days and about 200,000 for the two-hour Goober Parade on the final day.

The parade gives the festival its fame; the streets are paved with Alabama's gold—peanuts. A converted cement mixer spreads tons of peanuts along the entire parade route, and spectators scramble after them. And, of course, the parade has marching bands, floats, horses, clowns, and Miss and Little Miss National Peanut Festival waving regally.

The festival is now more like a county fair than a country social; there are livestock shows, homemaking and youth exhibits, carnival rides, big-name entertainment, sports tournaments, an antique-car show, and food vendors vending standard fair food. Yet the spotlight remains on the peanut.

There's a Peanut Recipe Contest designed to "demonstrate the versatility of peanuts, peanut butter, and peanut oil." This results in such creations as Chocolate Angel Food Peanut Roll, Bubba's Uptown Peanut Butter Brownies, Peanut Butter 'n' Jelly Coffee Cake, and Peanut Harvest Peach Pie.

And there are peanut foods to buy—peanut brittle, peanut fudge, peanut butter, and peanuts roasted, fried, raw, or boiled. Boiled peanuts are a Southern specialty, albeit possibly an acquired taste. They are usually picked when green and boiled unshelled in salted water. The nuts are moist and mealy and taste only vaguely like roasted or fresh peanuts.

The festival also has its small-town elements—greased-pig (the "grease" is peanut oil, of course) and calf scrambles, where the winner gets to keep the animal; square dancing, a choral festival, coloring and poster contests.

Dothan is a marketing center in the peanut country of southeastern Alabama, an area known as the Wiregrass Region for the prevalence of a tough spreading weed that looks wiry. Much of the land was cultivated for cotton toward the end of the nineteenth century, but around 1915, the boll weevil wiped out about two-thirds of the crop, and the Wiregrass moved into peanuts. Today, fields of soybeans, corn, and peanuts surround Dothan.

Location: Houston County Farm Center in Dothan, in the southeastern corner of Alabama, about 12 miles from both Florida and Georgia.   **Contact:** National Peanut Festival Assn., 1691 Ross Clark Circle, S.E., Dothan, AL 36301; Tel: (334)793-4323, Fax: (334) 793-3247.

While You're There: Landmark Park, on U.S. 431 north of Dothan, is an 1890s living-history farm, complete with a farmhouse, smokehouse, cane mill, and sheep, goats, and pigs. Many educational and cultural workshops and special events are held throughout the year.

See Also: Georgia Peanut Festival (Poulan, GA).

Elberta

Elberta Sausage Festival

Last Saturday of March and the last Saturday of October   Twice a year the volunteer fire department of this tiny town—one stop light, population about 500—serves up some 6,000 pounds of sausages, which is 16,000 to 18,000 individual sausages, to hungry crowds. The sausages, a more or less secret combination of beef, pork, German seasonings, and garlic, are grilled over open fires and served with sauerkraut. Other foods to keep appetites in check are German stuffed cabbage, German goulash, fried chicken, and such Southern staples as red beans and rice. For entertainment, bands and accordion players play gospel, polkas, and oompah, and there are rides and games. Proceeds from the event, held since 1977, have helped buy fire equipment and a new town hall.

Elberta was founded in the early 1900s when German colonization companies brought different ethnic groups to Alabama to settle what was largely virgin forest. The town was the center of a thriving agricultural area of oranges and peaches; the first child born in the settlement was named Elberta. But the Elberta peach, for whom the child and town were named, hasn't been grown here since a big freeze made growers decide the climate was too severe.

The Elberta water tower is decorated with a painting of German dancers and the words "Für das gute leben," which means "For the good life."

Location: Elberta is on U.S. 98, about 10 miles from the Alabama coast. **Contact:** Baldwin County Heritage Museum, P.O. Box 356, Elberta, AL 36530; Tel: (334)986-8375.

Gulf Shores

National Shrimp Festival

Second weekend of October (Thursday through Sunday)

Before the Spaniards found the coast of what's now Alabama in the sixteenth century, nomadic Indian tribes dined on the shrimp and oysters teeming in the Gulf of Mexico.

It wasn't until 1971, though, that the shrimpers of Gulf Shores decided to do some bragging about their industry. That year, they held the first shrimp festival as a one-day affair to liven up this resort area after Labor Day.

Today it attracts more than 200,000 people who stroll the white and fine-as-sugar beach and clog the Seafood Boardwalk for shrimp in every guise—steamed, fried, as kebabs, in gyros, in puffs, in gumbo and jambalaya. There are also crabs, oysters, shark. . . . "If it swims, they serve it," said a spokesman. Standard non-seafood festival foods are served at the other end of the boardwalk. Besides noshing, people can listen to continuous music, visit more than 200 fine arts and crafts booths, run in a 5K run, enter the sand-castle contest, sail in a regatta. For children, hands-on painting at the Children's Art Village is a favorite.

Shrimp is America's favorite shellfish, and there are hundreds of species of warm-water and cold-water shrimp. In the Gulf of Mexico, there are about thirty species, but only four are fished commercially—what are known as brown, white, pink, and royal red. It's confusing to non-shrimpers because the color can depend on where they are; for example, pink shrimp along the northern Gulf coast are often lemon-yellow.

Most shrimp spawn offshore in deep water and then the young shrimp are carried by currents into estuaries to mature. The shrimp boats—trawlers—pull cone-shaped nets through the water to catch the shrimp, then haul the catch on board to sort it into giant, jumbo, large, medium, and small.

Location: Gulf Shores is on the Gulf of Mexico, at the end of Alabama 59. **Contact:** Alabama Gulf Coast Area Chamber of Commerce, 3150 Gulf Shores Pkwy., P.O. Box 457, Gulf Shores, AL 36547; Tel: (334)968-6904.

Shrimp Puffs

8 ounces cream cheese	¼ teaspoon cayenne
2 teaspoons grated onion	½ cup Parmesan cheese
½ cup mayonnaise	1 cup cooked shrimp
2 tablespoons chopped chives	1 small loaf white bread

Grind shrimp in blender. In a bowl, combine all ingredients except bread. Mix well. Cut bread into desired shapes and spread each with shrimp/cheese mixture. Bake in 350 degree oven for 15 minutes (longer for a crisper puff). These may be done ahead of time and frozen. Bake when ready to use.

National Shrimp Festival

Mobile

Mardi Gras

Day before Ash Wednesday ☼ Mardi Gras a food festival? Well, in Mobile chants of "Moon Pie! Moon Pie!" fill the air during the parades leading up to Fat Tuesday.

The "throws" that marching mystic-society members toss to the crowds include not only doubloons and beads and balloons but also Moon Pies. It's hard for Mobilians to explain their devotion to the Moon Pie, but every Mobilian knows the Moon Pie is the top prize of Mardi Gras throws.

Guests see just chocolate-covered cookies with a marshmallow filling, wrapped in cellophane. A Mobilian, on the other hand, looks at a Moon Pie as a part of the Mobile Mardi Gras heritage.

Nobody quite knows why Mobile started associating Moon Pies with Mardi Gras, but it's been a tradition for decades.

Mobile claims to have the nation's oldest Mardi Gras, dating to 1705. (New Orleans didn't have its first Mardi Gras until 1827.) A few souls wore masks and painted their faces red for that first celebration, held a few miles upstream from present-day Mobile.

The Civil War put a temporary end to pre-Lenten celebrations in Mobile, but on Mardi Gras afternoon in 1866, Joseph Stillwell Cain dressed himself as a Chickasaw Indian chief and rode through the streets on a coal wagon pulled by a mule. The Chickasaws had been undefeated in battle, so Cain was both taunting Union troops occupying the city and raising the city's morale. And, inadvertently, re-starting Mardi Gras.

Location: Throughout Mobile.   **Contact:** Mobile Convention & Visitors Corp., P.O. Box 204, Mobile, AL 36601-0204; Tel: (334)415-2000 or (800)5-MOBILE; Fax: (334)415-2060.

See Also: Moon Pie Games and Country Fair (Bell Buckle, TN).

Red Snapper Festival

Saturday before Mardi Gras   No less than the great James Beard called red snapper a "magnificent fish," and Orange Beach is not about to dispute the great James Beard: Orange Beach is the Red Snapper Capital of the World.

Here's why: Alabama has only 53 miles of coastline but lands about 40 percent of the recreationally caught red snapper from the U.S. portion of the Gulf of Mexico; Orange

Beach, which abuts Gulf Shores on Pleasure Island, has one of the largest charterboat operations on the Gulf.

The annual snapper festival was founded in 1993 and is really a huge fish fry attended by 10,000 to 15,000 snapper fans. Charter-boat captains catch the fish for it, and on festival day, the snappers are fried and served with hush puppies, cole slaw, and grits. The festival also offers arts and crafts and musical entertainment.

One reason for the abundance of red snapper, grouper, amberjack, and other reef dwellers off Alabama is an artificial reef-building system that was started by the charter-boat captains in the 1950s. The reefs consist of obsolete tanks (one year, the federal government sank 100 tanks in the Gulf), Liberty ships, bridge rubble, old school buses, and wrecked automobiles, all providing snapper havens and nurseries. Snappers, incidentally, can grow to thirty-five pounds, but are usually marketed in the two-to-eight-pound range.

Location: Orange Beach is about five miles east of Gulf Shores on Alabama 180. **Contact:** Alabama Gulf Coast Convention & Visitors Bureau, P.O. Drawer 457, Gulf Shores, AL 36547; Tel: (334)968-6904.

Tuskegee

Sweet Potato Festival

Second Saturday of October George Washington Carver, the biochemist usually remembered for the many uses he found for the peanut, also developed more than 100 products or uses for sweet potatoes. This festival began in 1985 both to honor him and to promote sweet potatoes.

Dr. Carver, whose mother was a slave, worked to better the lives of farm people. His research into peanuts, soy beans, and sweet potatoes revolutionized southern agriculture by enabling farmers to shed their dependence on cotton after boll weevils ravaged the cotton crop. Among the sweet-potato products Carver developed were flour, rubber compound, ink, and library paste.

At Tuskegee Institute, where Dr. Carver headed the agricultural department from 1896 until his death in 1943, scientists and breeders are still studying this native American root vegetable. James Tarver Jr., a pharmacologist, is currently trying to document the estrogen content of a strain of sweet potato; women who eat it regularly seem to have lower rates of breast and vaginal cancer.

You learn this and more at the festival, and you can also try imaginative sweet-potato concoctions. The vegetable is traditionally eaten at winter holidays, but at Tuskegee, they want you to see how it can be a year-round treat. So besides familiar dishes like sweet-potato pie, you can sample sweet-potato ice cream (a big hit), cold sweet-potato punch (from the tips of the greens), and the vines cooked like spinach.

This is a down-home festival that attracts around 3,000 visitors. It has arts and crafts exhibits, band music, a plant sale, a show of antique farm implements, and contests for the best sweet potatoes and the best sweet-potato dish.

Location: Tuskegee Institute, Tuskegee, about 35 miles east of Montgomery, 5 miles south of I-95, on U.S. 29. 🔅 **Contact:** National Park Service, Tuskegee Institute National Historic Site, 520 Old Montgomery Rd., Tuskegee, AL 36088; Tel: (334)727-6390; Fax: (334)727-8201.

While You're There: The George Washington Carver Museum, near the entrance to Tuskegee Institute, has a section devoted to Dr. Carver's career, with displays of his laboratory equipment and samples of peanut and sweet-potato products. A second section traces the development of the Institute, founded in 1881, to the present.

See Also: Ham & Yam Festival (Smithfield, NC).

Arkansas

Alma

Spinach Festival

Third Saturday in April ☼ The Allen Canning Company in Alma cans 56 percent of all the spinach canned in the country, and that gives the town the right to claim the title of Spinach Capital of the World. Alma, a town of less than 3,000, takes its capitalism seriously, boasting not only an eight-foot statue of Popeye across from the municipal complex, but also what it calls the World's Largest Spinach Can. The can is actually the town water tower painted to resemble the label on Allen's Popeye Spinach.

With all this spinach sloganeering, the festival itself is a fairly subdued affair. On Friday night, a supper is held in the high school cafeteria with a menu of spinach, beans, and corn bread, and it's followed with a show of local talent. On Saturday, more than 100 vendors sell arts and crafts and food—largely standard festival food, like funnel cakes and dogs. For entertainment, there are antique-car and racing-car shows, country music and gospel music, and sometimes a spinach cook-off.

Location: Alma is about 8 miles northeast of Fort Smith, off I-40. ☼ **Contact:** Alma Chamber of Commerce, 235 W. Cherry St., Alma, AR 72921; Tel: (501)632-4127.

Atkins

Pickle Fest

Third weekend in May (Friday and Saturday) ☼ Arkansas isn't in the running for top pickle producer, but Atkins has a pickle plant (Dean Pickle and Specialty Products), so pickles were picked to pique people's interest in the town. The festival started in 1992, and about 10,000 come to celebrate, more than tripling the town's population.

In the eating department, honors go to fried dill pickles, made according to a secret recipe developed by a member of the VFW. Dean Pickle's booth offers all sorts of pickles for sampling: kosher, dill, bread-and-butter, okra, and gherkins.

This is, indeed, an eating fest; there are 147 food booths that offer standard festival fare (dogs, burgers, funnel cake) as well as homemade ice cream and fried pies, an Arkansas favorite.

Just contemplating the contests makes one's mouth pucker. There are pickle-eating contests for those 12 and under and for adults. One year, the winner in the adult group ate 46 ounces of pickles in three minutes and thirty-three seconds, and won $100. There are also pickle-juice-drinking contests, for under-12s and seniors, and one senior winner actually drank half a gallon in 42 seconds. The prize again was $100. The young people get prizes of $25.

Other events include a 5K run, a dance, contests for Little Miss Sweet Pickle and Mr. Dill Pickle, a rodeo, horseshoe-pitching competitions, sports tournaments, continuous music, a dance, and sometimes a pickling contest. Fest proceeds help fund such town projects as new sidewalks, a welcome sign, and a huge sign on the side of the mountain: Go Razorbacks.

Location: Downtown Atkins, about 50 miles northwest of Little Rock on I-40.
Contact: Pickle Fest, 9171 U.S. 64 East, Atkins, AR 72823; Tel: (501)641-2576.

Dardanelle

Mount Nebo Chicken Fry

Last Saturday in June This chicken fry began in 1949 to promote the poultry industry, and it seems to have worked. Arkansas is the number-one broiler producing state in the country, with cash receipts from broilers totaling almost two billion dollars.

They don't keep statistics on how many fried-chicken dinners are consumed here in the heart of the broiler region, but consumption is known to be high. The chickens are donated by Tyson Foods, one of the biggest poultry processors anywhere, and a couple of other companies in the area. To go with them, there are spear pickles from a nearby pickle plant, and rice, baked beans, and cole slaw. For beverages, there are old-fashioned lemonade and sarsaparilla.

In keeping with the theme, there are chicken-calling contests and raw-egg tosses. Other fun events are a most beautiful men's legs contest, in which men in shorts wear grocery bags over their heads to protect their identity; contests of crosscut sawing and log splitting; a 10K run and other sports events; arts and crafts; a Miss Nebo and Junior Miss Nebo pageant; a Little Mr. Rooster and Miss Pullet contest for youngsters aged five and six, and various children's activities. Singers and dancers entertain, and politicians are generally on hand to do a little glad-handing.

Mount Nebo is a state park a few miles from Dardanelle, and the festival takes its name and royal personages' names from the park.

Location: Dardanelle is at the junction of Arkansas 7 and 22, about 50 miles northwest of Little Rock. **Contact:** Dardanelle Chamber of Commerce, P.O. Box 208, Dardanelle, AR 72834; Tel: (501)229-3328.

See Also: Delmarva Chicken Festival (DE).

Hope

Hope Watermelon Festival

Third weekend in August (Thursday through Sunday) ◌

Hope is the place that you may think was made famous as the birthplace of President Bill Clinton, who memorably said "I still believe in a place called Hope."

But for the folks of Hope, the town has been famous since well before Mr. Clinton was born. The town's logo for quite some time has been Home of the World's Largest Watermelons, and they do not lie in Hope.

Hope watermelons are humongous. At the first festival in 1926, the biggest watermelon weighed 143¼ pounds and was grown by Hope farmer Edgar Lasseter. It was shipped to the Kiwanis Club in Little Rock, and the whole club wasn't able to finish it. Edgar Lasseter's big melons are what started the festival; the year before he grew a 136-pound melon that created such a sensation it was sent to President Calvin Coolidge. This prompted local boosters to start an annual watermelon festival.

The festival continued into the late 1930s, then lapsed for a number of years, but has been held annually since 1977, and the melons have kept on getting bigger. The 200-pound mark was reached in 1979; the growers were Lloyd and Ivan Bright of Hope. In 1985, Lloyd Bright's son Jason grew a champion 260 pounder, which made it into the *Guinness Book of World Records*. That weighty melon has since been eclipsed (by two pounds) by a Tennessee grower, but there's always hope in Hope. Good sandy soil, too, which promotes melon growth. So does chopping all the melons off a vine except one.

The festival isn't all about weighing; it's about eating, too. Volunteers slice up 22,000 watermelons, more normal ones, averaging 30 pounds each, and people sit at tables in a tent and eat slice after slice. There's a big fish fry, and vendors sell barbecue, bratwurst, sausages, funnel cake, and other fair food.

There are watermelon-eating, seed-spitting, watermelon-decorating, and Bill and Hillary look-alike contests; gospel and band concerts; sports competitions (softball, ping-pong, tug of war, etc.); children's games, square dancing, line dancing. This is a big, big event in Hope, attended by about 75,000 people.

Location: Fair Park in Hope, 120 miles southwest of Little Rock on I-30. ◌ **Contact:** Hope-Hempstead Chamber of Commerce, P.O. Box 250, Hope, AR 71801; Tel: (501)777-3640.

While You're There: Nashville, about 17 miles northwest of Hope, has the only diamond mine in North America open to the public. Amateur diamond hunters are

Members of the Bright family (from left, Jason, Richard, Lloyd, and Ivan) show off young Jason's 260-pound champion melon in 1985.

(Hope-Hempstead County Chamber of Commerce)

welcome to search the 35-acre field. Something to do when you can't look at another watermelon slice.

Wings Over the Prairie Festival and World's Championship Duck Calling Contest

Friday and Saturday after Thanksgiving ※ Stuttgart is the Rice and Duck Capital of the World, and the reason it's the duck capital is because of the abundance of rice.

Rice was first grown successfully on the Grand Prairie in the early 1900s, and it gradually became the foundation of Stuttgart's economy. About 103,000 acres are now grown in Arkansas County. The duck season usually begins in late November when the fields of rice have been harvested, and this gives the ducks lots to feed on.

Since Stuttgart has rice and ducks, it became logical to have this jawbreaker of a festival, which began in 1936 as a casual duck-calling contest among a few local hunters. Now 65,000 people show up, and there are dozens of callers who demonstrate specific kinds of calls, with very precise rules. There are also fun shoots, the crowning of Queen Mallard, an arts and crafts show, and a street dance.

Rice comes into the affair with the Duck Gumbo Cook-off in which 40 or more teams compete to produce the best gumbo. Spectators are invited to stop by each of the gumbo booths and have a taste. There is also standard fair food available.

The contest-festival has been listed as one of the top 100 parties by *Playboy* magazine.

Location: Stuttgart is at the intersection of U.S. 79 and 165, about 40 miles southeast of Little Rock. **Contact:** Stuttgart Chamber of Commerce, P.O. Box 932, Stuttgart, AR 72160; Tel: (501)673-1602.

While You're There: The Stuttgart Agricultural Museum (E. 4th and Park Ave.) displays a replica of a pioneer homestead as well as exhibits and slide shows on past methods of farming on the Grand Prairie, on duck hunting, and on rice and soybean growing.

Warren

Bradley County Pink Tomato Festival

Second weekend in June An all-tomato luncheon is the star attraction of this festival in the Pink Tomato Capital of the World.

The official verbatim menu: "Bradley County favorite drink [tomato juice, since Bradley County is dry], ham with Bradley County sauce, green tomato-beans with almonds, tomarinated carrots—pride of Bradley County, tomato finger rolls, heavenly tomato cake." The cake has tomato juice in both the cake and the icing. The tomarinated carrots are cooked carrots marinated in tomato soup, oil, vinegar, sugar, dry mustard, and Worcestershire sauce, and served cold. Bacon and tomato sandwiches and regular festival foods are also sold.

Twenty-pound boxes of tomatoes are auctioned and keep bringing record bids; in 1996, $2,500 was paid for a box. Proceeds are returned to the community.

The once-famous Bradley pink tomato, if the truth be told, is not as popular as it once was, and there are also not as many of them as there once were. When the festival started in 1957, there were more than 400 tomato farms in the area. Now there are about 100—still enough, however, to provide adequate numbers of pink tomatoes for the festival. About 15,000 attend.

The tomato has a pinkish tinge just before it's fully ripe and is considered (in Bradley County, anyway) the world's tastiest tomato. Its downside is that it doesn't ship well, but that's an upside for locals who get to eat plenty of Bradley pinks at their vine-ripened freshest.

Warren is a small town in southern Arkansas, and the festival has a hometown feel to it. There's a parade featuring horse-drawn farm wagons, and the festival includes other events such as a tomato-eating contest, a street dance, a cutest baby contest, and a talent

Heavenly Tomato Cake

½ cup margarine	1 teaspoon soda
½ cup shortening	½ cup tomato juice
2 cups sugar	1 cup hot water
2 eggs	1 teaspoon vanilla
¼ cup cocoa	1½ cups miniature marshmallows
2 cups flour	

Cake: Cream together margarine, shortening, and sugar. Add eggs one at a time, beating well after each. Sift together cocoa, flour, and soda. Add to creamed mixture, mixing thoroughly. Combine tomato juice, hot water, and marshmallows; add to batter. Add vanilla. Batter will be thin and marshmallows will come to top. Pour into 15½ x 10½ x 1 inch pan. Bake in 350-degree, preheated oven for 35 minutes. Ice while hot.

½ cup margarine	¼ teaspoon salt
¼ cup tomato juice	1 box powdered sugar, sifted
2 tablespoons water	1 cup chopped pecans (toasted)
4 tablespoons cocoa	

Icing: Combine margarine, tomato juice, water, cocoa, and salt; heat until boiling. Pour over powdered sugar and beat well. Add nuts and spread on hot cake.

Jean Frisby

contest. During the week before the festival, there are pageants to select Miss Pink Tomato, Little Miss Pink Tomato, and Miss Teen Pink Tomato. Fireworks end the weekend show.

Location: Warren is 40 miles south of Pine Bluff at the intersection of Arkansas 4 and 15.   Contact: Warren Chamber of Commerce, 104 N. Myrtle, Warren AR 71671; Tel: (501)226-5225.

Weiner

Arkansas Rice Festival

Second weekend in October   Poinsett County is the number-one rice-growing county in Arkansas, and Arkansas is by far the number-one rice-growing state, with well over a million acres in rice, more than twice as many acres as second-place Louisiana.

You might, then, expect to see rice here, but 200 different dishes? That's right. There's a tasting of these dishes, and it takes about three hours for the line to move past all of them. A sampling of the samples: duck, chicken, and pork with rice; vegetables with rice; rice custards with various toppings; salads, breads. Both white and brown rice are used, and sometimes wild rice is mixed in, even though wild rice isn't rice and isn't grown locally.

In a food cook-off the week before the festival, professional judges award honors in categories of main dish, bread, dessert, salad, and hors d'oeuvre. Cash prizes go to winners. Some of the more notable winning dishes have been soup in a pumpkin, rice-pudding cake, Chinatown lemon bread. Riceland Foods sponsors the cook-off and publishes the winning recipes.

Events illustrate the industry's history. There are demonstrations of threshing with an old threshing machine, and there are farm-related exhibits indoors and old farm machinery displayed outdoors. On Sunday, thanksgiving harvest services are held in area churches.

Additionally, there are three stages of entertainment, a beauty pageant, and toddlers modeling the rice festival T-shirt of the year.

Location: Weiner is on U.S. 49, about 60 miles northwest of Memphis, TN.
Contact: Arkansas Rice Festival, Box 186, Weiner, AR 72479; Tel: (501)684-7174.

See Also: International Rice Festival (Crowley, LA).

Florida

Arcadia Watermelon Festival

Memorial Day weekend (Friday through Monday) ❀ This is big watermelon country, and Florida is a big watermelon state, so there are lots of watermelons at the festival that can be bought for modest sums, whole or by the slice. In addition, you'll find watermelon ice cream, watermelon icies (like snow-cones in a cup, pronounced ice-ees), Italian watermelon ice, and watermelon jelly or pickled watermelon rind. And other food: fried ostrich legs, hot dogs, barbecued ribs, pork, and chicken—the usual.

About 30,000 come to the festival, which began in 1986. For those who like competition, there are watermelon-eating and seed-spitting contests, and raft, canoe, and bed races, in which all "vehicles" have to be decorated in watermelon themes. A queen, between the ages of 18 and 23, and four little queens, starting at age one, are chosen in the week before the festival and ride in glory in the watermelon-themed parade. The festival also has a "$1.99 queen," who is a man. The contestants for this dubious honor are local dignitaries—the mayor, councilmen, the sheriff—and they are required to dress like women.

Location: De Soto Park in Arcadia, on U.S. 17 and Florida 70, 45 miles east of Sarasota. ❀ **Contact:** Arcadia Watermelon Assn., 23 Elverano Ave., Arcadia, FL 34266; Tel: (941)494-9500, Fax: (941)494-6911.

See Also: Newberry Watermelon Festival (Newberry, FL).

Isle of Eight Flags Shrimp Festival

First weekend in May (Friday through Sunday, can include last days of April) ❀ Fernandina Beach, a community on Amelia Island dating from the 1500s, has been claimed by eight rulers whose flags have flown over the village. Ghosts are supposed to be regular residents, and it's believed pirates' treasures are buried somewhere in the Old Town.

More to the point of the shrimp festival is Fernandina's standing in the shrimp industry. Fernandina Beach is considered the birthplace of the modern shrimping industry; here shrimpers were first motorized, trawls were used instead of cast nets, and rowboats changed over to fleets of motored vessels.

Today the town is known for its shrimp and for Burbank Trawl Makers, locally called the Net House, the world's largest producer of handmade shrimp nets, with customers from Africa to South America. The Net House uses 24 miles of twine to weave just one shrimp net.

With these credentials, you can count on authenticity, real local color, and plenty of shrimp at the festival.

It started in 1964, and now 125,000 people flock to the barrier island, most of them looking for shrimp, a few for pirates' gold. It's the shrimp they find, though. More than 40 nonprofit food vendors sell shrimp boiled, fried, in salads. They sell it in a quiche-like pie, with a seven-grain crust. They sell it in pitas and gumbo. A big hit is the seafood platter, containing the catch of the day plus crab, oyster, and shrimp. Other foods include fried pickles, crawfish, and usual festival fare (hot dogs and the like).

The Georgia Bulldog, a teaching shrimp boat from Athens, Georgia, gives tours of the boat and has displays of salt-water fish and shellfish. Because of the history of pirates (the island made a fine hideaway), a Blackbeard impersonator strolls about looking fierce. There are two stages for entertainment, and there are displays of children's art and a Miss Shrimp Festival beauty contest. A parade kicks off the festivities.

On Sunday, the old tradition of the blessing of the fleet is held with a priest on the cabin of a shrimp boat blessing all the boats parading before him. There's a contest for best decorated boat.

The festival began when shrimpers gathered to race their boats, but the shrimpers race no more. Enough turbulence with Blackbeard in the crowd.

Oh, yes—the eight flags that have flown over Amelia Island have been those of the French, Spanish, English, Patriots (who overthrew Spain), the Green Cross of Florida (which also overthrew Spain), Mexicans, Confederates, and United States.

Location: Amelia Island is off the northeast corner of Florida, about 14 miles east of I-95. Follow signs for Fernandina Beach. ☀ **Contact:** Isle of Eight Flags Shrimp Festival, P.O. Box 6146, Amelia Island, FL 32035; Tel: (904)261-0203, or (800)2-AMELIA.

Homestead

Tropical Agricultural Fiesta

Second or third weekend in July ☀ For a fascinating introduction to tropical fruits and Oriental vegetables, visit the tropical fiesta. This is the only region in the United States where many of these fruits are grown, since the warm oceans surrounding Florida's tip create the tropical climate that lets them flourish.

Homestead is Florida's center of fruit and nursery growing. While Hurricane Andrew devastated the area in 1992, the groves have come back, in some cases more vigorously than before, and here you'll see fruits like papayas, longans, annonas (sugar apples), and carambolas. The fiesta began in the 1950s as a mango celebration, but has evolved to include other tropical fruits and also ornamental plants and Oriental vegetables.

The Dade County Extension Service sponsors an educational fruit tasting, identifies fruits, demonstrates how to slice or dice them, and sells cups of fruit. Usually a dozen or more fruits are featured. Among them: mameys, brown and football-shaped, with a sandpapery exterior, very sweet, often used in blender beverages; papayas, with juicy orange or salmon flesh; mangoes, very juicy, deep orange flesh; carambolas, also called star fruit because cross sections resemble five-pointed stars, in tart or sweet varieties. The sweet carambola is good raw in salads or desserts, while the tart carambola is baked with hams or roasts or used to make wine.

Demonstrations by local chefs might show tropical-fruit cooking, or the preparation of *som tom* (Thai salad made with green papaya), or the techniques of slicing and chopping vegetables for tempura or stir-frying. The Rare Fruit Council International displays exotic fruits that are not commercially grown but are for serious hobbyists, and some samples are usually available.

Tropical fruit ices, ethnic foods (Hispanic, West Indian, Jamaican, Chinese), and tropical-fruit jellies and jams are sold. Free seeds are a special bonus.

Another interesting event in the same location is the Taste of Asia, which takes place the first weekend in March. The Taste highlights the fruits (litchis, for example) and vegetables commonly used in Asian cookery and in season at the time.

Location: Fruit and Spice Park in Homestead, about 20 miles south of Miami, west of U.S. 1. **Contact:** Fruit and Spice Park, 24801 S.W. 187th Ave., Homestead, FL 33030; Tel: (305)247-5727.

While You're There: Be sure to wander around the 30-acre Fruit and Spice Park, which has more than 500 species of fruits, nuts, and spice trees from around the world.

La Belle

Swamp Cabbage Festival

Last full weekend in February Swamp cabbage, despite its name, has to be one of our more exotic foods. You have to cut down a whole tree to get it. Swamp cabbage is not a cabbage; it's the heart or core of the trunk of a sabal palmetto, a palm tree that the Florida legislature declared the state tree in 1953. You might think the state tree would be a protected species, but this is not a palm that needs protection—it covers the state, the way sagebrush covers Wyoming.

Also called hearts of palm, the cabbages can be eaten fresh in salads, but festival vendors most commonly offer it in fritters, or boiled and seasoned, or steamed and fried with white bacon (the fat of the bacon).

There are barbecued chicken and ribs and French fries to accompany the cabbage, and the Seminole Indians, who have a reservation about 25 miles from La Belle, are on hand with fruit-filled fry bread, pumpkin bread, and fried gator tail.

About 30,000 come to the festival, held on the banks of the Caloosahatchee River where there are live oak trees, making a shady, pretty setting. The celebration, started in the 1960s, honors the swamp cabbage because it was a staple during the early years of the state. And it was known to Seminole and Calusa Indians long before white settlers arrived.

About 800 palms are cut down for the festival by civic groups and high school students. After a tree is felled, the fronds are chopped off and then layers of fibrous sheathing are stripped from the trunk. The process, called booting out a cabbage, is demonstrated at the fair.

A parade, with a different theme each year, is the festival highlight, and there's a contest for best-decorated floats, which must have palmetto fronds in their decorations. Other attractions are country and western music, a Swamp Cabbage Queen, armadillo races, and Seminole handicrafts, including long flowing skirts, on display and for sale.

Location: Barron Park in La Belle, on Florida 80, about 20 miles east of Fort Myers, midway between the west coast and Lake Okeechobee.   **Contact:** Greater La Belle Chamber of Commerce, P.O. Box 456, La Belle, FL 33935; Tel: (813)675-0125.

Miami

Carnaval Miami

First Saturday in March through the second Sunday
Dancers, musicians, parades, wild costumes, Cuban food.

Carnaval has it all in a week of activities honoring Hispanic music, culture, and ethnic foods. The festival began in 1978 and keeps getting bigger. International performers, bands, and dance groups come to entertain the throngs in a week of fun that ends with the rousing Calle Ocho on 23 blocks of Eighth Street (Calle Ocho in Spanish) known as Little Havana. It's called the Biggest Street Party in the World.

The area becomes a sea of a million or more people, with about 600 food vendors to keep them nourished, and dozens of stages for performers. The food emphasizes Cuban cuisine—Cuban pork and ham sandwiches (which traditionally also include a dill pickle), paella, *plantanos* (fried sweet bananas), chicken and rice, black-bean cakes, shrimp sautéed with garlic. And there are also Central and South American foods and cheese tamales and Greek gyros and shish kebabs and Italian sausages. . . . You won't go hungry.

On Carnaval Night—the Saturday of the first weekend—there is a concert in the Orange Bowl at which they serve enormous quantities of a dish that includes garbanzos, meat, chicken, and shrimp.

Mark Hodge (kneeling) was the 1995 winner of Biggest Melon and Biggest Shipping Melon at the Newberry Watermelon Festival; watermelon broker Bob Kirby holds his trophies. (Newberry Watermelon Festival, Inc.)

Before the culminating Calle Ocho, there's a Miss Carnaval Miami pageant and coronation. There are a number of parades, sports events, and all kinds of entertainment from salsa concerts to performances by folkloric troupes to fireworks.

A cooking contest has two categories—one for students, one for the general public—and mouth-watering recipes pour in. Adults are awarded cash, and student winners receive U.S. savings bonds. The winning recipes are posted and samples of the dishes are dished up to first comers.

Location: Throughout Miami, largely in Little Havana, along S.W. 8th St. from S.W. 4th Ave. to S.W. 27th Ave.   **Contact:** Little Havana Kiwanis Club, 1312 S.W. 27th Ave., 3rd floor, Miami, FL 33145; Tel: (305)644-8888, Fax: (305)644-8693.

Newberry

Newberry Watermelon Festival

Second Saturday in June The American Legion of Newberry started this festival in 1946 as a community reunion, a welcome to returning World War II veterans, and a day to relax and eat watermelon, since a lot of watermelons of many varieties are grown here. The festival is now the Nation's Oldest Watermelon Festival, with attendance about 10,000, but it's still a down-home one-day get-together.

Events are of the old-fashioned fun type: contests for turkey calling, hog calling, and owl hooting, for watermelon eating and watermelon-seed spitting, for the biggest melon and biggest shipping melon (when they get too big, they aren't shipped).

Other activities include a parade, a Saturday-night dance, pony rides, a miniature train for kids, stagecoach rides, an arts and crafts show, a pageant for pretty babies, and the naming of the watermelon queen.

Farmers donate about 500 watermelons, and slices of them are given away all day. There's also a barbecue of chicken, pork, and ribs at midday, sometimes there are watermelon snow-cones, and vendors sell the standard hot dogs and hamburgers.

Florida is the number one producer of watermelons in the United States, with Georgia a close second, and California in third place.

There's some question about where the watermelon was first grown, but it does go back to ancient times. Pictures of watermelons have been found on Egyptian tombs of 5,000 years ago; the watermelon was naturalized in the Middle East and Russia in prehistoric times; by the 1600s, it was cultivated throughout Africa and had arrived in Europe and China. It's generally thought that enslaved west Africans brought watermelons to North America, but it's also possible they're native—French explorers found Indians growing watermelons in the Mississippi Valley.

Thomas Jefferson, who tried everything horticultural, grew watermelons at Monticello, and during the Civil War, soldiers in the Confederate Army boiled down watermelons for sugar and molasses.

They are universally known. And universally loved. Mark Twain wrote in *Pudd'nhead Wilson* that the watermelon "is chief of this world's luxuries, king by the grace of God over all the fruits of the earth."

Whatever their origin, they seem now to be a thoroughly American treat, and the Fourth of July is barely complete without watermelon.

Location: American Legion hall and grounds, Newberry, 12 miles west of I-75 at Gainesville.   **Contact:** Newberry Watermelon Festival Inc., P.O. Box 929, Newberry, FL 32669; Tel: (352)472-2161 (City Hall).

Niceville

Boggy Bayou Mullet Festival

Third weekend in October (Friday through Sunday)
Mullet is not a glamorous fish, but this mullet festival is a smash. The average attendance is 220,000, and about 10 tons of mullet—fried, smoked, and in chowder—are consumed. Mullet is a good source of protein, but its drawback is that it's a vegetarian bottom feeder that tastes like its food, which can be muddy. Of course, the people of Niceville say the bottom of the waters on Florida's Gulf Coast are pristine and sandy, making the mullets taste fine.

The festival has all kinds of sea and other food—but first a look at Niceville's somewhat picaresque history.

Boggy Bayou is a finger that goes from Niceville to the Choctawhatchee (pronounced chock-a-hatchie) Bay, between the barrier islands and the mainland. The east side of the bayou was known way back as Boggy Town, and the residents known as Boggy Boys. In the 1920s, in the Prohibition era, a wealthy Chicago businessman went flying around the country looking for places in the middle of nowhere to establish resorts or hideaways. He found the Boggy Bayou area, and he incorporated a town on the west side of the bayou that he named Valparaiso (vale of paradise), and some of Chicago's well-to-do people who needed privacy came for vacations. It is not true that Al Capone visited, but many of his pals did.

Boggy Town was called New Valparaiso, but nobody liked the name, so a contest was held for a new name. Niceville won.

Niceville, which is almost entirely surrounded by the Eglin Air Force Base, was fairly quiet after Prohibition ended and gangsters stopped visiting. Then in 1977, the mullet festival began, and suddenly Niceville was in the national news.

It could be the name or it could be the food, which is plentiful. About 60 booths sell alligator (usually fried on a skewer), crabmeat fritters, conch fritters, seafood paella, grouper, amberjack, shark, shrimp, red snapper, seafood pockets, oyster po' boys. On the non-seafood side are deep-fried turkey sandwiches (fried sandwiches are a southern thing), hush puppies, boudin, German foods, frosted fruit drinks, Mexican and Cajun foods.

The eating is accompanied by music, mostly country and western and Cajun. There are hot-air balloons, arts and crafts, a beauty pageant, a foot race, clowns, and other attractions for kids.

Location: At the intersection of Florida 85N and College Rd., just north of Niceville, on Florida's panhandle, about 40 miles east of Pensacola. **Contact:** Boggy Bayou Mullet Festival, P.O. Box 231, Niceville, FL 32588; Tel: (904)678-1615.

Palmetto

Tomato Fiesta

Weekend before Thanksgiving ⦿ Manatee County, where they have manatees and watermelons and tomatoes and tomato-packing plants, has celebrated tomatoes since the 1950s. At one time, the fiesta took place in the tomato fields, but now it's in town, where it's a little easier to have a parade.

The festival comes at the close of the county's Farm City Week, which celebrates the county's agriculture. Manatee ranks number 6 among the state's 63 counties in terms of agriculture cash receipts. And tomatoes, largely Roma and Beefsteak, grown in Florida for the fresh market rather than for processing (as in California), contribute about $600 million to the state's economy, second only to oranges.

The food available focuses on tomatoes and on tomato-rich Cuban and Mexican food, since there's a large Latino community here. You'll find fried green tomatoes and varieties of Hispanic food, which, besides tomato-flavored dishes, include favorites such as black beans and rice and black-bean soup. Other popular items are shaved rib-eye steak sandwiches, Polish sausage, and other standard fair items.

Cook-offs can include any kind of dish, so long as it contains tomatoes. There are cash prizes.

A children's parade for kids up to high school age starts the festivities on Saturday morning, and then a fair atmosphere prevails, with entertainment, arts and crafts, a 5K run, concessions booths selling tomato-motif T-shirts and mugs. There are also tours of tomato-packing plants on Saturday. About 20,000 attend.

Location: Palmetto is at the south end of the Skyway Bridge across Tampa Bay from St. Petersburg.   **Contact:** Tomato Fiesta Coordinator, 516 8th Ave West, Palmetto, FL 34221; Tel: (941)723-4704.

See Also: Tomato Fest (Jacksonville, TX).

Pensacola

Pensacola Seafood Festival

Fourth full weekend in September (Friday through Sunday)
  If you have a salt tooth (as opposed to sweet tooth), this is your thing. You'll be joined by about 200,000 other salt teeth.

The festival began in 1977 to celebrate the seafood industry, and it takes the pleasurable way of doing this with about two dozen vendors selling every imaginable type of fish and seafood. There are dishes that are not too unusual—boiled shrimp, barbecued shrimp, catfish sandwiches, and stuffed crab. And then there's the over-the-top food, the items you don't often see in a festival setting: blackened amberjack, baby lobster sandwiches, seafood gumbo, marinated octopus, seafood pastas, crawfish pie, seafood and alligator sausage, grilled grouper, grilled yellowfin tuna, crawfish étouffée.

At the Seafood Grill, local and visiting chefs demonstrate cooking with seafood. The demonstrations are outdoors, but people in bleachers can easily understand what's going on with the help of overhead mirrors and microphones. Cookbooks are sold and four of them contain tickets with the demonstrated recipes on them; those who get the tickets are also able to sample the demonstrated foods. Proceeds from the cookbook sales benefit a charity.

Something's always happening besides food; one of the park venues becomes Child's Place, with puppets, face painting, pony rides, and crafts-making. For adults, there's continuous music of all types, and almost 200 arts and crafts vendors display only handmade crafts.

Pensacola, known for its sugar-white beaches, also boasts restored nineteenth-century buildings, now used as shops, galleries, and restaurants, in the Seville Square area.

Location: Downtown Seville Square, Pensacola, on the western panhandle off I-10. Take the downtown exit.   **Contact:** Fiesta of Five Flags, P.O. Box 1943, Pensacola, FL 32589; Tel: (904)433-6512.

If you have a yen
for strawberry
anything and
everything, then
Plant City's
Florida Strawberry
Festival is the
place to go. (Courtesy
of the Florida Strawberry
Festival®)

While You're There: The Historic Preservation Society gives tours of historic buildings on Friday and Saturday.

Plant City

Florida Strawberry Festival

Usually first week in March (eleven days) Florida produces nearly 20 percent of the nation's table strawberries and most of them come from around Plant City, the Winter Strawberry Capital of the World. It's the *winter* capital because the season runs from December to April.

The festival began in 1930 to celebrate the strawberry harvest; today, it promotes all agriculture in Hillsborough County, one of the nation's largest agricultural counties, producing crops with an annual value of more than $400 million. Attendance is about 825,000, and there's something for everyone—assorted livestock shows, a cow-milking contest, a cow-chip throwing contest, a beef cook-off, a veggie cook-off.

But the strawberry is king. A quarter of a million strawberry shortcakes are consumed, along with strawberry milk shakes, sundaes, cobbler, ice cream, cheesecake, and just plain strawberries that can be bought by the flat or the quart. Of the many events, high on the popularity list are strawberry-stemming contests and a strawberry-shortcake-eating contest, in which participants have 10 minutes to consume four pounds of shortcake with whipped cream. Bibs are supplied.

Attractions include continuous big-name entertainment; the "Cracker Corner" featuring a log cabin built in 1858 and displaying artifacts of Florida's pioneer days; grand, youth, and baby parades; clogging contests and baby contests; and demonstrations of spinning, rope-making, and dog-obedience. A queen in a flowing red cape reigns over it all.

Interesting coincidence: Plant City was named for Henry B. Plant, a self-made tycoon who brought railroads to western Florida, controlled steamship lines, and built a grand Moorish-style hotel in Tampa. He was born in Branford, Connecticut, where his family raised strawberries—so many strawberries, in fact, that at one time Branford was the strawberry capital of New England.

Location: Plant City is 21 miles east of Tampa and 60 miles west of Orlando/Disney World, off I-4.   **Contact:** Florida Strawberry Festival, P.O. Box 1869, Plant City, FL 33564-1869; Tel: (813)752-9194; Fax: (813)754-4297.

Port Canaveral

Seafest

Usually last weekend in March (Friday through Sunday; a week earlier if it conflicts with Easter)   Variety is the spice of the Seafest: helicopter rides; hands-on demonstrations of wildlife, including alligators, crocodiles, turtles, and snakes; tours of a Navy ship; music and dancing; arts and crafts.

And, fresh from the ocean, all kinds of seafood specialties. The centerpiece is the chowder that earlier in the year is judged the best in a local-chef cook-off. One year, it was a chowder of shrimp, scallops, heavy cream, and secret spices; another year, a classic clam chowder from a New Bedford, Massachusetts, recipe handed down to the chef from her grandfather. Only the chowder that wins the cook-off is served at the seafest.

Among other seafood delicacies, you'll find octopus marinated, grilled, then chopped and blended into several different dishes, including seafood fajitas. Also on the menu are boiled shrimp, raw and steamed oysters, seafood pockets with shrimp, crab, or fish, king-crab fritters, fried calamari, blackened mahi-mahi sandwiches. Swamp denizens are allowed in, too—2,000 pounds of alligator tail are served. And there's regular fair food for non-seafood types.

The festival gets about 50,000 visitors.

Location: Port Canaveral, adjacent to Cruise Terminal No. 5, off Florida 407, 50 miles east of Orlando. ❀ **Contact:** Cocoa Beach Area Chamber of Commerce, 400 Fortenberry Rd., Merritt Island, FL 32952; Tel: (407)459-2200, Fax: (407)459-2232.

Tampa (Ybor City)

Fiesta Day

Second Saturday in February ❀ Six-hundred gallons of Spanish Bean Soup are dished out free to all comers on Fiesta Day in Tampa's Ybor City.

There's a reason.

Ybor City was once the Cigar Capital of the World. Millions of cigars were hand-rolled for almost 50 years after Cuban Vicente Martinez Ybor (pronounced EE-bor) opened a cigar factory in 1886. At the peak, there were more than 200 cigar factories, staffed largely by Cubans. They made Ybor City (once independent, later annexed into Tampa) a hotbed of the rebel forces fighting for Cuba's independence from Spain.

The community was multiethnic and still is, but the Cuban and Spanish influence dominates. And *that's* the reason for the free Spanish soup, which is served with Cuban bread (a long loaf baked with a palmetto leaf stuck down the middle) and cafe con leche.

The soup, a medley of garbanzo beans, Spanish sausage, and other ingredients, is made by Ybor's Columbia Restaurant, the oldest restaurant in Florida. The Columbia also sets up a 10½-foot-diameter pan in the middle of Seventh Avenue, the community's main drag, and sells about 2,000 servings of paella, which contains shrimp, grouper, clams, scallops, calamari, etc. Additionally, numerous booths and restaurants feature Cuban sandwiches of ham, pork, salami, and cheese.

Street entertainment includes Spanish flamenco dancers, brass bands, gospel singers. Capping it all is the Krewe of Knights of Sant' Yago Illuminated Night Parade, a Mardi Gras-type spectacle. About a quarter-million spectators scream and grab for glittery strands of beads tossed into the crowds by knights and pirates.

The fiesta and parade are the finale to the Tampa Bay area Gasparilla Festival started in 1904 to celebrate a pirate named José Gaspar. Historians say Gaspar is a total figment of the Tampa imagination—but who cares? The Ybor fiesta began in 1945.

Location: Ybor City, about a mile from downtown Tampa, is at the convergence of I-4 and I-275. ❀ **Contact:** Ybor City Chamber of Commerce, 1800 E. 9th Avenue, Tampa, FL 33605; Tel: (813)248-3712; Fax: (813)247-1764.

While You're There: Visit the Martinez de Ybor Art Gallery, 2027 E. 7th Ave., to see what are most likely some of the world's very few paintings that use Cuban coffee, tea, extract of Tampa tobacco, wine, and beer for pigment. The paintings by Arnold Martinez are largely of Ybor City, and the materials tie in with the subject matter.

Tarpon Springs

Greek Orthodox Epiphany Celebration

January 6 ☼ Greek divers who were experienced in the sponge industry came to this area early in the 1900s to ply their trade. They brought with them their traditional celebration of Epiphany, and its colorful rites combined with the traditional diving attract 10,000 to 30,000 people.

The activities begin with services at the Greek Orthodox Church of St. Nicholas, a replica of St. Sophia's in Constantinople. Following the services, the bishop leads a procession to the bayou a block away, where he throws a white cross into the waters; boys jump in to recover it. The boy who gets to the cross first will have a blessed year. The tradition of diving after a cross thrown into the sea is an ancient one, long practiced in Greece.

And then—time to eat. Greek restaurants set up booths along the bayou, and serve traditional Greek dishes. There are gyros galore—made here with spicy yogurt sauce over thinly sliced lamb or pork, with lettuce and tomatoes, all served in pita bread. And there is hearty fare such as moussaka, souvlaki, and spanakopita (a spinach pie made with filo, feta cheese, cottage cheese, and spices), Greek style lasagna, mountains of Greek salad, and much more. Drinks range from beers to traditional Greek drinks like ouzo and metaxa.

Other events include a parade and often a White House honor guard to carry flags.

Location: Tarpon Springs is on U.S. 19 about 30 miles north of St. Petersburg. ☼ **Contact:** St. Nicholas Cathedral, P.O.Box 248, Tarpon Springs, FL 34688; Tel: (813)937-3540 or, Tarpon Springs Chamber of Commerce; Tel: (813)937-6109.

Winter Haven

Florida Citrus Festival and Polk County Fair

Last week of January and first weekend of February (Thursday through second Sunday, eleven days) ☼ They don't have an Orange Bowl in Florida for nothing. They have an Orange Bowl because Florida is America's citrus leader.

The Sunshine State grows a bit more than 75 percent of all the oranges in the United States and ranks second only to Brazil in the production of oranges, providing 18.5 percent of the world supply. The state is the world leader in grapefruit production, accounting for about a third of the world supply. Florida grows all of America's tangelos and temple oranges. Most of the state's oranges—93 percent—are processed into orange juice.

Good reasons for the name of the bowl and for the Citrus Festival, which showcases the state's oranges and grapefruit with displays, educational exhibits, and food and drink that feature the fruits. You'll find, for example, Frozen Floridian, which is sponge cake with whipped cream and ice cream, topped with orange or grapefruit slices; orange juice; candies made from oranges, grapefruit, and tangelos; and citrus salsa. The salsa recipe calls for a red bell pepper, crushed canned pineapple, onions, jalapeño, cilantro leaves, cumin, lime juice, *and* a Florida red grapefruit and a Florida orange.

The Citrus Festival is part of the Polk County Fair, which began in 1923, gets crowds of about 140,000, and offers usual county-fair entertainment and shows—fine arts displays, livestock judging, a parade.

On the citrus side of things, there's a competition for most creative fresh-fruit display. There's a cooking contest. Tours of citrus groves can be arranged. Regally observing all the activity is Miss Florida Citrus.

Oranges boomed in the twentieth century. Before 1900, oranges were considered a luxury or a Christmas treat almost everywhere in the United States.

The orange is a native of southern China and Indochina, but spread to every part of the world that had a suitable climate. Orange trees are sensitive to frost; temperatures of even 25 degrees cause some injury.

The grapefruit probably originated in the Malay Archipelago, but the United States gets credit for developing it. The grapefruit was described growing in Barbados in 1750, finally got to Florida in 1840, and was shipped to northern markets in 1880. Although there has been a great growth in the grapefruit industry in southern Texas, Florida is considered the cradle of grapefruit culture, and remains the runaway leader.

Location: Winter Haven, in central Florida, is 16 miles east of Lakeland on U.S. 92. **Contact:** Florida Citrus Showcase, 70 Florida Showcase Blvd., Winter Haven, FL 33881; Tel: (941)967-3175, Fax: (941)967-8810.

See Also: Texas Citrus Festival (Mission, TX).

Georgia

Blueberry Festival

Last Saturday in June ☼ Rabbiteye blueberries are as big as a rabbit's eye, someone once said, and the name stuck.

This variety of berry, a type of highbush but different from the highbush berries bred in New Jersey, was developed by agricultural agent Tom Brightwell in 1973 to replace tobacco and corn, which were no longer money-makers on small farms. About 1,500 acres of berries, 98 percent of them Rabbiteyes, are grown in Bacon County, where Alma is located, making the county Georgia's biggest blueberry grower and Alma the Blueberry Capital of Georgia.

Something to celebrate, and they do with a blueberry pancake breakfast, food booths with blueberry treats, and a blueberry-cooking contest. Winning dishes have included blueberry-banana muffins, frozen blueberry fruit salad, a blueberry cream-puff ring, and blueberry pizza.

The fun and games part of the festival includes sports, an archery contest, arts and crafts, an antique-car show, and a motorcycle display. Fireworks at the airport round out the day.

About 5,000 attend the festival, which began in 1975.

Location: Downtown Alma, at the junction of U.S. 23 and Georgia 32, 30 miles north of Waycross. ☼ **Contact:** Alma/Bacon County Chamber of Commerce, P.O. Box 450, Alma, GA 31510; Tel: (912)632-5859.

See Also: Whitesbog Blueberry Festival (Whitesbog, NJ).

Pecan Harvest Festival

Third Saturday in November ☼ The first pecan trees in Georgia were planted in Baconton in the 1800s, which gives them a pretty long lineage. They are transplants, though; the pecan is native to Alabama and Mississippi. There American Indians used them in various ways—they roasted them to take on hunting trips, ground them to add to stewed meat. A number of Southern states are big growers of pecans, but Georgia—the state that adopted them—tops them all.

Pecans, which are related to hickory nuts, are associated with Southern cooking. Southerners glaze pecans, make pecan pie and bread and candies, stuff fowl with a bread-sausage-pecan mixture.

It seemed quite natural, then, when the Women's Club of Baconton began this festival in the 1970s, that they would name it for the trees that had been growing in their town so long. And they decided to sell pecan pies and pecan cookies to live up to the name.

The festival still offers pies and cookies but also heartier fare. On Friday night, before the festival is really under way, people enjoy a fish fry and street dance, and on Saturday, there are barbecued dishes, more fried fish, and standard festival foods. There are also interesting jellies, some made from cactus. Coming across cactus jelly at a pecan festival, though, is like finding a rare autograph at a flea market.

Festival events include clogging, performances by local singing groups, a parade on Saturday morning, and arts and crafts. The festival draws about 3,000 people to Baconton, where the resident population is just a few hundred.

Location: Baconton is about 12 miles south of Albany, at U.S. 19 and Georgia 93. **Contact:** Baconton City Hall, P.O. Box 399, Baconton, GA 31716; Tel: (912)787-5511.

Blairsville

Sorghum Festival

Second, third, and fourth weekends in October Sweet sorghum has almost disappeared in the United States, but there are places in the mountains of the Southeast where people still grow it for the syrup known as sorghum molasses.

Blairsville, in the North Georgia Mountains, is one of those places. The world's largest sorghum festival, a three-weekend event, is one of the most popular festivals in the area. Here you can see the whole process of syrup-making, which takes about three hours. Festival visitors buy the molasses to take home in commemorative plastic jugs, but they also buy it so they can sit a spell and sop biscuits in it. That's what sorghum molasses is all about.

The festival offers plain and sausage biscuits for sopping, as well as apple pies, jalapeño corn dogs, boiled peanuts, corn bread, and the more standard funnel cakes and hamburgers.

Four trailer loads of locally raised sorghum cane are used each weekend for grinding. Local folks estimate that a truckload yields about 300 gallons of juice, and when the juice is boiled down, the syrup comes to about half that amount.

The festival features "Biskit Contests" to see who, in 15 minutes, can eat the most biscuits sopped in sorghum syrup. There has been a bounty on one man who has won year after year; anyone who tops him wins $100. There are also contests of pole climbing, rock throwing, horseshoe throwing, "baccor" (tobacco) spitting, and log sawing with a cross-cut saw. Plaques, T-shirts, and ribbons are the prizes. The person who attends the fair from the greatest distance and the oldest person at the fair also win T-shirts. Additionally, there are demonstrations by a glass blower and blacksmith, and arts and crafts displays.

Sorghum molasses was a popular sweetener in the United States from the mid-1800s until the turn of the century, but its popularity declined because granulated sugar was so much handier.

Today, grain sorghum, used for livestock feed, is widely grown; sweet sorghum, with a juicier stalk, is a different variety. Both grow in tall, cornlike stalks. To make syrup, the stalks are cut down, their seeds and leaves removed, and then they're fed into cane mills or horse- or mule-driven grinders. Rollers squeeze the canes dry, and the juice flows into a tub where it's boiled into the molasses. Sorghum is a major cash crop in the Blairsville area, but acreage is down because growing and processing it take so much work.

The festival, held since 1969, is a Jaycees fund-raiser for the less fortunate in the community. About 12,000 attend each weekend.

Location: On Georgia 515, west of Blairsville, which is at the junction of U.S. 19 and 76. **Contact:** Blairsville Jaycees, P.O. Box 701, Blairsville, GA 30514; Tel: (706)745-4745.

Colquitt

National Mayhaw Festival

Third Saturday in April Colquitt, the Mayhaw Capital of the World, is not the only town with a mayhaw festival, but Colquitt does boast the *first* (it began in 1984).

What are mayhaws? They're trees in the rose family, growing to about 25 feet, having red, tart fruit about the size of cranberries. Mayhaws are generally found in swamps or along creeks, and there are more of them around Colquitt than anywhere, partly because the town has three aquifers running underneath it, according to India Taylor, who lives there. Several groves have been planted in the area, and the University of Georgia is working at hybridizing them.

Indians used to pound mayhaws into venison to preserve it, but nowadays, said India, the fruit makes excellent jellies and wine.

At the festival, you can buy mayhaw cheese pinwheels, which are biscuit dough and cheese rolled out and spread with mayhaw jelly and sprinkled with pecans, then refrigerated, sliced, and baked. Maude Wilkin developed the recipe some years ago, and they're made today in Wilkin's IGA store. The store also makes mayhaw jelly every Monday that it ships worldwide; it has sent jelly to the Pope. You can buy the jelly and syrup and juice to take home.

Events of the festival include a parade, entertainment, and children's activities. Vendors sell non-mayhaw food, too. Attendance is about 15,000.

Watermelon Spice Pie

1½ cup watermelon rind	1 cup sugar
1 teaspoon cinnamon	⅓ teaspoon nutmeg
¼ teaspoon cloves	⅛ teaspoon salt
2 teaspoons flour	¼ cup vinegar
½ cup raisins	½ cup pecans, chopped
1-2 crust pie pastry	

Cut green outer rind and most of pulp from watermelon rind; cut into ¼-inch cubes. Combine cubes with water to cover in saucepan; bring to boil, then simmer until tender. Drain. Add sugar, cinnamon, nutmeg, cloves, salt, flour, vinegar, raisins, and nuts to cubes; blend well. Pour into pastry shell; cover with pastry. Cut steam vents. Bake at 450 degrees until crust is browned. Reduce temperature to 350 degrees; bake until filling is set.

National Watermelon Association

Location: Colquitt, in southeast Georgia 60 miles north of Tallahassee, is off U.S. 27 at Georgia 91. **Contact:** Colquitt Chamber of Commerce, P.O. Box 253, Colquitt, GA 31737; Tel: (912)758-2400, Fax: (912)758-8140.

Cordele

Watermelon Days Festival

Last weekend in June through second weekend in July (major events on second weekend in July, Thursday through Saturday) Festival events are spread over the days in Cordele, the way seeds are spread through a melon. In June, you have a Mr. Melon Contest, the winner being the man who looks best dressed as a woman, and the election of four Miss Watermelon Festivals, one in each of four age groups. All week leading to the final weekend, there's a Watermelon Slice Give-Away, and other events include a "Whatta" Melon Decorating and Carving Contest, arts and crafts, a parade, tennis and horseshoe tournaments, junior and adult seed-spitting contests, and a big-melon contest.

Besides the many different food booths, this is a festival where you do not lack for watermelon. Cordele for years has called itself the Watermelon Capital of the World because more watermelons—some 200 millions pounds a year—are shipped from the Watermelon State Market here than from any other area. And while Florida is the top watermelon producer in the union, Georgia is a close second.

Furthermore, Cordele brags that its melons are the *best*. In the early 1990s, Arkansas and Texas sent challenging melons to Cordele, and in a blind test, with judges from all three states, Cordele's were judged the sweetest.

About 6,000 to 8,000 attend the festival, which began in 1949.

Location: On U.S. 280, off I-75, 60 miles south of Macon. ⸬ **Contact:** Cordele-Crisp Chamber of Commerce, P.O. Box 158, Cordele, GA 31010; Tel: (912)273-3526.

See Also: Newberry Watermelon Festival (Newberry, FL).

Fort Valley

Georgia Peach Festival

Third weekend in June (Friday through Sunday) ⸬ What would Ty Cobb, the Georgia Peach, be called today? The Georgia Peanut? Or maybe Georgia Pecan? Back in the early 1900s, the Detroit Tiger terror got his nickname because he was from Georgia, then the number-one grower of peaches.

Today, Georgia ranks third in peach production, behind top-ranking California and South Carolina. But Georgia officials insist that peaches have long been synonymous with Georgia, and that "Georgia still holds the title as the 'peach state.'" Georgia was one of the first states to produce peaches commercially in the 1800s. Two factors enabled the state to expand sales nationally: the development of the Elberta peach by the Rumph family in Macon County and the invention of refrigerated rail cars.

Fort Valley is in Peach County, which is in the heart of the peach-growing counties, and the festival shows there's no shame in some slippage.

The festival, which started in the peach glory days in the 1920s, then lapsed and resumed in 1987, isn't on its knees. About 5,000 attend, and they get to see and taste the World's Largest Peach Cobbler. Other treats are peach ice cream, peach sauce for ice cream, fresh peaches, and peach salsa and chutney to take home. There's a food cook-off for peach desserts, and spectators can sample the entries.

The over-sized cobbler is made in a specially constructed pan and cooked over six fish fryers at courthouse square. In the wee hours of the morning, the work starts by peeling 1,500 pounds of peaches. They're stirred constantly for eight hours until the peaches are cooked, then the pastry topping is added, and at lunchtime, the cobbler is served. Ta-da!

Other eating events are a pancake breakfast on Saturday, and two historical-society luncheons. There is also standard festival fare.

Miss Georgia Peach Festival and her court of younger princesses ride regally in a parade Saturday; there are performances by cloggers, jump ropers, gospel singers, a community chorus, and such attractions as an arts-and-crafts show and 5K and fun runs.

Georgia is now first among states in peanuts and pecans, so when you think about it, maybe today Ty Cobb would be the Georgia Nut. Probably more fitting than peach, anyway.

Location: Fort Valley is about 20 miles south of Macon, on Georgia 96, off I-75. **Contact:** Georgia Peach Festival, P.O. Box 2001, Fort Valley, GA 31030; Tel: (912)825-4002.

While You're There: Local peach-packing sheds offer tours and sell peach products—jams, jellies, etc.

Kudzu Takeover Day and Crafts Fair

Second Saturday in August When you stand in a kudzu patch at night, you can hear the kudzu grow. This vine from China and Japan grows a foot a day when the days are hot, and can creep 100 feet in a single summer. It has become something of the emblem of the South, climbing up telephone poles, sprawling over fields.

But it's not all bad, and the Providence Canyon State Park began this fair in 1985 to soften the killer-kudzu image. Not that it isn't a takeover vine; it is, which is the reason for the fair's name.

You'll learn that you can eat the kudzu—all of it but the vines, and those are good for making baskets and paper and jump ropes.

The fair's foods vary from year to year, but you might find kudzu quiche, made with the leaves, or leaves dipped in a tempura batter, then fried in hot oil. Some eat the leaves in salads, but they are fuzzy, like the pods, not to everyone's liking raw. Sometimes there's fried chicken, with a kudzu-powder batter made from the kudzu root. And kudzu juice, made by pouring boiling water over flower petals.

Diane Hoots, co-author with Juanitta Baldwin of the book, *The Vine to Love or Hate,* always has kudzu jellies and syrups for sale, made from the flower, as well as kudzu tchotchkes like green bean pods with googly eyes pasted on so they look like caterpillars.

Fair events include demonstrations in basket-making using the kudzu vine, country music, cloggers and line dancers, and a crafts show. There are also non-kudzu foods available.

Kudzu was brought to the United States in the late nineteenth century by the Japanese to decorate a national pavilion in a Philadelphia celebration. The Japanese have long used the kudzu in cooking, and also to make a cream that is supposed to be a remedy for upset stomach and sexual torpor.

In this country it was used decoratively until the United States Soil Conservation Services discovered kudzu was perfect for stopping soil erosion, so they planted it throughout the South. It stopped soil erosion, but kept traveling, and now creeps all over the Southeast, from Florida to Maryland to Louisiana.

Location: Providence Canyon State Park, on Georgia 39C, 7 miles west of Lumpkin at U.S. 27, 30 miles south of Columbus. **Contact:** Providence Canyon State Park, Box 158, Lumpkin, GA 31815; Tel: (912)838-6202.

Poulan

Georgia Peanut Festival

Fourth weekend in October ☼ Peanuts are one of Georgia's top crops, Georgia produces about 40 percent of all the peanuts grown in the country, and Worth County is the Peanut Capital of the World because it's the largest peanut producer per land capita (meaning that it produces the most peanuts for the land available).

That's why there's a Georgia Peanut Festival.

The festival began in 1964 and its great moment in history came in 1987 when the chief attraction was the World's Largest Peanut Butter and Jelly Sandwich—12½-feet square. It has since been eclipsed elsewhere, but its glory lingers on.

Today's festival highlight is a 2½-hour parade spotlighting Miss Georgia Peanut and Little Miss Peanut. Other attractions include music, cloggers, an arts and crafts show, children's events, a dessert-recipe contest, and the sale of a book of peanut recipes created by children. Food for sale runs the gamut from boiled peanuts, peanuts deep-fried in fat, and pink peanut divinity, to Southern favorites like black-eyed peas and corn bread, to fair staples like hamburgers, homemade cakes, and caramel popcorn. Attendance is about 30,000.

The story behind Georgia's peanut eminence has ancient beginnings. Peanuts originated in Brazil and Peru where Incan graves have been found with jars of peanuts. Explorers who found Indians growing them in North America spread them around the world in a jiffy. Peanuts became a staple food in Africa, and ironically African slaves brought peanuts back to North America.

The peanut today is one of the more common—and most fascinating—of native American foods. It's not a nut but a legume, related to peas and beans, and it grows in an unusual way, flowering above ground but fruiting underground. After the petals fall off, the peanut ovary, called a peg, begins to form and grows away from the plant on a vine and goes underground.

Peanuts weren't important economically in the United States for a long time; there were peanut patches on plantations and that was about it. During the Civil War, hungry soldiers ate peanuts, and toward the end of the century roasted peanuts were sold on the streets, but peanuts were still not money-making crops.

In 1896, George Washington Carver first went to Tuskegee Institute in Alabama, and in 1903 he began his research on the peanut, ultimately developing more than 300 products from it. He urged farmers to plant peanuts, teaching that peanuts and soybeans could restore nitrogen to the soil instead of depleting it as cotton did.

In the 1920s and 1930s, the boll weevil marched through the South, toppled king cotton, and was the impetus that pushed the peanut up the agricultural ladder. Today, in a good year, peanuts contribute more than $4 billion to the U.S. economy, and bring more than $500 million into Georgia's coffers.

Location: Possum Poke (where a Michigan governor had a hunting lodge, now preserved as it was in the early 1900s), Poulan, on U.S. 82, 20 miles west of I-75, three miles

Savannah's St. Patrick's Day parade is one of the largest and oldest in the United States. ©The Savannah Area Convention & Visitors Bureau)

east of Sylvester. ⊕ **Contact:** Georgia Peanut Festival, P.O. Box 60, Sylvester, GA 31791; Tel: (912)776-7718.

See Also: Sweet Potato Festival (Tuskegee, AL).

Savannah

St. Patrick's Day

Three days including March 17 ⊕ The Savannah Sinn Fein Society provides this recipe for green grits: "33 packages of instant grits, cooked, 33 drops of emerald green food coloring, 33 jiggers of Irish Whisky from Free Ireland. And carefully set afire."

They are kidding (maybe) about the grits recipe, but the Irish aren't kidding when they stage the St. Patrick's Day parade, one of the biggest and oldest parades in the United States, and the high point of the three-day St. Pat's celebration. About half a million people line the parade route, and many of the spectators are as colorful as the marchers, dressed in green, or painted green. Even dogs wear green.

The spirit extends to the riverfront for a celebration that features live entertainment, a speech by an official from Ireland, and food. The grits are green, the beer is green, and ven-

Savannah's Waterfront Plaza fills with festivalgoers in search of the fruits of the sea at the Savannah Seafood Festival. (Photo by Hawkeye Aerial Photo)

dors also sell Irish stew, potato soup, corned beef, and Irish sausages. A queen and her court preside. The Savannah Shamrock Rugby Club also gets some action, sponsoring a rugby tournament with more than 50 teams from around the nation competing.

The first St. Patrick's Day parade is thought to have been on March 17, 1824, when the Irish Jasper Greens provided a military escort for other Irish groups in a procession. The Irish have been marching ever since, with the exception of a few years when wars intervened.

Savannah has had a sizable Irish population for some time. The city is one of the oldest southern ports, going back to 1733 when James E. Oglethorpe sailed up the Savannah River and founded America's first planned city. The city prospered, and immigrants from Ireland and Scotland came long before the potato famine. The oldest Irish society in the United States, the Hibernian Society, was founded in 1812 in Savannah by 13 Irish Protestants.

Location: Downtown Savannah and Waterfront Plaza. ⚬ Contact: Savannah Waterfront Assn., P.O. Box 572, Savannah, GA 31402; Tel: (912)234-0295.

Savannah Seafood Festival

First weekend in May ⚬ Savannah is one of the 10 busiest ports in the United States, and this festival celebrates its sea heritage with a range of seafood, if not from A to Z, then at least from B (as in seafood bisque) to W (as in wahoo, a large tropical game fish). In between, you'll find seafood chowder and crawfish, tuna, lobster, shrimp, and rock shrimp cooked every way you can imagine.

There are also landlubberly desserts—peach cobblers, baked goods, and candies of the South like praline, divinity, and bear claws (similar to turtles with chopped nuts and a thick chocolate coating on top). These are all found in food tents lining the river.

The festival began in the late 1980s as a community and civic-organization festival, and has become increasingly popular, with attendance about 100,000. It offers headline bands and arts and crafts, and a fishing tournament is held concurrently with the festival. Non-participants can see the fish brought in, prizes awarded, and the cooking of the fish.

Location: Savannah's Waterfront Plaza, along River Street. **Contact:** Savannah Waterfront Assn., P.O. Box 572, Savannah, GA 31402; Tel: (912)234-0295.

St. Marys

Rock Shrimp Festival

First Saturday in October The rock shrimp is an interesting denizen of the deep. It's a cousin of the familiar pink, brown, and white shrimp, but with a tough, hard shell that makes it look something like a small lobster. This shell, or exoskeleton, limited its popularity, but then a machine was invented to split and de-vein the headed shrimp, and now St. Marys is the Rock Shrimp Capital of the United States, so named by Georgia's General Assembly in 1980.

The festival began in 1987, and gets about 20,000 people who come for dinners of fried rock shrimp, hush puppies, cole slaw, and French fries, served throughout the day. Rock shrimp cooks more quickly than other shrimp, the flesh turning opaque white. The taste is between that of a shrimp and lobster tail. Volunteers cook the shrimp dinners, but watermen supply the shrimp already peeled of the shells.

It's not just the exoskeleton that makes rock shrimp different from their cousins, but also their life cycle. Non-rock shrimp spawn in deep water but then drift to shallow estuaries to mature, but rock shrimp, like deep-sea lobsters, spawn and are harvested in water 120 to 140 feet deep. They're harvested with reinforced trawl nets.

Festival early birds can have a pancake breakfast, and standard festival food is available. Among the day's events are a riding-lawnmower race, a 5K (foot) race, amusement rides, arts and crafts, a parade, and street dancing to live bands.

St. Marys, settled by the English in 1787, is a fishing village, with shrimp boats lining St. Marys River. Its past includes treasure-smuggling pirates, but it's gotten respectable and is now the home of the Kings Bay Naval Submarine Base.

Location: St. Marys is on the southeastern tip of Georgia, six miles from the Florida border, just off I-75. **Contact:** Orange Hall House Museum and Welcome Center, P.O. Box 1291, St. Marys, GA 31558; Tel: (800)868-8687.

While You're There: The McIntosh Sugar Mill Tabby Ruin on Crooked River Road, built in the eighteenth century and used to grind and boil cane for sugar products, is one of the best preserved tabby structures on the coast. Tabby is a material made of oyster shells, sand, and water.

St. Simons Island

Georgia Sea Island Festival

Third weekend in October ☼ St. Simons is one of the barrier islands that lie just off the coasts of Georgia and South Carolina, where for many years the Gullah-speaking descendants of slaves made their homes. Georgia calls them the Golden Isles, and their allure has led to their development as resorts; St. Simons, where slaves once tilled the soil, has four golf courses.

Yet some of the Gullah speakers remain. Because they were isolated for so long, they retained their culture and language, the latter being a mixture of the English that was spoken by seventeenth- and eighteenth-century English colonists and various languages of West Africa. The festival, attended by about 5,000, was started in the early 1980s with the aim of demonstrating the culture in order to preserve it.

At islanders' family reunions, it's customary to have country boils of seafood and sausage that simmer for hours over wood fires. At the festival, food is prepared in a similar manner—outdoors so festival-goers can watch.

Some of the specialties are ribs, traditionally barbecued over oak logs though now often cooked on a grill; broiled chitlins, different from the mainland boiled or fried chitlins; smoked mullet; collard greens; sweet-potato pie. There's syrup bread, corn bread with syrup added before it's baked; and cracklin' bread, in which pieces of fried hog fat or skin are added to the bread dough before baking.

Cultural activities show the old ways: story-telling, music, demonstrations of making fish nets and soap and hanging a bucket from a tree to get tar. Children are taught traditional songs and dances. Craftspeople also display and sell their wares. Basketry, one of the oldest African crafts practiced in the United States, is a specialty of the Gullah speakers, and baskets, originally utilitarian, are now collectors' items.

Hundreds of Gullah words are taken directly from West African languages, but have been assimilated into American English. Some of these are goober—peanut, from the Kimbundu language; chigger—small flea, from Wolof; nana—grandmother, from Twi. Festival visitors will hear the language and explanations of some words.

Location: Neptune Park, St. Simons Island. Take the St. Simons Island causeway, and at the last bridge, turn right on King's Way, then right at the second light, then go to the pier area at the end of the street. ☼ **Contact:** St. Simons Visitor Center, 530 Beachview, St. Simons Island, GA 31522; Tel: (912)638-2723.

While You're There: Take a look around Neptune Park, named for Neptune Small, who was a slave in the King family. He fought with the Kings' youngest son in the Confederate Army. When the son was killed, Neptune ran out onto the battlefield, retrieved his body, and brought it home to the family. He then returned to war with another son. The family was so grateful that they gave him his freedom and the property that is now Neptune Park.

Judges survey the offerings in the 1996 Vidalia Onion Cook-off. (Vidalia Onion Festival)

Vidalia Onion Festival

Last weekend in April (Thursday through Sunday) ☼ The Vidalia onion is the "world's sweetest onion." So they say in Georgia, but growers of sweet onions in Texas, Washington, Hawaii, and California might beg to differ. The Vidalia, however, *is* sweet, very juicy, and can be diced without inducing tears.

It also has become widely known and bought (even though the price is higher), helped by astute marketing. The Vidalia festival, started in 1977 and attended by 40,000 or more, certainly doesn't hurt the onion's fame, either.

The festival has its own royalty—Miss Vidalia Onion Seed, Miss Vidalia Onion Sprout, Junior Miss Vidalia Onion, and Miss Vidalia Onion; these royal misses go from four years old to college age. Events include a children's parade, sports activities, an air show, a street dance, fireworks, an arts and crafts show, a gift shop where onion products—vinaigrettes, salsas, etc.—can be bought, and an onion-eating contest. Vendors sell all kinds of food, and it's no problem finding onions to eat.

For cooks, highlights are the Friday-night cooking demonstrations by chefs using Vidalia onions (with recipes distributed), and the onion cook-off, in which up to 50 contestants submit their dishes with recipes. A recent winning recipe was strawberry-onion pie; its chief ingredients are a quart of strawberries and half a cup of diced Vidalia onions.

Sweet onions, by act of the Georgia legislature in 1986, can only be called Vidalia onions if they are grown in Toombs County, where Vidalia is, and 19 other counties or parts of them in southeastern Georgia. The rationale is that the onion, a yellow Granex hybrid, gets its sweetness because of the climate and low-sulfur soil in this area. Spoilsports say the soil throughout southern Georgia is basically the same.

Vidalias began their path to prominence in 1931 when Mose Coleman, a farmer in Toombs County, discovered his onions were sweet. He managed to sell them at a good price during the Depression. In 1940, the state built a farmers' market in Vidalia, a crossroads

Vidalia's Favorite Onion Dip

3 cups chopped Vidalia onions   2½ cups Kraft mayonnaise
3 cups shredded Swiss cheese   garlic and salt to taste

Mix all ingredients and pour into greased 1½-quart baking dish. Bake at 350 degrees for 35–45 minutes until lightly brown. Serve with corn chips.

Ruth M. Underwood, 1996 Appetizer Winner and Grand Prize Winner,
Vidalia Onion Festival, Vidalia, Georgia

town, and the word spread about "those Vidalia onions." Production grew, reaching 600 acres by the mid-1970s. The production season is late April through mid-June, but developments in controlled-atmosphere storage have prolonged their lives. Today, about 275 growers cultivate Vidalia onions on more than 10,000 acres, bringing about $50 million into the Georgia economy. The growers don't even have to cry all the way to the bank.

Location: Vidalia is 84 miles east of Savannah, and 15 miles south of I-16 at exit 21. ⬡ Contact: Vidalia Onion Festival, P.O. Box 280, Vidalia, GA 30475; Tel: (912)538-8687, Fax: (912)537-1805.

See Also: Walla Walla Sweet Onion Fest (Walla Walla, WA).

Vienna

Big Pig Jig

Second weekend in October (Thursday through Saturday)
⬡ The Big Pig Jig is the state's oldest and largest pig-cooking contest, with better than 100 teams from all over the United States competing for the Georgia Barbecue Cooking Championship. It has also been cited as one of the top 100 events in North America by the American Bus Association. That's something to squeal about.

It began in 1982 as a contest to see who could barbecue the most succulent pig, combining the contest with an already established arts and crafts fair and with Dooly County's annual hog show. Twenty teams competed, cooking whole hogs only.

Now more than 100 teams compete, and over wood or charcoal fires, they prepare whole hogs, pork shoulders, and pork ribs *plus* Brunswick stew and barbecue sauce. It takes 450 judges to sort things out and name the champs.

About 35,000 people attend. Activities have expanded to include a parade, entertainment, rides, games, and more than 70 arts and crafts booths. Vendors sell not only barbecued pork but also barbecued chicken and beef and other standard fair nourishment.

Saturday, the Georgia Championship Hog Calling Contest is held. Conservative types might just call SOOO-eee or Here, piggie, but many contestants are pros who give a short lecture on the history of hog-calling. Their calls are snorts, grunts, oinks. Real hog sounds. The winner gets a trophy.

Location: Slosheye Trail Rd. in Vienna, 45 miles south of Macon, a mile west of I-75 at exit 36. **Contact:** Dooly County Chamber of Commerce, P.O. Box 376, Vienna, GA 31092; Tel: (912)268-8275, Fax: (912)268-8200.

Southern Wild Game & Chicken "Thang"

Spring (no set date) At varying times, Vienna (pronounced VY-anna) hosts this two-day barbecue cook-off that underscores the fact that this is one of the best hunting and fishing areas in the state. About 50 teams, quite a few from out of state, compete, and about 5,000 come to watch (and to eat the barbecued meat and chicken that vendors sell). Deer, wild turkey, and wild hog (boar) are abundant around here, and usually wind up on the grill, along with catfish and birds such as dove, pheasant, and quail. Among the dishes contestants have entered are bacon-wrapped dove, blackened fish, and deep-fried turkey, which is a whole turkey dropped in a vat of oil, making it very crispy.

Location and Contact: See above.

Kentucky

Kentucky Bourbon Festival

Eight days, third weekend through fourth weekend in September ☼ Bardstown has two claims to fame: Stephen Foster wrote "My Old Kentucky Home" here, and this is the Bourbon Capital of the World. The city's principal industry is bourbon, and four of the state's nine bourbon distilleries are in the area. Once, there were 22 distilleries in or around Bardstown.

This spirited festival of spirits began in 1993 to promote the bourbon industry, Kentucky's number-one export. The week is packed with non-whiskey activities, but it's hard to lose sight of the fact that this is a bourbon festival.

The Food Court is a festival highlight. Here you can sample the featured chocolate candy, made each year with a different bourbon. All the food vendors in the court have to use bourbon, and you'll find such delicacies as pork tenderloin marinated in bourbon, bourbon pork barbecue, ice cream with bourbon chocolate sauce, and funnel cake with bourbon syrup and whipped cream. Elsewhere, non-bourbon foods are available.

Special events include a seminar on bourbon's history, distillery tours, a cooking demonstration using bourbon, a waiters and waitresses race, and an excursion (reservations required) on My Old Kentucky Dinner Train, which has restored 1940s-era dining cars and offers guests food prepared with Kentucky bourbon.

Throughout the festival, there are displays of barrel making and walking tours that highlight bourbon memorabilia. And a not-to-miss event is the World's Championship Bourbon Barrel Relay; distillery barrel rollers compete for prizes by maneuvering 500-pound bourbon barrels through an obstacle course, demonstrating how they actually roll the barrels at work.

The festival begins with a 5K run and classic-car display and winds up with a country-music concert attended by about 10,000.

Bourbon, an original American drink, is named for Kentucky's Bourbon County, where bourbon whiskey was first produced in the eighteenth century. Later the bourbon industry moved west to Bardstown's Nelson County, about 80 miles distant, because of more fertile land for grain. Bardstown has distilling records dating back to 1776.

To be called straight bourbon, whiskey has to be distilled from a mash of at least 51 percent corn; blended bourbon has to contain no less than 51 percent straight bourbon. The famous mint julep, a trademark of Louisville's Derby Day, is made of bourbon, mint, sugar syrup, and crushed ice, and is properly served in a silver julep cup.

Location: Spalding Hall, North Fifth St., Bardstown, 45 miles south of Louisville on U.S. 150.   **Contact:** Bardstown-Nelson County Tourist & Convention Commission, P.O. Box 867B, Bardstown, KY 40004; Tel: (800)638-4877, Fax: (502)349-0804.

While You're There: Be sure to take a look at the Oscar Getz Museum of Whiskey History in Spalding Hall, where you'll see an 1854 E. C. Booz bottle, the brand that gave booze its name. Other exhibits and documents trace the history of the American whiskey industry.

Cadiz

Trigg County Country Ham Festival

Second weekend in October (Friday through Sunday)   At one time, farmers would come to Cadiz and sit around bragging about their hams being better than their neighbors'. Finally, in 1977, they asked the local packing company to judge their hams.

That was the start of a festival that now brings 35,000 people to town to pay homage to one of Kentucky's most distinguished products (bourbon is another)—the Kentucky country ham. The trademark of the festival is the World's Largest Ham and Cheese Sandwich.

The ham competition is still the central part of the festival. The rule is that the hams must be farm-cured by an amateur, not for commercial sale. The winner gets a silver tray. The winning ham isn't eaten at the fair; the winner takes it home and probably slices it at Christmas. In the festival's first 20 years, there were 16 winners—one man won five times.

Kentucky country hams, moldy and decidedly unappetising-looking when they're ready to eat, have a rich salt taste that comes from being soaked in salt for 21 days, then hung for about 16 days in a smokehouse where hickory chips smolder. After the smoking, the ham hangs for about 18 months. Mold grows, but not to worry—with warm water the mold is easily wiped away.

Country hams don't need refrigeration. People hang them in their pantries in a sock (cloth) and slice off whatever they need.

About the big sandwich: eight to ten people slice 16 country hams and roll out the biscuit dough. The process takes about three hours. At about 12:30, the sandwich, in a galvanized tin pan that has to be picked up with a fork lift and placed on rollers, is transported to a special oven in the town square to bake for an hour. The 1995 sandwich weighed 514 pounds and made 2,700 smaller sandwiches, which were all sold out in two hours.

Besides the sandwiches, available food runs largely to pig products: slices of country ham, beans and ham, ham and biscuits, ham and bean soup, pork sandwiches. You can also buy whole and half hams.

There are lots of country-style events: hog calling, with the county champion picked by crowd cheers; a Kiss-the-Pig Contest, a fundraiser, since people put money in jars with the names of local ministers, and the minister whose jar has the most money kisses the pig; a greased-pig contest; a hog-trough race, with the trough on wheels and prominent towns-people participating.

Other attractions: a parade, fiddling, tractor-pulling, contests for Miss and Mrs. Country Ham and for a King and Queen, who are six years old or younger, a country western concert, gospel quartets, a craft show, a kiddie carnival, hot-air balloons.

Location: Main Street, Cadiz, on U.S. 68, off I-24 at exit 65, about 40 miles southeast of Paducah. **Contact:** Cadiz Tourist Commission, P.O. Box 735, Cadiz, KY 42211; Tel: (502)522-6343.

London

World Chicken Festival

Last weekend in September (Thursday through Sunday)
If you have a hankering to make a Colonel Sanders pilgrimage the way people make Elvis pilgrimages, head for Laurel County at the time of London's World Chicken Festival.

The middle of town is closed down for the festival, and about 8,000 pieces of chicken are fried in what is claimed to be the World's Largest Skillet. (However, you might want to compare the skillets at the Delmarva Chicken Festival and the Central Maine Egg Festival.) The skillet is ten feet, six inches in diameter, eight inches deep, and weighs 700 pounds. It holds 892 quarters of chicken at one time. Here's what it takes to fry 8,000 pieces of chicken—375 pounds of flour, 75 pounds of salt, and 30 pounds each of pepper and paprika. Besides fried chicken, you can buy stewed chicken and dumplings, grilled chicken, grilled hamburgers, corn bread, and the usual festival foods.

The festival was founded in 1990 to promote the town, and the chicken theme was chosen because Harland Sanders started his first restaurant in Corbin, about 12 miles south of London. (For those who have been living on Mars during the twentieth century, Colonel Sanders was the gentleman with the white goatee who founded the chain of Kentucky Fried Chicken restaurants—now known as KFC—that dot the globe.)

Along with food, the festival offers bluegrass and country bands, street dances, arts and crafts, volleyball, magicians, a circus and rides, Chicken Man and the Red Hen Boogie Band, a mother/daughter look-alike contest, gospel music, a 5K run, and an antique-car show. You like to compete? There's a hot-wing-eating contest (the recipe for the sauce is a secret), and crowing, strutting, and clucking contests.

More than 200,000 attend the festival.

Owensboro calls itself the Barbecue Capital of the World with good reason: during the International Bar-B-Q Festival, they barbecue more than 10 tons of mutton and 5,000 chickens. (©Don Hardesty Photography, Evansville, IN)

Location: London is on I-75, about 60 miles south of Lexington. ☼ **Contact:** London Tourist Office, 140 W. Daniel Boone Parkway, London, KY 40741; Tel: (606)878-6900.

While You're There: The original restaurant started by Colonel Sanders in 1940 is south of Corbin on U.S. 25E off I-75 at exit 29. It has been restored, and is both a restaurant, serving standard Kentucky Fried Chicken dishes, and a museum, where you can see the colonel's old kitchen and artifacts such as old pressure cookers. Real Americana!

Owensboro

International Bar-B-Q Festival

Second full weekend in May, weekend after Derby Day (Friday and Saturday) ☼ Owensboro is Kentucky's third largest city, gracefully located on the banks of the Ohio River, home of the world's largest sassafras tree and the International Bluegrass Music Association Fan Fest in September. To foodies, all this pales beside Owensboro's unique glory: the city is not just the Barbecue Capital of the World, but the Barbecued-Mutton Capital of the World.

Owensboro calls itself just the Barbecue Capital, not Barbecued-Mutton Capital—something déclassé about mutton, perhaps. However, they barbecue more than 10 tons of mutton and only 5,000 chickens; there's no barbecued beef or ham.

Mutton is sheep more than two years old, having a stronger flavor and tougher flesh than lamb. However, 18 to 24 hours of slow cooking is a great tenderizer. On Friday night, cooking teams dig pits on the riverbanks, fill them with logs and hickory chips, and light their fires simultaneously. They cook all night, and the barbecue is served the next afternoon at about four o'clock.

Teams also prepare 1,500 gallons of burgoo, a western Kentucky specialty. According to indefatigable food researchers Jane and Michael Stern, it was invented during the Civil War by a Lexington chef for Confederate troops, or it was invented by a hungry Union soldier with a speech impediment who threw blackbirds in a pot and tried to call it bird stew. In Owensboro, burgoo is a thick stew of mutton, chicken, veal, pork, beef, and vegetables such as corn, cabbage, tomatoes, potatoes, okra, lima beans, green peppers, and celery.

Early stews were made with whatever game was available, and it's believed that original burgoo used squirrel. However, James T. Looney seems to be widely accepted as Kentucky's king of burgoo from 1900 up to the late 1930s, and if his word was a royal edict, then burgoo doesn't use squirrel. His recipe for burgoo for 5,000, as published in the Louisville *Courier-Journal,* called for 800 pounds of beef and 200 pounds of fowl, but no squirrel.

Prizes are awarded for the best barbecued mutton, chicken, and burgoo, as well as "Best Overall Bar-B-Q Cooking Team in the World."

The festival began in 1979, but its origins go back much farther. Dutch settlers in Daviess County raised sheep, not cattle, so mutton was a natural for barbecues. There are many Roman Catholic churches—Owensboro is now about 50 percent Catholic—and around the turn of the century, many parishes had barbecue picnics. After a while, the church teams vied with each other to come up with the best barbecue. Out of that grew today's festival, which is open to all but still includes competing church teams, and attracts as many as 40,000 people.

Other events of the festival are a backyard grilling contest, various sports events and road races, arts and crafts, four stages offering music, including country and bluegrass, a Little Miss and Mister Pageant, and mutton- and pie-eating contests.

Location: On the Ohio River banks in Owensboro, on the Tennessee border, just off the William H. Natcher Parkway, 111 miles from Louisville. **Contact:** Owensboro-Daviess County Tourist Commission, 326 St. Elizabeth St., Owensboro, KY 42301; Tel: (800)489-1131, Fax: (502)926-1161.

See Also: Burgoo Festival (Utica, IL).

Stanton

Stanton Corn Festival

First weekend in August You know you're in corn country when you look at the road leading to the park where the corn festival is held. It's stenciled with green and yellow six-foot-long ears of corn—always fresh, repainted annually. They get you in the mood for corn, and people eat a lot of it at the festival—roasted, boiled, and in corn bread.

Corn is the second largest crop in Kentucky, but grown largely as grain for feed, for bourbon, and for new industrial uses being developed. Still, they grow sweet corn, too, and the festival proves there are some prodigious eaters of sweet corn in the commonwealth. A long-standing record in the adult category of the corn-eating contests was 17 ears, eaten in about 10 minutes.

Other corn events are a corn-bread bake-off, with prizes from the Martha Washington cake-mix company, and a woman dressed like a corn cob touring the fair, sometimes in the cornmobile, a go-cart shaped like an ear of corn and running on ethanol, which is made from corn.

The festival began in 1990 as a community fundraiser, and about 15,000 attend. Besides corn, they can munch on country ham and biscuits, pork tenderloin sandwiches, and traditional festival fare. A Miss Corn Festival is chosen, and she has a court of princesses of various ages down to infants. A craft show and car show are held, and there's continuous music, from gospel to bluegrass.

Location: City Municipal Park in Stanton, off Mountain Parkway at exit 22, 45 miles southeast of Lexington. **Contact:** Stanton Corn Festival, P.O. Box 1100, Stanton, KY 40380; Tel: (606)663-2271.

Louisiana

Amite Oyster Day

Last weekend in March unless there is a conflict with Easter, in which case scheduled for second to last weekend (Friday through Sunday) Amite isn't on the coastline, but it has three oyster-shucking and packing houses, and has dubbed itself the Oyster Capital of the World. Oysters are generously used in Louisiana in all the varying cuisines of the state. They are often chief ingredients in gumbos, jambalayas, and soups, and they're revered as Oysters Rockefeller and Oysters Bienville, both invented in New Orleans. In the nineteenth century, according to food historian Evan Jones, Louisiana oysters were as famous as Puget Sound's Olympias and the Chincoteagues from Chesapeake Bay.

They haven't declined in popularity. At the festival, which began in 1975 and is attended by as many as 35,000, nonprofit groups sell oysters fried and on the half shell; one group might sell as many as 50 gallons of fried oysters.

In addition, you can fill up on boiled crawfish, barbecued goat, jambalaya, and ethnic foods such as Italian sausage and Asian dishes.

An oyster-cooking contest is held, and there's a not-too-serious chili cook-off, participated in by the parish officials—judges, sheriffs, and so on. Their entries are not necessarily anything to make chiliheads sit up and cheer, but it's a fun event, and the chilis are available for tasting after the judging (which the participants usually claim is rigged).

As at most Louisiana festivals, there's music ranging from Cajun to country to rock and roll, and there's a parade on Saturday where all six oyster queens (from different age groups) ride in glory along with an Oyster King and Pearl. The latter are mature individuals selected for their contributions to the community. Other attractions include displays of arts and crafts, a carnival midway, and a horseshoe tournament.

Location: Amite is 80 miles north of New Orleans and 50 miles east of Baton Rouge on I-55. **Contact:** Amite Oyster Day, P.O. Box 1064, Amite, LA 70422; Tel: (504)748-5161.

Creamy Oyster Stew

2	cups milk	1	teaspoon celery salt
2	cups light cream	4-5	dozen medium oysters
½	cup butter		oyster liquid
3	tablespoons flour		salt and cayenne pepper
½	cup green onions, chopped		oyster crackers
½	cup parsley, chopped		

In a large saucepan, melt butter. Stir in flour until blended. Add chopped green onions. Cook until soft. Stir in fresh chopped parsley and celery salt. Gradually add milk and cream. Blend in oyster liquid and simmer for 20–30 minutes. Add salt and cayenne pepper to taste. Do not allow to boil. About the last 10 minutes before serving, add oysters and cook until edges curl. Do not overcook. Top with oyster crackers and serve immediately. Makes 6 servings. Cooking time: 30 minutes.

Dairy Farmers of Louisiana

While You're There: Oyster shucking facilities are open for tours.

See Also: St. Mary's County Oyster Festival (Leonardtown, MD).

Breaux Bridge

Crawfish Festival

First full weekend in May (Friday through Sunday)
Louisiana Indians considered crawfish sacred.

Cajuns in early days thought crawfish was humble fare, certainly not something to be a symbol of their people. In the 1930s, saloons served crawfish free to encourage people to drink beer.

What goes around comes around.

Today the crawfish, a small fresh-water crustacean a few inches long that looks like a stunted lobster, is revered by Cajuns and just about everybody else in Louisiana. Sleepy little Breaux Bridge thumps the drums about being La Capitale Mondiale des Ecrevisses, or the World Capital of Crawfish.

In 1959 Breaux Bridge celebrated its centennial with such élan that it was named the crawfish capital. It's not an empty title. Townspeople have traditionally been big crawfish catchers and eaters. The festival began in 1960; about 30,000 now attend and consume about five tons of crawfish cooked in every way imaginable.

The standard way is boiled (usually with potatoes and spices). Boiled crawfish are eaten with the fingers, and the head can be sucked out. There is also Cajun popcorn—fried tail. Other crawfish dishes: crawfish étouffée, dogs, jambalaya, pies, bisque, gumbo, fettucini, boudin. Boudin is normally a pork sausage, but at this festival, the casing is stuffed with crawfish, rice, peppers, and onions. Your hosts also offer shrimp, crab, chicken, fried fish, and red beans and rice.

A crawfish-étouffée cook-off, with showmanship a part of the presentation, and a first prize of $200, is held on Sunday morning. Samples are available after the judging.

The shouts of, "Ils sont partis," means the crawfish have left the gate. It's the crawfish race, on an eight-foot-diameter track.

And there are also crawfish-eating contests, one for celebrities and one for regular folks. The winners are the ones who down the most boiled crawfish in a set time. A record was set by Andrew Thevenet of Breaux Bridge who ate 33⅓ pounds in an hour.

A top attraction is Cajun music—this is one of the largest gatherings of world-famous Cajun musicians. To go with it, there's a Cajun dance contest. And there are also exhibitions of crafts such as accordion-, fiddle-, and bonnet-making; story tellers telling about Cajun culture; a parade with the Crawfish Royalty (Queen, King, Ecrevette Ambassadors and little Miss and Mister Pincher) in places of honor; a carnival midway.

The one-time lowly status of the crawfish may be related to their habits; they burrow into mud, and therefore are sometimes called mudbugs. But there's a legend that may explain the fondness Cajuns have for mudbugs: After being exiled by the British from Nova Scotia, the Acadians wandered for years, and were followed by the North Atlantic lobster. When the Acadians finally settled in the swampy land of Louisiana, the lobsters settled with them. But the long, difficult travel had taken its toll; the lobsters had become tiny creatures—the crawfish.

Location: Breaux Bridge is off I-20 at exit 109, 6 miles from Lafayette. ☼ **Contact:** Breaux Bridge Crawfish Festival, P.O. Box 25, Breaux Bridge, LA 70517; Tel: (318)332-6655, Fax: (318)332-5917.

While You're There: The Breaux Bridge Creole Festival takes place at the national armory the same weekend. All music there is zydeco. Contact the Creole Festival Association, (318)394-2216.

Bridge City

Gumbo Festival

Second weekend of October (Friday through Sunday) ☼ If the dishes of the Cajun cuisine were an armada, gumbo would be their flagship. And Bridge City, across the Big Muddy from New Orleans, is its home port—the Gumbo Capital of the World, as proclaimed by the Louisiana governor in 1973.

Gumbo, if you consider its ancestors, like bouillabaisse, in shoreline countries, should be a seafood dish; but in Louisiana it is not only allowable but very popularly made with sausage or alligator or almost any kind of meat or fish. At the festival, volunteers from the Holy Guardian Angels Church stir 50-gallon pots in preparing more than 2,000 gallons of both seafood and chicken-sausage gumbo; they also make about 1,000 gallons of jambalaya, both shrimp and sausage. There are also plentiful red beans and rice with sausage. For dessert, look for pecan pie and pralines.

The festival began in 1971 and now draws about 120,000 people who are entertained with music (Cajun, country, zydeco, jazz, blues, rock), rides, games, a bridge run, dancing groups, and a fais-do-do (traditional Cajun dancing) area. Miss Creole Gumbo and King Creole Gumbo are on hand to greet visitors.

There's a Gumbo Cooking Contest, with contestants submitting two-gallon batches of gumbo in one of two categories—seafood or chicken. Judges are local chefs.

Gumbo is probably the best known of Cajun dishes. The name comes from the African word for okra, *ngombo* or *kingombo,* a plant brought to America with the slaves from Africa. Gumbo is thickened with okra, or sometimes with *filé,* the ground powder of sassafras leaves that was used by the Choctaws.

There are almost infinite varieties of gumbo. There is even a vegetarian "green gumbo" called *gumbo z'herbes* (gumbo des herbes), which has no meat or seafood and may contain as many as seven vegetables.

Gumbos begin with roux, a mix of flour and oil (about two parts flour to one part oil). This is slowly cooked and constantly stirred until it's a deep brown. The ingredients—shrimp and oyster, say, for the seafood gumbo, along with the trinity of onions, celery, and green bell peppers—are mixed together with the roux and spices and simmered a long time before being ladled over rice.

Location: Angel Park, behind the Holy Guardian Angels Church in Bridge City, across the Mississippi River from New Orleans, at the foot of the Huey P. Long Bridge.
Contact: Gumbo Festival, P.O. Box 9069, Bridge City, LA 70096; Tel: (504)436-4712, Fax: (504)436-4070.

See Also: Festivals Acadiens (Lafayette, LA).

Buras

Plaquemines Parish Fair & Orange Festival

First full weekend of December Plaquemines Parish is Louisiana's southernmost toe, jutting into the Gulf of Mexico, with the Mississippi River running down its middle to meet the Gulf. The parish harvests almost 250 million pounds of seafood, including about a third of all the state's oysters, and it also produces about 95 percent of the state's citrus.

The parish is famous in citrus circles because the first mandarin orange in the United States is thought to have been grown there in about 1850. The mandarin is a loose-skinned orange with a number of family members, among them the small, almost seedless satsuma.

As might be expected, the Orange Festival has fresh oranges, orange drinks, and homemade marmalade for sale, as well as oysters on the half shell, oyster po' boys, alligator burgers, shrimp Creole, and crawfish sausage. And more.

Citrus is center stage with an orange-eating contest and the coronation of the orange king and queen; seafood is acknowledged with catfish-skinning, oyster-shucking, and shrimp-peeling contests. Other events include children's games, an art display, music, and dancing. About 15,000 to 20,000 attend.

The first Orange Festival was organized in 1947 to promote the citrus crop, and, considering the string of disasters that followed, it's a wonder the festival and the oranges ever survived: 1951, a bad freeze; 1962 and 1963, snow and destructive freezes; 1965, Hurricane Betsy, and then Hurricane Camille; 1982, 1983, and 1985, crippling freezes. The festival, suspended a few years, resumed in 1978. Growers kept reviving the devastated citrus groves.

The seedless navel orange is the mainstay of the parish citrus industry, but satsumas rank second to the navel, and Plaquemines also grows tangerines, lemons, and grapefruit.

Location: Fort Jackson, on Louisiana 23, 6 miles south of Buras, about 60 miles south of New Orleans.   **Contact:** Plaquemines Parish Fair & Festival Assn., P.O. Box 3090, Port Sulphur, LA 70083; Tel: (504)564-2951, Fax: (504)564-2234.

See Also: Orange Blossom Festival (Riverside, CA).

Crowley

International Rice Festival

Usually third weekend of October (Friday and Saturday)
This is one of Louisiana's oldest festivals, first held in 1937. It's one of the biggest, too, attracting between 125,000 and 150,000 people who manage to put away a lot of rice.

Not plain, though. Crowley is the Rice Capital of America, and one-fourth of the nation's rice is produced here, but even in Crowley they admit that plain rice is bland. So they serve rice and crawfish étouffée (culinarily fitting, since rice and crawfish are cultivated in the same flooded fields) and jambalaya. You can also get rice pudding, rice cakes, rice casseroles, and basic rice and gravy.

The celebration is intended to call attention to the importance of rice as food and its place in the world economic picture. That means some serious goings-on, namely a rice-grading contest and a rice-cooking contest. Beyond that, the festival becomes a typical Louisiana music-and-fun affair. There are French accordion, fiddle, and harmonica contests, a children's parade on Friday and a grand parade on Saturday, an arts and crafts exhibit, a Junior King and Queen Contest, and a Queen's Ball.

Rice was introduced to North America in the latter part of the seventeenth century in the area of Charleston, South Carolina, with the original seed thought to have come from Madagascar. In time, an intricate system of dikes and ponds was built in the estuarine areas, and South Carolina became the country's principal rice-growing region.

As rice growing declined on the East Coast (it finally ended after some devastating storms in the early 1900s), the enterprising brothers W. W. and C. C. Duson formed a land

Crawfish and rice are both cultivated in these flooded fields in Louisiana; both can be found in abundance at Crowley's International Rice Festival. (Barbara W. Carlson)

company, and in 1886 bought 174 acres of Louisiana prairie land for a total of $80. They sold lots, the town of Crowley was founded, and families, many wheat farmers from the Midwest, came to raise rice. Soon Crowley was the country's rice capital by virtue of the fact that more rice was milled here than in all the cities of the United States put together.

The festival is held after the fields are drained and the rice is gathered.

Location: Crowley is off I-10, 23 miles west of Lafayette. **Contact:** International Rice Festival, P.O. Box 1900, Crowley, LA 70527; Tel: (318)783-3067.

While You're There: The Rice Museum, the first home of the Louisiana State University Rice Experiment Station, tells the history of rice with pictures, indoor and outdoor machinery displays, and a working model of a rice mill.

See Also: Arkansas Rice Festival (Weiner, AR).

Delcambre

Delcambre Shrimp Festival

Third weekend in August (Wednesday through Sunday)

Delcambre has long been a shrimping port, and because of that a shrimp festival seemed appropriate when it began in 1950. It started as a means to raise money for the Iberia Parish fire department, but has become lucrative enough to benefit a number of community projects.

If you come here to eat, you won't be disappointed: there's plenty of shrimp with sauce piquante, shrimp boiled, fried, and in étouffée and po' boys. There's also a shrimp cook-off, where contestants each cook a gallon of their shrimp dish, allowing generous samples for spectators after the judging.

A blessing of the fleet is an old tradition, and as the boats parade by the blessing boat, they're judged and awarded prizes. There are separate categories for best-decorated shrimp boat and sporting boat.

Other events of the weekend are music (Cajun, country, zydeco), a fais-do-do (street dancing), a carnival, and the coronation of a Delcambre Shrimp Queen and King. The king is someone in the shrimp industry; the queen is a pretty young woman.

Location: Delcambre is 21 miles south of Lafayette on Louisiana 14. **Contact:** Delcambre Shrimp Festival, P.O. Box 286, Delcambre, LA 20528; Tel: (318)685-2653 or (318)685-4239.

Des Allemands

Louisiana Catfish Festival

Second full weekend in July The catfish you get at this festival are fresh-water wild catfish, and there is a strongly partisan group that insists farmed catfish will never have the taste that the wild ones do. That's despite the fact that catfish farms are a fast-growing industry in Louisiana; you drive down a road in prairie country and see what looks like a sea—it's the ponds of catfish farms.

The Des Allemands catfish industry uses fish caught by local fishermen in the clean waters of the area. For the festival, members of St. Gertrude's Catholic Church clean and prepare the fish and feed them to 20,000 to 30,000 visitors. This is not just a fried-catfish event; you can get catfish with sauce piquante, or you can try catfish po' boys. There are also homemade jambalaya and seafood gumbo with crab and shrimp. A catfish-cooking contest is judged by agricultural extension agents, and there's also a canning and preserving contest.

Catfish are not normally caught with rod and reel. Fishermen often use baited coffee cans with mesh traps, hauling the fish out of the river after they swim into the cans.

To the complaint that catfish have a muddy taste (they are a bottom-feeding fish), a wild-fish partisan explains patiently that a 50-pound catfish would have a muddy taste, but the smaller ones, he says, have not acquired the taste. Louisiana harvests five to six million pounds of river catfish a year, leading the nation.

Location: St. Gertrude's Catholic Church, visible from Louisiana 631. Des Allemands is on U.S. 90 at Louisiana 631, about 30 miles west of New Orleans. **Contact:** St. Gertrude's Catholic Church, P.O. Box 767, Des Allemands, LA 70030; Tel: (504)758-7542.

World's Championship Crawfish Étouffée Cook-Off

Last Sunday in March (preceding Sunday if there is a conflict with Easter) ⊙ Étouffée is a stew, and one of the more popular Cajun dishes. Eunice, Louisiana's Prairie Cajun Capital, has made an icon of étouffée. The town has been holding this cook-off since 1986, and spectators number from 10,000 to 15,000.

The word étouffée means smothered, and an étouffée therefore is food, usually a crawfish or shrimp stew, cooked in a small amount of liquid in a tightly covered pot. The base is the Cajun holy trinity of chopped onions, bell peppers, and celery (it should be noted that the holy trinity can vary depending on the belief of the individual), and roux.

Cajun roux is a thickener of flour and oil, not butter, stirred and cooked slowly until it's molasses-brown.

The cook-off is a triumph of purity; only crawfish étouffée is allowed, and there are no other foods but the crawfish étouffée. No shrimp, no catfish, no—heaven forfend—funnel cake.

But that doesn't mean lack of variety. Between 60 and 90 teams compete, and rarely are there two étouffées that taste just the same. Proportions make the difference. And some contestants use cream of celery or cream of mushroom soup, or bay leaves, or tomato sauce, or garlic, or beer or wine in the gravy, or butter instead of oil, or Indian seasonings.

Judges seem to prefer traditional étouffée—crawfish tail, with the crawfish "fat," an orange glob that is actually the liver and pancreas and is considered a delicacy, the holy trinity, and salt and pepper.

Crawfish Étouffée "Lanse Aux Pailles" Style

1 stick butter or oleo	2 tablespoons flour
2 large chopped onions	1 cup water
1 large bell pepper, chopped	1 tablespoon tomato sauce
3 cloves garlic	½ cup green onion tops
1 pound crawfish tails	¼ cup chopped parsley
salt and pepper to taste	

Combine butter, onions, bell pepper, and garlic and cook until clear. Add crawfish tails, tomato sauce, flour, and water. Bring to a boil and lower fire to simmer. Cook 10 minutes. Add greens and cook one minute. Serve on hot rice.

Olga Manuel and Prairie Acadian Cultural Center, Eunice, LA

The étouffées are judged in categories for amateurs, professionals, and club organizations. The winners get plaques to which a local taxidermist attaches an embalmed crawfish and decorations that are different each year.

What's in it for spectators? Each contestant cooks at least 10 pounds of étouffée, some up to 50 pounds, and sells portions for a dollar. And the cook-off is a visual sensation; the cooking booths are all decorated, some outlandishly, and the winner of the best decorated booth also gets a crawfish plaque.

And, of course, there's Cajun and zydeco music all day—this is the Prairie Cajun Capital, remember? And there are a Miss Étouffée Pageant and a carnival for those who can drag themselves away from the étouffée aroma.

Location: Northwest Community Center Pavilion, Samuel Dr., Eunice, 45 miles northwest of Lafayette, on U.S. 190 at the intersection of Louisiana 13. ⬩ **Contact:** Eunice Chamber of Commerce, P.O. Box 508, Eunice, LA 70535; Tel: (318)457-2565.

While You're There: The Liberty Center for the Performing Arts is the site of the "Rendez Vous des Cajuns," a two-hour live radio show of music and jokes presented every Saturday from 6 to 8 p.m. Get there early; the hall fills up.

Gonzales

Jambalaya Festival

Memorial Day weekend (Thursday through Sunday) ⬩
Cajuns sometimes define jambalaya as what's left over: You take cubes of sausage, ham, chicken, onions, bell peppers, mix them in a pot, and put the pot in the oven until it's done.

It's not quite that simple, of course. Cuisine is a religion with Cajuns, and, as in most religions, controversy often exists. In Gonzales, the Jambalaya Capital of the World, jambalaya should be brown. That means tomatoes aren't used, but rice is, and rice is generally considered the base of jambalaya.

But in Mamou, in the prairies, you would never cook jambalaya with rice. To further confuse matters, some say that jambalaya isn't Cajun at all, but a Spanish-Creole dish, or simply a Creole dish. (Creole cuisine is sometimes called sophisticated Cajun; others say it melds the cuisines of the French who came to Louisiana earlier than the Cajuns with those of the Haitians, Africans, and Spanish.) It is also conjectured that the word comes from the Spanish jamón, meaning ham, and that it's related to paella—or that it's an African dish.

The jambalaya festival is basically a cook-off, and the winner is the World Jambalaya Cooking Champion. The festival association takes cooks on the road to do what might be called jambalaya missionary work; they've cooked for Jimmy Carter, they've been to Texas, to France.

About 50 cooks participate in three cook-offs on Saturday, preparing a basic chicken jambalaya. They must use a large iron pot and cook over a wood fire at the festival site. The festival gives the cooks the ingredients; their skill dictates the proportions, and the way ingredients are mixed. One rule is that no Kitchen Bouquet is allowed.

Audrey's Jambalaya

⅓ pound bacon
2 medium chopped onions
3 ribs of chopped celery
1 medium bell pepper
½ cup (4 ounces) green onion tops
2 teaspoons Kitchen Bouquet

2 pounds peeled shrimp
4 cups (32 ounces) long grain rice
8 cups (64 ounces) hot water
Red or black pepper to taste
1 teaspoon garlic powder
parsley

In a heavy six-quart pot, brown the bacon until crisp. Remove the bacon, leaving the drippings in which you will add the chopped onions, cooking until very dark brown in color. Then, add the bell pepper, celery, parsley, and green onion. Cook these about 10 minutes on a medium fire, stirring frequently. Add salt and pepper according to taste. Add water, Kitchen Bouquet for rich dark color, and the cooked bacon. When this mixture comes to a boil, add the raw shrimp, which you cook only five minutes before adding the raw long grain rice. Stir the rice only once while it cooks. If rice is not cooked well when juices are used up, simply add small amounts of boiling water to the pot until rice is cooked. For the shrimp you can substitute sausage, duck, ribs, etc. Brown the meat well, keeping the drippings and putting all in the place of the raw shrimp. Bon appetit!

To make Kitchen Bouquet: In a small heavy skillet put one cup of sugar, cook until dark brown, add one cup of warm water. If sugar hardens, cook until it liquefies and add about 3 tablespoons to water in jambalaya. This makes the bitter taste go away.

Audrey Babineaux-George, Cajun Bed and Breakfast Association, Houma, LA

The iron pots, by the way, are said to be essential in the preparation of proper jambalaya. Pots are by preference old and well-seasoned.

The cooks, who look very snappy in royal blue shirts, white pants, and white shoes, take about two-and-a-half hours to cook their jambalayas, usually using 45-quart pots.

For a modest sum, festival-goers get a heaping amount of the contestants' jambalaya with cole slaw and bread.

The festival, a Gonzales fixture since 1967, raises money for the community. Attendance at one time was close to 100,000, but it's now down to less than 10,000; the big crowds were getting too rowdy so the townsfolk took steps and introduced some restraints.

A king of the festival is someone honored for his community work, and other royal figures are a queen and junior queen. There's a carnival for entertainment, and music; a Cajun event would not be Cajun without music.

Location: American Legion grounds in Gonzales, 25 miles south of Baton Rouge on U.S. 61 off I-10. **Contact:** Jambalaya Festival Association, P.O. Box 1243, Gonzales, LA 70707; Tel: (505)647-7487.

Lafayette

Festivals Acadiens

Third weekend in September (Friday through Sunday)

In Lafayette, the Capital of French Louisiana, you can feel the rhythm of Cajun life—especially at the Festivals Acadiens.

The event is a combination of festivals. The Louisiana Native Crafts Festival started in the early 1970s to feature the work of craftspeople, cooks, storytellers, artisans, and singers. The Festival de Musique Acadienne began with a three-hour concert in 1975 to increase awareness of Cajun music and language.

In 1977, the festivals were combined, restaurants began the Bayou Food Festival, and then Downtown Alive! stepped in with its TGIF street concert. Today they're all happening at once, with more than 300 entertainers displaying the Cajun culture in all its facets for 100,000 visitors.

The cuisine—c'est bonne. It's rich and hearty and spicy. (Cajuns have a theory that the spices they use so freely counteract the fats they also use freely, keeping cholesterol counts from shooting through the ceiling.)

At the Bayou Food Festival, area restaurants serve up seafood gumbo, crawfish étouffée, boiled crawfish, crawfish fettucini, and Cajun popcorn—crawfish tails shelled, battered, and deep-fried. There's andouille (chitlins and tripe sausage) jambalaya, or gumbo. There's boudin, a pork and rice sausage. There are alligator-sausage po' boys and fried alligator. There's *fricot,* a potato soup with sausage or shredded meat.

There are stuffed catfish, fried bite-size catfish, crab cakes, shrimp-stuffed basil bread. There's shrimp-and-tasso pasta—tasso being smoked, spiced beef or pork usually used to flavor other dishes.

When you need a sweet, you'll find pralines and probably bread pudding, a favorite Cajun dessert.

While you eat, you'll hear the two-step music of accordions and fiddles, the mainstays of Cajun music.

Old crafts—indigo dying, saddle making, boat building, blanket making, basket weaving, alligator skinning—are demonstrated at the Lafayette Natural History Museum. And the Lafayette Beaver Club has a tent called How Men Cook where they demonstrate and give out free samples of such dishes as stews cooked in iron pots over open fires, grilled dishes, and wild game. They also have a cookbook, *Cajun Men Cook.*

The festivals are, moreover, a chance to learn the Cajun history. Simply put, a Cajun is someone whose ancestors left France and arrived in Louisiana by way of Canada.

These ancestors settled in Acadie, now Nova Scotia, in 1604, where they farmed and fished. When the British gained control of Acadie in 1713, the Acadians maintained their independence and Catholic religion, refusing to bow to the British crown. In 1755, the British removed them from their home in what was known as *Le Grand Derangement.* Thousands died during the dispersal, and some settled along the American East Coast, some in France, some in the Caribbean. Many found their way to south Louisiana, where 3,000 to 4,000 had settled by the beginning of the nineteenth century.

The state was not always hospitable to them. Not too many decades ago, the state forbade the speaking of French in schools. Yet the Acadian culture continued, a Cajun-French language evolved, the music and cuisine flourished. Lafayette is the place to learn the culture, eat it, hear it, and dance to it.

Location: Girard Park (exit 101 off I-10) for music festival and food festival; Parc de Lafayette in downtown Lafayette for Downtown Alive! and Kids Alive! (programs of free concerts); Lafayette Natural History Museum, 637 Girard Park Dr. Lafayette is in central Louisiana, at the intersection of I-10 and I-49.   **Contact:** Lafayette Visitors Center, P.O. Box 52066, Lafayette, LA 70707; Tel: (800)346-1958, or (318)232-3808; Fax (318)232-0161.

While You're There: Visit Randol's Restaurant and Cajun Dance Hall, 2320 Kaliste Saloom Rd., where there's Cajun music nightly and the dance floor is filled with men and women of all ages, adults dancing as they hold youngsters in their arms, people in jeans and boots, women in long swirly dresses.

LaPlace

Saint John the Baptist Parish Andouille Festival

First weekend in October (Saturday and Sunday)
Andouille is a spicy Cajun (that's redundant) sausage made of pork chitlins and tripe. It's used often in other dishes as a spicy accent—especially in jambalaya and gumbo—and is served cold as well. LaPlace calls itself the Andouille Capital of the World.

At the festival, nonprofit groups raise funds for the community, chiefly by selling andouille dishes—chicken-and-andouille gumbo, red-bean-and-andouille gumbo, pizza, jambalaya, and bayou pasta, which is andouille-chicken sauce over pasta. They also offer seafood po' boys, blackened chicken, onion mums (deep-fried, also known as blooming onions), deep-fried corn on the cob, hamburgers, and funnel cake.

There's an andouille cook-off for adults and youths, in categories of gumbo, jambalaya, and "other." One year, the winner came up with an "other" that was an andouille stuffing for artichokes and boneless chicken.

About 12,000 attend the festival, which began in 1972, lapsed, and then resumed in 1994. The mood is set with Cajun music, and by Miss, Mrs., Teen, and Tiny Tot Andouille, who reign over the festival.

Location: LaPlace is about 25 miles west of New Orleans on U.S. 61.   **Contact:** Saint John the Baptist Parish Andouille Festival, 1801 W. Airline Highway, LaPlace, LA 70068; Tel: (504)652-9567.

Mansura

Cochon de Lait Festival

Second weekend in May (Thursday through Sunday)

Cochon de lait means suckling pig. When the festival began in 1960 to celebrate the town's centennial, the idea was to revive a long unpracticed style of cooking sucklings by spit-roasting them over a wood fire.

The event got too popular for a town with a population of about 2,000 and was terminated in 1972. Revived in 1977, the festival initially attracted crowds of 100,000 to Mansura, but now 25,000 to 30,000 come—much easier on the town.

This is very much an eating fair; the cooked pork is served on a platter with sauce, dirty rice, candied yams, and shredded-cabbage salad. There are also such Cajun foods available as cracklin's, boudin, fried pork, jambalaya, and crawfish, and there are standard festival foods, too.

Today, the festival chefs roast about 40 corn-fed pigs of 60 to 100 pounds each, rather than the sucklings, because there are just too many people to be able to feed them with sucklings. They roast them over a wood fire for at least five hours; the fat drips into the fire and what's left is cracklin's and the meat.

Dirty rice, a ubiquitous Louisiana dish, is made by combining chicken liver and gizzards with the steamed rice, and adding various spices.

There's more than eating: a greased-pig race; a parade starring Miss Cochon de Lait; sporting events such as water-balloon tosses, raw-egg tosses, and horseshoe games; hot-air balloon rides; and street dancing to Cajun and zydeco music.

There are also what might be called ingesting contests. There are beer drinking contests, one for men and one for women, in which contestants vie to drink a can of beer the quickest. There's a boudin-eating contest, in which contestants are given a pound of the sausage and the winner is the one who consumes it the fastest. (The contest used to determine who could eat the most boudin in a set amount of time, but it got a bit too Rabelaisian when one champion ate seven pounds, or about six feet of sausage.) There's also a watermelon-eating contest.

Some background for information pigs: Mansura was named after El Mansura, a city in the Nile Delta, by former soldiers of Napoleon, who made exploratory expeditions to Egypt. The Louisiana site reminded them of the Egyptian town; both are flat and fertile.

"Cochon de lait" is how the festival is spelled here, though in the French of France one would have to say *"du* lait." The differences between the Cajun's French and France's French are attributable to the hundreds of years the Cajuns have been separated from their homeland; Cajun French both retained some usages that now seem archaic to European French speakers and added new words and pronunciations through interaction with other national groups.

Location: Mansura is in central Louisiana on Louisiana 1, about 150 miles north of New Orleans. **Contact:** Mansura Chamber of Commerce, P.O. Box 536, Mansura, LA 71350; Tel: (318)964-2887.

Louisiana Shrimp and Petroleum Festival

Labor Day weekend (Friday through Monday) ☼ In 1936, Morgan City alligator hunters, shrimpers, crabbers, oystermen, and dock workers put on a Labor Day celebration with beano games and a dance. That was the start of what is now Louisiana's oldest state-chartered festival.

Morgan City lies on the Atchafalaya River (pronounced Chaf-a-LIE-ya), and by 1948 its major industry was large gulf shrimp, and the port was calling itself the Jumbo Shrimp Capital of the World. The Labor Day celebration therefore became the Louisiana Shrimp Festival.

In 1967, the name was changed to Louisiana Shrimp and Petroleum Festival because offshore gas and oil production, which began in 1947, was booming and revolutionizing the local economy. While neither the oil nor shrimp industries are what they once were, the festival's name remains, as does the town logo, painted on levees and the water tower—a shrimp crawling up an oil derrick.

Some things stay the same. The blessing of the fleet began in 1937, and continues every year on Sunday, followed by a water parade of shrimp and pleasure boats. More recent parade additions are the biggest "muscle boats" of the oilpatch.

One of the most popular of the festival's many events is the Cajun Culinary Classic. This is Cajun country, and that means lots of food. More than 25 nonprofit booths feature Cajun food: gumbo, jambalaya, dirty rice, boiled crawfish, and the like. At the commercial food booths, you'll find fried shrimp on a stick, fried catfish, white beans, boiled shrimp, shrimp po' boys, Greek sandwiches.

There's also a shrimp cook-off for individuals and businesses, and after the judging by celebrity chefs, the food is sold to the public.

Cajun also means music, and it's continuous—Cajun, zydeco, swamp pop. And there are also a royal pageant and ball, arts and crafts, a children's parade, storytelling. About 100,000 attend.

Location: Downtown Morgan City, 90 miles from New Orleans, is at the intersection of U.S. 90 and Louisiana 70. ☼ **Contact:** Louisiana Shrimp & Petroleum Festival & Fair Assn., P.O. Box 103, Morgan City, LA 70381; Tel: (504)385-0703, or (800)256-2931.

New Orleans Jazz and Heritage Festival

Last weekend in April (Friday through Sunday) and first weekend in May (Thursday through Sunday), with concerts and workshops during the week ☼ "In New Orleans, heritage means eating," says that indomitable eater Calvin Trillin, and indeed the food at this jazz and heritage festival is an embarrassment of richness.

Almost half a million people attend the festival, and they're fed by about 65 vendors, whose food is judged before they can qualify as vendors. Each serves two or three specialties.

There are more than 30 crawfish dishes, including some created just for the festival and served here exclusively. One of the crawfish dishes is Crawfish Monica—crawfish, cream sauce, and pasta. People line up at the gate at the opening to rush for Crawfish Monica.

The point of coming is to try all of the food Louisiana is known for—a daunting task, but the fair-givers have tried to make it as easy as possible. The heritage part of the fair is held in the infield of the Fair Grounds' race track, and because the cost of food is kept low and small snacks are available, it's possible to try a lot of dishes, digesting each by sitting on the grass before staggering to the next food booth.

There's something to taste from every Louisiana cuisine: Cajun, Creole, Caribbean, African, Spanish, Italian, and Soul.

Besides several of the 30 kinds of crawfish dishes, dedicated visitors will try gumbos based on pheasant, quail, or andouille; jambalaya; étouffée; boudin (a sausage of pork, rice, and onions, unless it's red boudin, in which case blood is added). They will want at least a cup of oyster Rockefeller bisque. They will have an appetizer of oyster shooters (raw oysters), or an alligator-sausage po' boy. They will polish things off with pralines, pecan pie, and bread pudding.

If they want an idea of how to re-create the dishes, they'll visit the Food Heritage Tent where regional and local chefs demonstrate cooking, and samples are available.

In 1970, 300 musicians entertained a crowd of about 150 in the city's Congo Square, brought there by George Wein, the founder of the famed Newport Jazz Festival. That was the start of the festival that today sees 4,000 musicians and more than 600 bands of all types, from Cajun and zydeco to Caribbean, African, Brazilian, and Haitian, all playing up a storm. There's a Jazz Tent, there's a Gospel Tent. Something for everyone.

Altogether, some 10,000 musicians, cooks, and craftspeople join to make this a one-of-a-kind celebration.

Location: New Orleans Fairgrounds, next to City Park.   **Contact:** New Orleans Jazz and Heritage Festival, 1205 N. Rampart St., New Orleans, LA 70116; Tel: (504)522-4786.

Rayne

Rayne Frog Festival

Labor Day weekend (Friday through Sunday)   You know you're in the Frog Capital of the World as soon as you turn off the interstate into Rayne; there, greeting you from the highway's concrete abutments are giant-sized painted frogs. Throughout Rayne, which also calls itself the City of Murals, frogs jump out at you from the sides of buildings and even roads.

The festival began in 1973 to honor three French brothers, Jacques, Edmond, and Gautran Weil, who back in the 1880s recognized the culinary value of local bullfrogs and shipped them to restaurants all over the country. Their business is long gone, and, truth to tell, there are not a lot of frogs around Rayne any more. The Jaycees, who sponsor the festival, provide frogs for contests, and collecting the frogs is not as easy as it once was. The decline in the frog population is attributable to underground irrigation and chemicals.

However, the 30,000 to 40,000 people who show up for the frog festival would get hopping mad if they didn't find frog, and there are in fact about 350 pounds of fried frogs' legs—from Taiwan, imported through a Louisiana seafood broker.

Rayne is in the heart of Cajun country, so you can also count on Cajun specialties: crawfish étouffée, crawfish with rice and corn, jambalaya, boudin, and seafood-stuffed bread. There are also turkey legs, barbecued chicken, shrimp on a stick, and sausage and roast beef po' boys.

Despite dwindling numbers of frogs, the festival features frog-racing and jumping contests. A fais-do-do—traditional Cajun dancing—starts the merriment, and there are also a parade, the crowning of a Frog Festival Queen and Junior Frog Festival Queen and Little Mr. and Miss Tadpole, arts and crafts displays, and continuous foot-tapping music.

Location: Rayne is 14 miles west of Lafayette, off I-10 at exit 87. **Contact:** Rayne Chamber of Commerce, P.O. Box 2823; Tel: (318)334-2332, Fax (334)8381.

Mississippi

Bay St. Louis

Our Lady of the Gulf Crab Fest

Fourth of July weekend ☀ Because Bay St. Louis is a seaport not far from New Orleans, you might expect a festival here to have seafood and show a Cajun influence. You would be right.

The specialty is boiled blue-claw crab. This is the same hard crab that frequents Maryland's Chesapeake Bay, and the people here get a little defensive about Maryland's great reputation for blue crabs. The Gulf states produce more, they say.

They cook them differently in Mississippi and Louisiana, too—they boil them instead of steaming them as they do in Maryland. At the Bay St. Louis fest, they drop the crabs in a big boiling pot of water that's been seasoned with garlic and other herbs, and then they add more garlic, onions, potatoes, and corn on the cob, and boil everything for seven to nine minutes. The result is crabmeat with a softer texture than steamed crab, and with a more intense flavor. *Chacun à son goût.*

The festival began sometime in the 1940s as a humble church fair, and now 50,000 come, but not much has changed and it's still for the benefit of the church. About a dozen church families set up booths and bring their specialties to sell—dishes like fried crab claws, or potatoes stuffed with crab and shrimp meat, or étouffée, or red beans and rice.

As a diversion from food, there are amusement-park rides, arts and crafts booths, a flea market, country cloggers, and Cajun fiddlers.

Location: Our Lady of the Gulf Church, 126 S. Beach St., Bay St. Louis, which is on U.S. 90 about 50 miles from New Orleans. ☀ **Contact:** Our Lady of the Gulf Crab Fest, Bay St. Louis, MS 39520; Tel: (601)467-4721.

See Also: National Hard Crab Derby and Fair (Crisfield, MD).

World Catfish Festival

First Saturday of April (Second Saturday if the first is on Easter weekend) ⛲ Let's not argue with Humphreys County's self-designation—Catfish Capital of the World.

In 1965, the first catfish pond was dug in the county by J. B. Williams. Thirty years later, the county had about 117 farms and 35,000 acres of ponds, more catfish acreage than any other single state. Mississippi itself is the number-one catfish producer.

Belzoni, the county seat, is not surprisingly the site of the World's Largest Catfish Fry, which began in 1975 as a picnic to celebrate the growing farmed-catfish industry. More than 30,000 people come from all over the country and abroad, and most of them seem to line up for the genuine Southern midday dinner served on the Courthouse lawn—fried catfish, hush puppies, cole slaw, and a cold drink.

Festival features include crowning a Catfish Queen, arts and crafts, tours of catfish ponds, displays of catfish farm equipment, music, dance, and kids' activities. There are contests for catfish eating and catfish cooking.

Cooks prepare for the more than 30,000 visitors that flock to the World Catfish Festival for a classic Southern meal of fried catfish, hush puppies, and cole slaw. (World Catfish Festival)

Catfish and Goat Cheese Pastries

1 15-ounce package folded refrigerated
   unbaked pie crusts (2 crusts)
1 medium onion, chopped
1 clove garlic, minced
3 tablespoons butter
   or margarine

1½ pounds U.S. Farm-Raised Catfish
   fillets, cubed
8 ounces fresh goat cheese or soft-style
   cream cheese
2 tablespoons chopped fresh basil or 1
   teaspoon dried basil, crushed

Let pie crusts stand at room temperature for 10 to 15 minutes according to package
   directions. Unfold pie crusts. Place on ungreased baking sheet.
In a saucepan, cook onion and garlic in butter or margarine until tender. Add catfish;
   cook and stir about 5 minutes or until fish flakes easily. Use spoon to break fish
   into small pieces. Add goat cheese or cream cheese and basil. Cook and stir until
   cheese melts. Remove from heat.
Spoon half of the catfish mixture onto half of each pie crust. Moisten edges with water.
   Fold pie crusts in half, turn edges under. Seal edges with the tines of a fork. For
   smaller pastries, cut pie crusts into thirds.
Prick top of pie crust and brush with milk. Bake in 375-degree oven for 25 to 30 minutes or until pastry is brown. Cut into wedges and serve warm. Makes 2 pastries or
   8 servings.

The Catfish Cookbook, published by the Catfish Institute

Traditional Southern-style catfish was coated with corn meal, salt, and pepper and
then deep-fried. Now there are choices. Recipe books at the festival list a wealth of dishes,
including catfish pan-fried, grilled, baked, blackened, seared, in gumbo, as fingers or strips
served with mustard or barbecue sauce. A recent innovation is catfish pâté, which visitors
may buy at the festival to take home.

Catfish used to be eaten almost solely in the South. It didn't have much to recom-
mend it. It's ugly, with long feelers that look like a cat's whiskers hanging down from its
mouth. Some varieties are bottom-feeding scavengers, and detractors say older ones have a
muddy taste.

But now that channel catfish (predators, not scavengers) are netted from ponds and
fed high-protein food in pellets that float on the water's surface, they don't taste like mud.
(The wild-fish partisans say they are bland.) They have become the largest source of agricultural revenue for once-blighted Humphreys County. They're on dinner plates everywhere.

In ten years after the founding of the Catfish Institute in Belzoni in 1986, U.S. per
capita consumption went from 0.4 pounds to 0.9 pounds, catfish became the fifth most popular fish in the United States, and the fish is shipped to European and Far East markets.

From 1970 to 1995, catfish production in Mississippi, Arkansas, Alabama, and Louisiana, which raise 95 percent of the nation's catfish, grew from 5.7 million pounds to 447 million pounds, nearly an 80-fold increase. Catfish is high in protein, low in fat, full of vitamins and minerals.

Location: Belzoni is about 75 miles north of Jackson on U.S. 49W. **Contact:** World Catfish Festival Association, P.O. Box 385, Belzoni, MS 39038; Tel: (601)247-4838, or (800)408-4838, Fax: (601)247-4805.

While You're There: Visit the Catfish Capitol in an old railroad depot to see handcrafted exhibits and a video explaining various phases of catfish farming. King Cat, a 40-foot-long sculpted catfish, presides over a landscape of sculptures.

Biloxi

Shrimp Festival and Blessing of the Fleet

First weekend in May Seafood is the major industry in Biloxi, and the blessing of the fleet to ensure safe journeys and a bountiful harvest has been a tradition since 1929. Between 5,000 and 10,000 attend.

Saturday is festival day, with the major events the crowning of a shrimp king and queen, a mass at St. Michael's Roman Catholic Church (also known as the Church of the Fisherman), net-throwing and oyster-shucking contests, and a dinner of shrimp, corn on the cob, and potatoes, all boiled together to fuse the flavors. Other foods usually include mullet and Biloxi bacon and a dessert made by Slavic women of the area that's like a doughnut hole, with fillings of fruits and nuts, fried, then rolled in sugar. At night, bands play for dancing.

On Sunday, a helicopter drops a wreath in the water in honor of shrimpers who have died, and then as many as 80 decorated boats parade past the Blessing Boat, where the bishop bestows the blessing. The boats, with elaborate representations of mermaids and shrimps, are judged and cash prizes awarded.

Location: Biloxi is about midway between New Orleans and Mobile, a mile south of I-10. **Contact:** St. Michael's Church, P.O. Box 523, Biloxi, MS 39533; Tel: (601)435-5578.

While You're There: The Maritime & Seafood Industry Museum off U.S. 90 at the foot of the Ocean Springs Bridge has exhibits that tell the story of Biloxi's seafood industry.

Columbus

Possum Town Pigfest

Fourth weekend in September (Thursday through Saturday) The name of this festival is not as peculiar as it seems; Possum Town was the original name of Columbus. Spirus Roach built a tavern here around 1817, and the Indians thought he looked like a possum and named the town for him. But in 1821, the starchy cotton planters thought it was undignified to live in a place called Possum Town and renamed it Columbus. Then in 1983 along came some businessmen with a good P.R. sense and gave the new festival a historically correct title.

Columbus is in the center of a big agricultural area of soybeans, catfish, and cotton, but Mississippians like their pig, so this became a pigfest rather than a cotton fest. Sixty-five teams compete in barbecuing ribs, shoulders, and whole hogs for the official state championship, leading to the Memphis BBQ nationals. The general public, which numbers about 15,000, can't eat the contestants' dishes because of health regulations, but vendors have lots of barbecued foods as well as fried catfish, fried shrimp, gyros, shrimp po' boys, and the ever-present fair delicacies, funnel cake and ice cream.

Bands play blues, country, and rock; the barbecue teams put on skits; there are helicopter rides and children's games. Other events include a Pigs in Review Parade, a hog-calling contest, and a contest for Miss Possum Town Pig, won by the hairiest and all-round most ugly person; men usually win.

Such contests might suggest a lack of couth in Columbus, but in fact the city has more than 100 well-preserved antebellum homes; the campus of the Mississippi University for Women, which was the country's first state-supported college for women, founded in 1884; lush azalea gardens; and the historic Friendship Cemetery, where Civil War soldiers, both Union and Confederate, are buried. On April 25, 1886, local families decided to decorate the graves of all the war dead, on both sides, and from this gesture grew the national observance of Memorial Day.

Location: Columbus Fair Grounds, off I-82 East, 12 miles from the Alabama border. **Contact:** Possum Town Pigfest, Box 2099, Columbus, MS 39704; Tel: (601)328-4532.

See Also: Memphis in May Championship Barbecue Cooking Contest (Memphis, TN)

Forest

Mississippi Broiler Festival

First Saturday in June Back in the 1950s, a broiler producer wanted to show his gratitude to the town for its general support, so he threw a little party in the park. The picnic grew into a full-fledged broiler festival, celebrating an important industry here; Scott County is the state's top broiler producer, and Mississippi ranks fifth among states in broiler production.

The festival itself is a one-day affair, but Broiler Festival pageants are held Thursday and Friday. On Saturday, the local product, cooked in many ways, is for sale. You can taste battered deep-fried chicken, grilled chicken, chicken on a stick—a kebab with chunks of chicken, peppers, and onions. Steak and drinks like lemonade are also available.

A chicken-cooking contest is limited to about 20 cooks who prepare grilled, barbecued, and fried chicken. About 5,000 people attend to enjoy sports tournaments, a 5K race and one-mile fun run, pie-eating contests, a classic-car show, a talent show-down, professional entertainers, and a grand finale of fireworks.

Location: Forest is on U.S. 80, off I-20, about 50 miles east of Jackson. ☼ **Contact:** Forest Area Chamber of Commerce, P.O. Box 266, Forest, MS 39074; Tel: (601)469-4332.

See Also: Delmarva Chicken Festival (DE).

Gulfport

Highlands and Islands Scottish Games and Celtic Festival

First full weekend in October ☼ Aye, you'll find caber (a pole about the size of a telephone pole) tossing and stone and sheath tossing, and bonny Highland dancing and bagpiping, too. And you'll see Irish step dancing, and dressage exhibitions with what are called "warm-blooded" horses. These are thought to be of Celtic origin and are a mix of draft and Thoroughbred horses, giving them the elegance of Thoroughbreds and the sturdiness of draft horses.

The color of the festival comes from the kilt-wearing participants, and the flavor from the foods of the vendors: Scottish bridies, puff pastry with a ground-beef filling; meat pies, made with pie-crust pastry; Scotch eggs, hard-boiled eggs with a sausage batter; and haggis, the dish memorialized by Robert Burns in "To a Haggis," the poem in which he called haggis "Great chieftain o' the pudding race!" Haggis is made of "liver and lights"—sheep's organs, mixed with suet and oatmeal, cooked in a sheep's stomach.

The Mississippi coastal area was founded largely by the French and Spanish, but a good number of Scots and Irish made their way here, fleeing repression at home and the seizing of their property by English landowners. Scots and Celts are widely represented in the South, and Scottish games are held in numerous towns, so that people often make a circuit of the games.

The Gulfport games began in 1986, and a few thousand take part.

Location: Harrison County Fairgrounds, north of Gulfport and Long Beach, 6 miles north of I-10 at exit 28. ☼ **Contact:** Highlands and Islands Association of Celtic Gatherings Inc., Box 221, Gulfport, MS 39507; Tel: (601)864-5623.

Jackson

Trustmark Red Beans and Rice Celebration

A Saturday in October (no set date) ☼ No bands or dancing at this celebration; it's strictly a food festival, designed to raise money for the Mississippi Stew Pot, a shelter and soup kitchen.

The celebration is actually a cook-off, and what's cooked is red beans (kidney beans) and rice. Between 20 and 30 teams participate, all with their own recipes using different varieties of spices, sausage or beef or poke (a green) or whatever. Red beans and rice is considered a Louisiana dish, but the Louisiana flavor spills over into Mississippi.

Contestants each cook up sizable quantities of their own version of red beans and rice, and visitors get to sample the dish from each team. The cooking starts at 11 a.m., and the sampling lasts until it's all gone.

The cook-off is sponsored by one of Jackson's largest banks.

Location: Downtown Jackson, at One Jackson Place. Take the Pearl St. exit off I-55 and follow the signs to State St.; go right on State St. **Contact:** Events and Artists, P.O. Box 9201, Jackson, MS 39286; Tel: (601)362-5070.

North Carolina

Grifton Shad Festival

Second or third weekend in April (not Easter weekend)
About 20 hickory shad are caught in Grifton's Contentnea Creek for every American shad, and hickory shad are smaller and bonier than American shad, and not much fun to eat. When it was proposed to make hickory shad the theme of a festival, people hooted. But the mayor prevailed: "We don't have to *eat* shad," he said, "They don't eat azaleas at the Azalea Festival or mules at Mule Days."

Thus in 1971 the first Shad Festival was held as a one-day affair; now it stretches over a week and about 12,000 come to this town of 2,200 population. The festival's highlights—a parade, canoe race, street dance, art show, flea market, food—are on the weekend.

On Saturday, between 11 a.m. and 2 p.m., there's fried fish, fish stew, baked goods, and free bites of edible American shad. On Sunday, from noon on, there's a barbecue.

Eastern North Carolina barbecues are different from barbecues elsewhere; they are pork, not beef, and the barbecue sauce is based on vinegar and red pepper, not on tomato. People serve themselves, using long-handled forks to pick pieces off the pig as it's still over the coals. This is known as pig pickin'.

For the fish fry, herring fillets are generally used, and catfish or rockfish make up the stew. About 20 minutes before the stew is done, tomato soup is added, and then eggs are broken into the stew and cooked until the yokes are hard. The eggs are what make the fish stew *eastern* North Carolina stew.

Location: Grifton is off North Carolina 11, about 20 miles south of Greenville.
Contact: Grifton Shad Festival, P.O. Box 928, Grifton, NC 28530; Tel: (919)524-4934, or (919)524-4356.

See Also:: Shad Festival (Lambertville, NJ).

North Carolina Apple Festival

Labor Day weekend (Friday through Monday) ⊙ The people of Hendersonville began this festival in 1947 to celebrate springtime apple blossoms, but when they realized the trees could be ornery about blossoming at a specific time, they changed it to a harvest festival. If you like apples—lucky you.

You're now guaranteed plentiful fresh apples. This is the largest apple-growing county in North Carolina—65 percent of the state's apples are from Henderson County's 155 commercial orchards—and North Carolina is among the 10 largest apple-producing states. The most commonly grown apples here are the Red and Golden Delicious and the Rome.

On Friday and Saturday, early risers can fill up on apple pancakes, and through the weekend, the booths of local growers offer apple cake, apple fritters, caramel apples, cider, fried apple pie, and various other apple concoctions. The Ladies' Club bake sale is known for its apple specialties. And there are dozens of other food booths with everything from Greek and Chinese specialties to barbecued pork and hamburgers.

Contests spur competitive juices. Cooks have the Apple Recipe Contest, with an auction of the dishes after the judging. For kids, there's the Henderson County 4-H apple-decorating contest, and local growers compete in the apple-display contest.

Events of the weekend include tours to visit orchards, an apple-packing house, and roadside apple stands. There are exhibits of needle art, crafts, and antique cars; open house at the Western North Carolina Air Museum and the Henderson Depot for exhibits of model trains; concerts (great bluegrass); a carnival; and helicopter rides. Stamp collectors go for the apple festival postal cancellation; athletic types choose a 10K road race, a tennis tournament, or a bike tour. The festival winds down on Monday with the King Apple Parade, followed by a street dance. Attendance is 150,000 to 200,000.

Location: Along Main St. in Hendersonville, just off I-26 in western North Carolina, about 25 miles south of Asheville. ⊙ **Contact:** North Carolina Apple Festival, P.O. Box 886, Hendersonville, NC 28792; Tel: (704)697-4557.

While You're There: Connemara is a 240-acre goat farm where poet Carl Sandburg spent his last 22 years and his wife raised prize-winning goats. It's now part of the National Park Service and has hiking trails and guided tours of the house. On Little River Rd., 7 miles south of Hendersonville. Contact: (704)693-4178.

North Carolina Seafood Festival

First weekend in October (Friday through Sunday) ⊙ Seafood lovers—about 120,000 of them—travel from all over the country for this festival's fish. It's all here, from the mundane to the exotic. Try grilled mullet, deep-fried shark bites, conch stew, flounder sandwiches, and oysters on the half shell. Or sample burgers with a twist; they're made of crab, shrimp, or oyster. (There are boring beef burgers, too, if you're in that kind of mood.) Feel guilty about overeating? Don't. All the food stands are run by local nonprofit groups, who do good things with your money.

The festival began in 1987 because the locals wanted to show off their fishing industry; the city is a boatmaking center and the site of one of the two North Carolina State Ports (the other is Wilmington). The port becomes a sea-garden of colorful pennants on Sunday when boats are decorated for the blessing of the fleet.

There's a fishing tournament held off the local pier, and for youngsters, there's a kiddie fishing tournament. There are lots of activities for athletic types—softball, volleyball, basketball, and an 8K road race—and for the less athletically inclined, arts and crafts and the Miss Seafood Festival Pageant.

Pre-festival events include the King Neptune Ball, held the weekend before the festival to give Morehead City fishermen and others a chance to dress up and dance the night away.

Location: Between 4th and 9th Sts. on the waterfront in Morehead City, just across from the southern tip of the Outer Banks on U.S. 70. **Contact:** North Carolina Seafood Festival, P.O. Box 1812, Morehead City, NC 28557; Tel: (919)726-6273.

While You're There: Beaufort, separated from Morehead City only by a bridge, is a popular stop for boaters on the Intracoastal Waterway. Tours of historic Beaufort include a nineteenth-century apothecary shop and doctor's office and a typical early fisherman's cottage, plus the North Carolina Maritime Museum, 315 Front St., with ship models and exhibits of birds and fish.

Mount Airy

Sonker Festival

First Saturday in October An argument over the proper way to make sonkers led to this festival, which is small and cozy, about 400 people, because not many people know enough about sonkers to argue over them.

What's a sonker? It's a deep-dish pie that originated as a practical way to fix a treat using food on hand. Sonkers can be made with left-over biscuit dough or bread crumbs and whatever fruit is in the garden or, sometimes, sweet potatoes. Sonkers are a rarity in North Carolina other than in the remote mountains and hollows around Mount Airy, where the culture has been retained.

The festival began in 1984, and they still haven't agreed on the best sonker recipe, so you're on your own. Sample one of the many fruit sonkers. Be sure to have a sweet-potato sonker accompanied by "dip," which is not really a dip—it's a sauce made of milk, sugar, and vanilla and poured over the sonker.

As you sit back with a sonker and lemonade, listen to old-time string music, a blend of bluegrass, Irish, and Scottish music. And try some flatfoot dancing, a favorite mountain pastime.

Location: The Edwards-Franklin House, a 1789 plantation house on Haystack Rd., near the intersection of I-77 and North Carolina 89, about seven miles west of Mount Airy.

☼ **Contact:** Surry County Historical Society, 832 East Country Club Rd., Mount Airy, NC 27030; Tel: (910)786-8359.

While You're There: Mount Airy was the prototype for the town of Mayberry in the popular television program "The Andy Griffith Show." Griffith grew up here, and his former home is in the town's historic district. Remembering Mayberry with a visit to the district could enhance your enjoyment of sonkers.

Murfreesboro

North Carolina Watermelon Festival

First weekend in August (Wednesday through Saturday)

☼ Murfreesboro has an interesting history, but what festival-goers concentrate on is not history but eating and arguing, in a southern way, about whether the watermelon is a fruit or a vegetable.

Whichever, the festival serves as much of it as you can eat or drink: daiquiri-like watermelon drinks, watermelon ice cream, scoops of watermelon served in watermelons carved to look like baskets.

When you've had your fill of watermelon, try Carolina specialties like Carolina pulled-pork barbecue or a Carolina Burger, which natives eat topped with mustard, chili, cole slaw, and onions. Or sample blooming onions, huge Vidalia onions cut to look like chrysanthe-mums, deep-fried so the "petals" can be dipped in ranch, Cajun, or Thousand Island dressing. Or shrimp and lobster. Or hot fudge cakes.

The theme, despite all that other food, is unequivocally watermelon. There's a contest for the biggest watermelon, and the biggest grow up to 160 pounds. There are seed-spitting contests and watermelon-eating contests with contestants' hands tied behind their backs. A grand parade features the Watermelon Queen, watermelon floats, and local kids dressed as watermelon seeds.

The festival began in 1986 as a laid-back two-hour affair, but it now attracts some 20,000 visitors and has events like helicopter rides, a petting zoo, music and dancing every night, and fireworks on the last night.

Murfreesboro is a large watermelon distribution center, shipping watermelons all over the United States and Mexico. It got its rather odd name because the Murphy clan from New England settled in this area in the 1700s. They had changed their name to Murfree to celebrate their new-found religious freedom when they first arrived in the colonies and settled in the Boston area. The town was prosperous until 1820 when its shipping business died off because the river was too shallow for large ships. Most Murfrees moved to Tennessee to establish another Murfreesboro, and the ones who stayed behind are chiefly farmers.

Location: Murfreesboro, 20 miles south of the Virginia state line and 60 miles southwest of Norfolk, is at the intersection of U.S. 158 and U.S. 258. ☼ **Contact:** North Carolina Watermelon Festival, P.O. Box 3, Murfreesboro, NC 27855; Tel: (919)398-5922.

North Carolina Turkey Festival

Third full weekend in September (Thursday through Saturday) Turkey legs are a favorite dish of the South, but turkey producers still have a hard time persuading the rest of the country that turkey can be eaten on days other than Thanksgiving. This festival tries to dispel the notion that turkey is a one-day bird by providing all kinds of turkey dishes.

Turkey fare includes turkey sausage, turkey rolls, turkey with ham, smoked turkey, barbecued turkey, turkey hot dogs. And for traditionalists, there's a good old-fashioned turkey dinner with all the fixings.

There's also a turkey-cooking contest, where contestants have to prepare their offerings at the site. A recent winner was turkey lasagna.

Further festival events include a parade in which all the floats have a turkey theme, music and dancing after the big turkey dinner, sports events, and a concert by the Fort Bragg chorus and band (Fort Bragg is nearby).

North Carolina is America's number-one producer of turkeys, raising about 60 million of them, and Raeville is in the heart of turkey country. Raeville's other industries are textiles and cosmetics. When the festival began in 1983, the theme was a toss-up among the industries, but turkey seemed to lend itself to a festival better than the other industries. About 50,000 attend.

The wild turkeys that the Pilgrims and Indians ate at the first Thanksgiving were probably not the true ancestors of present-day cultivated turkeys in the United States. While wild turkeys were flying and gobbling all over North America, turkeys cultivated by the Aztecs in Mexico were taken back to the Old World by the Spanish. The turkey caught on fast with Europeans, was bred to be plumper, and came back to North America. These European commercial birds are supposedly the forefathers of today's commercial American turkeys.

Their name may have come about because Europeans thought they came from Turkey. Or the name may have come from the bird's call, which sounds sort of like "turk-turk."

Benjamin Franklin wanted to make the turkey our national bird instead of the eagle, which conjures up visions of a turkey on national seals. But he lost his campaign.

Location: Raeville is 23 miles west of Fayetteville on U.S. 401. Contact: North Carolina Turkey Festival, P.O. Box 1260, Raeford, NC 28376; Tel: (910)875-5929.

Ham & Yam Festival

Third weekend in April (Friday through Sunday) The name Ham & Yam Festival is misleading. Yams aren't even grown in the United States. But North Carolina produces more sweet potatoes, frequently confused with yams, than any other state (sometimes switching places with Louisiana). What's more, the state has the country's second highest hog inventory, behind Iowa. All this makes a ham and yam (sounds better than ham and sweet potato, the folks reasoned) festival just about mandatory.

Yams, grown largely in Africa, are white-fleshed members of the *Dioscorea* family. Sweet potatoes, which have yellow or orange flesh, belong to the *Ipomea* family, have about 35 varieties, and were discovered by Columbus. China, however, grows more sweet potatoes than any other country. Cherokees were cultivating sweet potatoes when settlers arrived in the Southeast, and the Spanish introduced them to Europe in the early sixteenth century. For some reason they became known as an aphrodisiac, and Henry VIII imported them from Spain and ate them in heavily spiced pies.

The 20,000 people who are more interested in eating at the festival than in learning about Henry VIII are not disappointed.

Johnston County's five local ham curers produce what are considered among the best hams in the country. Judge for yourself at the "Ham & Yam Supper" held at the local high school or the "Distinguished Hams Breakfast," a church breakfast that highlights country ham. Or wander among the more than 20 food vendors selling Carolina pulled-pork barbecue, hush puppies, fried sweet potatoes, and sweet-potato pie. Locals flock to the Kiwanis booth for ham biscuits.

For cooks, there's a Ham & Yam Cooking Contest, with cash prizes. For kids, there's "What's That Yam Thing," a children's sweet-potato-decorating contest.

The festival began in 1985 as a friendly competition between Smithfield, North Carolina, and Smithfield, Virginia, to see which town cured the best ham. A note here about Smithfield ham: The Virginia legislature decided a ham could only be called Smithfield if it's produced within Smithfield, Virginia. In fact, what makes a ham taste like a Smithfield ham is what the hog is fed—it must eat peanuts for part of its life—and how it's cured (rubbed with salt, among other steps in the process). Many hams of Virginia and the Carolinas and Kentucky are similar to Smithfield hams, but are often called country hams.

Anyway, there was this contest between the Smithfields of Virginia and North Carolina, and food and ham experts were brought in as judges. But after an eight-year winning streak for Smithfield, North Carolina, it apparently got depressing for the Virginia curers, and both the cured-ham contest and a festival in Smithfield, Virginia, ended.

The Smithfield, North Carolina, festival continues, with road races, 175 arts and crafts vendors, three stages for entertainment, agricultural exhibits, children's games, and a car show with a block-long display of antique cars. On Saturday night, there's a street dance with North Carolina "beach" music and a top-40 band in the center of historic downtown Smithfield.

Smithfield and Johnson County's points of pride are: 1) the county has the largest number of farms of any county in the state, and 2) Ava Gardner was born just outside Smithfield and is buried in a local graveyard. The Ava Gardner Museum tells the story of her life, from childhood up through movie stardom.

Location: Smithfield is about 25 miles southeast of Raleigh, a mile west of I-95 at exit 95.   **Contact:** Ham & Yam Festival, P.O. Box 761, Smithfield, NC 27577; Tel: (919)934-0887.

See Also: Sweet Potato Festival (Tuskegee, AL).

Ramp Convention

First Sunday in May ⬚ Waynesville's first official ramp-eating gathering was held in the late 1920s, then became a sporadic event, and has been held annually since 1968. The convention began when a band of mountaineers gathered to talk politics, listen to mountain hoedown music, dig ramps, and eat ramps to get rid of winter miseries and wash off spring colds.

What's a ramp?

It's *Alium tricoccum,* a wild vegetable that grows on shady slopes of Appalachia, is related to the onion but smells to high heaven, has an "assertive" flavor, and is supposed to have medicinal qualities. Old timers say it's the only preventative for a common cold.

The convention's ramp dinner should stave off colds for months. On the menu: ramp meatloaf, raw ramps, boiled ramps, sautéed ramps, scrambled eggs with ramps, country ham, barbecued chicken, buttermilk, and corn bread. Some bland stuff is needed as a sop.

A ramp-eating contest is held, and the record stands at 94 ramps eaten in 10 minutes.

Craftsmen display and sell their work, string bands and cloggers provide entertainment, and usually state and national representatives and sometimes the governor stop by to shake hands, do a little stumping, and eat.

Location: American Legion Field in Waynesville, 25 miles west of Asheville, off I-40. ⬚ **Contact:** Haywood County Tourism Development Authority, P.O. Box 1079, Maggie Valley, NC 28751; Tel: (704)926-5425, or (800)334-9036; Fax: (704)926-5427.

South Carolina

South Carolina Peach Festival

Eleven days, beginning second weekend in June ❁ Cotton was once the major crop in South Carolina, but now peaches are, and the state is the second largest grower of peaches in the United States, behind California. Besides that, a somewhat controversial water tank called a Peachoid looms over Gaffney. And besides *that,* a peach festival in Gaffney has been happening since 1947 and is attended by about 150,000 people. So you might say Gaffney is a peach of a place.

Festival visitors get to eat fresh peaches that are kept on ice, so they're almost frozen—refreshing on a warm June day. There are also peach pies and peach slushes—made with fresh peaches, ice, and sugar—and the usual festival foods.

A peach-dessert contest brings out numerous variations of pies and cobblers. Local growers also compete, submitting their peaches to a peach-eating panel of judges that determines the best-flavored and biggest peaches.

In its many years, the festival has accrued a host of activities. There are sports events—a bicycle race called the Tour de Pèche, football, softball, and golf tournaments. There are concerts of country and contemporary music, a swimsuit competition, a show of antique cars, a Little Miss South Carolina Peach Festival Pageant, a Giant Peach Festival Parade, and fireworks.

Location: Lake Wylie in Gaffney, about 30 miles northeast of Greenville, at the intersection of I-85 and I-26. ❁ **Contact:** Gaffney Chamber of Commerce, 225 S. Limestone Street, Gaffney, SC 29340; Tel: (864)489-5721, or (864)489-1353.

While You're There: Take a good look at the Peachoid, a water storage tank built in 1981 by the Board of Public Works in the shape of a peach. Its orangey color required 50 gallons of paint in 20 different colors. It took five months to design and mold the steel. After the peach shape was formed, a stem 12 feet long and 18 inches in diameter was added, and later a 60-by-16-foot leaf weighing 7 tons was added. It's visible (very) from

I-85, and probably the most photographed town water tank in the United States. But does it make everybody happy? No. Some people in Gaffney don't think the Peachoid looks that much like a peach.

Okra Strut

Last weekend in September (Friday and Saturday) ⊛ In 1974, the Irmo Women's Club decided Irmo needed a public library, so instead of holding a book sale or something else literary to raise funds they held the Okra Strut. Why not? Okra is grown here, and there's a song called "Okra Strut." Proceeds from the strut built the library, and now the strut's revenues are helping fund its expansion.

About 80,000 people come to the wingding. Quite a few actually eat okra. When the strut started getting big, the Women's Club turned it over to the town, but the club still has a booth where it sells fried okra in a cornmeal batter. Very popular. Other okra dishes usually available are pickled okra and a spicy Indian version of batter-coated fried okra. Okra has been known in India for many years.

The strut also offers more traditional fair food—hot dogs, corn dogs, pizza. But the gluey okra is center stage, figuring in okra-eating contests, which are truly gross, and a cooking contest. For the eating matches, okra is boiled, then put in the freezer so it gets "cold and slimy," as a strut official put it. The contestants are allowed to wash this down with Coca-Cola. A competition on Friday night is for police officers, and there are two contests on Saturday, one for adults, one for children. The law people have to eat two pounds, the civilians just one pound. Prizes are awarded.

In the Okra Delight Cooking Contest, contestants submit a recipe and a dish in one of four categories—salad, vegetable, main entree, hors d'oeuvre. The public can't sample the winning dishes, but recipes are usually published in local newspapers.

There are contests for the longest okra pod and the tallest plant. And there's a Miss Irmo Pageant and competitions for Little Miss Okras and Little Mister Okras. The Misses and Misters get to ride in the parade, while the president of the Women's Club and the daughter of the owners of the Garden Center, which sponsors the okra-growing contest, are also in the parade, dressed as okra pods.

Other events include arts and crafts, children's amusements, and two bands playing music for dancing. And Okra Man walks around the festival grounds dressed all in green, with an okra belt and necklace.

Location: Irmo is about six miles northwest of Columbia, off I-26 at the Irmo exit.
⊛ **Contact:** Okra Strut Commission, Irmo, SC 29063; Tel: (803)781-9878.

See Also: Okrafest (Checota, OK).

McClellanville

Lowcountry Shrimp Festival

First Saturday in May ☼ McClellanville is a village of a few hundred on the intracoastal waterway, and the industry here is shrimp. So loosen your belt.

The festival began in the late 1980s as a fundraiser for a school, Rutledge Academy, and it combines food and fun events with the color and ritual of a Blessing of the Fleet.

Shrimp dinners—boiled or fried shrimp, with hush puppies and cole slaw—are the main attraction; you can also fill up on clam chowder and fish stew, and if you wonder how it's done, there's a village cookbook of seafood recipes. Bagpipes play, there's country music, dancing, and there are arts and crafts displays and demonstrations by wood carvers and other crafters.

On Sunday, the shrimp boats, decorated from stem to stern, file past the blessing boat, where a priest dispenses benedictions. Festival-goers may ride on the shrimp boats during the parade.

Location: McClellanville is about 30 miles north of Charleston off U.S. 17. ☼ **Contact:** Archibald Rutledge Academy, P.O. Box 520, McClellanville, SC 29458; Tel: (803)887-3323.

While You're There: Visit the two large seafood markets in McClellanville for genuine local color.

Pageland

Pageland Watermelon Festival

Weekend closest to July 21 ☼ This isn't the nation's oldest watermelon festival, but it's been around since 1951, and in that time it's developed some pretty peculiar features. For instance:

The Melon Yellow Lawn Tractor Race, in which lawn-mower drivers have to complete 15 laps neither too fast nor too pokily, making two pit stops, one to drink a cup of Melon Yellow juice, and the other to eat a slice of melon. (Among the melons grown here are a variety with yellow flesh.)

The Melon Mile Relay Race, in which runners carry and hand off 25-pound watermelons instead of batons.

There are also contests for watermelon eating, watermelon-seed spitting, and watermelon carving.

About 75,000 people show up for this watermelon wackiness. They have their choice of watermelon drinks, pops, ice cream, and pickled watermelon rind, and four or five varieties of watermelon by the slice. Watermelons are a big crop in the area, running neck and neck with soybeans.

There is also a range of international food at the festival. Those who prefer to wear watermelons can find sweatshirts and T-shirts with painted watermelons in addition to watermelon necklaces and bracelets, or they can get their faces painted with watermelons.

A mammoth parade with about 400 units gets the festival rolling; other events include a Miss Watermelon World Pageant, carnival rides, an antique-car show, and arts and crafts. And there's that lawn-tractor race. These riding mowers can be rented models or rebuilt junk. The race tends to be suspenseful. One year, because his jalopy of a mower kept throwing oil, a driver had to keep leaning forward to pour oil in the engine; he was about to win when the contraption exploded on the last lap. This is not unusual.

Location: Farmers' Market on U.S. 601, just north of Pageland, about 50 miles northeast of Columbia. ⊛ **Contact:** Pageland Watermelon Festival, Rt. 1, Box 72, Mt. Croghan, SC 29727; Tel: (803)672-5257.

Salley

Chitlin Strut

Saturday after Thanksgiving ⊛ Chitlins are formally called chitterlings, but since the small intestines of pigs are not the most formal of foods, we'll stick with chitlins. Most chitlin recipes call for soaking them in running water and then removing all fat, which takes from 45 minutes to 2 hours for 10 pounds, and then boiling them for about 3 hours.

That's what they do at the strut in the World Chitlin Capital, and they also coat the chitlins in egg and crumbs and fry them. People scarf up more than 10,000 pounds of these things along with barbecued pork and chicken and roasted corn.

Salley has a population of about 500, and 40,000 to 60,000 come to the strut, such is the allure of chitlins. Of course, Salley also puts on a big country-music show, a dance, a parade (some people dress like pigs), a carnival, an arts and crafts show, and children's rides. And there's a hog-calling contest.

This strut is no joke. It began in 1966 because the town needed money for Christmas decorations. That first venture, with more than a thousand people coming and eating 600 pounds of chitlins, was such a success that it kept going and has funded, besides street decorations, a new fire truck—though the retired 1929 Buick still sparkles in the chitlin parade. Back in 1971, by the way, an official representative from the White House rode in the parade in a 1901 Oldsmobile.

Salley got its name because it was founded by Captain Dempsey Hammond Salley, who shoveled the first dirt from the roadbed upon which the first railroad train rode when it came to town on December 24, 1887.

Location: Salley is on South Carolina 394 and 39, about 35 miles south of Columbia. ⊛ **Contact:** Town of Salley, 161 Railroad Ave., North P.O. Box 484, Salley, SC 29137; Tel: (803)258-3485.

St. George

World Grits Festival

Weekend in April, depending on when Easter and festival in nearby town are (Friday through Sunday) ☼ This very Southern festival in the Grits Capital of the World is distinctive for several reasons. Here are a few:

Grits. Grits for breakfast, dinner, and supper. Grits, grits, grits.

Grown men and women rolling in mounds of wet grits.

Children and adults eating grits as fast as possible, with their choice of topping. Requests have included butter and margarine (normal enough), catsup, honey, peanut butter, Cheez Whiz, milk and sugar, grated cheese.

St. George's grits festival and its claim to the grits-capital title came about in 1985 when John Walters, owner of the local Piggly Wiggly, noticed the great quantity of grits he was selling. Suppliers confirmed that more grits are sold in the coastal plains of South Carolina than anyplace else in the world. Consumption in St. George itself is pushed up by six nearby religious campgrounds that hold annual "camp meetings" where there's always a pot of grits cooking at each cabin, and no one who comes by is turned away.

About 50,000 attend the festival to eat grits with eggs and bacon, ham, or sausage; with country-fried steak, fried chicken, or fried fish; with red-eye gravy and tomato gravy. Tomato gravy is created by frying bacon and onions, removing the bacon and crumbling it, then putting it back in the bacon fat with tomatoes.

The Rolling in the Grits Contest is one of those things that has to be seen. About 400 pounds of instant grits are put in a plastic swimming pool and wet down, and then stirred with a boat paddle. The contestants, who prefer knit sweatsuits because they're so absorbent, climb in and roll around. In ten seconds, they climb out and are weighed, and the person who weighs in with the most grits adhering is the winner. One year, the winner emerged weighing 27 pounds more than when she entered the pool.

Recipe contests tend to be an off-and-on thing. For possible future contests, Nell Bennett, the local doyenne of grits cooking, offered the advice that long cooking and stirring are the secret to good grits.

Celebrities at this grits gala are Wee Baby Grits, Baby Grits, Wee Miss Grits, Teen Miss Grits, Miss Grits, Wee Master Grits, Master Grits. They get to ride in a parade with dignitaries, firemen, and politicians.

The grits in St. George are made from dried yellow or white corn; demonstrations of grits grinding are given, and corn kernels are ground and sold. Strictly speaking, grits are any ground grain, but it has come to mean ground hominy. Hominy, which colonists picked up from Native Americans, is dried corn from which the hull and germ have been removed, usually by soaking in lye. The word is derived from the Algonquin *tackhummin,* meaning corn without skin. Southerners are generally willing to eat grits for any meal of the day, seven days a week.

Location: Downtown St. George, on I-95, 45 miles west of Charleston. ☼
Contact: World Grits Festival, P.O. Box 787, St. George, SC 29477; Tel: (803)563-3255.

Walterboro

Colleton County Rice Festival

Last full weekend in April (Friday through Sunday) ☼ The World's Largest Pot of Rice is cooked in a huge vat by the local Ruritan Club for this festival and sold by the cup. It's hard to prove the "world's-largest" claim, because the Ruritans don't know how much rice goes in the pot, but they do know that 500 pounds of rice are cooked for the festival. Some of it, however, goes in other dishes, like Hoppin' John, the southern good-luck dish.

Here Hoppin' John is made of rice, black-eyed peas, onions, and spices; traditional recipes also call for ham or salt pork. Other foods available are sausage pilaf, red rice (tomatoes make the red), ostrich burgers from locally raised birds, fried sweet potatoes, custom-cooked potatoes, funnel cake, elephant ears, apple dumplings, fried fish.

A cook-off is held, requiring at least one cup of rice in each recipe in five categories—dessert, salad, main dish with meat, rice with vegetables, most original. The public, on payment of a dollar, gets to judge, and the winner gets a ribbon with a rosette.

Attendance at this festival, which started in 1976, is 60,000, so there must be something besides rice. There is: fireworks, a parade, arts and crafts, street dances, road races, a softball tournament, a Civil War camp, a police-dog show, children's and adults' dog shows, cloggers, choruses, and more.

Rice was once a major crop in South Carolina, and the coastal area in the eighteenth- and nineteenth-centuries had more than 70,000 acres of intertidal land diked and built to grow rice. It's a labor-intensive crop, and it peaked about 1850 just as slave labor became unavailable. The rice that's still grown here is used mainly to feed wildlife and as a novelty (for throwing at weddings). Arkansas is now the country's major grower.

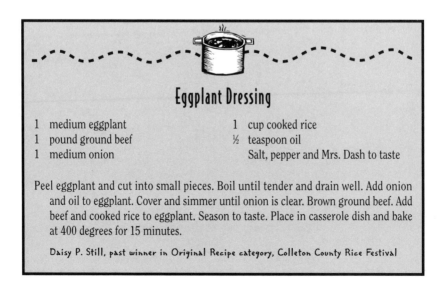

Eggplant Dressing

1 medium eggplant	1 cup cooked rice
1 pound ground beef	½ teaspoon oil
1 medium onion	Salt, pepper and Mrs. Dash to taste

Peel eggplant and cut into small pieces. Boil until tender and drain well. Add onion and oil to eggplant. Cover and simmer until onion is clear. Brown ground beef. Add beef and cooked rice to eggplant. Season to taste. Place in casserole dish and bake at 400 degrees for 15 minutes.

Daisy P. Still, past winner in Original Recipe category, Colleton County Rice Festival

Walterboro was founded because the rice growers on the coastal plantations were dying of malaria. Walterboro is inland and on higher ground, thus it didn't have the coast's malaria-bearing mosquitoes.

Location: Walterboro, 35 miles west of Charleston, is two miles east of I-95 on U.S. 17. ☼ **Contact:** Colleton County Rice Festival, Old Jail, 239 N. Jeffries Blvd., Walterboro, SC 29488; Tel: (803)549-1079.

While You're There: The Museum of Walterboro has exhibits on the coastal plantations and the history of rice-growing. Later, you might want to try a chicken-bog dinner. It's served Sunday on the banks of the Edisto River, and while it's intended for participants in the road races, anyone can attend. The broth from a stewed chicken is used to cook rice pilaf, and pieces of chicken are added: that's chicken bog.

See Also: International Rice Festival (Crowley, LA).

Tennessee

Moon Pie Games and Country Fair

Third Saturday in June ⦿ A town with the improbable name of Bell Buckle boasts an improbable festival drawing an improbable 80,000 people.

Actually, when you know the Moon Pie history, it's not so improbable. In the South, a Moon Pie with Royal Crown Cola is called the "working-class dessert," because during the Depression two nickels would buy a Moon Pie and an RC. Moon Pies remain one of those Southern passions that baffle people from other areas. They aren't pies; they are four-inch-diameter chocolate-covered graham-cracker-type cookies with marshmallow in the middle. Variations have banana, vanilla, and caramel icings. The Moon Pie's cellophane wrapping calls it "The Original Marshmallow Sandwich."

It's a Tennessee product. The Chattanooga Bakery in Chattanooga registered the Moon Pie trademark in 1919 and has been making Moon Pies ever since. The bakery now bakes about 75 million Moon Pies a year and nothing else. In a royalty agreement with Japan, Moon Pies are made there too, but are called Massi (meaning marshmallow) Pies because the moon is sacred to the Japanese.

Moon Pies abound at the festival. There's the World's Largest Moon Pie, 3 feet in diameter, weighing 40 pounds, specially created by the Chattanooga Bakery. You can get regular-sized Moon Pies in all four flavors, or desserts made with Moon Pies. Favorites are Moon Pies covered with whipped cream, crumbled nuts, and chocolate syrup, and Moon Pies heated and topped with ice cream. RC-and-ice-cream floats go along with the Moon Pies. Other standard festival food—funnel cakes, burgers, dogs—is also available.

A highlight is the Moon Pie–RC Recipe Competition. Past winners have created RC cake, RC punch, and Moon Pie pie.

The Moon Pie Games, spoofing the Olympic games, include boxing matches, in which boxers wrap boxes of Moon Pies, field hockey played with Moon Pie pucks, and Moon Pie throwing.

In the country-fair part of the day, there are more than 100 art and crafts booths, and ribbons are awarded for the best cakes, pies, canned goods, and produce.

Bell Buckle has a population of 453, many of them artists. In 1886, W. R. Webb, considered the father of preparatory schools in the South, opened the Webb School here that produced 10 Rhodes scholars and three state governors; it still exists.

There are different versions of where the town's name came from. The most prevalent version is that a cow strayed onto the property of an Indian who killed it and then fixed the cow's bell on a tree with a buckle as a warning to settlers to keep their cows home.

Location: Bell Buckle is about 40 miles south of Nashville, 7 miles west of I-24 on Tennessee 82. **Contact:** Moon Pie Games, 14 Railroad Sq., Bell Buckle, TN 37020; Tel: (615)389-9371.

See Also: Mardi Gras (Mobile, AL).

Covington

Tipton County Barbecue Festival

Third weekend in July (Thursday through Sunday) Tipton County claims that this barbecue, which began in 1973 as part of the county's sesquicentennial celebration, is the World's Oldest Barbecue Cooking Contest. Five teams competed in the '73 event, and now about 40 teams compete in three categories: whole hog, shoulders, and ribs.

The sweet scent of sizzling pork works up appetites, but the yearning goes unsatisfied unless the barbecuers invite you into their booth for a taste. On the other hand, especially in election years, politicians often compete, and they generally offer a sampling to anybody old enough to vote.

The winner goes on to compete in the Memphis in May World Championship Barbecue Cooking Contest, that very big pig cook-off. The winner is also entered in the lottery to win admission to the Jack Daniels Invitational Barbecue in Lynchburg, Tennessee, in October.

Besides the pig barbecuing at the festival, there's an "Anything But" cooking contest, which means anything but pork. Entries have included quail, dove, alligator, anything you can imagine. Again, samples are only by invitation.

This is a backwoodsy partying kind of competition, attended by about 15,000. There's other fun besides watching pigs and doves cook: bands play country and gospel music, there are truck and four-wheeler pulls and a demolition derby.

And food vendors are on hand if visitors get really hungry and the barbecue contestants take no pity.

Location: Covington is about 40 miles north of Memphis on U.S. 51. **Contact:** Tipton County Barbecue Festival, P.O. Box 768, Covington, TN 38019; Tel: (901)476-9613.

See Also: Memphis in May World Championship Barbecue Cooking Contest (Memphis, TN) and Jack Daniels Invitational Barbecue (Lynchburg, TN).

Gainesboro

Tennessee Annual Poke Sallet Festival

Second weekend in May (Thursday through Saturday) ⊛
In late April and early May, residents of Gainesboro start preparing for their festival by combing the mountainsides with 35-gallon trash bags. They're searching for poke sallet, a vegetable that grows wild in meadows. Its stalk and berries are poisonous but its leaves taste like turnip greens or spinach if they're cooked right. During the Depression many families depended on poke sallet for their survival, but poke is now considered something of a delicacy—at least by the people in the hilly hamlets around Gainesboro.

Proper cooking means boiling them, then discarding the juice and reboiling them. After boiling, the poke is usually cooked in grease, sometimes with eggs added. It tastes a lot better than it sounds; the food booths sell poke sallet as fast as they can cook it. For a real mountain dinner, get the poke sallet plate with dried beans and hoecakes (corn bread cooked like a pancake on a hoe over hot coals).

If poke sallet isn't your thing, there are burgers, dogs, and standard festival fare, too.

Among the festival highlights are a poke-sallet-eating contest—a prize goes to the person who eats the most in three minutes, not a pretty sight—and an outhouse race with privies on wheels racing to the finish line at the town's only stop light. Other attractions are arts and crafts, country and bluegrass music, a crosscut-sawing contest, an antique tractor show, a Miss Poke Sallet beauty pageant, a golf tournament, a terrapin race, and a quilt show.

The history of the word poke, sometimes called pokeweed, is somewhat hazy. Possibly the word originated because the greens were gathered in brown paper bags called pokes. Or poke may be an Algonquin Indian word. Sallet has Elizabethan origins as the word for salad.

The festival began in 1977 when some locals, who were sitting outside the courthouse whittling, chewing, and spitting, decided a poke sallet festival could make a nice get-together for the town's 1,000 residents and attract visitors, too. Sure enough. The festival brings together 5,000 people, and the entire county has a population of only 10,000.

Location: Gainesboro is 80 miles east of Nashville, 15 miles north of I-40 on Tennessee 56. ⊛ Contact: Jackson County Rescue Squad, P.O. Box 103, Gainesboro, TN; Tel: (615)268-3447.

Humboldt

West Tennessee Strawberry Festival

First full week in May (Monday through Saturday) ⊛ "The strawberry will be glorified by the celebration," a local newspaper wrote in 1934. That was the beginning of this festival that has been held ever since (except during World War II), and is now one of the oldest festivals in the Southeast, drawing more than 100,000 people and still glorifying the strawberry. This was once a major commercial strawberry-growing area. There's less commercial growing now, but there are pick-your-own farms, and, weather permitting, at least some of the berries at the festival are local.

One way the strawberry is glorified is with the World's Largest Strawberry Shortcake. Eating it is part of the opening ceremonies. They don't know for sure this is the world's biggest shortcake, but it's big—a lot of individual shortcakes (real biscuit shortcake, not sponge cake or some such impostor) in a ten-foot by eight-foot form. It feeds 500 to 600.

During the festival, strawberry pies, sundaes, and shortcake are sold, and food vendors sell usual fair food—Italian sausages, hot dogs, and fiddlesticks (ice cream on a stick). Local cooks compete in a recipe contest, and, while they make their share of shortcakes, they also come up with odder entries like strawberry pizza and chocolate-dipped strawberries that look like mice. As many as 40 or 50 people enter their strawberry concoctions, which can be sampled after the judging.

Other events include two parades with lavish strawberry-theme floats, a pet parade, an arts and crafts show, 5K and 10K runs, a Tennessee Walking Horse Show that is the kick-off show for the circuit, plus music and dancing. A queen in a red robe reigns over festivities with a court that includes tots and teenagers.

Location: Humboldt is 85 miles northwest of Memphis on U.S. 79. **Contact:** Humboldt Chamber of Commerce, 1200 Main St., Humboldt, TN 38343; Tel: (901)784-1842, Fax: (901)784-1573.

While You're There: The Strawberry Festival Historical Museum on the second floor of the renovated Humboldt City Hall building holds artifacts from the festival's and the community's early days.

See Also: California Strawberry Festival (Oxnard, CA).

Lynchburg

Jack Daniels Invitational Barbecue

Last Saturday in October While there are events that aren't strictly related to barbecues at this barbecue, cook-offs are the main thing. Thirty-five teams from around the world, which must each have won a championship elsewhere to enter, arrive on Friday and immediately start cooking. Judging is at noon Saturday, and after the judging, free samples are available for festival goers. Attendance tops 30,000.

The categories for contestants are pork—whole hog, shoulder, rib; poultry; beef brisket; barbecue sauce. The sauce can contain anything, but if the team wants to win, it will use Jack Daniels whiskey as one ingredient.

The winning sauce one year contained 22 ingredients, including pureed peaches, garlic, catsup, and Jack Daniels.

Those who get hungry smelling the meat as it cooks can assuage their hunger with vendors' food: barbecued pork, ribs, and chicken, roasted corn on the cob, and fried pies and other desserts.

Fun events include greased-pig contests, an "old country dog" contest for the ugliest dog, clog dancers, and musical entertainment.

Location: Town square, Lynchburg, 13 miles northeast of Fayetteville on Tennessee 55. **Contact:** Chamber of Commerce and Welcome Center, P.O. Box 421, Lynchburg, TN 37352; Tel: (615)759-4111.

While You're There: The Jack Daniels Distillery offers tours daily.

Memphis

Memphis in May World Championship Barbecue Cooking Contest

Third week in May (Thursday through Saturday) The barbecue contest, an event that fills most of Memphis with the tangy aroma of barbecued pork, is actually part of the Memphis in May International Festival, which lasts most of the month of May. But for BBQ aficionados, the contest days are the time to be in Memphis.

Carrying out the international theme, there are 250 teams from around the world competing for their share of the $25,000 purse. This is an all-pork barbecue, with contestants cooking 30 tons of whole hogs, shoulders, and ribs, using individually designed cookers and secret sauce recipes. Sauces are judged in the categories hot, sweet, tangy, thick, and thin.

After the judging, the drooling spectators—about 30,000 of them—are allowed to sample the entries, or they can buy barbecued tidbits from vendors who are often former contestants. Since the International Festival honors a different country each year, the traditional foods of that country are also available. And standard fair food—sausage on a stick, corn dogs, funnel cakes—are sold.

The BBQ team members are not just single-minded cooks; they entertain and cook with showmanship, and their booths are fancifully decorated. The weekend also features a hog-calling contest, a Miss Piggy contest, music, and chefs demonstrating cooking techniques.

Location: Tom Lee Park on the banks of the Mississippi River, Memphis. **Contact:** Memphis in May International Festival, 249 Wagner Pl., Ste. 220, Memphis, TN 38103; Tel: (901)525-4611, Fax: (901)525-4686.

Norris

Fall Festival Weekend

Second weekend in October This celebration of mountain folkways is held at the Museum of Appalachia, a 70-acre village and working farm, with 35 log buildings containing frontier artifacts. It's a perfect background for the many demonstrations: the crafts of soap-making, tinsmithing, blacksmithing, barrel-making, quilting; and the arts of banjo picking, fiddling, clog dancing, and playing the Jew's harp.

Foods are authentic mountain fare. Visitors may watch demonstrations of preparing these Appalachian specialties and then sample them: apple butter; sorghum molasses; sassafras tea, ground from the sassafras root and originally used as a spring tonic or medicinal drink but now more common as an herbal tea; dried apples. There are also home-baked country ham and biscuits, sausage and biscuits, fried country ham, fried pies, funnel cake, pinto beans.

Norris was founded by the Tennessee Valley Authority at the time the Norris Dam was built. The town and dam are named for Nebraska Senator George W. Norris, co-sponsor of the bill that created the TVA.

Location: Museum of Appalachia, 1 mile east of I-75 on Tennessee 61, 16 miles north of Knoxville. **Contact:** Museum of Appalachia, P.O. Box 0318, Norris, TN 37828; Tel: (423)494-7680.

While You're There: Don't miss the Appalachian Hall of Fame on the museum grounds. It contains a miscellany of belongings of famous and/or colorful people from the region.

See Also: Sassafras Tea Festival (Vernon, IN) and Sorghum Festival (Blairsville, GA).

Paris

World's Biggest Fish Fry

Last full week in April (Monday through Saturday) It seems strange, but this fish fry began in 1938 as Mule Day. On the first Monday in April, farmers came to town to shop, palaver, and trade mules and farm products. By the 1950s, the tractor was taking the place of the mule, and the Chamber of Commerce looked for a Mule Day replacement and came up with a one-day fish fry in 1953. It kept growing, and in 1961 the Jaycees took it over and served 1,600 pounds of catfish. Now they fry up better than 10,000 pounds, and crowds of 100,000 or so come to Paris, population 9,000.

The main entree of the fish fry is the all-you-can-eat catfish dinner. A small sum buys deep-fried catfish, hush puppies, French fries, cole slaw, white beans, and a drink.

There's lots happening during the week—five beauty pageants, a two-hour parade and a small fry parade, a carnival, rodeos, square dancing, a fishing rodeo with prizes for the biggest crappie and catfish caught in nearby Kentucky Lake, and a bed-race derby through downtown.

Location: Henry County Fairgrounds, Paris, on U.S. 641 in northwest Tennessee, 10 miles south of the Kentucky border. **Contact:** Henry County Chamber of Commerce, 2508 E. Wood St., P.O. Box 8, Paris, TN 38242; Tel: (901)642-3431.

Lauderdale County Tomato Festival

Weekend after Fourth of July (Thursday through Saturday) ❁ Located in the Mississippi River valley, Lauderdale County has wonderfully rich soil, and every crop grown in the state can be found in Lauderdale. But what the county is especially proud of is its tomatoes. More than a dozen varieties are grown; they are all referred to as Ripley tomatoes, and, according to the county agricultural extension leader, they are the best in the state, even though eastern Tennessee has more tomato acreage.

At the festival, held during the peak of the tomato season, tomatoes star in everything from appetizers to desserts: salsas, tomato salads, tomato fritters, fried green tomatoes, and green-tomato pie, which tastes sort of like a tart apple pie. There's also a tomato-tasting booth, where different varieties—Pik Rite, Pik Red, Mountain Pride, Mountain Spring, Solar Set, Sunrise, and on and on—can be sampled. Vendors sell everything from soul-food greens to Greek souvlaki to fruit kebabs.

A barbecue cook-off, which requires that the sauce be tomato-based, has categories for pork shoulders, pork ribs, and "anything but." In the "anything but" division, contestants have entered chicken and frogs' legs and mysterious somethings that you have to guess at.

Tomato growers also have contests—for best-tasting, oddest-shape, and largest tomatoes. And home canners enter their products in the exhibit of canned tomatoes.

This down-home celebration began in 1983 and attracts about 7,000 people who, if they didn't already know, certainly find out how important the tomato is to Ripley. There's a local cannery (one of two in the state), and, depending on the canning schedule, people with bumper crops can can them at the cannery, with employees guiding them through the steps.

This is a non-alcoholic fair, so you'll have to walk down the street to get . . . see below.

Location: South Main St. in Ripley, 50 miles north of Memphis, just off U.S. 51. ❁ **Contact:** Lauderdale County Chamber of Commerce, 103 East Jackson, Ripley, TN 38063; Tel: (901) 635-9541.

While You're There: A must! Lauderdale Cellars, 196 S. Washington St., a block or so from the fair, makes tomato wine. It's a white wine, called Tomate Blanche. Winemaker Roy Crowder, Jr. says the wine is a "strange product. You love the heck out of it or you can't stand it. Nothing else is comparable." The winery is open for tours and tastings, and Dr. Crowder also makes blueberry and pear wine, and in 1996 he started making—you won't believe this—grape wine. Crazy.

See Also: Tomato Fest (Jacksonville, TX).

Virginia

Chincoteague

Chincoteague Oyster Festival

Saturday of Columbus Day weekend ❀ Only 2,250 people can get tickets to this banquet of bivalves, so a lot of people buy them a year in advance. The festival has been a tradition since 1972; family reunions are planned around it. For some, because this is an all-you-can-eat affair, it becomes a Rabelaisian gorge-out; more genteel souls bring along elaborate table settings—candelabra, linen tablecloths, fine china, champagne and crystal to drink it from, and their own tables and chairs.

The oysters come in almost every guise: fried, steamed, in fritters, on the half shell, sometimes in stew, and as "angels on horseback" (wrapped in bacon and broiled). The menu, once solely oysters, has been expanded to include clam chowder, steamed hard-shell crabs, potato salad, cole slaw, and clam fritters.

The eating goes on from about 10 a.m. to 5 p.m. as shells pile up and up and up. A recent tally showed consumption of 144 gallons of shucked oysters and 225 bushels of oysters in the shell plus 60 bushels of steamed crabs, 70 gallons of clam chowder. . . . A band plays a mix of music all day, but that's it for frivolous events. People are here to eat; they are *serious* eaters.

Chincoteague oysters look like other eastern shore oysters but they have a saltier taste because Chincoteague Bay, from whence they come, has a high salt content. There are oyster connoisseurs who think Chincoteagues are as good as they come.

Location: Maddox Family Campground, Chincoteague, a few miles east of U.S. 13 on the eastern shore of the Delmarva Peninsula. ❀ **Contact:** Chincoteague Chamber of Commerce, Chincoteague, VA 23336; Tel: (804)336-6161.

See Also: St. Mary's County Oyster Festival (Leonardtown, MD).

Virginia Pork Festival

Second Wednesday in June More than 20 tons of pork are served in about 30 different dishes at this festival that dates back to 1974 and was started to promote what was Virginia's top product. The state is down on the pig list now, about eighth in the state rankings of pork producers, but Virginians still eat a lot of pork. They even like chitlins; the festival has four chitlin booths. Other favorites are country fried ham and red-eye gravy (ham drippings cooked with water and hot coffee to make red-eye beads), grilled loin chops, pork yummy (a pork and cheese sandwich), pork kebabs, pork skins, pit-cooked barbecue, sausage burgers, fresh roast-pork sandwiches, barbecued spareribs, ham biscuits, chitlin fritters, and festival pork stew. Since man and woman do not live by pork alone, there are also fried sweet potatoes, hush puppies, potato wedges.

The festival has an all-you-can-eat format, which means that the attendees—estimated at something over 16,000—really do pig out. In doing so, they contribute lots of money to Emporia; more than 30 nonprofit organizations prepare and sell the food, earning about $30,000 for community projects.

For entertainment, there are five stages always in use, and you'll hear all kinds of music—beach music, which began in Myrtle Beach, Virginia, Motown, rock and roll, R&B, old standards. Carrying out the festival motif, there's a pig on display that weighs more than 200 pounds and is called Little Mac, and there are piglets for petting.

Location: Greensville County Ruritan Club grounds in Emporia (see Great Peanut Bicycle Tour). **Contact:** Virginia Pork Festival, P.O. Box 1001, Emporia, VA 23847; Tel: (800)4VA-PORK, Fax: (804)348-0119.

Great Peanut Bicycle Tour and Virginia Peanut Festival

Weekends in September (Thursday through Sunday) If you spread them out over the four weekends in September, about 30,000 people come to Emporia for events linked to peanuts, an important crop in Virginia.

The first weekend (Thursday through Sunday) is known far and wide to bicyclists, and is generally a sellout, limited to 1,500 cyclists. The Bicycle Tour combines bike touring in Virginia and North Carolina with hearty eating: a pasta dinner the first day, a fish fry the second (with a harpist), a barbecued dinner on Saturday (with bagpipe music), and a hearty breakfast Sunday morning. The focal point is the Great Peanut Tour on Saturday, a 13-mile ride through peanut country, with two stops—one to discuss peanut farming, harvesting, and marketing, and the second at a peanut farmer's home to sample a large variety of peanuts and other products.

Events of the Virginia Peanut Festival, which began in 1963, are scattered over the three weekends after the bike tour. They include an archery shoot and pig pickin' (barbecue) on the second weekend, and, on the final weekend, a carnival, arts and crafts show, parade, classic-car show, jazz, and country music. Edible offerings include Cajun peanuts, Spanish peanuts, and all sorts of other foods.

Location: Bicycle tour begins at Cattail Creek R.V. Park and Campground, on Virginia 629, three miles west of I-95. Peanut Festival events are chiefly in Veterans Memorial Park, Main St., Emporia, off I-95, 13 miles north of the North Carolina border. **Contact:** For the bike tour, contact the Emporia Bicycle Club Inc., P.O. Box 668, Emporia, VA 23847; Tel: (800)449-BIKE. For the Virginia Peanut Festival, contact P.O. Box 868, Emporia, VA 23847; Tel: (804)634-6611.

Ferrum

Blue Ridge Folklife Festival

Fourth Saturday in October For those who delight in genuine regional foods, and especially foods that have stayed regional and not wandered across America, this is a festival to bring joy.

It's called Virginia's largest showcase of regional traditions, and that covers a lot of ground: Coon-dog contests, where the dogs swim across a lake and tree a rag that smells like a raccoon. A marble-shooting tournament. Demonstrations of crafts such as chair caning, dulcimer making, rug braiding, herb drying, quilting, cane carving. Demonstrations of Border Collie herding. Cloggers, ballad singers, and storytellers. Log-skidding, mule-jumping, and horse-pulling contests.

Note: Mules don't jump fences the way horses do. They go up to a fence, size it up, then clamber over, hind legs first.

Since traditions include food, prepare to eat. Civic organizations and churches demonstrate how to make certain dishes and then sell them.

You'll be able to choose from black-pot chicken (chicken fried in a black pot), country ham biscuits, chitterlings (a.k.a. chitlins), Brunswick stew, fried apple pie.

A word about those last two:

Like so many of our dishes, the provenance of the stew is misty. Some say it originated in Brunswick County, Virginia, and was made primarily of squirrel and onions. Georgians claim it was born in Brunswick, Georgia. It is now generally a stew of chicken, beef, rabbit, and vegetables.

Fried pie, like Brunswick stew, is still popular, found largely in the mountain areas of the Southeast. To store apples, mountain people sliced them and dried them in the sun. When they wanted to make a pie, they stewed the apples, sweetened them, and filled dough that had been rolled to a saucer-sized circle. The dough was folded in half and crimped, then deep fried. Frying most likely was easier than heating up an oven for baking. Today, while it isn't necessarily more convenient to fry pie, the taste of this dessert has made it a favorite part of mountain cookery.

There are also demonstrations of making apple, peach, and pear butter, and there's homemade bread, and fish and barbecued-pork dinners.

The festival began in 1975 and focuses on age-old traditions that are still part of daily life in the community.

Location: Ferrum College, Ferrum, VA, 35 miles southwest of Roanoke, on Virginia 40, off U.S. 220. ⚜ Contact: Blue Ridge Institute, Ferrum College, Ferrum, VA 24088; Tel: (540)365-4418.

Fredericksburg

Cheesecake Festival

First Saturday in October ⚜ This is a festival for the committed cheesecake fan who thinks cheesecake is one of the world's noblest inventions. It began on a slow Saturday in 1989 when the staff at Karla's Great Cheesecakes thought offering free tastings might liven things up. About ten people came in for tastes, the next year 100 came, and now more than 1,000 show up.

The only food available is cheesecake, served with complimentary coffee. (The cheesecake is no longer free; you pay and get a plate but then you eat all you want.)

Karla's serves cheesecake in three categories—sweet, specialty, and savory.

There are 20 to 25 kinds of sweet cake, from New York cheesecake to such fancy flavors as white chocolate, butterscotch, Cointreau, cappuccino, and fudge brownie. Each year, new flavors are introduced, like creamsicle, key lime, milk chocolate Amaretto mousse, pink squirrel (with an almond flavor, like the cocktail), grasshopper (creme de menthe flavor, like the after-dinner drink), apple strudel, pumpkin, blueberry pie (with real pie inside, baked by Karla's).

In the specialty category, there are cheesecake "truffles"—walnut-sized pieces of cheesecake dipped in various toppings: chocolate, raspberry, peanut, butterscotch, butter pecan, mocha.

Savory, simply meaning not sweet, cheesecakes are intended to be eaten as hors d'oeuvres. The spinach and garlic varieties are good with crackers or tossed with warm fettucine. Others in the savory class are cheddar cheese, Swiss apple and pecan, pesto, sun-dried tomato, and chutney.

A dessert recipe book is available for purchase as well as a cheesecake-truffle-making kit and video, and Karla's has been working on a cheesecake-wedding-cake kit.

The event, as noted, is for the truly committed.

Location: Karla's Great Cheesecakes, 41 Cool Springs Rd., just outside the historic district of Fredericksburg. From downtown, follow William St. east, across Chatham Bridge; turn left onto Cool Springs at the second light after the bridge. ⚜ Contact: Karla's Great Cheesecakes, 41 Cool Springs Rd., Fredericksburg, VA 22405; Tel: (540)373-4260.

Front Royal

Virginia Mushroom and Wine Festival

Third Saturday in May ⚜ Mushrooms and wine make a perfect marriage at the Front Royal festival. Mushroom growers from Virginia, West Virginia, and Pennsylvania are on hand to explain how mushrooms are grown (shiitakes are grown in holes in logs); vendors provide breaded mushrooms, stir-fried mushrooms, and portobellos marinated and grilled on a bun; and Virginia vintners will sell you a glass, bottle, or case of wine.

Additionally, more than 100 craftspeople sell their handmade goods, and there's live music at the gazebo area of the town commons. The festival began in 1987 and brings together about 15,000 mushroom and wine lovers.

Location: Front Royal, at the foot of the Blue Ridge Mountains, is 70 miles west of Washington, just south of I-66. **Contact:** Front Royal–Warren County Chamber of Commerce, 414 Main St., Front Royal, VA 22630; Tel: (703)635-3185, or (800)338-2576.

Hampton

Afrikan-American Festival

Fourth Saturday in June At night, it's the Hampton Jazz Festival; during the day, the Afrikan-American Festival, which has been pulling in crowds of 25,000 to 30,000 since 1990. A highlight is the lively "African market." Talking drums, kente cloth, and African masks are for sale, jazz musicians play for free, and the food is authentic African American and Caribbean: fried fish, Caribbean blackened fish and yellow rice, red beans and rice, Jamaican jerk chicken, crab cakes, soft-shell crabs, steamed hard-shell crabs, shrimp. To cool the throat, there's nonalcoholic guava beer. (This is an alcohol-free event.)

The festival benefits the Peninsula Association for Sickle Cell Anemia. The Hampton Roads area that comprises Hampton and Newport News (the Peninsula) and Norfolk and Portsmouth on the other side of the bay has a large community of African Americans who have often found positions in the fishing and shipbuilding industries, the Norfolk Naval Base, and at Hampton University.

A local claim to fame is that Booker T. Washington attended Hampton University.

Location: Millpoint Park in downtown Hampton, in the City Hall area. Hampton is about 30 miles south of Williamsburg off I-64. **Contact:** Peninsula Association for Sickle Cell Anemia, 2021 Cunningham Dr., Hampton, VA 23666; Tel: (804)838-4721, Fax: (804)838-0836.

While You're There: The Hampton University Museum, one of the oldest museums in Virginia, displays art objects and various artifacts from sub-Saharan Africa, as well as works by contemporary African and African American artists.

Meadows of Dan

Cabbage Festival

Fourth Saturday of August Fried mountain cabbage is the big drawing card at this homey festival. Meadows of Dan is up in the mountains, and the cool nights and loamy soil produce the "sweetest cabbage in the world," according to Ronnie Green, one of a dwindling number of local cabbage farmers.

This was once a big cabbage area, but the acreage in Patrick and Carroll Counties has dropped to only about 500 acres. When the festival began in the mid-1980s, there used to be food cook-offs, but now the festivities are leaner.

Still, about 3,000 people show up for fried cabbage. Farmer Green makes it by frying fatback in two-foot-diameter frying pans, and putting cabbage, pepper, sugar, and maybe hot peppers in the fat. The cabbage is served with corn bread, and Green doesn't keep track of how much he bakes, but he does know he cuts up 600 pounds of cabbage to fry. He also offers hot dogs with cole slaw and sauerkraut made from local cabbage, a barbecue, and homemade fudge, candies, and apples, which can be dipped in fudge. Sometimes he offers cabbage fudge. No joke. He squeezes cabbage juice into the fudge and adds green coloring.

Mountain music is played all day, and there are children's games such as rolling a cabbage a certain distance. Baskets, plants, Native American goods, and pottery in the shape of cabbages are sold.

Explorer Jacques Cartier introduced cabbage to North America in 1541, planting it in Canada on his third voyage.

Location: Meadows of Dan, five miles east of the Blue Ridge Parkway on U.S. 58. **Contact:** Cabbage Festival, Poor Farmers Farm, U.S. 58, Meadows of Dan, VA 24120; Tel: (540)952-2560.

Reedville

Watermen's Festival

First full weekend in May Reedville, near the end of what's called Virginia's Northern Neck between the Potomac and Rappahannock Rivers, is a fishing village founded in 1874 by Captain Elijah Reed, who came down from Maine to harvest menhaden. There's a menhaden-processing plant here, and the mainstay of the village is menhaden, a junk fish. It's not a fish for eating, unless you're another fish, but its oil has numerous uses and in Europe is used for cooking.

The folks here also like to *eat* some of the bounty of the sea, so they started the Watermen's Festival in 1996 as a good excuse to gorge on fried-oyster sandwiches and soft-shell crab sandwiches. The festival also features a crab-recipe contest and demonstrations of building crab pots, harvesting hard crabs from pots and soft-shell crabs from floats, and a Coast Guard search-and-rescue operation. There are tours of a menhaden fishing boat and a "creek peek" tour—seeing the river from a pontoon boat. For kids, there's a hard-crab derby, in which it's legal for the children to cheat by throwing water on the crabs. And for sailors, small handmade wooden sailboats of the Nutshell Class open their racing season with a regatta.

This is followed Sunday with a boat parade and blessing of the fleet.

Location: From the north, take I-95 to Fredericksburg, go east on Virginia 3, which becomes Virginia 360, ending at Reedville. **Contact:** Reedville Museum, P.O. Box 306, Reedville, VA 22539; Tel: (804)453-6529.

While You're There: The Reedville Museum consists of the Walker House, the oldest house in Reedville, built in 1874, restored as a turn-of-the-century fisherman's home, and the new Covington Building. A permanent exhibit tells the history of menhaden fishing and processing.

Bluefish Derby

Second full weekend in June (Thursday through Saturday)

A few weeks after the Watermen's Festival, Reedville sponsors a Bluefish Derby that ends Saturday night with a dinner of fish caught that day. During the derby, local groups sell local seafood and some non-seafood dishes, and there are crafts, music, and dancing. People have to register in advance to fish in the derby, competing for cash prizes that add up to $25,000. There's a *big* prize that keeps getting bigger with add-ons, and is now $50,000 in cash plus a pickup truck and boat and trailer. Nobody has won this since the derby began in 1983. It's for the person who catches a bluefish bigger than the biggest ever caught in Virginia. The state record is 25 pounds and 4 ounces, and the biggest ever caught off Reedville was something over 19 pounds. But greed and hope and fishing reels spring eternal.

The derby is a fundraiser for the Smith Point Sea Rescue Service, and the Watermen's Festival benefits the Reedville Museum.

Location and contact: See above.

Surry

Pork, Peanut, and Pine Festival

Third weekend in July Pork, peanuts, and pine are combined in this festival not for the alliteration but because they account for the three major industries of Surry County.

Pork goes way back. The Indians taught the Jamestown settlers how to cure meat, especially venison, by salting, smoking, and aging, and the colonists used this method in preserving hog meat. The meat acquired a distinct flavor because pigs roamed loose and ate peanuts, which were being more and more widely planted.

At the festival, some home-style favorites you can sample are pit-cooked barbecue, grilled pork chops, pork rinds, hickory-smoked sausages, Virginia ham sandwiches, chitlins, and pigs' feet.

Peanuts, a major cash crop in Virginia, have a long lineage, going from the New World to the Old World and back to the New World. In the Civil War, peanuts provided food for starving soldiers and was widely used as a coffee substitute. Today, peanuts, the versatile legume, are used in all kinds of food. Festival favorites are peanut-raisin pie, peanut soup, peanut brittle, chocolate-covered peanuts, peanut cookies, and plain roasted peanuts.

As for the pine, Virginia has dense forests of pine, which is widely used in pulp products and furniture.

The festival attracts about 70,000 people and has been held since 1976 at Chippokes Plantation on the James River. The oldest continuously operated plantation in the nation, it was established in the early 1600s.

Besides foodstuffs, there are pig races, a lumberjack show, bands, displays of pine crafts, pine furniture, paintings, and antique machinery (things like peanut shellers), as well as demonstrations of soap making, broom making, and other useful trades. The Farm & Forestry Museum is open to tell the story of Virginia's agricultural and forestry industries.

Location: The Chippokes Plantation State Park is on Virginia 31, about 12 miles south of Williamsburg via the Colonial Parkway and James River ferry. **Contact:** Chippokes Plantation State Park, P.O. Box 116, Surry, VA 23883; Tel: (804)294-3344.

See Also: Georgia Peanut Festival (Poulan, GA).

Urbanna

Urbanna Oyster Festival

First weekend in November (Friday and Saturday) The tiny town of Urbanna (population 750) hosts the *official* Oyster Festival of the Commonwealth of Virginia, so decreed by the Virginia General Assembly. That translates to attendance of 80,000, 30 to 40 food vendors, and oysters that are fried, on the half shell, roasted, steamed, in fritters, in stew. You like clams? They come the same way.

As an example of how much oysterphiles eat in Urbanna, one year just one booth cooked and sold 315 gallons of shucked oysters, and another single booth sold 15,200 oysters on the half shell.

Steamed shrimp is also on hand, although it's not local, and there's an assortment of Mediterranean food, Philadelphia cheese steaks, pastries, funnel cake, and so on.

The Virginia State Oyster Shucking Championship is a major part of the festival. The winner goes to the national shucking contest, held in Leonardtown, Maryland, and the winner of that contest travels to Ireland to compete for the world championship. It happens that Deborah Pratt of nearby Jamaica, Virginia, has won several times in Urbanna and has won the national three times, and placed in the top three in the international. Urbanna is very proud of that.

Other competitions are for Oyster Festival Queen, which is open to high school students, and for Little Miss Spat, for which a first-grader is selected. (A spat is a very young oyster.)

The two days bulge with activities: two parades (the Fireman's Parade on Friday night with about 100 fire companies coming from throughout the state, and the Festival Parade on Saturday afternoon), a dance, music, arts and crafts, ships open for tours.

The town, once a thriving commercial port and the heart of the oyster industry for the lower Rappahannock, is now more of a resort and harbor for recreational boating. The predecessor of the festival was Urbanna Days; it began in 1958 as a kind of community pick-me-up, and the festival remains that.

Location: Urbanna is 64 miles east of Richmond, on the Rappahannock River, about 5 miles east of U.S. 17. ⚙ **Contact:** Urbanna Oyster Festival Foundation, Drawer C, Urbanna, VA 23175; Tel: (804)758-0368.

While You're There: Urbanna looks like the good old days. Visit Marshall's Drug Store; it was established in 1929 and still has an old-fashioned lunch counter where you can get an old-fashioned malted shake.

See Also: St. Mary's County Oyster Festival (Leonardtown, MD).

Great Lakes & Ohio Valley

Illinois

Indiana

Michigan

Minnesota

Ohio

West Virginia

Wisconsin

Illinois

International Horseradish Festival

First weekend of June ❀ A giant white balloon that looks like a big white horseradish gives you a clue—you're at the horseradish festival in the Horseradish Capital of the World.

Collinsville and the area around it are part of what are known as the American Bottom Lands, a Mississippi River basin adjacent to St. Louis, Missouri. It was carved out by glaciers in the ice age, and the soil is sandy and rich in potash, the chemical nutrient that makes horseradish thrive.

It thrives so much that farmers harvest about 10 million pounds a year, close to 85 percent of the world's supply, even though it's a native of eastern Europe and the Orient.

The festival started in 1988 and attracts about 35,000 visitors. Here you can buy products made with horseradish to take home—fresh ground mustard, catsup, and jellies—and there are lots of brats, hot dogs, and such to be eaten on the spot, preferably spiced up with horseradish. Food producers sometimes test-market products; horseradish cheesecake was tried out one year.

A Horseradish Recipe Contest has produced garlic-and-horseradish mashed potatoes, horseradish-apple pie, apple-horseradish jelly, shrimp pizza, and broiled salmon with smoked horseradish sauce.

One of the final events of the weekend is the Horseradish Eating Contest, where mounds of fresh horseradish are piled on hot dogs and eaten to beat the clock. Other horseradish-related events are a root toss (roots grow about a foot long) for distance, root golf (the roots are carved into ball shapes and frozen), root sacking. The Little Miss Horseradish Festival Pageant is open to girls from ages three to five; other activities include music, dancing, a 5K run, a kiddie-tractor pull, crafts booths.

Horseradish, related to mustard, has a colorful lore. Centuries ago, it was claimed that horseradish would stimulate the appetite, relieve colic, rid children of worms, and act as an aphrodisiac. It's the bitter herb placed with other symbolic foods at the Seder table at the

Hot Reuben Dip

1 cup mayonnaise	2 cups Swiss cheese, shredded
1 16-ounce can Bavarian sauerkraut, drained, squeezed, dried	4 packages (2½ oz. each) dried corned beef, finely chopped
1 small onion, finely chopped	2 tablespoons prepared horseradish

Mix all ingredients in a 1½-quart casserole dish. Bake in oven 30–40 minutes at 350 degrees. Serve with toasty rye bagel chips or party rye bread. Serves 32.

Doris Chiste, 1993 First Place Winner, International Horseradish Festival; from brochure prepared by Horseradish Information Council, Atlanta, GA

start of the Jewish Passover. For Polish Catholics, it's a tradition to take horseradish to church on Easter to have it blessed.

The first person to grind horseradish for profit is supposed to have been Henry J. Heinz, who was better known for his catsup and wasn't even from Collinsville.

Location: Woodland Park, at the intersection of I-70 and Beltline Rd., in Collinsville, about eight miles east of St. Louis. ☼ **Contact:** International Horseradish Festival, 211 W. Main St., Collinsville, IL 62234; Tel: (618)344-2884.

Fulton

Fulton Dutch Days

First Friday and Saturday in May ☼ Fulton is predominantly Dutch, though it's never quite been known why so many immigrants from Holland found their way to this small Midwestern town, a transfer port in the days of steamboating.

The first Dutch settler came in 1835, and by 1890 there were 198 families, most members of the Dutch Reformed Church. A reporter later wrote, "Their great fortune then was that they were all about evenly poor."

The festival began in 1974 when the Community Christian School Auxiliary organized its first Dutch Dinner. The dinner has expanded to a major festival, visited by about 15,000, but with the Friday-night dinner still the center attraction.

Dinner dishes include *gewekte vlees,* home-canned beef (meat baked in an oven, then chilled in fruit jars to preserve it); *hutspot,* a potato-carrot dish; *boes kool,* a potato-cabbage dish; *snert,* pea soup. Generally you'll also find Holland stew, brimming with beef, pork, beef liver, and dumplings, and *kippesoep,* chicken and noodles. And *aardappel*

Horseradish: it's not just for eating. These competitors vie for first place in the "Root Sacking" contest. (International Horseradish Festival)

puree, which translates as mashed potatoes, but also contains celery, onions, bread, and eggs. And *bitterballen,* small meat balls served at the "bitter hour" known to others as happy hour.

You can top it off with *Jan in de Zak* (John in the Sack), a steamed pudding with raisins and currants, or *chocolade en vanille vla,* chocolate and vanilla pudding.

The festival is more than the dinner. Events now include a Parade of Provinces, where marchers wear authentic costumes from all the Netherlands provinces and Sinterklass, the Dutch Santa Claus, marches in red robe and biretta; a demonstration of traditional street scrubbing, where rows of women take long-handled scrub brushes and pails of water and scrub down the street; klompen dancing, where you hear 200 klompen (wooden shoes) pounding in unison on the pavement.

At the quilt show, you'll see quilts more than 100 years old. The Dutch dress-a-doll contest showcases Dutch miniature costumes on porcelain dolls. After the judging, the dolls are auctioned to the highest bidders. There are also demonstrations by klompen makers and hindenloopen painters who paint small wooden pieces.

All told, this is an authentic Dutch treat.

Location: Downtown Fulton, on Illinois 84, just off U.S. 30, about 30 miles north of Davenport, Iowa.   **Contact:** Fulton Dutch Days Festival, P.O. Box 14, Fulton, IL 61252; Tel: (815)589-4545.

While You're There: Heritage Canyon nearby is a 12-acre reconstructed country village in an abandoned rock quarry, with a log cabin and root cellar, a blacksmith shop, a country church, and more.

Kewanee

Hog Capital of the World Festival

Labor Day weekend (Saturday through Monday) They serve 37,000 grilled pork chops on a bun with a special sauce at this festival, making it the World's Largest Pork Chop Festival. Henry County, which Kewanee is within, is the World's Largest Producer of Hogs, they claim, so it seems reasonable to have the biggest chop festival in Kewanee.

However: Illinois raises close to 5 million hogs, way behind Iowa, which raises more than 14 million and is the number-one producer in the United States. Illinois usually ranks fourth. And statistics from the National Pork Producers Council puts Henry County about twelfth on the list of top hog counties. But aren't we being rather *pig*ayune about all this fact stuff? They've got a lot of pigs here.

After all, the festival is an old one; it's been held since 1954, and pulls in more than 50,000 people. It sells pork patties and butterflied pork chops on buns, and the Jaycees

Bitterballen (Bit-tur-ball-un) Cocktail Balls

Combine two cups of finely ground cold cooked beef with one medium minced onion, fried until wilted, and one cup of thick brown sauce. The darker and tastier the sauce, the better. Use meat juices, worcestershire or soy sauce, beef bouillon, even brown gravy mix to achieve this. Add a tablespoon minced parsley and seasoning to taste. Stir in one package of softened unflavored gelatine. Spread this mixture over a large platter and chill until a piece of it comes off without sticking (about one hour).

Cut into ¾-inch squares and roll each into a ball. Roll in bread or cornflake crumbs, dip in beaten egg mixed with some water, and roll in crumbs again. Chill once more.

Just before serving, fry in 370 degree deep fat, a few at a time. Serve at once with a choice of prepared mustard and ketchup for dipping.

Recipe brought to U.S. in the 1950s from the Netherlands by Patty Ritzema

serve a pork-chop dinner with chips and apple sauce. Vendors offer bratwurst, potato chippers (French fries), and other standard fair food.

The theme is definitely swinish. Townspeople decorate their houses with hog paintings and carvings for the Hog House Decorating Contest, and there are Hog Mud Wallow Classic Volleyball Tourneys (slip, slide, splat). Other events include contests for Little Miss Bar-Be-Q (ages 8 to 12) and Queen (ages 18 to 23), a carnival, a Ford Model-T race, flea market, parade, arts and crafts, music, a tractor pull for kids, entertainers.

Location: Kewanee is on Illinois 78, 10 miles south of I-80 at exit 33. ░
Contact: Kewanee Chamber of Commerce, 113 E. 2nd St., Kewanee, IL 61443; Tel: (309)852-2175, Fax: (309)852-2176.

Mattoon

Bagel Fest

Last weekend in July (Friday through Saturday) ░ When you eat one of the 70,000 bagels with cream cheese and jelly given away at this festival, you might like to know that bagels are considered lucky because they're round, and that bagels are becoming more popular in the United States than doughnuts. Want some stats? The Commerce Department says bagel consumption rose from 2.5 pounds per person in 1988 to 4.5 pounds in 1995. Retail sales of bagels rose from $429 million in 1993 to $2.3 billion in 1996.

Bagels, yeast rolls shaped like doughnuts but with a hard exterior, are simmered in almost boiling water for a couple of minutes, and then baked. The water dip produces the hard crust. They were originally a Jewish food; the word came into English from the Yiddish *beygel,* which came from the German *Beugel,* meaning a round loaf of bread. But the soaring per capita consumption is making them everyman's nosh.

About 40,000 people attend the festival to get the bagel handout from Lender's Bagel Bakery, which has a factory in town. The festival began in 1986 with a cozy breakfast of bagels and cream cheese on tables in the center of town.

Events vary. There have been recipe contests and there may be again. One past entry was a pudding-ish dessert that consisted of crushed pineapples, pieces of bagel, butterscotch morsels, eggs, and nuts.

In 1996, Lender's made a special oven and baked a bagel that weighed 564 pounds, hoping to set a record. Will they make a colossal bagel again? Maybe. Another event of the past that may reappear is the bagel-buggy derby, wherein soapboxes are decorated with bagels or constructed to look like bagels.

Regular festival events are a messy cream-pie-eating contest; 5K and 10K runs; and the crowning of Little Miss Bagel Fest, Miss Pre-teen Bagel Fest, and Miss Teen Bagel Fest, who participate in the annual parade. Food vendors sell food other than bagels.

When the Bagel Fest began in 1986, it was a cozy, small affair. Today, 40,000 people consume 70,000 bagels on the streets of downtown Mattoon. (Mattoon Chamber of Commerce)

The belief that bagels bring luck because of their roundness is classic; Greeks thought a circle was the perfect form because it had no beginning or end. Jews traditionally served bagels and hard-boiled eggs at funerals to symbolize the "unending 'round' processes of life and the world," according to Yiddish scholar Leo Rosten. The 1610 community regulations of Cracow, Poland—which Rosten says are the first printed mention of bagels—stated that bagels were to be given to women in childbirth.

Other bagel bagatelles: It's believed the bagel was born in Poland, and made the passage to America with Eastern European Jews in the late 1800s, but not to Palestine. It has long been said that you can't get a good bagel in Israel. A bagel and lox for breakfast is not an ancient Jewish tradition; it was created in America after World War II.

Location: Mattoon is off I-57 on Illinois 16, about 50 miles south of Champaign.
Contact: Mattoon Chamber of Commerce, 1701 Wabash Avenue, Mattoon, IL 61938; Tel: (217)235-5661.

National Sweet Corn Festival

Second weekend in August (Friday through Sunday) About 161,000 ears of steamed sweet corn—that's 60 tons—are given to all comers at Mendota's corn fest, one of the Midwest's oldest and largest harvest festivals. They have healthy appetites here. Festival attendance is about 55,000; divide that into 161,000 . . . well, that's big per capita consumption.

The maize days began in 1948, and the following year the local Del Monte Corporation plant contributed more than 20 tons of corn to the festival. The company has been contributing ever since and the big giveaway comes at 2:30 on Sunday afternoon. The corn is steamed in boilers heated by an antique steam engine, and then slathered with 400 pounds of Shedd's Spread Country Crock margarine.

To go with the corn, 80 vendors sell old-time favorites like fruited funnel cakes, as well as ostrich burgers and gator tail. The Optimist Club sells roast corn each day of the festival, and if you're still not corned out, Del Monte sweet corn is sold by the bag to take home.

Each year, Del Monte produces some 13 million cases of canned whole-kernel corn and creamed corn, and Illinois is one of the top ten states in the harvesting of sweet corn both for processing and for the fresh market. So this is corn-belt country, and you know it when you visit the festival. Kids wear funny hats that look like ears of corn, and the mile-long parade just before the free corn handout features corny floats and walking ears of corn.

Numerous other events include a pet show, marionettes, a Crafters Market Place and Flea Market, a display of antique and classic cars, music, tumblers, and line dancers.

Location: Washington, Illinois, and Jefferson Sts. in downtown Mendota, 3 miles west of I-39, about 80 miles west of Chicago. **Contact:** Mendota Chamber of Commerce, P.O. Box 620, Mendota, IL 61342; Tel: (815)539-6507.

Morton Pumpkin Festival

Second weekend after Labor Day (Wednesday through Saturday) Morton rolls out the orange carpet for 100,000 guests at this festival and proclaims to all that it's the Pumpkin Capital of the World. At the end of the festival, there's not much doubt.

All kinds of pumpkin food are featured, and among the pumpkin contests are window decorating, pumpkin decorating, "punkin chuckin'," contests to judge the biggest pumpkin, and a cooking contest. The cooking contest has eight categories and three age divisions and requires that each entry contain at least half a cup of Libby's processed pumpkin.

That's not unreasonable, since Nestlé-Libby's pumpkin-packing plant, the largest in the country, is in town, and during the pumpkin season turns out about 30,000 cases, or 720,000 cans, of pumpkin each day. That would be enough to make pumpkin pies that

Good Morning Pumpkin Pancakes

2 cups biscuit mix
2 tablespoons packed light brown sugar
2 teaspoons ground cinnamon
1 teaspoon ground allspice

1½ cups (12-ounce can) *undiluted* Carnation Evaporated Milk
½ cup Libby's Solid Pack Pumpkin
2 tablespoons vegetable oil
2 eggs
1 teaspoon vanilla extract

In large mixer bowl, combine biscuit mix, brown sugar, cinnamon, and allspice. Add evaporated milk, pumpkin, oil, eggs, and vanilla; beat until smooth. Pour ¼ to ½ cup batter (depending on size of pancake desired) onto heated and lightly greased griddle. Cook until top surface is bubbly and edges are dry. Turn; cook until golden. Keep pancakes warm. Serve with syrup, honey, or jam. Makes 16 pancakes.

Libby's Favorite Pumpkin Recipes

would stretch the 160 miles from Morton to Chicago. Libby's provides farmers with seed, and all the pumpkins processed are grown within 50 miles of Morton.

The contest produces dishes that are sometimes peculiar, usually interesting: A recent winning dish for the under-12 kids was a peanut-butter-pumpkin dip, with brown sugar, served in a pumpkin shell; adults have come up with pumpkin party salsa and pumpkin potato boats.

As for food to graze on, the headliners are butterfly pork chops (this is pig-rich country) and pumpkin pies. On Saturday morning, there are pumpkin pancakes, and each day pumpkin chili (pumpkin is used instead of tomato, but V-8 juice is added for a better consistency), pumpkin fudge, ice cream, giant cookies, and nachos with pumpkin chili. There are hot dogs, too.

Entertainment includes a carnival, a pageant for Miss Morton and for little princesses, a parade in which the princesses are driven by a top-hatted coachman in a horse-drawn pumpkin coach, a flower and garden show, a carnival, music, and entertainers.

In 1996, a new event was added—"Punkin Chuckin'." Based on the long-standing Punkin Chunkin' in Lewes, Delaware (they *chunk* in Delaware and *chuck* in Illinois), it's a contest in which non-explosive machines vie to hurl a pumpkin the farthest. In the contest's first year, a consortium of builders constructed a compressed-air contraption with a 60-foot-long barrel that tossed a pumpkin 2,500 feet.

Pumpkins as food rather than missiles go back to pre-colonial days. They're among the oldest edible plants in the Northern Hemisphere and were a staple of Native Americans. The first settlers found them good eating, and Amelia Simmons, America's first cookbook

This prize-winning pumpkin with the nice hat was grown by George Young in 1994. (Morton Pumpkin Festival)

writer, provided a "pumpkin" recipe: "One quart of milk, 1 pint pumpkin, 4 eggs, molaffes, allfpice and ginger in a cruft, bake 1 hour."

Because of its processing, Illinois leads the country as pumpkin producer, although California is the leading supplier for the fresh market. Fresh-market pumpkins are sold almost exclusively during the Halloween season. Illinois tops the list in numbers of acres harvested, with California second.

Location: Morton is 13 miles southeast of Peoria, on I-155. ☼ Contact: Morton Chamber of Commerce, 415 W. Jefferson, Morton, IL 61550; Tel: (309)263-2491, Fax: (309)263-2401.

Utica

Burgoo Festival

Second Sunday in October ☼ Most burgoo authorities agree that burgoo became famous in Lexington, Kentucky, though nobody knows for sure just who first threw meat and vegetables in a pot and called it burgoo. Burgoo is commonly cooked up in great quantities in Kentucky, Indiana, and Illinois at political rallies or other large-scale gatherings, and the burgoo feed in Utica is a continuation of an old tradition.

The Utica burgoo consists of beef and a long list of vegetables, including carrots, cabbage, beans, tomato, onions, and peppers. Like most such stews that are cooked out-of-doors for the multitudes, it is simmered and stirred for hours.

The preparation is overseen by a Burgoo Meister. His helpers begin the cooking at about 10 on Saturday night, and start serving it at 11 the next morning. A Burgoo Meister-in-training stays at the Meister's elbow, learning the secrets. To go along with the burgoo, there are pork chop dinners, butterfly pork chop sandwiches, pork burgers, and steak burgers. Desserts are also served.

About 20,000 attend the festival, which began in 1970 as a small affair, and is now a major fund-raiser for the LaSalle County Historical Society. More than 200 artisans and crafters display their goods, and many demonstrate crafts. There are also blacksmith demonstrations, and tours of a one-room schoolhouse and the museum. German bands play, and the high school band marches and performs.

Location: Utica is about 100 miles southwest of Chicago, on Illinois 178, 2 miles south of I-80.   **Contact:** LaSalle County Historical Society, P.O. Box 278, Utica, IL 61373; Tel: (815)667-4861.

See Also: International Bar-B-Q Festival (Owensboro, KY).

Indiana

Johnny Appleseed Festival

Third full weekend in September ❋ John Chapman is buried in Fort Wayne. The festival, going strong since 1975, honors his memory in a fittingly happy way, with about 300,000 people coming to town to pay homage to the fruit of the trees that Mr. Chapman, better known as Johnny Appleseed, planted throughout the Ohio Valley.

Apples are on or in everything imaginable—roll-ups, pancakes, apple sauce made at the festival, turnovers, pies, caramel-apple breads. There are, of course, also fresh apples, and there are apples with caramel sauce, and, if you have a thirst, there's cider.

An apple-pie recipe contest brings gift certificates to the winners, and slices of contest pies are sold to raise funds.

Johnny Appleseed himself (or a good imitation) walks around the festival grounds, telling apple stories and explaining how he planted seedlings by the thousands in his travels. He might even acknowledge that he played a major role in helping to settle the Midwest and turn America into an apple-loving nation. He is reticent, however, about why he sometimes wore a frying pan for a hat.

John Chapman was born in Massachusetts in 1774 and died in Fort Wayne in 1845. His birthday on September 26 is close to the time of the festival.

In addition to all the apple dishes, the many crafts booths incorporate the apple theme, and pioneer crafts and daily tasks are demonstrated by participants in 1880s garb. A farmers' market and an Indian encampment help complete the apple and pioneer motifs.

Location: Archer Park, behind the Memorial Coliseum and the baseball stadium. ❋ **Contact:** Johnny Appleseed Festival, Fort Wayne Parks and Recreation Dept., 705 E. State Street, Fort Wayne, IN 46805; Tel: (219)427-6003.

Frankfort

Hot Dog Festival

Last weekend in July ☼ Hot dogs are as quintessentially American as baseball. Is the experience of a game really complete without those wonderful wieners, slathered with yellow mustard? Food historians say the hot dog is just a German wurst, and the National Hot Dog and Sausage Council says the hot dog originated in Vienna about a thousand years ago.

Who cares? In America, the hot dog has been called a hot dog since 1901. Yet Frankfort, Indiana, is one of the few places where they fete the hot dog. They should: the Frankfort high school team is the Fighting Hot Dogs, and its mascot is a dachshund.

The festival began in 1995 and about 10,000 people come and line up for seven kinds of hot dogs, from standard-sized ones to foot-long dogs to mastiff half-pounders, as well as bratwurst and smoked sausage and a Puppy Dog, which is peanut butter and jelly on a roll, not a dog at all. Side orders of chips, baked beans, and salsa are available, but there are no hamburgers; this is a purist's festival.

Entertainment includes a four-mile Bun Run, a Puppy Park for the kids, the Bowzer Bash Car Show, a Parade of Pooches, and Arfs and Crafts booths.

For a cultural perspective, you should know that hot dogs are served in various ways in various places. In Chicago, people like them on poppy-seed buns, with yellow mustard, raw onion, pickle relish, a slice of tomato, and celery salt. In Kansas City, they like their dogs with sauerkraut and melted Swiss cheese. New Yorkers take their dogs steamed with yellow mustard—the ballpark hot dog.

Speaking of ballparks, T. A. Dorgan, a cartoonist known as Tad, was at a game in New York's old Polo Grounds in 1901 on a cold day when the vendors' ice cream wasn't selling. The vendors switched to hot sausages. Dorgan drew a cartoon, putting a tail and legs on the sausage, making it look like a dachshund, but he couldn't spell dachshund, so he captioned the cartoon, "Get your red hot dogs." Thus does the language evolve.

Vendors sold the hot dog at the St. Louis World's Fair in 1904 with white gloves, but the white gloves got really messy so the hot dog bun was invented. Marlene Dietrich said her favorite meal was hot dogs and champagne.

Location: Frankfort is about 30 miles north of Indianapolis, 10 miles east of I-65. ☼ **Contact:** Frankfort Main Street, 301 E. Clinton St., Frankfort, IN 46041; Tel: (317)654-4081, Fax: (317)654-7773.

Ligonier

Ligonier Marshmallow Festival

Labor Day weekend (Friday evening through Monday) ☼ Here you are back home in Indiana, celebrating that soft, white candy of childhood, and little do you think you have something in common with ancient Egyptians. But they ate marshmallows, too.

Egyptian records dating to 2000 B.C. depict a confection of honey flavored with an extract of the mallow root, which was common to Egyptian marshes. That was probably the earliest marshmallow candy.

The modern marshmallow was created in France in the mid-nineteenth century. The sap of the marshmallow shrub was bound by egg whites, corn syrup, and water, and whipped and molded into a light, fluffy confection. If you live near brackish marshes, you've seen marshmallows—shrubs with pink hibiscus-like flowers. They're not endangered; gelatin and other agents have replaced mallow root in marshmallow candies, and they're made now by extrusion, a quicker and more efficient process than the original casting.

Perhaps because marshmallows are such a common candy, Ligonier, which has had a festival since 1956, didn't think to honor the marshmallow until 1992, even though Kidd & Company in Ligonier and Kraft in a nearby town produce more than half of the marshmallows in the United States. That makes Noble County the Marshmallow Capital of the World.

Recognizing this, the festival goes all out. There's usually some kind of marshmallowy drama. In 1993, the World's Largest Marshmallow, made in a drum, weighed 671 pounds. In 1994, the World's Largest Bag of Marshmallows was created, with marshmallow candies the size of basketballs.

For a snack, you can try caramel cream served over marshmallows and apples, never-fail fudge made with Kidd's Marshmallow Creme, Rice Krispies-and-marshmallow candies, Samores, the marshmallow cookie that Girl Scouts sell. And there's hearty fair food, too.

There's also a Marshmallow Cook-off. Contestants produce salads, pies, cakes, cookies, candies. And there's a marshmallow roast on Friday night accompanied by fireworks. Tip: To keep marshmallows from burning, use non-stick cooking spray.

For those interested in other kinds of food, there's a pizza-eating contest, and on Monday a pancake-and-sausage breakfast and a chicken barbecue put on by the Rotary Club.

Events include a kiddie parade and a grand parade featuring a jet-puffed marshmallow mascot, mud volleyball, a car show, a garden-tractor pull, marshmallow golf and other sports, and concerts. About 15,000 attend the party.

Location: Ligonier is on U.S. 6, near the junction with U.S. 33, about 23 miles south of Elkart. ☼ **Contact:** Ligonier Chamber of Commerce, P.O. Box 121, Ligonier IN 46767; Tel: (219)894-4113.

While You're There: Kidd's Marshmallow factory gives tours and a free bag of marshmallows on the Saturday of the festival.

Mitchell

Persimmon Festival

Last full week in September that includes two Saturdays (eight days, Saturday through Saturday) ☼ When the Persimmon Festival debuted in 1947, Mitchell was a tiny Hoosier town with a two-block-long main street. It's still small, and friendly, with a population of less than 5,000, making it the perfect place for a festival celebrating an indigenous American fruit with an Algonquin name. It's thought to be the only persimmon festival in the world.

Persimmon Pudding

2   cups persimmon pulp
2   cups sugar
2   eggs
1½ cups flour
1   teaspoon baking powder
1   teaspoon cinnamon

1   teaspoon baking soda
1½ cup   buttermilk
½   cup cream or canned milk
1   tablespoon honey
4   tablespoons melted butter

Mix persimmon pulp and sugar in large mixing bowl (it's better to mix manually rather than with an electric beater). Add two beaten eggs. Mix soda with buttermilk; set aside. Alternate mixing dry ingredients and buttermilk mixture into the pulp mixture. Add cream (or milk) and honey. Add butter. Pour into 9-inch by 13-inch buttered dish (preferably glass). Bake at 350 degrees for approximately one hour. The pudding is done when it feels firm in the middle. Serve with whipped cream. Makes 12 servings.

Dymple Green, owner of Dymple's Delight persimmon-processing plant

Women brought persimmon puddings to the first festival; that was the birth of the best-persimmon-pudding competition, now the heart of the festival.

More than 100 contestants enter, and their puddings vary from solid and cake-like to creamy. Some contestants use only the fruit from their favorite persimmon trees, believing that the taste of the pudding depends on the particular persimmons used. It's considered a high honor to take home the best-pudding prize, and the winning recipe is published in the local newspaper.

A second contest is held for persimmon novelty desserts—which can be anything but cookies, because they're considered too easy.

Civic and church groups staff food booths and serve persimmon puddings, cookies, pies, cakes, fudge, and ice cream, as well as locally grown apples and pumpkin dishes, and standard festival food. Suppers of chicken and dumplings; ham, beans, and corn bread; and other Heartland favorites are served each evening. You can also buy persimmon pulp to take home for cooking.

Highlights are the selection of the Persimmon Festival Queen and three Miss Persimmons, and a parade on the last day that's the second largest in the state (after the Indy 500). In addition, bands play, and there are carnival rides, a 5K run, a quilt exhibit, and a car rally. About 10,000 attend each day, and about 30,000 crowd Mitchell on the last day.

American persimmons (*Diospyros virginiana*) are not to be confused with the Oriental persimmons commonly seen in grocery stores. Those are *Diospyros kaki,* which have long been cultivated in Asia, especially Japan, and are heart-shaped and much larger than the

American fruit, which is about the size of a cherry tomato. American persimmons are short-trunked trees that flower in May or June.

To food historian Raymond Sokolov, the American persimmons are far superior, "powerfully fragrant, sweet and luscious, and taste like dates." But they aren't cultivated, they grow wild. An old belief that they're not worth eating until the first frost has made them fall to the ground, Sokolov says, is a canard; they taste just as good if they're cut and ripened off the tree. They are very sour when not ripe.

Settlers discovered the persimmon early on; Hernando DeSoto wrote the first description of one in 1539 in Florida. John Smith said that a ripe persimmon was as "delicious as an Apricock." Settlers in Pennsylvania made persimmon wine, and in Maryland and Virginia they made persimmon brandy.

Location: Mitchell is about 30 miles south of Bloomington, at the intersection of Indiana 37 and 60. **Contact:** Mitchell Chamber of Commerce, P.O. Box 216, Mitchell, IN 47446; Tel: (800)580-1985.

While You're There: Dymple's Delight, the only persimmon-processing plant in the United States, is just outside of town. It's a family operation on a farm, and visitors are welcome to tour the plant.

Plymouth

Marshall County Blueberry Festival

Labor Day weekend (Friday through Monday) Almost three million pounds of blueberries are grown in Indiana, and Marshall County is a center of blueberry farming, and a lot of people like blueberries, all of which could explain why more than half a million people turn out for Plymouth's blueberry festival.

They have the opportunity to eat blueberry pancakes, muffins, shakes, cheesecake, pies, bagels, and fizz. You'll have to visit the festival to find out what blueberry fizz is; the recipe is top secret.

To take home with you, there are ample supplies of blueberry jams, jellies, and pies for sale. There is also the usual festival food—dogs, burgers, and the like.

To emphasize the blueberriness of the gathering, a costumed "Blueberry Hank" walks around the festival grounds greeting people. And blueberries strewn across the starting lines of the 5K, 15K, and one-mile runs turn these races into blueberry stomps.

There's a plethora of other activities—a parade with Miss Blueberry Festival, Little Mr. Blueberry Festival and Little Miss Blueberry Festival (ages three to six) riding in splendor; sports; truck, tractor, and horse pulling; a carnival and a circus; a car show; fireworks.

The festival was started by the Jaycees in 1967 as a sesquicentennial celebration and has become the community's major event.

Location: Centennial Park in downtown Plymouth, 25 miles south of Sound Bend on U.S. 30 and U.S. 31. ✦ **Contact:** Marshall County Blueberry Festival, P.O. Box 639, Plymouth, IN 46563; Tel: (888)936-5020.

Valparaiso

Popcorn Festival

Saturday after Labor Day ✦ Each year, Americans consume a total of 17.3 billion quarts of popped popcorn, which is 68 quarts for every man, woman, and child. Mind-boggling.

The average-consumption numbers are plumped out at festivals like the one in Valparaiso, which is Orville Redenbacher's birthplace and the spot where he developed large, fluffy popcorn with a low percentage of "spinsters" or "duds" (kernels that don't pop). He produced it as Orville Redenbacher's Gourmet Popcorn, and eventually sold the patent to Hunt Wesson Foods, which continues to make the Gourmet Popcorn in Valparaiso with corn from Indiana fields.

Until his death in 1995, Orville always attended the festival. His grandson Gary now rides on a float with the festival queen, princess, and prince, and also signs a biography of his grandfather, which is for sale.

The festival, attended by about 50,000, began in 1979 and has kept its corniness. Crafts include popcorn items such as mugs with handles of glazed popcorn, popcorn picture frames, and popcorn-shaped jewelry. Floats in the two-hour parade must have a popcorn theme, and people use all parts of the popcorn plant—stalks, leaves, tassels, cobs, and, of course, the kernels, popped and unpopped.

Popcorn Pizza

1 box 12.5 oz. Applan Way® Pizza Mix	1 cup shredded Colby cheese
1 pound ground hamburger	½ cup chopped onions (optional)
1 cup shredded mozzarella cheese	5 cups popped popcorn

Grease a 12-inch pizza pan. Spread dough on pan. Add sauce (included in pizza mix). Spread evenly. Sprinkle meat over sauce. Spread mozzarella cheese over meat. Bake in oven at 425 degrees for 15 minutes. Take out of oven. Add popcorn. Add Colby cheese. Place back in oven for 3 minutes. Let cool 10 minutes.

Rick Steuer, Kouts, Indiana, First Prize Winner, Valparaiso Popcorn Festival

It's no surprise that Indiana is home to more than one popcorn festival: it's the top producer in the world, with almost 80,000 acres devoted just to popcorn. (Courtesy of Hunt Wesson and The Valparaiso Popcorn Festival)

About 50 food vendors sell the usual fare, hot dogs and such, but many also sell popcorn and popcorn balls. Hunt Wesson provides the vendors with popcorn, including about 400 pounds used by the kettle-corn vendor. Kettle corn is old-fashioned caramel popcorn, made by putting popcorn, sugar, and oil in a huge kettle over an open fire, and stirring it with a paddle. As the corn pops, it gets coated, and it doesn't fly out of the kettle because the caramelized sugar makes it heavy. Yet it's surprisingly light and dry when it emerges.

Popcorn is a genuinely American food. At that first Thanksgiving feast in Plymouth, Massachusetts, Quadequina, brother of the Wampanoag chief, brought a deerskin bag of popped corn. Earlier, Columbus found West Indians wearing popcorn leis, and for other Indians popcorn was a dietary staple as well as a good material for headdresses and for offerings to gods.

But popcorn goes even farther back. Archaeologists have found ears of popcorn in the Bat Cave in west-central New Mexico that are about 5,600 years old; they know it's popcorn because botanists have determined that the original maize or corn was popcorn.

There are now five types of corn—sweet, dent, flint, pod, and popcorn—and popcorn is the only one that pops. The reason it pops is because each kernel stores water in a small circle of soft starch. As it heats, the pressure builds until the hard surface surrounding the starch explodes, and the soft starch pops out.

Today popcorn is grown in 19 states and in Ontario, Canada, but Indiana is way ahead of the pack, with almost 80,000 acres devoted to popcorn. Illinois and Nebraska are second and third. Almost all popcorn is grown in the United States, and Americans eat more than the people of any other country.

Location: In the blocks around the courthouse, downtown Valparaiso, off U.S. 80 in the northwest corner of the state.   **Contact:** Valparaiso Popcorn Festival, Inc., 204 E. Lincolnway, P.O. Box 189, Valparaiso, IN 46384; Tel: (219)464-8332, Fax: (219)464-2343.

Van Buren

Popcorn Festival

Second weekend in August (Thursday through Saturday)
Van Buren calls itself the Popcorn Center of the World because Weaver's, the world's largest popcorn-processing company, is in Van Buren, and because a lot of popcorn is grown around here. Popcorn is poppin' out all over at the festival; it's made in giant poppers and sold in bags for 25 cents in the Weaver Popcorn Tent. You can also buy unpopped corn and caramel corn at the information booth. To go with the popcorn, vendors sell a range of fair food, including grilled steak, hot dogs, and elephant ears.

Festivities begin with a 150-unit parade and the crowning of a prince, princess, and queen on Thursday night. Before the weekend ends, there are bed races, a 5K run, musical entertainment, a magic show, a garden-tractor pull, crafts, line dancing, and clogging.

The festival began in 1973 and draws about 15,000.

Location: Van Buren is about 30 miles north of Indianapolis, just off I-69.   **Contact:** Van Buren Popcorn Festival, 5046 W. Main St., Van Buren, IN 46991; Tel: (317)934-4888.

See Also: Valparaiso Popcorn Festival (Valparaiso, IN).

Vernon

Sassafras Tea Festival

Last weekend in April   The local historical society puts on this tea festival as a fund raiser, which seems appropriate since sassafras is a North American native tree with good historic roots: it was one of the earliest exports from the New World to England. The festival began in 1963, and about 7,000 attend for free tea and cookies. In addition, ham-and-bean dinners with corn bread and pie are sold, plus hundreds of homemade

These costumed visitors whip up a batch of good old-fashioned sassafras tea, celebrating the long history of the sassafras plant and raising money for the local historical society. (Courtesy of the Jennings County Visitors Center)

pies and more than 500 loaves of homemade bread of all kinds—white, whole wheat, lemon, poppy-seed, pumpkin, banana-nut, persimmon, and blueberry, among others. Ninety pounds of beans are cooked for the dinners.

Other attractions are weaving demonstrations, a working blacksmith shop, and a Civil War encampment, with participants in uniform, a reminder of the Civil War battle fought here.

To make the tea, the roots of sassafras trees or shrubs, native in this area, are dug, cleaned, split, dried, and bundled, and then boiled into tea. The best roots are red and saturated with sap; they must be dug before the sap starts to run.

The root has a strong, sweet smell and, besides being used for tea, provides a flavoring for certain medicines and candies and is an ingredient in root beer and sauces. After settlers introduced the pig to North America, Plains Indians used sassafras to give flavor to ham.

Location: Vernon is about 30 miles southeast of Columbus, on Indiana 7, just south of U.S. 50. **Contact:** Jennings County Visitors Center, P.O. Box 415, Vernon, IN 47282; Tel: (800)928-3667, Fax: (812)346-8928.

Michigan

Battle Creek

Cereal Festival

First weekend in June (Thursday through Saturday) ❀ It began with the Seventh Day Adventists suffering from dyspepsia, or indigestion.

Now Battle Creek, the Cereal City, has the World's Longest Breakfast Table (Springfield, Massachusetts, claims the longest, too), a line of picnic tables stretching down Michigan Avenue on Saturday morning. The table is loaded with the products of the local cereal companies—about 20 kinds of cereal, Tang orange drink, and Pop-Tarts—plus milk, bananas, and doughnut holes. Civic clubs set up coffee stations. It's all free, and between 60,000 and 65,000 people, more than the population of Battle Creek, have their breakfast downtown.

The breakfast began in 1956 as a Golden Jubilee celebration of the Kellogg Company's founding, and 14,000 people sat down for cereal, twice as many as expected. Thirty years later, Springfield, Massachusetts, celebrating an anniversary, decided to challenge Battle Creek. The competition continued through 1995, but then Battle Creek opted out of competing for either longest-table or most-breakfasts honors, because the Battle Creek breakfast had become a festival, with more events than just stuff that went snap-crackle-pop, and because the cereal-company hosts wanted to put the emphasis back on the city's cereal heritage.

Events begin on Thursday night with the Miss Cereal City Pageant, which is affiliated with the Miss Michigan/Miss America Pageant. Friday's highlights are two evening parades—a grand parade followed by a children's parade, where the kids dress like their favorite cereal characters. Saturday's highlight is still the World's Longest Breakfast Table, which 600 volunteers keep stocked. Wandering around while people eat are cereal characters: Kellogg's Tony the Tiger; Snap, Crackle, and Pop; Toucan Sam; and Post's Sugar Bear.

The breakfast segues into a fair with an arts and crafts show, and entertainment that varies from year to year but always includes music, kids' games, family walks and runs, and sometimes thunderous events such as a parade of 500 motorcyclists.

Back to the Adventists. In the 1800s they had their world headquarters in Battle Creek. Their leader, Ellen White, had a vision in 1865 that there should be a sanitarium to treat the flock for dyspepsia. Adventist John Harvey Kellogg was appointed director of the sanitarium, and was charged to treat people with all kinds of ailments. Some of the treatments were a bit faddish. Patients with high blood pressure, for example, were served nothing but grapes.

Kellogg was not exactly flaky, but while he was studying medicine, his daily breakfast was seven graham crackers and an apple. This was the start of his crusade to get people eating dietetic, already-cooked breakfast cereals to replace what he called "dyspepsia producing breakfast mush."

He came up with Granola, and then with his brother developed a method of flaking wheat kernels, and pretty soon they were marketing corn flakes. In 1906 the Kellogg Company was founded.

In the meantime, Charles Post had gone to the Battle Creek Sanatorium for ulcers. Kellogg didn't cure them, but his cereals gave Post the inspiration to market cereal as a health aid, and he came up with Postum and Grape Nuts.

When the Golden Jubilee of the Kellogg Company was being planned, someone came up with the idea for the World's Longest Breakfast Table. Now it's an institution, and Kellogg, Ralston Foods, and the Post Division of Kraft General Foods, all with local plants, get together to serve their breakfasts of champions.

Location: Michigan Avenue in downtown Battle Creek. Take exit 98B off I-94. ⊛ **Contact:** Greater Battle Creek/Calhoun County Visitors and Convention Bureau, 35 W. Jackson St., Battle Creek, MI 49017; Tel: (616)962-2240, or (800)397-2240, Fax: (616)962-6917.

See Also: World's Largest Pancake Breakfast (Springfield, MA).

<hr>

Berrien Springs

Christmas Pickle Festival

First weekend in December ⊛ They cheer the Pickle Queen, sing Christmas carols, listen to string quartets, and eat chocolate-covered pickles. An unusual way to evoke the Yuletide spirit?

Not in Berrien Springs, which is the Christmas Pickle Capital of the World.

This event began in 1992 as a way to celebrate the town's pickle heritage and to revive, in a way, an old German Christmas custom: on Christmas Eve parents hang a blown-glass pickle ornament on the Christmas tree, and on Christmas morning, the child who first discovers the pickle receives an extra gift.

The 1839 Courthouse Museum sells pickle ornaments in several sizes that are made in Germany from antique molds. While you're in town, you can also buy wonderful Christmasy foods: dill-pickle sausages, pickle bread, pickle relishes, and sweet gherkins covered with chocolate, which are the official festival confection. And to do it yourself, there are pickle-making mixes for sale.

The festival features a recipe contest for pickle dishes; performances by instrumental and choral groups; museum displays of decorated trees and a Victorian holiday dining room; demonstrations of blacksmithing (the smithy makes magic stocking hooks for Santa). The highlight is a parade that's almost longer than the town; it's led by the Grand Dillmeister, who's chosen by the townspeople, accompanied by real camels and a huge (unreal) Rudolph the Red Nosed Pickle, whose nose flashes like police-car lights.

About 3,000 come to the pickle festival, which isn't bad when you figure that only 2,000 people live in Berrien Springs. Many are of German descent and are fond of pickles. The town is in the heart of cucumber farms, and at one time had several pickle-bottling plants, although now there's only one. The old farmers call the cucumber plants raised for pickles "pickle vines."

Location: Berrien Springs is about 10 miles from I-94 at exit 28, about 15 miles north of the Indiana border. **Contact:** Christmas Pickle Festival, 1839 Courthouse Museum, P.O. Box 261, Berrien Springs, MI 49103; Tel: (616)471-1202.

Boyne City

National Mushroom Festival

Weekend of third Sunday in May (Friday through Sunday)
 American morels are considered the most delicious—and elusive—of mushrooms. Boyne City, which calls itself the Mushroom Capital of the World (as do some other cities), celebrates the morels hiding in its woodlands with a mushroom festival held since 1961.

Its major event is the hunt. Buses take about 450 hunters to morel-hunting grounds where they vie for the National Mushroom Hunting Championship awarded to the person who finds the most morels in 90 minutes. Residents and non-residents compete in separate categories for the awards, which include wooden morel trophies.

Sometimes very few morels are found, but once a hunter gathered 961. You never know. Morels are supposedly most plentiful under ash and poplar trees. One expert said he had never found them near a pine or oak tree.

About 15,000 gather for events other than the hunt. A carnival kicks off the festival on Thursday night. Friday's lineup includes a welcome seminar and free guided tour; instructions on hunting, cooking, and preserving morels; and free cream-of-morel soup. Saturday begins with a morel breakfast, continues with the hunt, and is followed by the "Taste of Boyne," in which area restaurants offer samples of morel specialties under a big top. Dishes include sautéed morels, morel-and-wild-asparagus frittata, morel hash, wild game with morels, chicken morel, morel custard.

Morels are found in woodlands in the Midwest and Northwest, but are most abundant in Michigan. There are several types of morels, but all "true" morels have honeycomb or pitted heads that look like sponges or coral. Morels fruit most heavily in May; thus, May is Morel Month in Michigan, and the state has several morel festivals, all featuring morel hunts. Among them are the Lewiston Morel Festival, on the second Saturday in May; for information call (517)786-2293. Another is the Mushroom Festival in Mesick, on the second weekend in May; for information call (616)885-1280.

Location: Boyne City, 20 miles south of Petoskey on the Lower Peninsula, is six miles west of U.S. 131. **Contact:** Boyne City Chamber of Commerce, 28 South Lake St., Boyne City, MI 49712; Tel: (616)582-6222, or (800)230-2739.

National Pickle Festival

Third weekend in August (Thursday through Sunday)
There are a number of pickle-packing factories and cucumber farmers and pickers in the Linwood area, and Michigan is the number-one state in growing cucumbers for pickles, so the idea of a pickle party seemed perfect. The party began in 1977 as a fund raiser for the Linwood Bi-Centennial Park (that's the Linwood spelling) completed in 1976. It still supports the park, in part with a raffle of a ton—that's a lot of pecks—of sweet, dill, bread and butter, and sour pickles, plus pickle cubes and relish. Pickles are also sold with barbecued chicken, roast pig, sloppy joes, and hot dogs.

Other events of the festival include a grand parade and a children's parade; a pickle-eating contest, in which contestants eat a pickle and then try to whistle; a designing-strange-or-interesting-objects-with-cucumbers contest; judging of home pickle canning; karaoke and dancing; magic shows. Attendance is 6,000 to 8,000.

Location: Linwood, on the edge of Saginaw Bay, is four miles east of I-75 at the Linwood Road exit. **Contact:** Pickle Festival, 2374 Linwood Rd., Linwood, MI 48634; Tel: (517)697-3868.

Seafood Festival

First weekend in September (Friday through Sunday)
Marquette, on the southern shore of Lake Superior, was founded as a shipping center in 1849, so seafood seemed an apt centerpiece when the Rotary Club founded this festival in 1984.

It's now a seafood satiation event: in three days, more than 5,000 pounds of seafood—shrimp and crab legs, chowder, frog legs, lake trout, Cajun catfish, whitefish, lobster, mussels, and seafood salad—are consumed, along with 800 pounds of bratwursts and hot dogs, 1,500 ears of corn, 1,200 baked potatoes, and vast quantities of other edibles. As they feast, festivalgoers are entertained with music, kids' games, and sky divers if the weather permits.

Location: Matson Lower Harbor Park on Lakeshore Blvd., Marquette, on I-41 on the Upper Peninsula. **Contact:** Marquette Chamber of Commerce, 501 S. Front St., Marquette, MI 49855; Tel: (906)226-6591.

While You're There: The Marquette Maritime Museum, in an 1890s waterworks building at East Ridge and Lake Shore Drive, outlines the maritime heritage of Marquette and Lake Superior with displays of boats, antique engines, and photos, as well as replicas of a fishing shanty and the dockside offices of Marquette's first commercial fishing and passenger companies.

Montrose

Montrose Blueberry Festival

Third weekend in August (Friday through Sunday) A local berry grower, Montrose Orchards, donates 300 pounds of berries for a breakfast of blueberry pancakes and sausage on Saturday and Sunday, and that's just the start of the blueberry eating. Various berry products—pies, cakes, cookies, ice cream, candy, and doughnuts—are available throughout the weekend. And the blueberry is also celebrated with a blueberry-pie eating contest (messy) and a blueberry bake-off (tasty); contestants auction off their entries after the judging.

Festival events include a 100-unit Super Parade and a children's costume parade, a gospel sing, a carnival, softball, volleyball, horseshoes, and teen dances. Between 30,000 and 35,000 attend the festival, which began in 1971 to raise money for a school pool.

Michigan is the leading producer of highbush blueberries in North America. Depending on the variety, the berries are tart, mild, medium, or sweet.

Location: Montrose is about 20 miles northwest of Flint, six miles west of I-75 at exit 131. **Contact:** Montrose Blueberry Festival, P.O. Box 316, Montrose, MI 48457; Tel: (810)639-3475.

See Also: Whitesbog Blueberry Festival (Whitesbog, NJ).

Niles

Apple Festival

Usually third weekend in September You can start the day with apple pancakes, apple fritters, and baked apples with ice cream. And you can follow up with slices of apple pie, apple dumplings, apple taffy, caramel apples, and apple cider. There are also plenty of vendors on hand offering food other than apples—gator tails, clam chowder, fried rice, walleye sandwiches, to name a few.

The festival celebrates the abundance of apple orchards (growing 14 varieties of apples) in what's known as the Four Flags Area, and Michigan's standing as the fourth-ranking apple-producing state. About 75,000 people attend the festival, which began in 1973.

The theme rarely swerves from apples. There's an apple-pie-cooking contest, in which aroma is one of the criteria for judging, and an apple-pie-eating contest. The apple queen is a contestant in this event, and has to eat the pie with her hands behind her back. There are also contests for apple-seed popping and apple peeling, and a biggest-apple contest for growers. Tours of orchards and wineries in the area are offered.

Entertainment is pretty much non-stop and includes the crowning of the queen, king, and princess, puppet shows, a beard and moustache contest, a scarecrow contest, line dancing, and a parade.

Niles is in the center of the Four Flags Area, called this because the flags of France, England, Spain, and the United States have flown here. A fort completed in 1691, manned by French soldiers, was the first permanent European community in Michigan. The city is named for the publisher of a newspaper in Maryland who never visited Niles.

Location: Lake and 17th Sts., adjacent to Niles airport, 5 miles north of South Bend, IN. **Contact:** Apple Festival, P.O. Box 672, Niles, MI 49120; Tel: (616)663-8870.

Romeo

Peach Festival

Labor Day weekend (Saturday through Monday) The peach crop goes up and down in Michigan, but generally the state is one of the top ten producers of peaches in the country. This long-time festival, started in 1930, is attended by 400,000 to 500,000 people, making it a close second-runner to the colossal National Cherry Festival in Traverse City.

The purpose of the festival, started by peach growers, is to salute the peach. You'll find, therefore, civic groups selling homemade peach pies, service clubs offering peach-pancake breakfasts, other vendors selling peach cobbler, doughnuts, strudel, cakes, jams, jellies, ice cream, and yogurt. Some also sell apple strudel—not an interloper, since apples are grown in the area, too.

If you stroll around the shopping area, you can stop for a cup of peach-flavored tea or coffee at the Peaches 'n' Creame shop, or try peach fudge and peach pie at the Ice Cream Saloon.

To augment the peach menu, there are Italian sausages, German bratwurst, barbecued ribs, steak sandwiches, and Oriental and Mexican foods, and beers from around the world. Different church groups traditionally hold suppers or cook-offs; for instance, the Baptist Church has a chili cook-off, with samples for tasting. Other eating events: an ice-cream social and pie-eating contests for kids and adults.

Romeo is north of Detroit's northern suburbs and on the edge of the fertile land of Michigan's Thumb, where the waters of Lake Huron temper the climatic extremes of summer and winter. Peaches are not the hardiest trees, but they thrive in California, in the Great Lakes regions of New York, Ohio, and Michigan, and along the Atlantic seaboard from Georgia as far north as Massachusetts.

The Thumb area—a description made meaningful by the fact that Michigan is shaped like a right-handed mitten, palm-up—was once covered by forests, but now it's farm and orchard land. Peaches, apples, blueberries, and sugar beets are grown here, and 14 orchards are in the Romeo area. You can take tours of the orchards and buy fresh fruit at orchard stands.

The festival is packed with events, including plenty of activities for youngsters, plenty of games, sports, and 300 crafts booths. A children's parade Monday morning and the Peach Festival Floral Parade Monday afternoon bring the celebration to a close.

Location: Romeo is about 30 miles north of downtown Detroit, off Michigan 53. **Contact:** Romeo Chamber of Commerce, P.O. Box 175, Romeo, MI 48065; Tel: (810)752-4436.

Sebewaing

Michigan Sugar Festival

Last weekend in June (Friday through Sunday) A chemist named Andreas Marggraf produced sugar from beets in 1747. Despite the fact that this sugar was shown to be chemically the same as sugar from sugar cane, it was many years before people wanted to use beet sugar as sugar. But then in 1811, Napoleon ordered 70,000 acres planted in beets, and factories were established to process it. This was out of necessity; the French were sugar-starved because a British blockade had cut off their supply of sugar cane from the West Indies.

Today beets are second to cane as the world's sugar source, and the United States, along with Russia, France, and Germany, are major producers of sugar beets. The industry is important because it frees countries in temperate climates from having to rely solely on tropical countries where sugar cane grows.

In the United States, about 30 million tons of sugar beets are produced each year, mostly in states in the northern part of the corn belt. Minnesota grows the most, and Michigan ranks fifth. In Michigan's Thumb area, it's the most important crop.

At the sugar festival, the sugary food helps people recognize the importance of the crop to the economy. There's free cotton candy, made from sugar beets, of course. And nearly everything else you eat at the festival contains sugar-beet sugar, from the ever popular elephant ears to homemade baked beans, pies, popcorn, and barbecued pork, beef, and chicken. Pancake breakfasts are sweetened with sugar-beet sugar, and you will be reminded that the sweetness of a strawberry ice cream social comes from *Beta vulgaris*.

The festival has been held since 1965 and features a road race, children's games, entertainers, sports, music. And sugar.

Location: Sebewaing is on Michigan 25, on the Saginaw Bay side of the Thumb. ⊕
Contact: Sugar Beet Festival, P.O. Box 622, Sebewaing, MI 48759; Tel: (517)883-2150.

Shelby and Hart

National Asparagus Festival

Second weekend in June (Friday through Sunday) ⊕ Shelby and Hart in Oceana County alternate as hosts of this festival, which celebrates the county's standing as Asparagus Capital of the World. The state of Michigan ranks third in the United States in growing asparagus, but the county harvests 9,700 acres of asparagus, and the Michigan legislature has proclaimed the county the asparagus capital, so that's that.

The festival, held in the "Spear-It of Elegance" since 1974, is attended by 10,000 to 15,000 people. Farm tours show folks how asparagus is grown and harvested, the wife of a grower is named Mrs. Asparagus, there's a parade and other entertainment.

There's usually both an asparagus luncheon and an asparagus dinner. A food show is held Saturday, and dishes prepared by professional and homebody cooks can be sampled. Michigan State University puts out a recipe book of favorites from the show, and these favorites have included asparagus delight (cold asparagus, sour cream, and salted peanuts), asparagus cakes, turnovers, souffle, meatballs, jelly, asparagus in shrimp sauce, and pickled asparagus.

The recipe book relates an odd bit of history: "The first assembly line processing plant in Oceana County was improvised in 1874 when the carrier pigeons arrived in such numbers they darkened the skies. Men, women and children all did their part as they captured the birds, plucked and packed them with ice in barrels and shipped them to New York for consumption in fancy restaurants." Strange doings in Oceana County.

Location: Hart is six miles north of Shelby, which is about 55 miles northwest of Grand Rapids. Both towns are just off U.S. 31. ⊕ **Contact:** National Asparagus Festival, P.O. Box 117, Shelby, MI 49455; Tel: (616)873-2129.

See Also: Stockton Asparagus Festival (Stockton, CA).

St. Johns

Mint Festival

Second weekend in August (Friday through Sunday) ⊕ Does the spearmint lose its flavor on the bedpost overnight?

You may not find the answer to that old song line at the Mint Festival, but you'll be able to sample mint ice cream, peppermint milk shakes, and minty tea. And you can buy bags of chocolate mints or hard mint candy and bottles of peppermint and spearmint oil for cooking. There's a chicken barbecue, too.

About 60,000 people attend the festival to celebrate the mint crop. Clinton County annually grows about 400,000 pounds of spearmint and peppermint on 12,000 acres and is Michigan's top mint producer, supplying about five percent of the world's total. St. Johns, which has mint farms, mint distilleries, and mint-candy factories, calls itself the Mint City.

The first commercial mint production in the United States began in the late 1700s. By the end of the Civil War, Michigan, with its rich black soil, was the primary supplier of mint. In the 1930s, verticillium wilt struck, and production in Clinton County practically stopped. But wilt-resistant strains were developed, saving the industry.

Oil for flavoring is produced in glands of the mint leaves and stems and is collected by distilling the mint hay in special condensers. Peppermint oil is used in chewing gum, candy, toothpaste, and medicines. Spearmint oil, with a smaller market, is used mostly in toothpaste and chewing gum.

Festival events include a mint parade, mint farm tours, a Kiss-the-Cow contest, arts and crafts exhibits, a teen dance, sports tournaments, bands, and a gospel sing-along.

A cookbook is available with recipes for dishes like Mint Melt-Away Cookies and Pink Peppermint Pie. It also has mint facts: One drop of oil will flavor a pitcher of lemonade, and one pound of oil will flavor 135,000 sticks of gum.

It doesn't say anything about what happens to spearmint on the bedpost.

Location: St. Johns is 20 miles north of Lansing at the crossroads of U.S. 27 and Michigan 21. **Contact:** St. Johns Area Chamber of Commerce, P.O. Box 61, St. Johns, MI 48879; Tel: (517)224-7248.

Traverse City

National Cherry Festival

Eight days, beginning the Saturday after the Fourth of July It's all because a Presbyterian missionary took time out from saving souls to plant some cherry trees that half a million people converge on Traverse City, the Cherry Capital of the World, in July.

Here's the story. Cherries originated in Asia, and then spread around the world. The Roman general Lucullus celebrated a victory in Cerasus, Pontus (now Giresun, Turkey), by bringing a sour cherry tree from there to Italy. That's why the sour cherry is *Prunus cerasus*. When settlers arrived in the New World, they found Cree Indians using sour cherries in pemmican.

Fast forward to 1852, when Peter Dougherty, the missionary, planted the first orchard of Montmorency cherries—a sour or tart cherry—on the Old Mission Peninsula on Lake Michigan. The winds off the lake tempered the cold of winter and heat of summer, the trees thrived, and in 1893 the first commercial orchard was planted near Dougherty's original plot.

The Cherry Prince and Princess preside over the festival (along with the Cherry Queen, of course). Note the young princess's professional beauty queen wave. (National Cherry Festival, Traverse City, Michigan)

The Montmorency was developed in the seventeenth century and brought to North America by French settlers. It's the principal tart cherry grown because it's very juicy and excellent for pies, preserves, jellies, and juices.

The region around Traverse City, at the base of the peninsula, has more than two million cherry trees, the densest concentration of cherry trees in the world, producing more than half of Michigan's tart cherries. Michigan leads the nation in tart-cherry production, annually harvesting well over 200 million pounds, three-fourths of the U.S. crop. When it comes to sweet cherries, Michigan is among the top four producers.

The National Cherry Queen reigns over the festival, which has nearly 150 events, many of them free. Cherry-related events include cherry-pie-eating and pit-spitting contests, tours of cherry orchards, a photo exhibit of the cherry industry, week-long tasting at the Cherry Product Sampling Pavilion, ice-cream socials with cherry sundaes, a Very Cherry Luncheon, and a Taste of Cherries Food Fair.

Cherry dishes visitors might want to try include nuggets (sugar-coated dried cherries), bread, pizza, pudding, cobbler, salsa, soup, cherry-bran "chewies," tarts, pies, cheesecake, and cherries in combination with other foods—for example, cherry-chicken-almond casserole.

And then there are three parades, drum-and-bugle-corps competitions, an air show, sporting events, an arts and crafts show, concerts, a milk-carton-boat regatta, rides, and clowns.

Location: Throughout downtown Traverse City in northwestern Michigan on U.S. 31. ☼ Contact: National Cherry Festival, 108 W. Grandview Parkway, Traverse City, MI 49684; Tel: (616)947-4230, Fax: (616)947-7435.

Vermontville

Maple Syrup Festival

Last weekend in April (Friday through Sunday) ☼ Michigan is usually only sixth in the state rankings of maple-sugar production, but since Vermont is first, a town named Vermontville in Michigan deserves to celebrate maple.

Not just for the name. This little village of 800 people is the home of 15 maple-syrup producers. It was settled by Vermonters who were looking for a new place to live and farm, because the Vermont soil was getting worn out. They started tapping maples, and in 1942 decided to have a festival. Vermonters are steadfast; they're still having the festival.

About 20,000 people visit and get to see the maple sugaring process, have a pancake breakfast with syrup, buy maple fudge, cream, and syrup. To counteract all those calories, there are contests for wood chopping, egg tossing, and arm wrestling. Those who would rather watch than act can enjoy clog dancing, bagpipes, arts and crafts displays, a petting zoo, and carnival rides.

Location: Vermontville is 30 miles southwest of Lansing, 12 miles west of I-69. ☼ Contact: Maple Syrup Festival, 8413 Brown Rd., Vermontville, MI 49096; Tel: (517)726-0394).

See Also: Vermont Maple Festival (St. Albans, VT).

Yale

Yale Bologna Festival

Last full weekend in July (Friday through Sunday) ☼ The World's Biggest Bologna Bash. That's what they call this event, and who's to argue with people who have the slogan, "We're Full of Bologna and Proud of It"?

Yale has been producing bologna, pronounced baloney, since 1906, largely for local consumption, with recipes handed down through the generations. Only one bologna plant remains, but that's enough for a festival. It started in 1989, has an attendance of 15,000, and features the crowning of a Bologna King and Queen, dancing, a magic show, a craft show, a pancake and sausage breakfast on Sunday, and plenty of bologna sandwiches every day.

On Saturday there occurs what may be America's most incongruous combination of events: outhouse races, a fashion show, and high tea. This is true.

Location: Yale is about 60 miles east of Flint, on Michigan 19, about 10 miles north of I-69. ☼ Contact: Yale Area Chamber of Commerce, 112 E. Mechanic St., Yale, MI 48097; Tel: (810)387-YALE.

Minnesota

Big Island Rendezvous and Festival

First full weekend in October ☼ In the days of the fur trade, the rendezvous was a time of trading, exchanging information about the land, and, of course, companionship and feasting after the days and months trappers spent alone in the wilderness.

This festival gives a glimpse of those early rendezvous, and at the same time shows the heritage of different ethnic groups who pioneered in North America in mountain-man days.

An encampment of 250 tents, with almost 1,000 costumed performers, lets visitors relive the fur-trading era from 1750 to the 1840s. Foods of the period, as well as later regional foods, are available: buffalo—a staple to the trappers, Native American fry bread, beef stew, barbecued pork, sourdough bread, cheese curds, Pennsylvania Dutch funnel cakes, pork and beef sandwiches, kettle corn—popcorn cooked over an open fire. Homemade root beer and sarsaparilla are favorites.

Visitors are encouraged to try to start a fire by scraping flint and steel over dry kindling, and there are demonstrations of rope making and knife and tomahawk throwing. Entertainment includes clogging to old-time stringband music, Minnesota folk singers, and folk musicians playing guitars, harmonicas, and the autoharp.

Location: Bancroft Bay Park in Albert Lea, at the junction of I-90 and I-35, about 12 miles north of the Iowa border. ☼ **Contact:** Big Island Rendezvous and Festival, 202 North Broadway, Albert Lea, MN 56007; Tel: (800)659-2526, or (507)373-3938.

Rutabaga Festival

Fourth weekend in August (Friday and Saturday) ☼ There are only two Askovs in the world, one in Minnesota and one in Denmark. This is a tip-off that, besides rutabagas, you're going to find a lot of *aebelskivers* at the Rutabaga Festival. In

Rutabaga Cookies

1 egg	2 tablespoons grated orange rind
1 cup oleo or butter	3 tablespoons orange juice
½ cup sugar	⅓ cup mashed rutabagas
1½ cups flour	½ cup raisins
⅔ teaspoon baking power	½ teaspoon ground ginger
¼ teaspoon salt	

Beat egg and add the oleo and sugar. Combine flour, baking powder, salt, and ginger and sift. Mix with remaining ingredients. Grease cookie sheet, drip a teaspoon of batter and space. Bake 12 minutes at 350 degrees.

Edna Petersen, Askov, MN

fact, this town of 350 manages to bake more than 7,000 aebelskivers—round fluffy pastries made with a buttermilk batter that look like small tennis balls and are eaten with chokecherry or blueberry syrup, or applesauce or jam, or rolled in brown sugar. Aebelskivers, need it be said, are a Danish favorite, and Askov has a large percentage of people with Danish ancestors.

This festival was started in the 1920s or 1930s when Askov was the Rutabaga Capital of the World because, Askovians say, the finest and largest rutabagas—turnip-like vegetables—were grown here. In the 1960s, the factory that wax-coated and packaged the rutabagas burned down, and rutabaga growing, which is labor-intensive, declined and now barely exists in Askov.

For the festival, about 1,300 pounds of rutabagas are picked up in Cumberland, Wisconsin, and sold by the bag or used in the Danish dinner served on Saturday evening. The dinner menu: mashed rutabagas, red cabbage, Danish meatballs.

A rutabaga-cooking contest rewards creativity. Entries have included rutabaga cole slaw, jam, stew, and Bloody Marys—puréed rutabaga with V-8 juice and Tabasco, with or without alcohol.

Church and other local groups, which count on the festival for raising funds, sell traditional offerings like hamburgers and hot dogs. And there are other events going on—a parade, a talent show, clowns, music, a pageant to crown a queen. The festival is also a homecoming of sorts, in that high-school class reunions are invariably held to coincide with it.

Rutabagas are not turnips but are often confused with them; rutabagas are more nutritious than turnips and have more chromosomes. What the average consumer is more likely to notice than chromosomes is that rutabagas can be as much as a foot in diameter and have yellow to orange flesh, whereas turnips are generally white-fleshed.

The name rutabaga is from the Swedish *rotabagge,* and in Minnesota, people pronounce the vegetable rutabaggy. Rutabagas are often called Swedes, or Swede turnips. Other tidbits: it's believed in Askov that Danes brought the first seeds to the area; in the Scandinavian countries rutabagas were fed to cows. It isn't known for sure where the rutabaga originated; the turnip is prehistoric, but the Swede is thought to be a cabbage-turnip hybrid that appeared in the Middle Ages.

Location: Askov is about midway between Minneapolis and Duluth, off I-35.
Contact: Askov City Offices, 6369 Merchant St., Askov, MN 55704; Tel: (320)838-3616.

While You're There: Wander around town to get a sense of its founders; the main cross street is named Hans Christian Andersen, and street signs give names in English and Danish.

Barnesville Potato Days

Third week in August (Friday and Saturday) There are contests during Potato Days for potato peeling and potato picking. There's an "Eyes of Fashion" Potato Sack Fashion Show, where people compete to create the most creative costume from potato sacks. There's potato golf and potato billiards. There's a potato cook-off and a *lefse* cook-off (read on). People like to compete in Barnesville.

Mashed Potato Fudge

This recipe is quick and easy, requires no cooking, and is a great way to use leftover mashed potatoes.

½ cup chilled leftover mashed potatoes
2 ounces unsweetened baking chocolate
2 tablespoons butter
½ teaspoon salt
1 teaspoon vanilla
4¼ cups powdered sugar
½ cup chopped walnuts

Put mashed potatoes in a mixing bowl. Melt butter and chocolate in a small bowl in microwave and add to mashed potatoes. Blend with a rubber spatula until smooth. Add salt and vanilla. Blend in powdered sugar ½ cup at a time. Add chopped walnuts. Note: Amount of powdered sugar can be adjusted as moisture content of mashed potatoes varies from time to time. Mixture should be soft but not sticky to the touch. Spread into a buttered 8" x 8" pan. Chill and cut into squares.

Dorothy Garvin, 1994 Potato Days Festival Cook Off Recipe

This well-dressed (tater) tot takes a break from the glamorous world of the Potato Sack Fashion Show during Barnesville's Potato Days. (Photo by Mike Kossick)

The festival began in 1938 and was held sporadically until it was officially revived in 1992. Barnesville is in the Red River Valley, noted for potatoes, and potatoes are definitely what you'll find to eat: potato dumplings, baked potatoes, potato doughnuts, potato sausage, French fries, German potato salad. There's a potato-pancake feed Saturday morning, and a Buck-a-Bowl potato-soup feed in the afternoon.

The potato cook-off allows any kind of dish so long as the main ingredient is potatoes; creativity wins.

The lefse contest is more rigid, since lefses don't allow for much variation in ingredients. The predominant ethnic group in Barnesville is Norwegian, and lefses are popular Norwegian delicacies. They are tortilla-like, plate-sized crepes, made of potato, flour, shortening, salt, and pepper. They are eaten with sugar or sometimes rolled around meat or other fillings, but the judges eat them plain so the lefse taste is unadulterated.

Contestants make up a batch of lefses, and the ones the judges don't eat are sold to visitors. Usually that means hundreds of lefses are for sale, but you need to get in line early because they go fast.

When the first potato celebration was held, the main focus was a potato-picking contest. Louis Ernst was the champion in that first contest, picking 25½ bushels of potatoes in

38 minutes. The following year, a women-only potato-peeling contest was added. The two contests remain big events, but the potato peeling is now open to both men and women.

The spud days also feature a street fair, with arts and crafts and fresh produce and stage entertainment, and a 160-unit parade on Saturday morning.

Clay County, where Barnesville is located, has been growing potatoes since the latter part of the nineteenth century. At one time, more potatoes were produced and shipped from within Clay County than any other county in the United States except Maine's famed Aroostook County.

Location: Barnesville is off I-94, about 15 miles southeast of Fargo, ND.
Contact: City of Barnesville, P.O. Box 550, Barnesville, MN 56514; Tel: (218)354-2145, Fax: (218)354-7600.

See Also: Potato Bowl (Grand Forks, ND).

Hopkins

Hopkins Raspberry Festival

Ten days ending on the third Sunday in July When this tribute to the raspberry began in 1937, Hopkins, a four-square-mile suburb of Minneapolis with a main street named Mainstreet (one word, like Broadway), was surrounded by raspberry fields. Now the area is filled with apartment buildings and businesses and a few remaining farms, but the festival continues as a reminder of the suburb's earlier days.

The reminders come with a cookbook of raspberry (and other) recipes updated every few years by a senior citizens' group, and in raspberry drinks, like raspberry lemonade, and in a bake-off of raspberry pies, cakes, and tarts. The farmers' market has raspberries on hand, and some groups sell raspberry treats. Otherwise, the food is usual festival food.

The last Sunday is the festival's big day, featuring a parade of more than 200 units; it's the state's longest continuously running parade. The days before the parade day are filled with a cornucopia of events: sporting events like softball, in-line skating (Rollerblades has its headquarters here), and bicycle races; the coronation of a queen and princess; a fishing contest in Shady Oak Lake for kids aged 6 to 12; and a pie-eating contest. There are also lots of children's events and contests on Family Day, the day before the parade: baby-crawl and toddler-walk contests, safety demonstrations presented by the fire and police departments, a lip-sync contest, and a big arts and crafts display. About 50,000 attend the parade, and 10,000 to 20,000 are present on other days.

Location: Mainstreet, Hopkins, about a mile southwest of Minneapolis on Minnesota 7 and U.S. 169. **Contact:** Hopkins Raspberry Festival, P.O. Box 504, Hopkins, MN 55343; Tel: (612)931-0878.

Moorhead

Scandinavian Hjemkomst Festival

Last week in June (Wednesday through Sunday) ⊛ This major Scandinavian festival, held jointly with Fargo, North Dakota, takes place largely in Fargo, but many special events are also held in Moorhead. See details under Fargo.

New Ulm

Heritagefest

Second and third weekends in July (Friday through Sunday) ⊛ New Ulm is one of the least ethnically diverse communities with a population over 10,000 in the United States. The town is almost completely populated by people of German descent.

That pretty much guarantees authenticity when it comes to a festival of German heritage. And authenticity is what you get. It comes in the form of bratwurst, *landjaegers*

Authentic German food, dancing, crafts, and music: all are available in abundance at New Ulm's Heritagefest. You can also see lots of men in lederhosen. (©Minnesota Office of Tourism)

(spicy sausages cooked on open grills and served on special buns), brat patties, German potato salad, *spaetzle* (noodles) served with gravy or butter, chicken breast, pork, rib sandwiches, apple strudel, *schmier kuchen* (prune and cottage-cheese cake), and German chocolate cake. Traditional festival food is also at hand.

The authenticity continues with folk crafts, a Bavarian gift shop with upscale imported items, a kinderfest with Old World games for children (plus a castle to explore), entertainers from Germany and Austria, and OOMPAH. Very loud. It's called Tuba Mania—hundreds of brass players putting on a concert and parade. You hear it in the pit of your stomach.

Thinking that the New Ulm area on the Minnesota River looked like Ulm on the Danube, the early settlers created some German ambience. They did this most marvelously with a free-standing glockenspiel, one of the few carillon clocks in the world. It has 37 bells in the carillon tower, the largest weighing 595 pounds; altogether, they weigh 2½ tons. Almost 400 German tunes are programmed into the glockenspiel and are played in order before they repeat. Sliding doors in the tower open to animated figures that show the Native American, brewing, and farming cultures of New Ulm. Normally there are glockenspiel concerts with the figurines' performances three times a day, but they do their mechanical magic five times a day during Heritagefest.

Location: Brown County Fairgrounds, New Ulm, in south central Minnesota, at Minnesota 15 and 68. **Contact:** Heritagefest, P.O. Box 461, New Ulm, MN 56073; Tel: (507)354-8850.

While You're There: The August Schnell Brewery, on the national registry of historic sites, is the oldest business in New Ulm, and gives tours daily. It has gardens with peacocks and deer.

South St. Paul

World's Championship Booya Competition & On the Road Again Festival

First Saturday in October Booya, you've never heard of booya?

Lots of other people have never heard of booya either, but in the St. Paul–Minneapolis area, booya is a stew, a cult, a part of the pioneer heritage. No one seems positive of its origins but the best bet is that it originated with the French *voyageurs* who explored the West and trapped beaver and boiled up whatever there was to garner from the wilds. The theory of French antecedents for booya seems convincing; *bouillir* means to boil.

Walt Books, who has been cooking booya for some time, started the booya competition in 1982 and is quite sure there's no place in the world where they have another booya competition. Usually, eight to ten cooks take part, and each is required to cook at least 30 gallons of booya (though sometimes someone will make as much as 200 gallons). There are no left-overs.

The cooks begin their cooking on Friday and don't start serving until noon on Saturday. Folks are lined up at 9 o'clock Saturday morning, and the booya is sold out by 3 p.m.—enough is saved to let the judges have a taste, though.

Okay, what is booya? The secret, said Mr. Books: "Do it your own way."

Up to a point. Basic booya consists of ox tails (a must), beef, pork, chicken, vegetables, and spices. It must be cooked until the meat is stringy and falls off the bones. Bones and skin are removed, the fat skimmed, and vegetables added. Corn should never be added—it sours the soup. Mr. Books likes to use rutabagas and goes heavily on carrots, which sweeten the stew and are a "staple of good booya," he says. As for spices, Mr. Books has seen people use chocolate and catsup, and, while he would never use catsup, the catsup fellow won the competition one year.

The booya can be bought by the bucket or bowl, and when the booya is ladled into a bowl, the stringy meat "should hang over the side of the bowl." That makes it booya.

Booya is not simply a once-a-year competition stew. At a number of parks, facilities have been created with big iron pots so that people can cook booya on weekends. Families send their kids to buy jugs of it.

The On the Road Again Festival, also started by Mr. Books, features ethnic foods—Greek, Mexican, Serbian. Nearby farmers bring in their pumpkins and gourds to sell, and there are also carnival events for children and adults, a car show, and live bands. The festival began in 1988 to celebrate the re-opening of Southview Boulevard, a main drag, that had been closed for repairs for 18 months. The food reflects the mixed ethnicity of the area.

The festivals are held simultaneously and attract about 14,000 hungry patrons.

Location: South St. Paul is a suburb just south of St. Paul. The festivals are held on Southview Blvd., the Booya Competition at 8th Avenue and the boulevard, the On the Road Again from 4th to 13th Avenues. **Contact:** Booya Competition, 44 6th Avenue South, South St. Paul, MN 55075; Tel: (612)455-4273.

Tower

Wild Rice Festival

Last weekend in August To gourmets, wild rice is a nutty-tasting marvel of a grain, good for eating plain, like rice, or as an ingredient in breads or stuffings or other foods.

It has an aura to it. It's America's only native grain and Native Americans still harvest it as they did a few hundred years ago. Near Tower, Chippewa Indians paddle out in canoes on Lake Big Rice or Lost Lake (lakes with murky bottoms); there are two people to a canoe: one maneuvers and the other threshes the grain into the canoe by bending the stalks and shaking them or striking them with a stick. On shore, the rice is sun-cured or dried over smoky fires and dehusked.

Wild rice is not actually rice—it's an aquatic grass that grows in the lakes and rivers of Minnesota, upper Michigan, Wisconsin, and adjoining parts of Canada, usually in places that are not readily accessible. The Latin name for wild rice translates as "water weed," and the early French explorers called it crazy oat (*folle avoine*). How it got to be wild rice is unclear.

What's very clear is the deliciousness of the wild-rice dishes, winners in a rice cook-off, that can be sampled at the festival. A dollar buys tastes of 12 dishes—such mouth-waterers as stuffed pea pods, popped wild rice (like popcorn), pork chops and wild-rice apple cake, glorified rice (rice with cherry or pineapple syrup and heavy cream), rice omelet, pancakes and muffins made with wild rice, wild-rice soup, and so on. Bags of wild rice are also sold.

The festival features historical demonstrations, twig-furniture making, beading, displays in the history and culture of the Chippewas, and story-telling for children and adults as Indian elders did years ago.

Indians harvest wild rice on their own land. The wild rice you see on your grocery shelf comes from commercial processors who, though they may have bought some of the grain from Indians, for the most part grow it in artificial paddies, not lakes.

Location: Tower is on the southern shore of Vermilion Lake on Minnesota 1, about 60 miles north of Duluth. **Contact:** Wild Rice Festival, P.O. Box 776, Tower, MN 57790; Tel: (218)753-6941.

Ohio

Amanda

American Soya Festival

Week after Labor Day (Wednesday through Saturday) ⊛
The soybean (or soya bean) is one of the most important agricultural products in the world. In the United States it's used largely for cooking oil; but other countries, especially in Asia, use it to make various foods, such as tofu.

Since a lot of it grows around Amanda, local farmers chose soy as the theme for their festival, which brings about 5,000 to this tiny hamlet. You won't, however, find a soy banquet. There's soybean soup, courtesy of the local Grange, and vendors of standard festival foods are encouraged to cook them in soy oil.

The festival does promote soybeans. Soy plants are presented for judging on their overall quality and on the number of pods per plant, and the Ohio Soybean Association displays educational materials, including methods of soybean cooking and recipes. Cooking demonstrations are also presented.

There are also tests of skill such as a nail-driving contest and a soybean-spitting contest (which uses yogurt-covered beans). Other events include a baby-crawling contest; kiddy tractor pulls; the coronation of Miss Soya, Little Miss Soya, and Junior Miss Soya; three parades; and on Friday night both square-dancing and gospel music.

The first festival was in 1978. Festival proceeds are used for scholarships and educational grants.

Location: Amanda (population 750) is between Lancaster and Circleville off U.S. 22. ⊛ **Contact:** American Soya Festival, P.O. Box 7, Amanda, OH 43102; Tel: (614)969-4525.

Ohio Pumpkin Festival

Last weekend in September (Thursday through Sunday)

Corn is a bigger crop than pumpkins around Barnesville, but pumpkins lend themselves to funnier or odder events, and Barnesville people seem to like odd things.

Like the Pumpkin Roll, a high point of the festival. It's a contest in which pumpkins are rolled to the finish line by prodding them with orange-colored sticks. The racetrack length is about 50 feet and uphill, and the bigger the pumpkin the more difficult it is to steer, or to keep from wobbling backwards, so contestants rummage through a pile of pumpkins looking for the smallest roundest ones. The Roll is a serious event, and no wonder—the winner gets a cash prize of $20.

The festival does culinary things with pumpkins that prosaic cooks could never imagine. Pumpkin dishes range from traditional to inventive, starting with standard pumpkin pies, moving on to pumpkin soup, bread, cookies, doughnuts, and cake, and then to pumpkin fudge, ice cream, blizzard (soft ice cream), milk shakes, burgers, pancakes, and puddings. There are also a few tons of pumpkins for people to take home.

A Miss Ohio Pumpkin Queen is crowned and contenders for King Pumpkin, which is a pumpkin, are weighed in. They can run 600 to 700 pounds. The King is mounted on a "throne" for the festival duration, and the King's grower gets a trophy.

About 100,000 people, most of them wearing pumpkin-orange attire, attend the festival, which began in 1963 and offers, amidst innumerable festival events, displays of pumpkin crafts. It's easy to find Barnesville because of its permanently pumpkin-colored water tower.

Location: Barnesville is 6 miles south of I-70, about 25 miles west of Wheeling, WV.   Contact: Barnesville Chamber of Commerce, Box 462, Barnesville, OH 42713; Tel: (614)425-4300.

Oktoberfest Zinzinnati

Third weekend in September (Friday through Sunday)

There's no way that Bavaria's Crown Prince Ludwig, who was joyfully married in 1810, could have imagined that the people of Cincinnati would still be celebrating his wedding almost 200 years later. And putting a couple of z's in the city's name—on the theory that it sounds more German that way—might have confused him, too.

Yet half a million celebrators make this bash the Nation's Largest Authentic Oktoberfest. Downtown Cincinnati becomes a Bavarian village of accordion players, polka dancers, folk dancers; there's also a Hansel and Gretel Play Garden for kids. About 90 food and beverage booths serve up miles of wurst and oceans of domestic, German, and microbrewed beer. In short, these are days of *Gutes Essen und Bier* and *Singen und Tanzen*.

The *Essen* includes all kinds of wurst, pigs' feet, potato pancakes, *frikadellen* (pork patties), wiener schnitzel, goulash soup, sauerkraut balls, redskin potato salad, rye *brot*, and sweets such as Viennese cheesecake, Alpine mountain cookies, buttercreme tortes, apple strudel. Beer tents offer oompah music with the suds.

The festival begins with a traditional parade and ceremonies where the mayor taps the first keg of beer and declares, "Opzapft ist!" (it's open). Old World activities of log-sawing and costume and dance contests lead to the World's Largest Chicken Dance Saturday evening. One year 48,000 took part, creating an international flap.

On Sunday, food vendors serve what is called the most authentic buffet outside of Munich, and a German mass is said at old St. Mary's Catholic Church. Earlier in the week, the Gemutlichkeit (Goodwill) Games provide the spectacle of men in lederhosen competing in a beer-barrel-rolling contest; there are also pretzel-making competitions and stein-sprint contests where women in dirndls race carrying six full beer steins.

The festival began in 1977, but Germans first began arriving in Cincinnati in the 1830s. By 1850, the city was the world's largest pork-packing center and had the nickname Porkopolis. Today more than half the city's population is of German ancestry.

Cincinnati's Oktoberfest is the world's second biggest—the biggest being the one in Munich where Ludwig began the whole thing. He arranged a Volksfest (people's festival) in a meadow to celebrate his marriage; there were horse races, farm-equipment exhibits, and food and drink, although the records don't mention beer.

The fest was a hit, so Ludwig issued a royal proclamation that it be repeated every year. As the years passed, the festival became more popular and more beery. Today it's a 16-day beer bust, where more than 6 million raucous people drink more than 5 million liters of beer and eat about 80 whole spit-roasted oxen and more than 200,000 pairs of pork sausages. Any other Oktoberfest is a piker by comparison, but Zinzinnati does pretty well.

Location: Fifth Street in downtown Cincinnati, off I-71 and I-75. To avoid city driving, take the Wunderbus leaving from various suburban locations every half hour. **Contact:** Greater Cincinnati Chamber of Commerce, 300 Carew Tower, 441 Vine St., Cincinnati, OH 45202; Tel: (513)579-3191, or (800)CINCYUSA.

While You're There: Visit a chili parlor in this city of chiliheads. The local chili is in a class of its own, possibly having Greek origins; it's made with ground beef, cinnamon, and chocolate. Five-way chili is a mound of noodles, kidney beans, meat, onions, and cheddar cheese.

Circleville

Circleville Pumpkin Show

Third Wednesday in October through following Saturday
Talk about continuity. Talk about tradition.

Circleville's pumpkin festival is the oldest and largest festival in Ohio, going back to the start of the twentieth century and pulling in crowds of up to half a million. It started in 1903, and has been held ever since except for a couple of lapses during the world wars.

What's more, the World's Largest Pumpkin Pie has been baked by the local Lindsey's Bakery since 1952. It's five feet in diameter, weighs 350 pounds, and is baked for hours in a giant pan. It's on display during the festival, and afterwards is fed to pigs.

The food available is inventive and pumpkin-themed, you might say: there are pumpkin pies, cookies, bread, pancakes, waffles, taffy, fudge, brittle, burgers (actually hamburgers with pumpkin-pie spice), ice cream, chili, doughnuts, pizza. Tons of pumpkins are for sale, too.

Continuing with the pumpkin theme, there are pumpkin-pie-eating contests (biggest gluttons get a ribbon), a pumpkin toss for distance, a contest for the heaviest pumpkin. The weigh-in is at noon on Wednesday before the show starts, because the pumpkins are so heavy they have to be brought downtown on trucks. A record was set in 1991 with a pumpkin weighing 589½ pounds.

Among other events are seven parades, the first, on Wednesday, for first-graders; a Miss Pumpkin Show pageant; an egg toss, in which raw eggs are tossed back and forth; hog-calling contests; concerts; and arts and crafts displays.

This all began when Mayor Haswell, who owned a store in town, invited the farmers of the area to display the fruits of the harvest at his store. The display kept growing—and now look at what Mayor Haswell started.

Pumpkins are a big crop in the Circleville region. You guessed that?

Location: Circleville is just off U.S. 23, about 30 miles south of Columbus. ⬚
Contact: The Pumpkin Show, 159 E. Franklin St., Circleville, OH 43113; Tel: (614)474-7000.

Cleveland

Slavic Village Harvest Festival

Third weekend in August ⬚ Polish immigrants settled in Cleveland to work in the rolling mills of the steel industry, and many people of Polish descent still live in the south Cleveland area, known as the Slavic Village. In 1978, village merchants and a community development group got together to promote this section of the city and, at the same time, pay homage to the Old World heritage.

What better way than with kielbasa? And indeed, there's a kielbasa cook-off, with judging based on appearance, taste, and texture. Food vendors sell almost every imaginable Slavic walk-around food: kielbasa (of course), pierogis, kolaches, strudels, Bohemian *listy* (pastries), and Slovenian *potica* (nut rolls). There's sit-and-savor food, too: blintzes, duck soup, cabbage and noodles, stuffed cabbage, potato pancakes, sauerkraut and dumplings.

The continuous ethnic entertainment is largely Polish, but you'll also hear banjo music and string quartets. Homemade crafts are on display.

This festive weekend draws about 100,000. No count on how many kielbasas disappear.

Location: Fleet Ave. in Slavic Village. Take the Fleet Ave. exit from U.S. 77 in Cleveland. ⊛ **Contact:** Slavic Village Broadway Development Corporation, 7100 Broadway, Ste. 200, Cleveland, OH 44105; Tel: (216)271-5591, Fax: (216)271-5503.

Dover

Dandelion Mayfest

First Saturday in May ⊛ "If you can't beat 'em, eat 'em!" That's the motto of the Defenders of Dandelions, and the theme of the Mayfest. The fest began in 1994, drew 1,000 people, had 5,000 visitors two years later, and keeps growing.

The object is both to promote dandelion wine and to educate people about the nutritional value and many uses of dandelions. The highlight is the National Dandelion Cook-off. One year, a dandelion polenta lasagna won in the division for professional chefs, and dandelion matzo-ball soup took first prize in the amateur category. Cash prizes are awarded.

Vendors offer all kinds of dandelion dishes: roasted peppers with goat cheese and dandelions; wedding soup (dandelion greens in a spicy broth with rice and meatballs); fritters (dandelion blossoms fried in batter, served with a dip); dandelion gravy served with potatoes; and dandelion soup, bread, pizza, sausage, and ice cream. Food without dandelions is sold, too.

Dandelion Matzo Ball Soup

2   tablespoons melted chicken fat (or oil)
2   eggs (slightly beaten)
1½ cup matzo meal
1   tablespoon salt
2   tablespoons chicken broth

3   quarts chicken broth (will be used at different times)
¼   cup diced carrots
¼   cup fresh onions (chopped)
1   cup fresh dandelion (chopped)
    Croutons and additional chopped dandelions

Blend fat or oil with eggs. Add to matzo meal and salt. Blend well. Then add 2 tablespoons broth. Mix until uniform. Refrigerate for 15 minutes. Bring broth, carrots, onions, and one cup dandelion to boil. Add matzo balls by dropping teaspoon making a ball. Turn heat down to gentle boil for 30 to 40 minutes, serve in bowls. Garnish with croutons and a little chopped fresh dandelion. Happy eating! Serves 6–8. Note: Can add ¼ cup dandelion to matzo meal mixture.

Doris Hootman, Dover, Ohio, First Place Winner, Dandelion Mayfest Cookoff

For beverages, there is a dandelion wine made by Breitenbach Wine Cellars, where the fest is held, and a coffee-like beverage (but without the caffeine) made from the dandelion's roasted roots.

Breitenbach makes 35 wines, most of them available to be tasted, and they include, besides dandelion and grape wines, wines made from black and red raspberries, elderberries, peaches, plums, rhubarb, apricots, strawberries, blackberries, spiced apples, and cherries. It takes about a gallon of dandelion flowers to make a gallon of dandelion wine, and the winery makes about 1,500 gallons each spring. The flowers are gathered by local Amish families—the area around Dover is heavily Amish.

The fest also has cooking demonstrations and fun events: games, pony rides, clowns, horse-drawn carriage rides, arts and crafts, and band music.

Dandelions are botanically known as *Taraxacum officinale,* which means "official remedy for disorders." They are rich in nutrients, are a natural diuretic (which is why the French sometimes call them pissenlits), and are supposed to be particularly good for the liver.

The man behind the burgeoning movement to use the nutrition that lurks in common weeds is Dr. Peter A. Gail. An ethnobotanist, he has been studying dandelions since the 1960s, has an extensive collection of recipes for wild plants, and says his inspiration is George Washington Carver, who discovered hundreds of products for the once useless weed called the peanut.

He established Goosefoot Acres Inc. in Cleveland to publish books and sell Dandy Line Products, which range from dandelion jellies to the coffee alternative called Dandy Blend. He also founded the Defenders of Dandelions to provide dandelion lovers with a forum to learn about the virtues of this "mistakenly maligned plant."

For people who complain that the dandelion is bitter, Dr. Gail advises masking the bitterness by cooking greens with ingredients like tomato sauce or dressing the raw greens with a sweet and sour or raspberry vinaigrette dressing.

Dandelions are not quite a major cash crop in Ohio. The area around Vineland, New Jersey, contains the largest commercial growers of dandelion greens in the United States.

Location: Breitenbach Wine Cellars (a big purple building), on County Road 139 in Dover, off I-77, 20 miles south of Canton.   **Contact:** Goosefoot Acres, P.O. Box 18016, Cleveland, OH 44118; Tel: (216)932-2145, or (800)697-4858. Or call Anita Davis at Breitenbach Wine Cellars, (330) 343-3603.

See Also: Dandelion Festival (Vineland, NJ).

Dublin

Irish Festival

First weekend in August (Friday through Sunday)   In a town with the name of Dublin, it's not too surprising to find an Irish festival with Irish bangers and mash (sausage and mashed potatoes), scones, Irish stew, soda bread, and corned beef and cabbage.

All that and non-Irish dishes—like barbecued chicken, lemon shake-ups, brats, and funnel cakes—are available at the festival. But the atmosphere is definitely Irish green.

The Columbus Feis draws some of the best Irish dancers in the Midwest and Canada for this annual Irish folk dancing festival and competition.

The Genealogy Tent helps you discover any Irish blood in your past.

The Marketplace features Irish wares such as heraldic ornaments, tin whistles, sweaters, and crystal. Cultural exhibits and workshops feature quilting, storytelling, lace, bodhran-making (a bodhran is a tunable Irish drum), and thatching, which has to do with how to keep dry when you come out of the green mist (rain in other languages).

And there are also darts matches, contests for reddest hair and greenest eyes, a soccer classic, three stages with entertainment from Ireland, including music and step dancing, and an Irish dog display, where you'll see the official dog of Ireland, the Kerry Blue Terrier.

Everything about the festival is so Irish that you expect, at the least, that Dublin owes its founding to the Irish. Not so. John Sells came from Pennsylvania in 1810 to claim land bought by his brothers. An Irish surveyor named John Shields helped him survey the town lots, and Sells asked the surveyor to name the new town.

Mr. Shields is supposed to have said, "If I have the honor conferred upon me to name your village, with the brightness of the morn, and the beaming of the sun on the hills and dales surrounding this beautiful valley, it would give me great pleasure to name your new town after my birthplace, Dublin, Ireland."

Dublin has been Irish ever since, and about 40,000 attend this very Irish celebration.

Location: Coffman Park in Dublin, 20 minutes northwest of downtown Columbus. Take Ohio 33/161 off I-270, go east on 161 to Post Rd., follow shamrocks to park. **Contact:** City of Dublin, 6665 Coffman Road, Dublin, OH 43017; Tel: (614)761-6500, or (800)245-8387, FAX: (614)761-1995.

Eldorado

Zucchini Festival

Third weekend in July (Friday through Sunday) Zucchini is supposed to have originated in South Africa, but it grows everywhere now, and is the kind of vegetable left on your doorstep in the dark of night by neighbors embarrassed to give it to you. Zucchini is prolific, and it seems to ripen all at once.

When a community group in Eldorado, a town of only about 650, began thinking of a food festival to raise money for community projects, zucchini seemed like a good theme because everybody has it in their yards. So the festival got under way in 1992, and the town practically turns green for it. Zucchini is in breads, shakes, and hamburgers, which you can doctor with zucchini relish. There's zucchini casserole for breakfast. And there's a zucchini cook-off, with categories for pies, cookies, casseroles, cakes, and brownies. After the judging, what's left is auctioned off. Food vendors sell non-zucchini foods.

A zucchini-carving contest is a favorite; people carve odd characters, and winners get ribbons. Other events include music, arts and crafts, a Saturday-morning parade that stars Little Miss Zucchini (up to age 4), a kiddie-tractor pull, and old-car and old-tractor shows.

Festival attendance is about 10,000.

Location: Eldorado is about 25 miles northwest of Dayton on Ohio 726, 4 miles north of U.S. 40. **Contact:** Zucchini Festival, P.O. Box 136, Eldorado, OH 45321; Tel: (513)273-2791.

Hamilton

Ohio Honey Festival

Second weekend in August (Friday through Sunday)
Probably the most extraordinary thing about this festival is the Living Bee Beard.

Three times a day, a volunteer gets bee-bearded. Here's how: A queen cage—a match-box-sized screen box—is hung under the chin of a volunteer. Then six to nine pounds of bees are dumped into the person's lap. The bees crawl up the volunteer's body and swarm around the queen cage. Simple as that.

The now bee-bearded volunteer exits from the screened-in launching area and walks around, rather gingerly, to give everyone the opportunity to look—and do double-takes. The American Honey Queen traditionally kisses the beard-wearer, and anybody else who wants to smooch with a swarm of bees can, too.

This makes people start thinking about bees, which is the point of the festival. It's a celebration of amateur beekeepers that started in 1968 and now attracts 25,000 people. There are 70 to 90 food booths to feed them, and the vendors, encouraged to use honey, offer specialty coffees sweetened with honey, lemonade with honey, honey-crusted pizza, honey ice cream, Greek pastries gooey with honey, and honey with waffles.

The beekeepers have their own booths with about 25 different bee products—raw honey, honeycombs, honey candy, honey in jars, strained honey, bee pollen, honey sticks (honey in plastic straws), beeswax, beeswax candles. They give demonstrations of extracting honey from frames, and spectators get samples.

The festival also buzzes with music, rides, a kiddy-tractor pull, an antique-car parade, and a grand parade.

About 18 million gallons of honey are produced in the United States each year. The value of bees, however, is not so much their honey and beeswax as it is their pollinating abilities. As the worker bees zoom about gathering nectar from flowers, pollen sticks to their body hair and is transferred from bloom to bloom. Some plants are totally dependent on bees for pollination; others find the bees helpful but not necessary. As a result, some beekeepers migrate with hives of millions of bees from blossoming crop to blossoming crop. On the East Coast, for instance, they help out in the citrus groves, then head north for blueberries, cranberries, apples.

It's alive! This beekeeper actually volunteered to have six to nine pounds of bees swarm around his face, creating a living beard of bees. (Ohio Honey Festival)

Most beekeepers make more money from honey and wax than from fees for pollination, but studies have shown that honeybee pollination, by increasing the yield of certain crops, has added billions of dollars to their value. A beekeepers' association is active in the Hamilton area, and a handful of the keepers rent out their bees for pollination.

The honeybee was a royal symbol in ancient Egypt, Norsemen fermented honey to make mead, and European monasteries were prime honey producers because of their need for beeswax candles. When the Reformation led to the closing of monasteries, beekeeping fell off. Honeybees were introduced to North America in about 1640; there were bees here before then, but they didn't produce honey.

Location: Hamilton is about 25 miles north of Cincinnati on U.S. 127. ❁ **Contact:** Ohio Honey Festival, Inc., P.O. Box 754, Hamilton, OH 45012; Tel: (513)868-5891.

West Virginia

West Virginia Strawberry Festival

Memorial Day weekend (Wednesday through Sunday) Buckhannon is festooned with red and green banners for this major fair, attended by about 100,000, that dates back to 1936. Strawberry growing is not as big as it was then, but there are still plenty of berries and berry dishes to go around. Take your choice: strawberry-banana "frosty flips" (like slushes), non-alcoholic strawberry daiquiris, strawberry pies, shortcakes, pancakes, muffins, ice cream, jam, and syrup. And fresh strawberries, of course.

The festival begins with a blessing of the berries at the courthouse and the coronation of a king and queen. The king is the berry grower judged in the prior year to have the best berries, and the queen. is the winner of a personality and appearance pageant; the queen is presented a basket of berries by the king. There are parades on three days; crafts, quilt, photo, car, and horse shows; a carnival; the Strawberry Party Gras featuring music and dance; a country hoedown; a gospel sing; the state marble-shooters tournament; strawberry-blonde contests for youngsters and adults; a strawberry-capping contest for seniors; and a strawberry-pie-eating contest for all ages. There are also a sweetest-berry contest and a recipe contest, which in the past has produced such delights as chicken glazed with strawberries and strawberry-and-kiwi pizza.

Location: Buckhannon, in the center of West Virginia, is about 13 miles from exit 99 on I-79. **Contact:** West Virginia Strawberry Festival, P.O. Box 117, Buckhannon, WV 26201; Tel: (204)472-9036.

See Also: California Strawberry Festival (Oxnard, CA).

Italian Heritage Festival

Labor Day weekend (Friday through Sunday) They greet you with "Benvenuti" at this festival, but they should be saying, "Mangia." There's lots of eating here—of things you might expect, like spaghetti and meatballs, lasagna, hoagies, pizza. But there are also pasta *fagiole* (pasta with beans), *minestra* (soup of spinach, potatoes, and beans), fried bread dough, Italian steak sandwiches (Italian bread with steak and mozzarella and hot peppers), and Italian bread baked outdoors on a brick hearth. For dessert, there are Italian ices, biscotti, tiramisu, cannolis. And there's a wine garden and a homemade-wine contest.

And more: a pasta cook-off, open to both professionals and amateurs, determines the best white sauce and best red sauce. Spectators who buy tickets can sample entries and vote, and the people's choice also wins a prize.

The festival was founded in 1979 to preserve the Italian heritage of Clarksburg and to showcase Italian-American culture. In the early 1900s, with the rail system expanding, railroads and industries advertised throughout southern Europe for workers, and Italians, looking for a way out of poverty at home, were one of the groups that poured into remote areas where there was work. They came to this mountainous area, which reminded them of northeastern Italy, to seek jobs in the coal mines and on the railways, and later in the glass industry. Today more than half the population of Harrison County is of Italian descent.

The old ways are remembered with a bocci tournament and contests of morra, a guessing game played by teams of four in which participants hold up any number of fingers behind their backs, and the teams have to guess the number. It can get heated. There's also the coronation of a queen, with the title Regina Maria, folk dancing, an Italian film festival, a parade, children's games, and operatic presentations.

About 175,000 attend the festival.

Location: Main St. in Clarksburg, at the intersection of I-79 and U.S. 50.
Contact: West Virginia Italian Heritage Festival, P.O. Box 1632, Clarksburg, WV 26302; Tel: (304)622-7314.

Kingwood

Preston County Buckwheat Festival

Last Thursday of September through Sunday Buckwheat cakes are the food of choice at this festival, held since 1938. The idea was to promote the county by highlighting one of its products, and it happens that Preston County is a mountainous, damp, short-summer place, just right for buckwheat.

Buckwheat grows fast, so it can be planted late in the season; it acts as a fertilizer, enriching soil for other crops; it grows well in sour soil on rocky, hilly land; and, finally, it seldom blights or is bothered by insects. Great crop.

The Volunteer Fire Department sponsors the fair and cooks up all-you-can-eat dinners of buckwheat cakes with syrup and applesauce and Preston-produced whole-hog sausage patties. They're served each day, all day, beginning at 8 a.m. In 1994, a record was set when 16,129 dinners were served, requiring two tons of buckwheat and nearly six tons of pork.

Preston County Raised Buckwheat Cakes

½ cup warm water
1 package dry yeast
2 cups buckwheat flour

¾ cup white flour
1 teaspoon salt
2 cups buttermilk

Mix ingredients and let rise overnight or mix in morning for evening meal. Before baking, mix 1 tablespoon brown sugar and 1 teaspoon soda with 1 cup hot water, stir
in the batter and mix well. Use some canned milk to make the batter thin enough
to spread.

Preston County Buckwheat Festival

The work involved is prodigious. Buckwheat cakes aren't just mixed—the batter has to
rise overnight, and then, before baking, brown sugar, baking soda, and hot water are added
to the batter.

The festival has a county-fair side with events such as agricultural and livestock
exhibits, livestock judging, a turkey-calling contest, and a farmer's-skills contest. Other
highlights are the Firemen's Gigantic Parade, the Farmers' Day Parade, the coronation of
Queen Ceres and King Buckwheat, a banjo and fiddlers' contest, a pet show, arts and crafts,
and antique-car shows.

Attendance averages 100,000.

Location: Kingwood is in the northeast part of the state, 22 miles south of I-68, on
West Virginia 26. **Contact:** Kingwood Volunteer Fire Department, P.O. Box 74,
Kingwood, WV 26537; Tel: (304)329-0021.

See Also: Buckwheat Harvest Festival (Penn Yan, NY).

Spencer

West Virginia Black Walnut Festival

Second weekend in October (Thursday through Sunday)
In 1955 there was a bumper crop of black walnuts in the Spencer area, and Henry
Young decided to gather them and sell them to promote Spencer. The festival has been held
ever since, providing a great and rare opportunity to fill up on black-walnut cakes, candies,
cookies, cupcakes, bars, and pies by the slice or whole.

And Spencer doesn't stop there. It also gets a tad exotic with strawberry shortcake with walnuts and pumpkin ice cream with walnuts. Standard festival foods are also on hand.

To stimulate further interest in the nut, there's a walnut bake-off, with rules stating that recipes must call for at least one-quarter cup of real Eastern black walnuts. Judging of the dishes and recipes is based on taste, texture, and the amount of time it takes to make the dish. Prizes are United States savings bonds. A cookbook of past winning recipes is available at the festival.

The festival, attended by 60,000 to 75,000, is like a county fair, with country-western music, band and majorette competitions, the coronation of a queen, a grand parade and kids' parade, a carnival, a livestock show, gospel singers, football, and displays of quilts and arts and crafts.

Eastern black walnuts are a breed apart; they grow wild, and the nuts must be hand-gathered after they fall. The nuts are something of a scarce commodity for those and other reasons, and West Virginia is one of the places where they are still somewhat plentiful. But after the festival the nuts are gone. Hammons Products Company in Stockton, Missouri, the only walnut-processing company in the world, has a buying station in the state, and it will buy as many walnuts as anyone wants to sell.

Location: Spencer is about 50 miles north of Charleston on U.S. 33. ⊛ **Contact:** Walnut Festival, P.O. Box 1, Spencer, WV 25276; Tel: (304)927-1780.

See Also: Black Walnut Festival (Stockton, MO).

Wisconsin

Applefest

First full weekend in October About 700 people live in Bayfield on the northernmost tip of Wisconsin on Lake Superior, and in 1962 they decided to promote their apples with a festival. Four thousand people showed up then. Now 60,000 come.

Applefest apples are presented in pies (served with warm caramel sauce), dumplings, fritters, strudels, apple butter; they are puréed into knockwurst; rendered as cider and dried apple rings; and wrapped in caramel. You can also get fresh apples. Other area specialties available are wild-rice soup, blackened whitefish, and whitefish livers.

Besides the food, people come for the coronation of the Apple King and Queen; a Scottish marching band with bagpipes playing at dusk, followed by the nighttime Venetian Boat Parade in the harbor; Big Top Chautauqua performances; a talent show; a pet parade; and the two-hour Sunday afternoon parade that ends with about 800 kids in high school bands blasting out "On, Wisconsin!"

There's also an apple-peeling contest, in which winners carve single peels 300 inches long and longer. Sometimes wrestling matches are held in small swimming pools filled with apple mash. Apple-pie and apple-cider contests are held during the week before the festival.

Bayfield, founded in 1856 with hopes of becoming a great port, flourished from the region's harvest of fish, lumber, and brownstone. But by the turn of the century, the forests were depleted and brownstone was no longer in demand. Along came William Knight, who planted a 30-acre apple orchard in 1905, and Bayfield County now contains some of Wisconsin's most concentrated commercial apple acreage.

Pale yellow tart apples called Transparents signal the beginning of the apple season here, and other locally grown apples are Cortlands, McIntoshes, Wealthys (the area's traditional baking apple), and Firesides, which are mostly green and almost as big as grapefruit.

Location: Bayfield is 85 miles east of Duluth, by way of Wisconsin 13, which winds along the lakeshore. **Contact:** Bayfield Chamber of Commerce, P.O. Box 138, Bayfield, WI 54814; Tel: (800)447-4094.

About 60,000 people come to Bayfield, a town with a population of 700, to celebrate—and of course, eat—apples. (Wisconsin Division of Tourism)

Burlington

Chocolate City Festival

Third weekend in May (Friday through Sunday) ⊛ Burlington was proclaimed Chocolate City USA by the Wisconsin legislature in what might strike some people as a burst of braggadocio. But there *is* a large Nestlé chocolate plant in town, and there certainly is a chocolate festival.

About 100,000 chocoholics come to the festival, and Nestlé apparently figures it has to satisfy their cravings, so every year since the festival began in 1987 the company has created something big. Once it was an 1,800-pound Nestlé crunch bar. Other times: a 2,700-pound mound in the shape of a chocolate kiss . . . an enormous chocolate dinosaur . . . a huge castle . . . a colossal clock. The chocolate sculpture is broken up with a jackhammer on Sunday, and then eaten.

At the Taste of Chocolate Tent, people line up to buy chocolate cookies, cheesecake, éclairs, ice cream, fudge and other candies, chocolate-covered pretzels and strawberries, and varieties of chocolate drinks. (No alcohol is allowed.) On Sunday morning there's a pancake breakfast; the flapjacks are served with—what else?—chocolate sauce. Help.

There are all sorts of other events, including a parade, a petting zoo for children, the Miss Burlington pageant, music groups, and clowns.

Location: Burlington Festival Grounds, Wisconsin 36 and Maryland Ave. Burlington is about 30 miles southwest of Milwaukee on 36.   **Contact:** Burlington Area Chamber of Commerce, 112 E. Chestnut St., P.O. Box 156, Burlington, WI 53105; Tel: (414)763-6044.

Cedarburg

Strawberry Festival

Fourth weekend in June   One of the top ten strawberry-producers in the country, Wisconsin celebrates the strawberry's arrival in towns all over the state. Cedarburg's bash draws about 25,000 people for a weekend of strawberries in all forms. There's a strawberry-pancake breakfast on Sunday, a "Block Party Pig Roast," and brats, burgers, and such.

Ripe berries are king, but also featured are strawberry pie, shortcake, cheesecake, schaum torte (baked meringue layers filled with berries and topped with whipped cream), burritos, popcorn, ice cream, and chocolate-covered strawberries. And strawberry slush and strawberry wine.

There are goofy contests, too—a "bubblicious" strawberry-bubblegum-blowing contest, a strawberry-pie eating contest, a berry bob (like bobbing for apples, only with berries), and Sunday's sundae-eating contest. Add to all this hayrides, music, a folk-art show, a minnow derby, a children's carnival, and the location—Cedarburg's historic district, with buildings from the 1850s—and you've got a jim-dandy old-fashioned strawberry social.

A Strawberry Fest in Waupaca on the third weekend in June is smaller but boasts the Longest Strawberry Shortcake, which runs about 300 feet (the length of a football field) and serves 1,500 people or more. For information, contact the Waupaca Area Chamber of Commerce at (800)236-2222.

Location: Cedarburg is about 15 miles north of Milwaukee off I-43.   **Contact:** Cedarburg Festivals, P.O. Box 104, Cedarburg, WI 53012; Tel: (414)377-9620, or (800)827-8020.

While You're There: The Cedar Creek Winery produces strawberry and grape wine and cranberry blush, offers winery tours, and has a museum on the site with winemaking implements. Cedarburg also has one of the two remaining covered bridges in Wisconsin.

See Also: California Strawberry Festival (Oxnard, CA).

Eagle River

Eagle River Cranberry Fest

First weekend in October   The North Woods of Wisconsin has abundant water and acidic peat soils. Result: cranberries, and in Eagle River the World's Longest

Cranberry-Sauerkraut Meatballs

½ cup water
1 cup finely crushed cracker crumbs
2 pounds ground beef

2 eggs
1 envelope regular onion soup mix

Mix together and shape into meatballs. Brown in a skillet. Mix together:

1 16 oz. can sauerkraut, drained and
   snipped
1 8 oz. can cranberry sauce, whole or
   strained

¾ cup chili sauce or catsup
2 cups water
⅓ cup brown sugar

Pour half of the sauce into a 9-inch by 13-inch baking dish. Arrange meatballs on sauce. Pour remaining sauce over meatballs. Cover with foil and bake for one hour at 325 degrees. Remove foil. Bake another 30 to 40 minutes. Serve hot over noodles or rice.

1994 Eagle River Cranberry Festival Bake-Off Winning Recipe

Cranberry Cheesecake. It's 100 feet long, contains 800 pounds of cream cheese (the herds that produce the cheese are farther south in the state) and 100 pounds of cranberries, and is baked in two-foot-by-three-foot pans. After the pieces are laid out end to end on Saturday, people line up to pay $1.25 a slice, and in six hours, it's gone.

A cranberry bake-off inspires dishes like cranberry-sauerkraut meatballs, and other festival attractions include a farmers' market, a petting zoo, folk music, arts and crafts exhibits, and tours of cranberry bogs and a winery where one can taste a variety of wines, including cranberry wine.

If cranberry wine sounds odd, how about espresso with cranberry and chocolate flavors? The fest has it, along with cranberry chili, muffins, pancakes, slush, cranberry and cheddar-cheese spread, strawberry/cranberry preserves, cranberry mustard, and hundreds of pounds of fresh cranberries.

The festival stresses fitness with a walk, a run, a bicycle tour, a golf tournament, and reminders that cranberries are high in fiber and vitamin C.

Location: Vilas County Fairgrounds in Eagle River off Wisconsin 70, at the junction of I-45. **Contact:** Eagle River Area Chamber of Commerce, P.O. Box 1917, Eagle River, WI 54521; Tel: (715)479-6400.

See Also: Warrens Cranberry Festival (Warrens, WI) and Massachusetts Cranberry Harvest Festival (South Carver, MA).

Fyr Bal Festival

Third weekend in June (Friday through Sunday) ☼ Fyr Bals are held all over Door County, which is at the end of Wisconsin's Thumb area that has Green Bay on one side and Lake Michigan on the other. "Fyr bal" means bonfire, and the festivals hark back to Scandinavian celebrations of the summer solstice and to the building of huge fires to scare off the witches that come in winter.

Today the solstice festivals are fish boils. But they still come with dramatic bonfires. No point in taking chances.

Ephraim's Fyr Bal Festival is representative of the others, with the fish boil held Saturday night. Whitefish steaks (a favorite in the area) are placed in a wire basket in a big kettle over an outdoor wood fire. The water is heavily salted, and little red potatoes, onions, and carrots are added, and then the "stew" is brought to a boil. The fish must boil at all times. When the fish and vegetables are done after about 20 minutes, kerosene is poured on the fire, and huge flames, as high as 35 feet, leap up. The kettle, of course, boils over, thus boiling away any oils of the fish.

And then the diners dive in. Among the other foods available are Door County cherry pie (this is cherry country), brats served by the fire department, and general festival food from other vendors.

What makes the fish boil a sort of mystic event, more than just a fish boil, is the ambience. Some 15 to 20 fyr bals (bonfires, as we know) are lighted around the lake. They're made of piles of timber, shaped like tepees, and the sight of them is mesmerizing. The bonfires are lit after the fish boil, which takes place at the village hall over one huge fire. Fireworks follow the fyr bals, to doubly protect against the witches.

Other events of the weekend include a community sing at the old village hall on Sunday evening and Scandinavian dancing by children. There is also a ceremony honoring someone who has served the community. This chieftain or chieftess of the village arrives at the festival by boat and lights the first fyr bal.

Location: Ephraim is on Wisconsin 42, about 14 miles from the end of the Thumb. ☼ **Contact:** Ephraim Business Council, Ephraim, WI 54211; Tel:(414)743-4456.

Kraut Festival

Third weekend in June (Friday through Sunday) ☼ Since 1951, Franksville has been celebrating sauerkraut with a festival that highlights the World Championship Kraut Eating Contest. The one who eats the most kraut in three minutes is the world champ. Not for the timid.

About 30,000 show up for the festival and are able to try kraut in standard and non-standard dishes—with brats, of course, but also in desserts, including chocolate cake. Kraut cookbooks are for sale.

Events include the crowning of a queen, a giant midway, a petting zoo, bingo, and country, polka, and German music.

Cabbage and corn are the main crops in the area, and many of the people are of German and Bohemian descent, traditional kraut eaters. A kraut-processing plant was located here but has since moved to Ohio.

But the cabbage keeps growing. Wisconsin is the number-one state in kraut production, with New York, a one-time leader, in second place.

Location: Downtown Franksville on County Rte. K, 20 miles south of Milwaukee, 2½ miles east of I-94.   **Contact:** Racine County Convention and Visitors Bureau, 345 Main St., Racine, WI 53403; Tel. (414)634-3293.

See Also: Phelps Sauerkraut Festival (Phelps, NY).

Little Chute

Great Wisconsin Cheese Festival

First weekend in June (Friday through Sunday)   Wisconsin, the Dairy State, has about two million cows and ranks first in the nation in the production of milk, cheese, butter, and sweetened condensed milk. About 75 percent of Wisconsin's milk goes into cheese, adding up to more than two billion pounds produced. More than 40 percent of the cheese consumed in the United States comes from Wisconsin.

And Little Chute is in the heart of the state's highest per capita milk and cheese producing areas.

Ergo, this is legitimately a *great* cheese festival. Food booths sell cheeseburgers, cheddarwurst (bratwurst with cheese mixed in), deep-fried cheese curds and nuggets, pizza, nachos, chili-cheese dogs, and cheese tacos.

Among the cheeses for free sampling are gouda, muenster, cream cheese, cheddar, string cheese, mild provolone, Swiss, Monterey Jack, shaved parmesan, semi-soft brick cheese with vegetables, and Colby.

Wisconsin makes 200 or more cheeses, but Colby is the only Wisconsin original. Moist, mild, and yellow, it was developed in 1885 by Joseph Steinwald near the town of Colby. Brick cheese is a variation of a German-Swiss cheese, in which curds were traditionally pressed under brick, and was first produced in Wisconsin in the 1870s.

Curds are a Dairy State specialty. When milk coagulates, it separates into whey, a watery liquid, and semi-solid curds, which cheese is made from. Best when really fresh, the curds are deep-fried to make them crisp on the outside and soft on the inside. People love them in Wisconsin.

The festival features several contests: A cheese-carving contest; once, a farm scene was carved from 720 pounds of cheese (it was the world's largest such scene). Curd-eating contests. And a cheesecake-recipe contest, after which slices are sold to whoever gets there first.

There used to be a Miss Cheese Queen contest, but this was discontinued because the contestants were increasingly uncooperative cows; "it got too hard to find cows willing to put up with makeup and nylons," according to a festival official.

Also offered are tours of dairy farms and cheese plants, a parade, children's activities, bluegrass music, rides, and craft/novelty booths.

But cheese is the big cheese of the festival.

Location: Little Chute is about 30 miles south of Green Bay on U.S. 41. ⬚
Contact: Great Wisconsin Cheese Festival, 1940 Buchanan St., Little Chute, WI 54140; Tel: (414)788-7390.

Milwaukee

United Festivals

Summer, June through September ⬚ Milwaukee calls itself the City of Festivals, and it certainly has a waterfront park that's ideal for showcasing such events. Milwaukee also boasts great ethnic diversity, bringing a rainbow of color to their festivals. The first inhabitants of the area, of course, were the American Indians. In the 1700s, the Potawami lived in villages in Milwaukee's Menominee Valley, and there were also Ojibwa, Ottawa, and Menominee.

In the nineteenth century, immigrants from more than 30 European countries came to Milwaukee; a river port, the city was a magnet in part because of the variety of jobs it offered at the time. Milwaukee was a manufacturing center, the brewing industry was king for years, and the area was ideally suited for both farming and fishing.

Throughout the summer, different groups celebrate their heritage and culture.

The ethnic season begins with the Asian Moon Festival (second weekend in June), started in 1994 by more than 20 of the city's Asian-American communities. The festival's symbol is the moon because many Asian celebrations revolve around the lunar calendar, and because the moon is a part of many Asian folk tales. Chefs from Asian restaurants provide tastes of Chinese, Filipino, Hmong, Indian, Indonesian, Japanese, Korean, Laotian, Malaysian, Taiwanese, Thai, and Vietnamese cuisines. There are demonstrations of calligraphy, origami, and martial arts; and performances by dancers in traditional costume. For information, call (414)273-5090.

Better than a third of Milwaukee's population is of Polish extraction, and their culture is celebrated at Polish Fest (third weekend in June) with folk and polka dancing, a traditional mass with both English and Polish hymns, and displays of traditional art such as painted eggs. There is also food! Kielbasa is prepared on a 45-foot grill, and other specialties include pierogis, *czarnina* (duck soup with noodles), and roast pig; for dessert there's *paczhi* (doughnuts with prune filling), or a crisp *chrusciki* (batter dipped in oil and sprinkled with sugar). For information, call (414)529-2140.

Festa Italiana (third weekend in July) is rooted in street festivals first held in 1906 by immigrants from the Sicilian town of Santo Stefano de Camastra. A mass is followed by a traditional religious procession; and there are—as in the past—brass bands, dancing, fireworks, and mounds of Italian specialties. Besides the familiar meatballs and ravioli, booths sell *arancini* (rice balls), *sfincione* (thick-crust Sicilian-style pizza), *froccia* (spinach) pie, *gnocci* (thumb-size potato dumplings), and octopus and squid, and sweets like tiramisu, amaretto cheesecake, and cream puffs. Games include old ones like bocci and newer ones like pizza tosses. For information, call (414)223-2180.

Germans began settling in Milwaukee in 1836 and largely shaped the culture and industry of the city. The German Fest (fourth weekend in July) honors the German tradition of *Gemutlichkeit*—geniality, good cheer—as well as good music, and good food: sauerbraten, *schnitzel* (veal cutlet), *rollbraten, spanfurkel* (roast suckling pig), potato pancakes, tortes, and strudels. For entertainment, there's a goulash of events—oompah bands, dachshund shows, and yodeling. For information, call (414)464-9444.

African American community leaders inaugurated the African World Festival (first weekend in August) to celebrate contributions of blacks throughout America, the Caribbean, and Africa. In a village of thatch-roofed buildings, artisans demonstrate basketmaking and weaving, and *girots* (storytellers) weave tales. The food reflects the old and new continents; there are barbecued ribs, fried chicken, fried catfish, goat, black-eyed peas, greens, sweet-potato pie, corn bread, peanut soup, and gumbo. For information, call (414)372-4567.

The Irish Fest (third weekend in August) is a grand Irish *ceili,* with music by top Gaelic performers, harpists, and bagpipers; displays of Irish dogs, and contests for the reddest red hair and the most freckles. Foods include cheesecakes, shamrock cookies, and lots of breads—raisin and currant soda bread, whiskey bread, shortbread—and Irish fish and chips, bridies (meat pies), boiled bacon and cabbage, bangers and mash (sausages and mashed potatoes), Irish stew with a baked potato. You can even get a "bookmaker's sandwich" of roast beef and sweet onions on a crusty roll, wrapped in the racing form, because that's traditionally how Irish bookmakers carried their lunch. For information, call (414)476-3378.

South of the Border comes north for the Mexican Fiesta (fourth weekend in August), sponsored by the city's sizable Mexican American community. Many originally came to the city as migrant agricultural workers. The festival resounds with music—the soaring brass of mariachi bands and get-up-and-dance Tex-Mex rhythms. Food ranges from hot-hot to warm and includes burritos, tacos with uncountable types of fillings, and other Mexican specialties; and there are jalapeño-eating and tortilla-making competitions. For information, call (414)383-7066.

A swirl of beads, fringe, and feathers ushers in Indian Summer (first weekend after Labor Day). Powwows are staged twice a day and are followed by dance competitions. Artisans create corn-husk dolls and weave rugs; vendors sell Native-American crafts such as silver jewelry and dream catchers. For food, there are buffalo burgers, fry bread, wild rice, wild-rice soup, corn soup, and venison. For information, call (414)774-7119.

All festivals are Friday through Sunday except for Festa Italiana, which is Thursday through Sunday.

Location: Henry Maier Festival Park (also known as Summerfest Grounds), off I-794 at Lincoln Memorial Drive. Look for "smiling face" signs to the park. ☼ **Contact:** For general festival information—Greater Milwaukee Convention & Visitors Bureau, 501 Kilbourn Ave., Milwaukee, WI 53203; Tel: (414)273-3950, or (800)231-0903.

Oktoberfest

Three weekends following Labor Day ☼ There are Oktoberfests and there are Bavarian Oktoberfests. Five Bavarian groups that make up the United German Societies of Milwaukee sponsor this fest and claim it's the oldest and most authentic Bavarian Oktoberfest in the Midwest. They say Oktoberfests run by Bavarians are closest to the real thing, since Oktoberfest originated in Munich, Bavaria's capital.

The fest has been held since 1943, and 18,000 to 20,000 attend. They celebrate with brass bands, yodeling, sing-alongs, the selection of an Oktoberfest queen, and *Schuhplattler* dancing, in which men clap their shoes together, slap the backs of their heels, slap their lederhosen, and slap the ground, while women twirl. And they celebrate with food: *spanfurkel* (piglet roasted over an open pit), bratwurst, char-broiled chicken, *rollbraten* (sliced roast pork on a kaiser roll), pretzels, fruit strudel. And, of course, beer and wine.

Location: Old Heidelberg Park, 700 W. Lexington Blvd., in northern Milwaukee, off I-43 at Silver Spring Dr. exit. ☼ **Contact:** United German Societies of Milwaukee, 700 W. Lexington Ave., Milwaukee, WI 53217; Tel: (414)462-9147.

See Also: Oktoberfest Zinzinnati (Cincinnati, OH).

Monroe

Green County Cheese Days

Third weekend in September in even numbered years (Friday through Sunday) ☼ The factories of Green County produce about 55 million pounds of cheese a year. And the county is the *only* place in the United States where they make that smelly Limburger cheese. For these reasons—and the fact that many people here are of Swiss descent—Monroe, the county seat, is called the Swiss Cheese Capital of the United States.

Cheese Days are a Swiss-style saturnalia of cheese-eating and music (by yodelers, polka bands, alpenhorn players, and drum and bugle corps) and sports (flag throwing and Swiss wrestling) and parades and dancers in costume. For learning about cheese, there are cheese-factory tours and cheese-making demonstrations. And there's a cow-milking contest.

About 120,000 come to the festival and line up for free samples of locally produced cheese, including, of course, Swiss and Limburger, originally a Belgian cheese, named for the town of Limbourg. A few words about the latter: It continues to age and develop flavor after you buy it, and the strong flavor is caused by bacteria that break down proteins into amino acids. The bacteria also form a red slime on the surface, giving the cheese a red-yellow color. The Chalet Cheese Co-op makes about a million pounds of Limburger a year, which supplies the entire United States.

Available in the Cheese Sales Tent are cheese sandwiches, cheese fondue, homemade pies with cheese, and deep-fried cheese curds (chunks of very young Cheddar dipped in beer batter and fried into crispy puffs).

Cheese making came here after a crop failure in Switzerland in 1844. Farmers from the Swiss canton of Glaurus emigrated to Wisconsin, settled what is now New Glaurus in 1845, and began building dairy herds and making cheese. Later they moved to Monroe, which had better rail connections.

Location: Courthouse square in downtown Monroe, 70 miles south of Madison at the junction of Wisconsin 69 and 11. **Contact:** Green County Cheese Days, Inc., P.O. Box 606, Monroe, WI 53566; Tel: (608)325-7771.

While You're There: New Glaurus, 16 miles north of Monroe on Wisconsin 69, is called America's Little Switzerland. The village's Swiss Historical Village Museum includes 12 buildings (some originals, some replicas) that provide a backdrop to demonstrations of Swiss pioneer life.

Mount Horeb

National Mustard Day

First Saturday in August This festival was inaugurated in the early 1990s to celebrate National Mustard Day and to promote mustard and the Mount Horeb Mustard Museum, which displays and sells mustard and mustard paraphernalia. It has turned into an Event, still small, but with attendance growing exponentially.

Hot dogs are free, and you're invited to try any one of about 200 mustards on your dog. Additionally, about 400 different kinds of mustard, combined with every spice imaginable, may be bought by the jar. Among the flavors are cranberry, orange espresso, chocolate fudge; these are considered better on ice cream (or pretzels), if you are the sort to put mustard on ice cream. Designed more for hot dogs are olive, balsamic-vinegar, dill-and-garlic, hot-pepper, and curry mustards. As is the custom at vineyards, there are tastings of the product, with explanations of each mustard's provenance.

Sometimes there are chefs who demonstrate cooking with mustard, but, if not, there are recipe books and books on how to make mustard. Entertainment varies. One year, a local personality wearing white ran a gauntlet of children squirting mustard from squeeze bottles at him.

Other entertainment comes just from inspecting the display of more than 2,500 mustards from around the world. Some have intriguing names: The Two Virgin Maidens' Breath Mustard, Blue Coyote Howlin' Good Pepper Mustard Relish.

Curators will tell you that very little mustard is grown in the United States, that much of the world's mustard comes from Canada, especially Saskatchewan and Alberta. That's because mustard plants need a short growing season and a long growing day, which Saskatchewan and Alberta both provide.

Location: Mount Horeb is 20 miles west of Madison, off Wisconsin 18 and 151. **Contact:** Mount Horeb Mustard Museum, P.O. Box 468, Mount Horeb, WI 53572; Tel: (800)438-6878.

Seymour

Burger Fest

First Saturday in August Seymour has two major bragging points: It's the Home of the Hamburger, America's favorite food, and it made *The Guinness Book of World Records* for the largest hamburger—5,520 pounds, 21 feet in diameter—created at its first fest in 1989.

The record hamburger is fact, but pinpointing the home of the hamburger gets you on sticky ground.

Here's some history, most of it unconfirmed and some of it contradictory:

The hamburger was named for the city of Hamburg, Germany, where they made a *chopped* beef steak that was imported to this country and called the Hamburg steak. (Dubious theory; hamburgers are ground meat, not chopped.)

The hamburger was invented in Hamburg, New York, in 1885 by Frank and Charles Menche.

The hamburger was invented by Louis Lassen at Louis' Lunch in New Haven, Connecticut. In 1900, a man dashed into the luncheonette and asked for a meal he could eat on the run. Lassen broiled a beef patty and put it between two slices of bread. Or—Lassen invented hamburgers because he hated throwing away scraps from his specialty, lean steak sandwiches, so he ground up the scraps, cooked them, and served them on toast. This concoction got its name, according to food mavens Jane and Michael Stern, because "a bunch of sailors from Hamburg, Germany, liked it so much they wouldn't stop talking about it." Louis' Lunch was going strong at the end of the twentieth century, run by younger generations of Lassens, still serving broiled hamburgers between slices of toast.

The hamburger was introduced to the world at the St. Louis World's Fair of 1904 by Fletcher Davis of Athens, Texas. A group of Athens businessmen financed Uncle Fletch's trip to the fair; he had invented hamburgers much earlier.

The hamburger was created by Charles R. Nagreen in 1885, when he set up a food stand at Seymour's first fair. His specialty was meatballs, but people wanted something more portable, so he flattened the meatballs and put them between bread. The dish was very popular, and he started taking the flat meatballs to fairs around the Midwest and got the nickname Hamburger Charlie. He died in 1951.

That last story is the one promulgated every year to the 10,000 who attend the Seymour Burger Fest.

Whatever the facts, the fest people try to do something different and big each year, although they haven't tried to make a bigger hamburger than that first 1989 whopper. In 1991, they made a 2,000-pound cheeseburger, and had to use a fork lift to hoist a 325-pound roll of American cheese over the burger. The truck holding the hamburger started sinking, and all kinds of problems arose. The next year, 10,000 baby burgers were distributed to honor the birth of the imaginary twins, Barbie Q and Chuckie Weldon.

The Hotel Seymour serves a buffet breakfast starring—this day only—a cheeseburger omelet. Throughout the day, there's a pickle buffet where people can help themselves.

Other events are a parade and a Hamburger Meet that features a catsup slide (catsup and water are smeared on a plastic strip and contestants take a flying leap and then slide for distance) and a discus-style bun toss.

Location: Outagamie County Fairgrounds, Main St., Seymour, 17 miles west of Green Bay on Wisconsin 54. **Contact:** Home of the Hamburger, Inc., P.O. Box 173, Seymour, WI 54165; Tel: (414)833-2517.

While You're There: The Hamburger Hall of Fame on Main Street has all kinds of hamburger memorabilia.

See Also: Burgerfest (Hamburg, NY).

Sheboygan

Bratwurst Days

First Friday and Saturday of August Sheboygan calls itself the "Wurst" City of the World and the Bratwurst Capital of the World. That's something when you consider the antiquity and ubiquity of sausages; ancient Romans cooked sausages over open fires at festivals.

Brats (rhymes with hots) are spiced sausages, four to six inches long, made of pork or a mixture of pork and beef. Sometimes they're boiled in beer before being charred over hot coals. Germans, who have been eating sausage almost forever, brought the brat to Sheboygan in the mid-1880s, and somebody figured out in 1987 that more than 70,200 miles of wurst had been produced in the city since then. Large commercial manufacturers and neighborhood butchers still grind them out.

Natives invariably take a "a double brat with the works," two brats split and charbroiled, eaten on a hard roll with pickles, stone-ground mustard, onions, and sometimes catsup. The hard roll is a round bun rolled in cornmeal and baked until the outside is crusty but not *hard*.

At the fair, attended by 50,000, you can get the classic double and also bratwurst tacos, bratwurst reuben sandwiches, "bratzas" (mini pizzas), and "bratsagna."

The festival, which began in 1953, had been suspended for a time, then was resurrected as a family festival. There is children's entertainment in the Fountain Park area, which is non-alcoholic, and other events at Kiwanis Park, where beer is sold. Events include a parade, flea market, dancers, singers, clowns, magicians, and a brat-eating contest.

Then there's the annual Stumpf Fiddling Contest. A stumpf fiddle is a combination of bells, springs, BB-filled pie plates, wood blocks, and taxi horns all mounted on a wooden pole with a rubber ball at the bottom. When you bounce the pole on its ball bottom, the whole contraption jingles and clangs and honks.

Location: Sheboygan is 55 miles north of Milwaukee. To both parks, take the Wisconsin 23 exit. At 17th St., go right to Kiwanis Park; at 9th St., go right to Fountain Park.

Contact: Sheboygan County Chamber of Commerce, 712 Riverfront Dr., Ste. 101, Sheboygan, WI 53081; Tel: (414)457-9495.

While You're There: Take a break from brats to visit the Sheboygan County Museum, where there's an 1867 cheese factory on the grounds. The museum was originally a judge's home built in 1852.

Sun Prairie

Sweet Corn Festival
Third weekend in August (Thursday through Sunday)
This corny festival began in 1952 when some Lions Club members who worked for a corn-canning factory brought some corn from the factory to a Lions picnic. The picnic grew into a community event, and now Sun Prairie puts on the state's biggest corn festival and serves 100,000 visitors 70 tons of corn, half a ton of butter, and three cases of salt.

To cook all that corn, volunteers fill half-ton-capacity buckets with corn, steam it in the husk, then peel the ears and roll them in butter. Diners fill cardboard boats with all they want for $2, take their corn to "salt trees"—clotheslines hung with salt shakers—and find a grassy slope where they can sit and chomp away.

If the corn isn't enough, there are hamburgers, brats, and pizza.

For non-gustatory pleasure, there are fireworks, a carnival, a parade, music, variety acts, games, midget auto racing, a crafts fair, sports events, children's activities, clowns, jugglers.

P.S. Painter Georgia O'Keeffe was born on a farm near Sun Prairie.

Location: Angell Park, near the intersection of Wisconsin 19 and I-151, about 10 miles north of Madison.   **Contact:** Sun Prairie Chamber of Commerce, 109 Main St., Sun Prairie, WI 53590; Tel: (608)837-4547.

Warrens

Warrens Cranberry Festival
Third weekend in September (Friday through Sunday)
Warrens, the Cranberry Capital of Wisconsin, has a population of 400, but at festival time it

bulges with crowds of about 100,000. That makes this the Biggest Cranberry Festival in the World.

The throngs come for the parade, the flea and farmers' markets, the arts and crafts show, and the carnival. They come to see the judges judge the cranberry cook-off, and to eat the famous Warrens cranberry cream puffs.

Cranberries, native to Wisconsin, are the state's number-one fruit crop, grown in 20 counties by about 150 growers. For quite a while Warrens was *almost* the cranberry capital of the world, second to Massachusetts. Then in the mid-1990s, Wisconsin surpassed Massachusetts in cranberry production, and the states were expected to see-saw for a while. But Wisconsin growers have expanded their acreage, and predict that by the late 1990s (it takes three years from planting to first production), the state will be permanently number one in cranberries.

The festival is big on contests. There's a contest for the biggest cranberry; some have weighed well over 5 grams. There are also scarecrow, photography, vegetable, needlework, and quilt contests. In the cranberry-recipe contest, cooks have come up with cranberry-raspberry brunch cake, cranberry-stuffed pork loin, wild rice and cranberry salad.

Food booths sell cranberries in muffins, fudge, fritters, pies, cheesecake, shortcake—and cream puffs. There are cranberries covered with chocolate or caramel, and on sundaes. The Catholic Church serves pancakes with cranberry syrup, and the Baptist Church provides cranberry pies. There are take-home delicacies like cranberry jellies, jams, candy, mustard, vinegar, and catsup. There are fresh berries. There's also standard fair food, which in Wisconsin includes cheese curds, and vegetables of all sorts at the 100 farmers' market booths.

The cranberry is always center stage, and tour leaders on Saturday show people the bogs and explain the growing and harvesting process.

Location: Warrens is about 70 miles southeast of Eau Claire, off I-94. ⚬ **Contact:** Warrens Cranberry Festival, P.O. Box 146, Warrens, WI 54666; Tel: (608)378-4200, Fax: (608)378-4250.

See Also: Massachusetts Cranberry Harvest Festival (South Carver, MA).

Great Plains

Iowa

Kansas

Missouri

Nebraska

North Dakota

Oklahoma

South Dakota

Texas

Iowa

Anamosa

Pumpkinfest

First weekend in October The focus of this fest is big—very big—pumpkins, but people more interested in eating pumpkins than weighing them will go away happy, too. After all, this is the Pumpkin Capital of Iowa.

The event began as a weigh-off in 1989, started by Tom Norlin, a long-time pumpkin grower whose goal was to grow a pumpkin that would tip the scales at 1,000 pounds. Pumpkin growers come to the weigh-off from eight or so states, and pumpkins over 900 pounds have gotten fairly common.

The original weigh-off was greeted with such enthusiasm that community leaders organized other events to go with it, and in 1994 the combined fest/weigh-off was born.

Vendors try to keep in the spirit of things with pumpkin cakes and breads and fried pumpkin blossoms, which are a big hit, tasting something like scalloped cabbage. Standard festival food is also available—turkey legs, bratwurst, sausage on a stick.

A pumpkin-recipe contest is held Saturday, and other pumpkin events are a pumpkin-carving contest and a pumpkin toss. A parade is the big draw on Saturday afternoon, but people manage to survive Saturday for a pumpkin-pancake breakfast Sunday morning. More than 10,000 attend the affair and help swell the proceeds, which are earmarked for community projects.

Location: Anamosa is about 15 miles northeast of Cedar Rapids, off U.S. 151. **Contact:** Anamosa Chamber of Commerce, 124 E. Main St., Anamosa, IA 52205; Tel: (319)462-4879.

Centerville

Pancake Day

Third Saturday in September Centerville is a rural town that once had 37 coal mines and a flour mill in the area, all now long gone. But weep not; the town has become a thriving retail center. Because there is no sales tax, people drive in from Missouri and other towns to shop. The town's population is 6,000, but it has four supermarkets.

In 1949, the owners of the flour mill decided to do something nice for the people of this little town, so it treated them to a big pancake breakfast. This continued for years, and when the factory finally closed, the people decided they liked their pancake day so much they would keep it.

And so they did. Donations from local businesses and festival friends pay for supplies. Thirty grills are set up, and 80,000 free pancakes with syrup are served, requiring 2,000 pounds of flour and 1,000 cases of syrup. To go with the pancakes are 900 gallons of coffee plus lots of milk for kids.

The day is more than just pancakes now. There is a parade, with Miss Pancake Queen and her court smiling at spectators. There are local bands, a carnival, arts and crafts, and food vendors. Between 20,000 and 30,000 people come to the breakfast-party.

Location: In the town square in Centerville, on Iowa 2, about 50 miles east of I-35, in southern Iowa near the Missouri border. **Contact:** Centerville Chamber of Commerce, 128 N. 12th St., Centerville, IA 52544; Tel: (515)437-4102.

While You're There: Visit the Historical and Coal Mining Museum in the 1903 post office. Exhibits show a pioneer farm and village and a coal-mine replica.

See Also: World's Largest Pancake Breakfast (Springfield, MA).

Orange City

Tulip Festival

Third Weekend in May (Thursday through Sunday) Is it the *saucijzebroodjes* that bring 125,000 to 150,000 people to this jaunty festival? Or the tapestry-like colors of the tulips?

Most likely it's a combination of the pigs in a blanket (another name for *saucijzebroodjes*) and the masses of tulips in bloom and two parades a day and authentic Dutch folk singing and dancing by people in Dutch costumes.

Orange City has a population of about 5,000 people, many of whom are of Dutch heritage. Their ancestors went first to Michigan and then settled in Iowa, and the business section of the town has colorful Dutch-style storefronts. And, because Holland made a gift of tulip bulbs to the city, there are now masses of tulips through the city, and 50,000 in the Vander Wel test gardens.

The festival has been observed since 1941 as a celebration of spring and of the town's Dutch legacy. Besides the typical dancing and singing of Holland, local restaurants offer ethnic food, including the sausages, pea soup, and *poffertjes* (pastries or crepes, somewhat like fried dough), as well as standard festival fare. Of all the food, one could say, " *Alles Smaakt Je Well Leker,* " which means, roughly, "Everything tastes very good."

A Dutch vegetable vendor rides through the streets of Orange City during a Tulip Festival parade. *(Courtesy of the Orange City, Iowa, Dutch Tulip Festival Committee and the Orange City Chamber of Commerce)*

The festival takes people on a trip to the Netherlands: For children, there are demonstrations of making wooden shoes, and for everybody there are art displays, a *straat markt*—a street market that looks like a miniature Dutch village—a quilt show, the queen and her court dressed in authentic Dutch costumes. There are also rousing band contests, the bands coming from Nebraska, South Dakota, and Iowa.

Location: Orange City is in northwest Iowa, on Iowa 10, 7 miles east of U.S. 75, about 40 miles north of Sioux City.   **Contact:** Orange City Chamber of Commerce, P.O. Box 36, Orange City, IA 51041; Tel: (712)737-4510.

West Point

West Point Sweet Corn Festival

Second weekend in September (Friday through Sunday)

Iowa grows more corn for grain than any other state, but statistically it's not important in sweet corn. That doesn't mean Iowans can't have sweet-corn festivals, and they have a big one in West Point: 30,000 people chomp through about 15 tons of free steamed and buttered sweet corn.

On the day before the festival, the corn, imported from other areas, is brought to the town center, and volunteers gather to shuck it. (The husks are loaded into dump trucks and taken to farms for cattle feed.) An antique steam engine heats the water for the corn, and when the corn is done, it's dipped in a huge vat of butter. A barbecued chicken dinner, chicken sandwiches, corn dogs, and other festival food round out the eats department.

In 1953, farmers with some acreage in sweet corn brought baskets of it to town to share. The sharing became a festival and kept getting bigger, and the local Community Club took over and now uses proceeds for community improvements.

Entertainment is oriented toward family activities: junior water-hose fights, pee-wee drag races, horseshoes, a mini-garden-tractor pull, 5K and 10K races, country and western music, carnival rides, a teen dance, and a parade, where the Sweet Corn Queen stars.

Location: West Point is in the southeast corner of Iowa on Iowa 16, about 12 miles west of Burlington. **Contact:** West Point Sweet Corn Festival, P.O. Box 305, West Point, IA 52656; Tel: (319)837-6178.

Kansas

Beef Empire Days

Early June (10 days, usually including first two weekends) ⊙ Beef Empire Days began in 1968 as a two-day educational event "to improve appraisal methods of economic values of slaughter steers and heifers." Since Kansas ranks first among states in cattle slaughtered, economic values of slaughter steers are of prime importance.

The main focus of the present show is education, both for the public and beef-industry insiders, but it has also become a festival, with a carnival, parade, rodeos, pancake feeds, and a cowboy-poetry gathering. Attendance is about 100,000 over the ten days.

One of the most popular events for the public is Chuckwagons in the Park, held on the show's second Saturday, following the parade. Businesses and organizations cook beef in a variety of ways, competing for cash prizes, and hand out bite-sized samples of their creations to the folks.

Family Night Rodeo is a food-cum-spectacle event. Ticket holders get barbecued hamburgers to go with the thrills of watching bronc riding and steer roping.

Location: Garden City is in western Kansas at the junction of U.S. 50 and 83. ⊙ **Contact:** Beef Empire Days Inc., 1511 E. Fulton Terrace, Garden City, KS 67846; Tel: (316)275-6807.

Oktoberfest

Friday in October preceding the Fort Hays State University homecoming ⊙ Like most Oktoberfests, this one is rich in food and music. Unlike some, it celebrates a Volga-German heritage: Six communities in Ellis County,

Kansas, were settled in 1873 by German Catholics who came from southern Russia on the Volga River. They had emigrated there at the invitation of Catherine the Great who promised exemption from military service. (One of the Ellis County towns is named Catherine.) The Germans stayed almost 100 years, but the exemption was ending, and so they set sail, a number arriving in Kansas.

The festival began in 1973 in conjunction with homecoming for Fort Hayes State University, and about 900 people came. Now about 10,000 show up.

Events begin with the tapping of a keg, and then people dig in. The foods reflect the dual Russian-German influence. *Bierocks,* for example, are a German version of the Russian *pirozhki,* a mix of hamburger, cabbage, and onion baked in a dough pocket.

Other foods offered include bratwurst; sauerkraut; crock pickles; *bierwurst,* a pork sausage cooked in beer; creamed-bean and noodle soup; *galushkies,* also spelled *kaluskies* and *galuschejes* and in English pigs-in-a-blanket (ground beef and pork with rice, rolled into a sausage shape, wrapped in a cabbage leaf, and boiled). On the sweet side are *herzen* (heart-shaped cookies); *kuchen,* bread dough covered with fruit and crumbs—a sort of coffee cake—and *spitzbuben,* diamond-shaped cookies filled with jellies and sprinkled with sugar.

When people aren't eating, they sing German songs and dance—polkas, the broom dance, and the chicken dance, a fast dance in which the dancers flap their arms and generally imitate chickens. Except for the chicken dance, popular in the Midwest, the dances are reminders of the old country. The festival also has arts and crafts exhibits and commemorative steins for sale.

Location: Hays is midway between Kansas City and Denver at the junction of I-70 and U.S. 183. **Contact:** Hays Convention and Visitors Bureau, 1301 Pine St., Hays, KS 67601; Tel: (913)628-8202, or (800)569-4504; Fax: (913)628-1471.

Lenexa

Lenexa Spinach Festival

First Saturday after Labor Day Popeye, the cartoon sailor who gulped down cans of spinach to make his biceps pop, and his lady friend Olive Oyl, are always on hand at the Spinach Festival to oversee the building of the World's Largest Spinach Salad. The salad—500 pounds of spinach and 30 gallons of dressing—is tossed in a plastic swimming pool with pitchforks.

Lenexa, which in the 1920s, '30s, and '40s claimed the title "Spinach Capital of the World," is a bedroom suburb of Kansas City, which may explain why a "briefcase throw" is one of the festival events.

The festival began in 1982 to celebrate Lenexa's Belgian heritage, as well as its history with spinach. From the early 1900s on, Belgian farmers in Lenexa produced more spinach than any other farmers in the world. The all-time spinach king is John Van Keirsbilck, who raised 1,250 pounds of spinach on one acre of land in 1946.

Swedish folkdancing is a favorite activity at Lindsborg's Hyllningsfest; colorful folk dress and musical strains from fiddles and accordions complete the scene. (Kansas Travel and Tourism)

This history is remembered with a spinach cook-off, in which contestants have come up with spinach milk shakes and Popeye pizzas; with food vendors selling spinach dips, spinach-meatloaf sandwiches, spinach balls, and spinach tortillas. Games emphasize the green or horticultural theme: there are green rock skipping contests, a green bubble-gum blowing contest, a vegetable-creations contest (hats, wreaths, etc.), a largest-sunflower contest, and fruit and vegetable bobbing. There's also a beer garden and Belgian polka dancing on the Friday eve of the festival, and pigeon racing on Saturday, because Belgian farmers liked to race pigeons and polka. The festival has an attendance of about 10,000.

Location: Sar-Ko-Par Trails Park, two miles west of I-35 after the 87th Street Parkway exit, in Lenexa, southwest of Kansas City. ❦ **Contact:** Lenexa Spinach Festival, 13420 Oak St., Lenexa, KS 66215; Tel: (913)541-0209, or (800)950-7867.

Lindsborg

Svensk Hyllningsfest (Swedish Homage Festival)

Second weekend in October (Friday through Sunday), in odd-numbered years ❦ In the spring of 1869, 200 Swedish immigrants from the province of Varmland arrived in central Kansas and founded Lindsborg, now known as

Little Sweden, U.S.A. The town retains a Swedish flavor; buildings bear such Swedish names as Apotek (pharmacy) and Bibliotek (library). Many residents are descendants of the original pioneers, who are honored during Hyllningsfest.

Lindsborg has a population of only 3,100, but about 50,000 visitors attend the Hyllningsfest, first held in 1941. It's all authentically Swedish. Folk art in crafts tents includes the popular Dala Horses, wooden horses painted with a flower-patterned saddle, and folk dancing is by costumed children and the adult Lindsborg Folkdanslag.

High points are a parade on Saturday morning and the Saturday night smorgasbord, a groaning board of more than 30 different Swedish foods—salads, pickled herring, *kroppkaka* (a potato-flour dumpling), cheese, poppyseed bread, Swedish meatballs and brown beans, cookies, and *ostkaka* (a creamy cheesecake topped with lingonberries). Advance tickets are required for the smorgasbord.

Location: Lindsborg is 2 miles west of I-135, 20 miles south of Salina. ⬥ **Contact:** Lindsborg Chamber of Commerce, P.O. Box 191, Lindsborg, KS 67456; Tel: (913)227-3706.

Lucia Fest

Second Saturday in December ⬥ Lucia Fest brings in the Christmas season with music, folk dancing, the crowning of St. Lucia, and baked goods. The festival, called *Luciadag* in Swedish, celebrates the saint who was burned at the stake in Sicily in the fourth century, but later appeared in Sweden carrying food and drink to the hungry during a famine. She returns each year on December 13 to herald Christmas. Traditionally, Lucia is portrayed by a family's oldest daughter, who wakes up early and, wearing a crown of lighted candles, carries a tray of ginger cookies to each member of the family and sings *Santa Lucia*. This ancient Swedish tradition is re-enacted in Lindsborg, with embellishments.

North Newton

Fall Festival

A Saturday on one of the first weekends in October (exact date determined by Bethel College homecoming) ⬥ The Fall Festival began in 1971 as an inaugural celebration for a new president of Bethel College, the oldest Mennonite college in the United States, founded in 1887. Its scope has expanded to honor Mennonite culture, and it now attracts about 10,000 visitors.

Mennonites have a reputation for good cooking, creating dishes with old-country roots. You'll find German bratwurst; *verenike* (soft-dough pockets filled with cottage cheese, a German dish); *pirozhki* (flaky pastry filled with ground meat, a Russian dish); and New Year's cookies that are a traditional Low German delicacy.

Highlights, besides the food, include a crafts show, athletic competitions, children's activities, and cooking demonstrations.

Mennonites first came to Kansas in the 1870s, and Harvey County now has the largest settlement of Mennonites in the country. They have forsaken their white bonnets and buggies, but their influence remains not only in schools and churches but in the prairies waving with wheat. The Mennonites were pioneer sodbusters.

The Mennonite movement stems from the sixteenth-century radical reform movement of the Anabaptists and takes its name from Menno Simons, a Catholic priest who provided leadership in Anabaptism's early days. Mennonites were originally pacifist Germans, who fled Germany to escape military service. Many migrated to Ukraine, where they were exempted from the military. In 1873, with the military exemption ending, the Mennonites emigrated *en masse*, settling largely in the U.S. and Canadian plains.

Bernhard Warkentin, born in Ukraine, visited central Kansas in 1872 and wrote home about the fertile fields, persuading more than 5,000 Mennonites to join him. They brought parcels of seeds of the wheat strain called Turkey Red—a hard winter wheat that had flourished on the European steppes. It grew well in Kansas. Neighbors bought it from the Mennonites, and it spread all over the plains and made Kansas the Breadbasket of the World.

Location: Bethel College campus in North Newtown, south of exit 34 on I-135, 20 miles north of Wichita. **Contact:** Events Coordinator, Bethel College, N. Main and 27th, North Newton, KS 67117; Tel: (316)283-2500, Fax: (316)283-5286.

While You're There: The Warkentin House at 211 E. First St. is a 16-room Victorian home built in 1886 by Bernard Warkentin. The oak dining table, which can seat 20, is in the home along with close to 90 percent of the original furnishings.

Sharon Springs

Kansas Rattlesnake Roundup and Prairie Folk Festival

Second weekend in May (Friday night through Sunday)
Rattlesnake chili, chicken-fried snake—that's enough to make this sound like a, well, *different* food festival. It's distinctive for another reason, too, and I quote: "This is the only rattlesnake roundup in the USA instigated entirely by women."

There's a no-nonsense reason for the festival, which began in 1992 and has an attendance of 2,000 to 3,000. The economy was declining in rural Kansas, Sharon Springs isn't on an interstate, and something was needed to draw visitors to the community. Members of PRIDE (a women's group) brainstormed and decided they had a regenerating resource, i.e., a generous supply of rattlesnakes.

Most roundups concentrate on big rattlesnakes, but in Sharon Springs they go for the prairie rattlesnake, a "small but extremely feisty animal." The sponsors have worked with university research teams and provide festival-goers with information on the prairie rattlesnake, including instructions on cooking it. If snake talk palls, there are fiddlers, special entertainment on Saturday night, crafts and, for those with timid appetites, non-snake food.

As the roundup grows, the women in the roundup crew—known as the Pit Hissers—are finding a need for more men to help. It might be hard, though, to find anyone—man or woman—like the grandmother on the staff who climbs into a sleeping bag with live rattlers.

Location: Sharon Springs is at the junction of U.S. 40 and Kansas 27, 17 miles from the Colorado border. ◌ **Contact:** Rattlesnake Roundup, HC 1, No. 485, Sharon Springs, KS 67758; Tel: (913)852-4473; Fax: (913)852-4228.

Topeka

Fiesta Mexicana

Third week of July (Tuesday through Saturday) ◌ This is a genuine south-of-the-border festival, put on by a good part of Topeka's population of 10,000 Mexican Americans to benefit the grade school of Our Lady of Guadalupe Church. Mexicans came to Topeka in about 1910 to escape the Revolution in Mexico, and many went to work on the Atchison, Topeka & Santa Fe Railway.

The fiesta days are filled with a parade, a 5K race, a coronation ball (contestants raise money throughout the year and the one raising the most is crowned Fiesta Princess), folkloric dancing, a carnival, kids' games, a jalapeño-pepper eating contest . . . and food. The food court specializes in five items: tacos, enchiladas, tostadas, tamales, and burritos, all home-cooked. In outlying food booths, there are non-Hispanic items like Polish sausage.

The fiesta began in 1933 and has been going strong ever since—except for the year a tornado wiped it out. It has become one of the largest celebrations of Hispanic culture in the Midwest. Attendance is about 40,000.

Location: The area of Our Lady of Guadalupe Church on the corner of Chandler and Atchison Streets, in the Oakland area of Topeka. ◌ **Contact:** Our Lady of Guadalupe Church—Fiesta Mexicana, 1008 N. Atchison Ave., Topeka, KA 66616-1196; Tel: (913)232-5088.

Shawnee County Allied Tribes Intertribal Pow Wow

Labor Day weekend (Friday through Sunday) ◌ Native-American dances—war dances, grass dances—are the main attraction for most visitors to this powwow, but for hungry carnivores, the attraction is buffalo stew and buffalo burgers. The concessions food includes many of the dishes American Indians have been eating for years and years: buffalo (a lean, sweet meat), Indian tacos, corn soup, popcorn (a Native American specialty), roast corn, and sometimes wild rice, though it's not native to Kansas.

Kansas is the home of four Native-American tribes, but some 30 to 35 tribes from all over the country come for the powwow, which began in 1991 and is attended by about 10,000. Crafts booths display silverwork, and seminars are conducted on Indian culture. A princess is chosen to reign for a year.

Location: Shawnee Lake Park on E. 29th St. just outside the Topeka city limits. ◌ **Contact:** Shawnee County Allied Tribes Intertribal Pow Wow Inc., P.O. Box 750284, Topeka, KS 66675; Tel: (913)272-5489.

Wellington

Kansas Wheat Festival

Weekend following Fourth of July (Wednesday through Sunday) Kansas isn't all waving fields of wheat, but more than 11 million acres of it are, and those are enough to keep Kansans celebrating wheat in Wellington year after year after year. The town is a processing and distribution center for Sumner County's wheat.

The first festival, called a Wheat Jubilee, was held in 1900 and celebrated a particularly good wheat harvest. Good harvest or bad, there's been a festival ever since. About 6,000 attend.

The festival begins Wednesday night with a picnic in the park—a meal of barbecued beef, potato salad, beans, and a wheat roll, accompanied by children's games and entertainment.

The Taste of Sumner County occupies Thursday and Friday. In the restaurant competition, in which chefs usually include wheat in their dishes, festival-goers vote for their favorite by putting a bean in the restaurant's jar. Typical foods are croissants with chicken and ham salad, apple strudel, and *bierocks,* a dough pocket filled with hamburger, cabbage, and onion.

Wheat Capital Festivities comprise a baking contest, a Mayor's Cookie Jar contest, and a cakewalk. Categories in the baking contest are cakes, pies, rolls, and bread; samples are available, and the leftovers are auctioned off.

For hizzoner (or herroner), contestants bake cookies and place them in a decorated jar. The jar and cookies deemed best by the judges is given to the mayor, and the winner gets cash.

The winner of the cakewalk gets a cake, which is an old tradition. The cakewalk originated in the South as a promenade in which couples who performed the most intricate steps won cakes. The promenade evolved into a dance.

Top honors go to three queens (different ages) and a king, whose wheat is judged the best by judges in Wichita. Other events are a carnival, arts and crafts, kids' games, music each evening, and a gospel sing.

Location: Wellington is 17 miles north of the Oklahoma border, 3 miles west of I-35. **Contact:** Wellington Chamber of Commerce, 207 S. Washington, Wellington, KS 67152; Tel: (316)326-7466.

See also: Fall Festival (North Newton, KS).

Missouri

Pecan Festival

First weekend in October (Friday through Sunday) ⊙ The Home of the World's Largest Pecan puts on a zany festival with backwoods events like mud runs (trucks drive through mud pits), a floozy contest (for men dressed as women), and a "nutty" parade with every imaginable kind of float.

But about 15 farms, most of them growing pecans, are in the area, so you'll also find an abundance of pecan pies, candies, cookies, and cakes. And you can buy five-pound bags of baked pecans topped with cinnamon and sugar or glazed with honey. There are country-ham and pecan-pie auctions, and bids for the pies run up to $700. One recent year, $4,000 was taken in on pies.

The pecans, by the way, are hard-shelled pecans, which the folks around here like to differentiate from Southern soft shells; the hard-shelled varieties, they say, are *moist* because they contain more natural oil.

For more general sustenance at the festival, there's Missouri fare—barbecued chicken, porkburgers, country ham, and a fish fry. And there's a beer garden to slake thirst.

The festival started in 1981, and is attended by about 5,000. Brunswick itself boasts a population of 1,500.

About the world's largest pecan: It's made of wire mesh covered with concrete and is the size of a subcompact car, about 12 feet long, 7 feet in diameter, weighing 6 tons. It's permanently installed at the James Pecan Farm, but has been seen on the Oprah Winfrey Show.

Festival proceeds are kept in the community for needy families. These funds helped victims of the great floods in 1993 and 1996.

Location: Brunswick is on U.S. 24, about 65 miles east of Kansas City. ⊙ **Contact:** Pecan Festival, 211 E. Broadway, Brunswick 65236; Tel: (816)548-3636.

While You're There: Don't miss the big cement pecan. The James Farm is two miles east of town.

California

Ozark Ham and Turkey Festival

Third Saturday in September ❉ Turkey and pork are the two biggest industries in California's Moniteau County, and this festival was started in 1991 to express the folks' appreciation of gobblers and oinkers. So about 18,000 people get together and eat a lot of pork and turkey and have a whopping good time.

In the turkey department, big sellers are smoked turkey drumsticks, a marinated turkey-breast dinner (the marinade is made with a secret recipe), and batter-dipped turkey strips. The ham division starts out with breakfasts of ham, biscuits, and ham-milk gravy, and moves on to country smoked ham.

There's a competition of grilled pork steaks, with trophies and cash prizes awarded. The steaks are judged on taste, texture, color, and showmanship, and festival-goers get to sample them after the judging.

Other edibles includes beef and steak sandwiches (beef production is also big in the area), burgers, and bratwurst with sauerkraut.

Some of the events have a distinctly regional hue. For example, the washer-board tournament, in which large washers are thrown at holes in a board, is popular in this area but barely known in many other parts of the country. Motorcycle poker is also a type of poker that's not widespread. Cyclists riding a course have to stop at designated locations to pick up a card, and the winner is the one who winds up with the best poker hand.

There are also other sports events, three stages for entertainers, country dancers, square dancers, an "anything-goes" parade, car and tractor shows, stock-car races, and arts-and-crafts displays.

Location: California is on U.S. 50 about 20 miles west of Jefferson City. ❉ **Contact:** California Chamber of Commerce, P.O. Box 85, California, MO 65018; Tel: (573)796-3040.

While You're There: Two plants offer tours showing the processing of their products. They are Cargill, which processes Honeysuckle white turkeys (a brand that is said to have a lot of white meat), and Burger's Smoke House, which produces country smoked hams.

Hermann

Wurstfest

Third full weekend in March ❉ The Sausage Capital of Missouri has been making sausages since about 1836; they've gotten pretty good at it, so if you're in Hermann, you're in the right spot for wurst.

Local sausage makers, wineries, restaurants, and shops all get together to show off their prime products. Sausages for sampling and purchase include leberwurst, bratwurst, blutwurst, schwartenmagen, sommerwurst, and other specialty wursts.

Sausage makers of the state compete for best sausage, and amateurs compete in the Best Wurst contest.

Because this is an area of both wine making and sausage making, there's a competition for amateur wine makers, and wineries offer tours of their cellars and samples of their fine wines.

In case you're still worried about getting enough wurst, the Hermann Fire Department serves a whole hog sausage breakfast Sunday morning starting at 7:30. And to reinforce the German-heritage theme, you will hear live German music and see German folk dancers.

Location: Hermann is about 60 miles west of St. Louis on Missouri 19. ⬡ **Contact:** Wurstfest Committee, 207A Schiller St., Hermann, MO 65041; Tel: (314)486-2120.

While You're There: Much of Hermann's downtown is on the National Register of Historic Places because of its distinctive German architecture. Streets have such names as Mozart and Goethe. Take a look.

Kansas City

American Royal Barbecue

First Friday and Saturday in October ⬡ This is the World's Biggest Barbecue, and the barbecue sauce that's chosen the best is declared the "Best Barbecue Sauce of the Planet." Modesty is not the hallmark of the KC barbecue.

More than 300 teams take part, and anywhere from 35,000 to 50,000 attend, partly to eat (the food of vendors, not of contestants), partly to watch the antics of the barbecuers (barbecuing is a long, slow process, so there's time for antics), partly to see the art.

The art may be one of the odder aspects of the American Royal. It's called bone art. Contestants use rib bones and fashion them into so-called art, which may be embellished with any kind of decoration, such as feathers or sequins. The finished work must be at least 75 percent bones.

The barbecue, which began in 1979, consists of five contests: the American Royal/KC Masterpiece International Invitational Barbecue Contest, limited to 40 to 60 teams; the Open Barbecue Contest, the original event and the biggest contest, in which teams compete for cash, a trophy, and everlasting fame; a sauce contest; a contest for side dishes, with categories of baked beans, potatoes, and vegetables; and the bone-art contest.

The categories sanctioned by the sanctioning organization, the Kansas City Barbecue Society, are ribs, chicken, pork, and beef brisket.

Attractions outside the barbecue complex include lots of food, live bands, a petting zoo, and other events for children.

The barbecuers all bring the prejudices of their regions. Generally, for example, a vinegar-based barbecue sauce is preferred in the South; in the East, they like mustard; in the Midwest and Texas, tomato-based sauces prevail.

Barbecues are probably as ancient as fire, but the Indians are believed to have taught European settlers the method. The word barbecue is supposed to be from the Spanish *barbacoa*; the Spanish probably picked it up from Arawak Indians who cooked game over pits where fires burned down to embers.

The Kansas City Barbeque Society is adamant about what barbecue means (and about how to spell it; they spell it with a "q"): meat cooked over a hardwood or charcoal fire for a long period of time; it is *not* meat cooked directly over a hot searing fire—that's grilling. That's what Californians do, they say.

There are about 200 KCBS-sanctioned barbecues in the United States; for a calendar of them, contact the Kansas City Barbeque Society, 11514 Hickman Mills Dr., Kansas City, MO 64134; Tel: (800)963-5227 or (816)765-5891.

Location: American Royal Complex, off I-35 and I-670, east of downtown near the Kemper Arena. **Contact:** American Royal Complex, 1701 American Royal Court, Kansas City, MO 64102; Tel: (816)221-9800.

Stockton

Black Walnut Festival

Last full weekend in September (Wednesday through Saturday) The Eastern black walnut is sort of a maverick loner tree, growing wild, sometimes in backyards or on farms but rarely in groves. Considering this untamed quality of the tree, it's nice to know it has a home: Stockton is not only the Black Walnut Capital of the World but also the home of the Hammons Products Company, the Largest (and only) Walnut-Processing Plant in the World.

That makes Stockton a likely place for a black-walnut festival. Here you can get a slice of genuine black-walnut pie and try other baked goods, also improved with black walnuts. You can also get the usual festival food.

A highlight of the festival is an Eastern black walnut contest, sponsored by Hammons. Nuts are judged according to a complex set of factors: the ideal nut should have a nutmeat near white in color, plump, crisp, and aromatic, without "bite." The shell should be thin, the nutmeat about 25 percent of the nut's total dry weight, husk removed. Samples are available for tasting.

Less nut-focused events include a carnival, music (from big band to country), the crowning of Miss Black Walnut Festival, a contest for prettiest baby, and demonstrations by a quilter, painter, banjo maker, wood carver, broom maker, and a chair-rush weaver. There are also special events for youngsters. About 15,000 attend the festival, which began in 1961.

The Latin term for the Eastern black walnut is *Juglans nigra,* meaning Jove's black acorn. It's acclaimed for its rich, earthy flavor and aroma, and has been used for a long, long time: Eastern and Midwestern Indians, according to Raymond Sokolov in *Fading Feast,* ate the nuts raw, pounded them into a butter for baking, and spiced up pumpkin soup with them.

Early pioneers learned from the Indians to like black walnuts, but they also discovered that black-walnut wood made fine furniture, and Sokolov observed in 1981 that "most of the great old trees, over 100 feet high, have been cut for timber." Consequently, there is some fear for the black walnut's future.

Besides its qualifications as a furniture wood, the nut has some contrary aspects. The California black walnut and the Eastern black walnut, which are slightly different genetically, both have extremely hard shells, very hard to crack. Furthermore, the shells are rich in black dye that gets all over everything and is indelible.

It's not the most economical of nuts. According to the Hammons company, the yield of nutmeats to the overall weight of the nut is about 8 percent, while many nuts yield 40 to 50 percent. And then there's its wild side. Nuts are harvested almost exclusively by hand, picked from the ground, since there aren't any large stands that might lend themselves to mechanical picking.

Nonetheless, they have been processed since the 1930s, and millions of trees grow unmanaged and untamed across a large part of the Midwest and eastern United States, providing Hammons Products with raw material.

Location: Stockton, in southwestern Missouri, is about 40 miles northwest of Springfield on Missouri 39 and 32. ❁ **Contact:** Stockton Area Chamber of Commerce, P.O. Box 410, Stockton, MO 65785; Tel: (417)276-5213.

While You're There: Hammons, the walnut-processor, gives tours every afternoon during the processing season, which begins in September and lasts about nine months.

See Also: West Virginia Black Walnut Festival (Spencer, WV).

Nebraska

Grand Island

Central Nebraska Ethnic Festival

Last weekend in July (Friday through Sunday) Grand Island is the community (now the state's third-biggest city) that sprang up near the island in the Platte River that French fur traders named La Grande Isle in the late 1770s. Those traders were the forerunners of 300,000 immigrants who traveled the Mormon and Oregon trails through Nebraska in the 1800s. Many stayed and made Nebraska their home. All of these, and newer immigrants as well, are honored at the ethnic festival by more than 40,000 visitors.

The festival features ethnic music and dance groups, among them Scottish bagpipers, Irish pipe players, and Vietnamese dragon dancers; an educational pavilion where you can investigate your genealogy on a computer; a street bazaar with ethnic arts and crafts; nightly street dances; and what are called Adventures in Eating. The adventurous menu lineup can include Indian tacos and fry bread, Swedish rosettes, Mexican burritos, crab Rangoon, Pennsylvania Dutch funnel cake, Greek gyros and baklava, Laotian egg rolls, Caribbean fruit drinks, and Italian sausage sandwiches. And there are hot dogs and hamburgers, roasted sweet corn, and homemade ice cream.

A few blocks from the festival, the Liederkranz Club of Grand Island holds its yearly Sommerfest on the same weekend, with German food, entertainment, and beer in an outdoor Beer Garden.

Location: Third and Wheelers Sts. in Grand Island, 80 miles west of Lincoln. Take exit 312 off I-80. **Contact:** Central Nebraska Ethnic Festival, P.O. Box 1306, Grand Island, NE 68802; Tel: (308)385-5444. For Sommerfest information, call (308) 382-9337.

Nebraska City

Applejack Celebration

Third weekend in September More than 36,000 bushels of apples, largely Jonathans and Red and Golden Delicious, are grown in local orchards, and this bounty has been celebrated since 1969. About 40,000 people come for the various activities and edibles, which include a pancake breakfast and barbecue on Saturday, and plain apples, caramel apples, and cider on both days. What they don't get at the Applejack Celebration is applejack, which is probably a good thing: applejack, a brandy made from apple cider, is 80- to 100-proof. It's called Calvados in France, and sometimes Jersey Lightning in the United States, supposedly because it was first made in New Jersey. The reason the festival has its name is because one of the founders was named Jack.

Activities and attractions include contests for apple-pie baking, apple peeling, and seed spitting; a parade and marching-band competition; antique, quilt, and needlework shows; a crafts fair; Go-Kart races; and a street dance on Saturday night.

Location: Nebraska City is 45 miles south of Omaha on Rt. 75. **Contact:** Nebraska City Chamber of Commerce, 806 1st Ave., Nebraska City, NE 68410; Tel: (800)514- 9113, or (402)873-3000.

While You're There: Tour the 200-acre Morton Orchard where you'll see a working beehive and, in the fall, demonstrations of cider making. The orchard was planted by Julius Sterling Morton, who originated Arbor Day in 1872. You can also visit the Morton homestead, a 52-room mansion in Arbor Lodge State Historical Park. It was once a four-room house but was added to after Morton's death in 1902 by his son who got very rich producing Morton Salt.

Wayne

Chicken Show

Second weekend in July (Friday and Saturday) Cheep Fun for the Family. Take the Whole Brood.

That gives you an idea of what this show is all about—fun and terrible puns and, not incidentally, omelets and barbecued chicken.

A show highlight, which has brought national publicity to Wayne, is Saturday's National Cluck-Off, a cockaphony (it's catching) of clucks and crows and cackles as people imitate chickens. To get the cluckers in the mood, 2,000 omelets, ham or vegetable, are served for breakfast, and beginning shortly after noon there's the chicken feed—a barbecued chicken dinner with fresh corn. There's a small charge for the omelets and chicken feed, but ice cream bars are free.

Other events include a fly-in and plane display at Wayne Municipal Airport, a street dance, an egg drop-catch, a parade, and a best-chicken-legs-on-human contest.

Nebraska produces more than two billion eggs each year, and ranks thirteenth in egg laying among the states.

Location: Most events at Bressler Park in Wayne, at the junction of Nebraska 35 and 15 in the northeastern part of the state. **Contact:** Wayne Area Chamber of Commerce, 108 West 3rd, Wayne, NE 68787; Tel: (402)375-2240, Fax: (402)375-2246.

Wilber

Nebraska Czech Festival

First weekend in August (Friday through Sunday) ⁣ Down-town Wilber looks like the quintessential Midwestern small town most days. In early August, however, it becomes unrestrained and Czech. As many as 35,000 people come to Wilber, population 1,500, to celebrate Czech heritage and eat Czech food in the Czech Capital of the U.S.A.

The Czechs began this festival in 1962, and it's now crammed with activities—Czech historical pageants and heritage demonstrations, a parade, accordion jamborees, polka dancing, folk dancers, the Miss Czech-Slovak U.S.A. Pageant, to name a few. And a kolache-eating contest, which brings us to Czech delicacies.

Kolaches are round buns with fillings that might typically be dried prunes or dried apricots and sweetened cottage cheese. In America, it is the most popular of Czech baked goods, and many Czech-American women still spend their Saturday mornings preparing them. They're everywhere at the festival.

A Czech dinner requires dumplings, and a number of restaurants and nonprofit groups offer duck dinners that include dumplings and kraut, usually flavored with onions and caraway seeds, and, surprise, kolaches. You'll also find *jaternice,* a type of headcheese; *jelita,* a blood and barley sausage; and *houska,* rye bread.

When the railroads and the Homestead Act opened the West, waves of Czechs (and Poles and Italians) came to Nebraska to work on ranches and in the Omaha stockyards. The population of Wilber remains almost 90 percent Czech in ancestry.

Location: Wilber is 35 miles southwest of Lincoln, at the intersection of Nebraska 41 and 103. ⁣ Contact: Nebraska Czechs of Wilber, P.O. Box 652, Wilber, NE 68465; Tel: (402)821-2812.

While You're There: The Wilber Czech Museum, 3rd and Main Sts., has all sorts of Czech artifacts, books, and cookbooks. And kolaches and coffee.

See Also: Kolache Festival (Caldwell, TX).

North Dakota

Scandinavian Hjemkomst Festival

Last week in June (Wednesday through Sunday) *Hjemkomst,* which means homecoming, is the name of the replica of a Viking ship that sailed from Duluth to make a homecoming in Norway in 1982. The festival takes the name since it's a kind of homecoming for the Scandinavians of the area.

Certainly the food and the sounds of the food's names provide a Scandinavian homecoming. Listen to the words: Danish smorrebrod (sandwich) and *kringle* (pastry); Norwegian *rommegrot* (cream mush or pudding); Icelandic *kleinur* (doughnuts) and *reyktur lax* (smoked salmon); Swedish *knackebrod* (hardtack), *kottbullar* (meatballs), *inlagd sill* (pickled herring), and *rysgryngrot* (rice pudding); and Finnish *pulla* (cardamom bread) with *puolukkas* (lingonberries), and *suolalohi* (salt salmon).

And that's just a small sampling. There are also plenty of *lefses,* the Norwegian crepes, and potato sausages and rhubarb pudding and pastries and cakes.

The festival, put on jointly by Fargo and sister city Moorhead, Minnesota, celebrates a different Scandinavian country each year with costumed dancers, musicians, crafts displays, and demonstrations of Scandinavian arts such as rosemaling, woodcarving, weaving, glass-blowing, and embroidery.

The annual Swedish *midsommars dans,* a ring dance around a Maypole, is a regular feature of the festival, and a Norwegian worship service on Sunday is also an annual event. Hymns are sung in Norwegian, and the pastor preaches the sermon in Norwegian.

Most of the events take place in Fargo, but there are also mini-fests in Moorhead. About 20,000 attend the festival, which has been held since 1978 and has been cited by the American Bus Association as one of North America's top events.

Location: Throughout Fargo and Moorhead. **Contact:** Scandinavian Hjemkomst Festival, 3107 S. Rivershore Dr., Moorhead, MN 56560; Tel: (701)282-3653 or (800)235-7654.

While You're There: Learn more about the Scandinavian heritage and local history at the Heritage Hjemkomst Interpretive Center, 202 First Ave. North, Moorhead. The center features the *Hjemkomst,* the 77-foot Viking ship replica; the story of its voyage to Bergen, Norway, is told through photographs and a videotape presentation.

Grand Forks

Potato Bowl

Second or third Week in September (Seven days, Saturday to Saturday) A ton of French fries is given away on French Fri-Day during this homage to the potato. If that's not enough to make eyes pop, the week is filled with all kinds of potato food: potato pancake breakfasts, and lunches with dishes such as potato salad, potato dumplings with cheese filling, potato soup, potato chips, French fries, and baked potatoes with every imaginable topping—cheese, sour cream, salsa, vegetables, sauces.

The event, started in 1966 and attended by 30,000 to 40,000, honors the 150,000 acres of potatoes grown in the fertile black soil of the Red River Valley, on North Dakota's eastern border. While the state ranks seventh in potato production, the valley area of North Dakota and Minnesota takes third place. They grow white potatoes, red potatoes, and russets here, and the valley is the world's largest supplier of so-called chipping potatoes—the russets used for potato chips, because they are rounder, smoother, and less watery than some varieties.

North Dakota became one of the most highly mechanized agricultural areas in the world because the homesteaders who cultivated huge tracts, called bonanza farms, were pioneers in farming techniques.

Events of the festival include the crowning of a Potato Bowl Queen, a parade, fireworks, music, and a potato-picking contest. The University of North Dakota is located here, and the festival culminates with a football game, preceded by a grand rally with marching bands and cheerleaders.

Location: Grand Forks is on I-29, about 80 miles from Canada. **Contact:** Tourist Promotion Division, 600 E. Boulevard Ave., Bismarck, ND 58505; Tel: (800)437-2077.

While You're There: Relive early days at the Myra Museum and Campbell House, 2405 Belmont Rd., where there are artifacts and restored buildings from the 1800s. The Campbell House, with furnishings from the 1890s, is dedicated to pioneer women.

See Also: Idaho Spud Day (Shelley, ID).

Minot

Norsk Hostfest

Second week in October (Tuesday through Saturday) The first Norwegians began coming to the United States in 1825. After the Homestead Act of 1862 and the building of the Great Northern Railway through the Dakota Territory in 1887, they came in great waves, and in the early 1900s, about one-third of North Dakota's immigrant population was Norwegian. Other Scandinavians came, too, and North Dakota has the largest numbers of both Norwegian and Icelandic communities in the country.

Hence Norsk Hostfest, North America's Largest Scandinavian Festival.

It began as a Norwegian celebration in 1978, and later became a pan-Scandinavian affair, honoring the heritage of Norway, Sweden, Denmark, Iceland, and Finland. Attendance is about 60,000 to 70,000, or roughly one out of every ten men, women, and children in North Dakota.

The Hostfest food reflects Scandinavia's geography; it's stick-to-the-ribs food for a cold climate.

For example: Norwegian meatballs; *potet klub,* potato dumpling; *keela forthum,* Norwegian hot dogs; Swedish pea soup; Finnish stew; *rommegrot,* a sour-cream pudding; vegetable soup with flatbread; fish plates. Swedes offer a lutefisk dinner, lutefisk being cod cured in lye and then soaked and soaked and finally boiled with a white sauce, traditionally served at Christmas time. The Danes check in with their famous *smorrebrods,* open-face sandwiches.

Sweets include *kringle,* a ring-shaped sweet bread; *smultringer,* doughnuts; *sot suppe,* sweet fruit soup; and *lefse,* the popular Norwegian crepe, dusted with cinnamon and sugar, which is everywhere.

A dessert contest brings forth more lefse. The three dessert categories are cookies and bars, cakes and puddings, and lefse and breads. There are also cooking demonstrations given by chefs in individual national pavilions.

Beyond all the food, there are crafts demonstrations—of rosemaling, for example, the Norwegian art of painting wooden objects with floral motifs. Entertainment includes dancing, singing, band music, specialty acts. Markets sell the stuff of Scandinavia—Dala horses, dolls, trolls, rosemaling, sweaters, and food to take home.

Location: State Fair Grounds, Minot, 100 miles north of Bismarck on U.S. 83. **Contact:** Norsk Hostfest Assn., 15 Second Ave., S.W., P.O. Box 1347, Minot, ND 58702; Tel: (701)852-2368, Fax: (701)838-7873.

Rutland

Uff-Da Day

First Sunday in October Uff-da is an exclamation that can signify either great delight, as in "Uff-da, what a great dinner," or unpleasant surprise, in which case it's stronger than "tch, tch," more akin to "Oy vay"—oh, woe.

It's heard often in the Dakotas and Minnesota, places where many Norwegians settled and their descendants still speak with the rhythms of Scandinavia.

Uff-Da Day, then, celebrates the community's Scandinavian and particularly Norwegian roots, and pioneer heritage. Work begins well before the festival as a crew prepares—

uff-da!—4,000 to 5,000 lefses, the tortilla-like Norwegian staple. There are only 250 people in Rutland.

About 3,000 to 3,500 come to the festival from all over, and often the governor, especially in an election year, puts in an appearance.

Visitors find lots to eat besides lefses—the Danish *aebelskivers,* a fluffy ball eaten with chokecherry jelly or dusted with powdered sugar; *krumkake,* crumbcake baked in a special pan and then rolled around a cone to make it cone-shaped; *sandbakkels,* cooked in cupcake tins, but more pie-crusty in texture; *fattigman,* deep-fried triangles of pie crust with powdered sugar; *rommegrot,* which is similar to hot ice-cream pudding.

And what would a Scandinavian festival be without Uff-da tacos? Nada. The Rutland tacos are deep-fried bread dough smothered with hamburger, tomatoes, lettuce, black olives, and cheese.

There are demonstrations of making homemade ice cream, and samples of the ice cream. In the Little Pioneer House, the cook makes rolls and muffins on an old wood stove, as great-grandma did; these can be sampled, too.

And there are more than snack foods; a Scandinavian smorgasbord with scalloped potatoes and ham, homemade bread, and rice pudding is served at city hall from 11 o'clock on.

A parade, usually including a Viking ship, begins the festivities. Other attractions are a classic-car show, a plowing demonstration with antique tractors, demonstrations of rope making and sausage making, horse-drawn wagon rides, rides for children on the Uff-da train, craft sales, and a quilt show.

Families plan reunions around the day, which began in 1985.

Location: Rutland is in southeastern North Dakota, 35 miles west of I-29, about 15 miles north of the South Dakota border. ❂ **Contact:** Uff-Da Day, P.O. Box 67, Rutland, ND 58067; Tel: (701)724-3467.

Oklahoma

Okrafest!

Second Saturday in September ⚙ Just about everybody grows okra in Checotah, so an Okrafest seemed the way to go. Related to both cotton and hibiscus, okra is not your everybody-loves-it vegetable, since it has a gelatinous (i.e., slimy) quality, but it makes for a pretty funny Slime Toss. And it has historical standing: Thomas Jefferson grew it. Okra is thought to have originated in what is now Ethiopia, and it came to this country with African slaves.

The fest, started in 1994, draws 7,500 attendees who get free okra at the Okra Pot, where volunteers fry 250 to 300 pounds of okra. Food booths lining Main Street offer okradogs (pickled okra deep-fried in a spicy batter, like corndogs on a stick), gumbo, okra salad (a warm salad of fried okra with bacon, onion, sweet pepper, and tomato), okra casserole, and sometimes okra ice cream.

Okra Cook-off cooks have concocted okra fritters, sautéed okra-and-cheese polenta, and okratalian stew, which combines, among other ingredients, Italian sausage, garlic, okra, and rice. Cook-off entries can be sampled by the public.

Major events are the Slime Toss and the boiled-okra eating contest. In the Toss, contestants throw balloons filled with okra slime, the water that's left after boiling okra, at each other, and the winner is the last unslimed person. The eating contest was characterized by the winner one year as "gross, nasty and disgusting."

Other events: Competitions for the longest okra stalk and longest pod; okra bobbing; live music; a tractor show; a rodeo; crowning, with okra pods, of the Okra Chief; and dancing. There are also beadwork demonstrations and an arts and crafts sale by the Checotah Indian community.

Checotah is not an okra capital, although it is 100 miles from Temple, Oklahoma, the largest supplier of okra seeds in the Southwest. Checotah, which has produced many rodeo champions, is the Steer Wrestling Capital of the World.

Location: Checotah is about 20 miles south of Muskogee on U.S. 69, just north of I-40.   **Contact:** Checotah Chamber of Commerce, Box 96, Checota, OK 74426; Tel: (918)473-2070.

Jay

Huckleberry Festival

Fourth of July weekend (four days) Free ice cream and huckleberry sauce, made with a secret recipe. A huckleberry-pie-baking contest, with the pies auctioned off after the judging. Huckleberry jam, pancakes, cake, milk shakes. Sounds like a huckleberry festival, and it has been since 1967, drawing up to 5,000 people.

Jay is within the boundaries of the Cherokee Nation, and a powwow is held in conjunction with the festival, featuring crafts displays and dancing by Native Americans in traditional costume.

Other events include a parade, a carnival, fireworks, bull riding (at the Delaware County Fairgrounds just north of Jay), kids' races, a dunk tank, and a gun and knife show.

The names huckleberry and blueberry are sometimes used interchangeably, but while they are closely related they are not the same. Huckleberries grow only wild, on low bushes. The berries are very small and have large seeds. The blueberry—both the wild lowbush and cultivated highbush—has tiny, almost imperceptible seeds.

It's never known how many huckleberries are going to be harvested for the festival. Late freezes kill off new berries. One terrible year, a Jayite recalls, "we had to substitute blueberries." But the show goes on.

Location: Jay is 85 miles northeast of Tulsa, at the intersection of Oklahoma 20 and U.S. 59.   **Contact:** Jay Chamber of Commerce, P.O. Box 806, Jay, OK 74346; Tel: (918)253-8698.

Okra Fritters

4 cups cornmeal mix	2 eggs
2 tablespoons baking powder	3 cups milk
2 cups chopped fresh okra	½ cup sugar
2 cups chopped onion	

Mix all ingredients. Make into small palm-sized flat cakes. Fry in ½-inch oil until browned. Serve warm.

Nichols' Super Thrift Corporate Winner, Okrafest! Cook-Off, 1995

This generous cowboy offers some tasty vittles to a lucky visitor at the Chuck Wagon Festival. (1992 Cowboy Chuck Wagon Gathering, National Cowboy Hall of Fame, Oklahoma City, Oklahoma)

Oklahoma City

Chuck Wagon Festival

Memorial Day weekend (Saturday through Monday) ⊛ A tantalizing aroma hangs over this festival. It comes from cowboy vittles stirred over open fires by cooks in period attire, using only ingredients available in the late 1800s. Their chuck wagons are actual 1800s wagons or replicas, adding to the ambience of cattle-drive days.

Visitors, numbering about 10,000, may buy a bowl for a dollar and then stoke up on brisket, beans, sourdough biscuits cooked in dutch ovens, cobblers, speckled pup (rice pudding with raisins in it), and son-of-a-gun stew.

Stew was a staple in cattle-drive days. One version, son-of-a-bitch stew, grew out of the need to waste not, want not, and the ingredients were largely internal organs—tongue, liver, heart, sweetbreads, and the marrow gut of a calf. This is the tube connecting a ruminant's four stomachs, and in calves it's filled with a substance that looks like marrow but is a digestive substance for the mother's milk.

Son-of-a-gun stew, as its more polite name suggests, is more genteel; it's made with beef, carrots, onions, and potatoes.

Besides food, the festival, which began in 1990, offers stagecoach rides, story telling, cowboy music, and other westernalia.

Originally cowboys carried provisions in sacks slung on their saddles, but the chuck wagon developed when large roundups and trail drives became commonplace and a mobile kitchen essential. Usually the cook hurried the wagon ahead of the drive and had the food cooking by the time the cowpokes rode in.

Location: The Western Heritage Center, in the northeast of Oklahoma City, on Northeast 63rd St., off I-44 between Martin Luther King and Kelly Sts. ☼ **Contact:** National Cowboy Hall of Fame, 1700 Northeast 63rd St., Oklahoma City, OK 73111; Tel: (405)478-2250, Fax: (405)478-4714.

While You're There: The National Cowboy Hall of Fame and Western Heritage Center hold the world's largest roundup of western art and historical displays. The center's Old West Town is a reproduced turn-of-the-century village with a marshal's office, telegraph office, and general store.

Okmulgee

Okmulgee Pecan Festival

Third weekend in June ☼ There may be places that grow more pecans, but not many that bake bigger pecan desserts.

The festival claimed the world's record in 1988 for the World's Largest Pecan Pie—it had a diameter of 40 feet and weighed about 33,000 pounds. A pecan cookie 32 feet in diameter, weighing more than 7,500 pounds, set another record. In 1991, Okmulgee downsized and merely threw the World's Largest Pecan Cookie and Ice Cream Party by dishing up 5,000 servings of ice cream and more than 15,000 cookies. The idea is to be big every year, and in 1996, for instance, two 20-foot pies were baked.

Festival-goers, of course, get to sample these gargantuan bakings.

The pecan, a member of the hickory family, is a popular native American nut, barely known outside the United States. It's grown largely in the South, and there are about 30 pecan growers in the Okmulgee area. One of the best known pecan desserts is pecan pie, and it's always on the Okmulgee festival menu along with brownies, cookies, and other pecan desserts.

The festival began in 1984, and offers a carnival, the crowning of a prince and princess (usually tykes about three), a pecan bake-off, music, and arts and crafts. About 30,000 attend.

Location: Okmulgee is 25 miles south of Tulsa on U.S. 75. ☼ **Contact:** Okmulgee Chamber of Commerce, P.O. Box 609, 112 North Morton, Okmulgee, OK 74447; Tel: (918)756-6172, or (800)355-5552; Fax: (918)756-6441.

While You're There: Okmulgee, meaning "bubbling waters" in the Creek language, was the capital of the Muskogee Creek nation long before Oklahoma was a state. The Creek Council House on 6th Street was built by the Creeks in 1878 and now houses a museum displaying Creek craftwork, weapons, clothing, and early documents.

Tulsa

Oktoberfest

Third week of October (Thursday through Sunday) Here's an Oktoberfest that's about as German as you can get, but it started not because Tulsa's German community was burning to celebrate, but because Tulsa has a nice park on the Arkansas River and needed a festival.

It began in 1979 and is now Tulsa's oldest and largest festival, with attendance at 175,000 to 200,000. There are bands from Germany, puppeteers, jugglers, a crafts show, and *Das Kinder Zelt*—a children's tent with games and crafts. Besides *Der Bier Garten,* there's also *Der Root Bier Garten* and there are about 20 food booths selling giant pretzels, pastries, sausages, and *Fleischkaese,* a sausage-shaped meatloaf famous in Munich, where Oktoberfests began.

Location: River West Festival Park, 2100 South Jackson on the banks of the Arkansas River. **Contact:** Oktoberfest, c/o River Parks Authority, 707 S. Houston, Ste. 202, Tulsa, OK 74127-9033; Tel: (918)596-7249, Fax: (918)596-7249.

See Also: Oktoberfest Zinzinnati (Cincinnati, OH).

Vinita

Calf Fry Festival

First Saturday after Labor Day A calf fry is a fry of calf testicles, a.k.a. Rocky Mountain oysters or prairie oysters. This one began in 1980 when town boosters thought a calf fry would be appropriate for a festival in cattle country, which this is, and would also attract gourmets who don't often have the chance to eat the real thing. Well, it did. Attendance is now about 10,000 in this town of less than 6,000, and 700 pounds of calf fries are served at the one-day affair, billed as the World's Oldest Calf Fry Festival.

The testicles are marinated with secret ingredients to make them sweet or mild or spicy, then sliced, dipped in a batter, deep-fried, and served with butter or sauces. "Tasting kits" with variously marinated fries, along with a vegetable, are sold. Proceeds go to community development.

"Gonads," according to food enthusiasts Jane and Michael Stern, "are a highly regarded delicacy in much of the West; when young livestock is castrated on the range, it is traditional for cowboys to fry up their harvest at the end of the day." Lamb testicles are eaten as well as calf.

The French village Domèvre-en-Haye also has a calf fry, and in 1996, Jean François Degault, mayor of this town of 800, came to Vinita to swap notes. Mayor Degault said the Vinita fried tidbits are quite different from those in his village, where they are boiled and sautéed. But he liked the Vinita version. In French, prairie oysters are called *roubignoles,* which translates roughly to family jewels.

Events at the Vinita fry include a bull-riding contest and other rodeo games, a hairiest-legs contest, arts and crafts, and kids' games like bubble-gum-blowing contests.

Founded in 1871, Vinita is one of the oldest towns in Oklahoma. Vinita and Domèvre-en-Haye claim to be the only towns in the world that hold testicle festivals. But they're mistaken. (See "See Also" below.)

Location: Vinita is on I-44, 56 miles northeast of Tulsa. **Contact:** Vinita Chamber of Commerce, P.O. Box 882, Vinita, OK 74301; Tel: (918)256-7133.

See Also: Rocky Mountain Oyster Feed (Clinton, MT).

Weatherford

World Championship Hog Calling Contest

First weekend in February You'll find food (as expected, mostly pork) and entertainment at this affair, and you will also hear some pretty strange sounds. Don't laugh, though—it's hog calling, and it's serious.

Hog calling goes back to pioneer days when a farmer didn't fence in his hogs, often because he didn't have the time or material to build fences. So the pigs were kept by a pond or a muddy place (pigs like to roll in mud because it cools them), and when the farmer wanted to get them back to the barn, he called them with certain sounds that the hogs recognized, and the hogs then followed the farmer home. Incidental note: some people think pigs are smarter than dogs.

Contestants don't just stand there and make noises; the hog has to come when the caller calls. Callers compete in adult, teen, and children's categories.

The day begins with a ham and egg breakfast, and later there are pork sandwiches, barbecued ribs, hot dogs, pork burgers, and chopped-pork sandwiches. Other events are a Miss Pig Tail contest, storytelling for children, square dancing, country music.

The festival began in 1989 and draws several thousand people.

Location: Weatherford is 70 miles west of Oklahoma City on I-40. **Contact:** World Championship Hog Calling Contest, 118 S. Broad St., Weatherford, OK 73096; Tel: (405)772-3301.

South Dakota

Clear Lake

Hot Dog Day

A Friday in mid-August ☼ This dog day began in 1988 as a promotion of the town by its retailers, the big draw being free hot dogs. Clear Lake is a town of about 1,300, and the first year of the promotion, they gave away 300 or 400 dogs. Now it's closer to 8,000. A town bank also has a popcorn wagon with free popcorn; more than 100 pounds of popcorn gets popped. Who said there are no more free lunches?

There are hot dogs of all kinds—brats, ballpark dogs, German wieners, all-beef dogs. It's what's done to them that makes them different. Each business picks a theme for its dogs and invents toppings to carry out the theme. If the theme is the circus, the business will have Fuzzy Dogs, dogs swathed in cotton candy. Others offer hot dogs rolled in Norwegian lefses, German dogs with sauerkraut, chili dogs, dogs with purple or white onions, dogs with hot-hot mustard.

To generate excitement, a radio announcer samples all the hot dogs and picks his favorites. There are also crafts displayed and a flea market, and pie socials with homemade pies and ice cream; admission is charged for the socials.

Location: Clear Lake is in eastern South Dakota on South Dakota 15, 9 miles east of I-29, 75 miles north of Sioux Falls. ☼ **Contact:** Clear Lake Community Club, Box 860, Clear Lake, SD 57226; Tel: (605)874-2191.

Tabor

Czech Days

Third weekend in June (Friday and Saturday) ☼ This town of a few hundred people draws between 15,000 and 20,000 to its Czech Days. In 1949, when the festival began, the town was about 98 percent Czech, and now it's only 75 percent, so a lot of the people at Czech Days are old residents coming back to visit. But the rest are people who never lived here and come for the dancing, the parades, and, above all, the food.

There are Czech pork and roast-beef dinners, typically with dumplings and sauerkraut. There are kolaches, the pastry that no Czech event is without, both served with the dinners and available to buy by the dozen to take home.

Demonstrations of Czech dancing have up to 16 or 17 rings of eight people, who range in age from six to seventy-something. There's also dancing to polka music. A kiddie parade is followed by a grand parade, with a prince and princess between the ages of eight and twelve, and two queens—Miss Czech Day and the South Dakota Czech-Slovak Queen.

Location: Tabor is about 70 miles southwest of Sioux City, IA, on South Dakota 50, just across the Nebraska line. **Contact:** Tabor Chamber of Commerce, Box 21, Tabor, SD 57063; Tel: (605)463-2476.

See Also: Nebraska Czech Festival (Wilber, NE).

Texas

Anahuac

Texas Gatorfest

Second weekend in September (Friday through Sunday) ☼

By decree of the Texas legislature, Anahuac—because it has three times as many alligators as people (that's 5,400 to 1,800)—is the Alligator Capital of Texas.

With all those alligators, the town decided in 1989 to have a gatorfest, combining, as the Anahuacans put it, "the alligator, family and good old-fashioned Texas two-stepping fun!" About 25,000 people come.

The fun is more than just two-stepping; there's food (lots of gator dishes), live-alligator displays, a petting zoo (not the same thing as the gator displays), airboat rides, arts-and-crafts booths, music ranging from country to zydeco. The fun highlight is the Great Texas Alligator Roundup that gives alligator hunters from across the state a chance to show off their catch and compete for cash prizes with weigh-ins for the longest and heaviest gators. Some of the critters are better than 13 feet long.

The fest is held at the start of the 30-day alligator roundup, when about 10 percent of the wild alligators in Texas are harvested and auctioned off for their hides and meat. Once on the endangered list, alligators are now so numerous they are controlled by organized hunting.

After visiting the live and dead gators, visitors can eat fried gator legs with French fries, gator balls (bits of alligator meat, breaded or dough-encased), Cajun alligator links on a stick or bun, gator sauce piquante, fried gator, a gator-link plate with dirty rice and cole slaw. Additionally, there are various Cajun, Mexican, seafood, regional (po' boys), and standard fair dishes.

Alligators court at night, the bulls roaring to attract females. The male swims in circles around his intended, and then comes alongside her, grips her in his jaws, and places his limbs over her body. The mother-to-be lays her eggs in a nest of damp, rotting vegetation and mud. When the eggs hatch two to three months later, the young, only eight inches long, are independent and quickly take to the water.

Location: Fort Anahuac Park, 8 miles south of I-10 at exit 810, 45 miles east of Houston. ⊛ **Contact:** Anahuac Area Chamber of Commerce, P.O. Box R, Anahuac, TX 77514; Tel: (409)267-4190.

Athens

Black-Eyed Pea Jamboree

Third weekend in July (Friday through Sunday) ⊛ The black-eyed pea, a small beige bean, gets its name from the black circular "eye" on its inner curve. Growing, processing, canning, and eating these beans/peas, also called cowpeas, was for years the central part of life in Athens, but now the city is industrialized and produces things like bricks and TV sets.

Still, the jamboree began in 1971 because Athens wanted to boast about being the Black-Eyed Pea Capital of the World, and nobody is about to end it just because the pea-canning factory is gone and the town produces more bricks than peas. The high spot of the jamboree, attended by 18,000 to 25,000, continues to be the black-eyed pea cook-off that

Pea-Pea Bueno

1 16 oz. can black-eyed peas	1 cup shredded Provolone cheese or
⅔ cup beer or water	mozzarella
¼ cup margarine or butter	2 tablespoons grated onion
2 cloves garlic, pressed	1 tablespoon plus 1 teaspoon chili
1 teaspoon finely chopped jalapeño	powder
peppers without seeds*	Dash of salt
	Dash of hot sauce

Thoroughly drain and mash black-eyed peas with fork or potato masher. (Do not purée peas, as the dip should have texture of mashed consistency.) Combine all ingredients in a heavy saucepan or 10-inch Teflon-coated skillet. Cook over low heat, stirring constantly, until cheese is melted and mixture is hot. Place in chafing dish and serve with tortilla or corn chips.

*Note: Omit the jalapeño peppers if a milder dip is desired or use peppers with seeds if a hotter dip is preferred.

Mary Ann Davis, Leonard, Texas, 3rd Place Winner, 1982; published in "Reci-Peas," Black-Eyed Pea Jamboree, Athens, Texas gets as many as 100 entrants. Until you see it, you wouldn't believe what people do to black-eyed peas: they make things like ice cream, stuffed jala*peaños, butter rum pea bars, pea ravioli, and pea-luha, which has ingredients that include "inexpensive California brandy," Yuban coffee, and liquid glycerine.

The contest has categories of appetizers, salads, vegetables/main dish, and "pea-nique" for foods that don't fit the other categories; for a small fee, visitors can sample the offerings. A "Reci-Peas" booklet with more than 20 years of winning recipes can be purchased. A children's cook-off is also held.

Jamboree volunteers boil a big pot of peas to serve with corn bread, and vendors sell beef-and-vegetable kebabs, funnel cake, ice cream, soft drinks (no alcohol), blooming onions with dip, and a variety of pea dishes. Attractions and events include carnival rides, pony rides, arts and crafts, clowns, a square dance on Friday night, a pea-rade on Saturday, and the Little Miss Black-Eyed Pea Beauty Pageant. There are contests for pea eating, pea shelling, and pea popping—in which competitors flick the peas from shells; the pea traveling the farthest wins. The National Terrapin Races close the jamboree.

Black-eyed peas, a sort of staff of life in the South, originated in India, traveled to Arabia and then to Africa; they came to America with the slaves. There's a legend that they were good-luck omens in Egypt in the days of the pharaohs; today's custom calls for eating black-eyed peas, usually in the form of Hoppin' John, on New Year's Day for good fortune. Hoppin' John is a casserole made with the peas, ham or bacon, and rice.

Location: Athens is 75 miles southeast of Dallas, at the intersection of U.S. 175 and Texas 19. **Contact:** Athens Chamber of Commerce, P.O. Box 2600, Athens, TX 75751; Tel: (903)675-5181.

While You're There: Don't miss the marker on the north side of the town square, between the Boswell-Fowler Building and the Crafters' Mall. The marker notes that it was on this spot that Fletcher Davis, a potter who thought he could make more money on food than pots, invented and first sold the hamburger, topping it with a slice of Bermuda onion. In 1904, local businessmen sent him to the St. Louis World's Fair to sell it. Eat your hearts out, Seymour, Wisconsin, Hamburg, New York, and New Haven, Connecticut. While you're on the square, stop at the New York Cheesecake Outlet, where they make about 20 different flavors of a light and fluffy secret-recipe cheesecake. It's genuine *New York* cheesecake, too—New York is a little town (population of 12) near Athens.

Brady

World Championship Barbecue Goat Cook-off

Saturday before Labor Day Goats are raised in Brady for their hair, but they eat them too. The cook-off has been held since 1974, and now about 125 teams, composed of anywhere from 1 to 20 chefs, each grill half a goat (a kid). Each team has a secret recipe; some like their goats mild, some hot and spicy. Some use sauces, some use only seasoning.

From 14,000 to 16,000 attend this cook-off, and after the judging, they can sample the meat or sit down to a heaping plate of barbecued goat, pinto beans, potato salad, and bread, all prepared by the Chamber of Commerce. At least 2,500 plates of barbecued goat are served on this one day.

Besides watching goats being grilled, visitors can browse through the 150 arts and crafts booths, listen to fiddlers and bands, dance, and play children's games. If they're children, that is.

Although it doesn't have much to do with goats, it might be of interest while you're there to realize that Brady is almost the exact geographical center of Texas. A historical marker on the courthouse square mentions this, as does another marker 15 miles north.

Location: Brady is at the juncture of U.S. 87 and U.S. 190, about 125 miles north of San Antonio. **Contact:** Brady Chamber of Commerce, 101 E. First St., Brady, TX 76825; Tel: (915)597-3491.

Brownsville and Matamoros, Mexico

Charro Days

Fourth Thursday in February through Sunday Charro is the word for a Mexican cowboy, especially an elaborately dressed cowboy, and you will see lots of splendiferously dressed charros at Charro Days. The word charro is from the Spanish-Mexican word for flashy, and the festival, begun in 1938 to promote international good will, has become a grand and flashy affair. Held before Lent, it's a sort of four-day Mardi Gras, a showcase of cowboy-variety Latin and Texas culture, and a time for 100,000 people to dance, dine, and shout olé.

Brownsville, on the Mexican border and only a few miles up the Rio Grande from the Gulf of Mexico, is both a railhead and a major seaport with a big shrimp fleet. It is intertwined economically with Matamoros on the other side of the river; in fact, the cities think of themselves as one.

The color of the festival extends to the food. It's Mexican and American with Native-American influences. There are baked and fried shrimp, shrimp in all sorts of sauces, and lots of other seafood dishes. There are also chicken and beef fajitas, Texas chili, hot salsa, tamales, tacos, nachos, grilled tripe, and *cabrito* (grilled baby goat).

There's *mole* (from the Nahuatl word *molli*, meaning concoction), a spicy sauce poured over chicken, pork, or shredded beef, made with various ingredients depending on the cook, with its best-known ingredient being a small amount of chocolate.

You'll also find *menudo*, Mexico's traditional hangover cure, a spicy soup made of hominy, chili, and assorted cow innards and odd bits, like calf's feet. Continuing with the hot theme, there's a jalapeño-eating contest.

There are also costume contests. Men wear costumes that are a cross between a Mexican cowboy's outfit and the gaudy garb worn by the Spanish dons who once ruled Mexico. Women often wear the *china poblana,* a costume supposedly worn by a Chinese girl who was befriended by Mexicans and thought of as a kind of fairy princess.

Attractions include street dancing, costume balls, mariachi bands, cowboy bands, parades, and children's activities. Rodeos and bullfights give cowboys and matadors a chance to show their grit.

Brownsville was founded in 1846 when Fort Brown was built to confirm the Rio Grande as the national boundary; unfortunately, that set off the Mexican-American War. But now there's true friendship across the border here.

Location: Brownsville is about 150 miles south of Corpus Christi, by way of U.S. 77. **Contact:** Brownsville Convention Bureau, 101 E. First St., Brownsville, TX 78523; Tel: (800)626-2639, or (210)546-3721.

While You're There: Browse in Matamoros's Mercado Juarez, an enclosed marketplace with bargains in housewares, table linens, pottery, and glassware.

Caldwell

Kolache Festival

Second Saturday in September Kolaches are sweet buns filled with various fruits or sausage, cheese, ham, ham and cheese, you name it. They are the original Czech wedding pastry, but have become a favorite snack for Czechs everywhere, and especially in Caldwell, the Kolache Capital of Texas, as proclaimed by the Texas legislature.

In Caldwell, where about 20 percent of the population of 3,500 has Czech names, the Kolache Bake Off (kolache is pronounced with the "e" silent) is the major event. Prizes for non-professional cooks are awarded to a Burleson County champion and a state champion (entrants not from the county), and there's also a prize for the grand champion professional cook, who can be from anywhere.

About 40,000 attend the festival, which started in 1985, and they eat a lot of kolaches. One recent year, bakers at kolache booths sold more than 7,000 dozen. Laid end to end, these kolaches would stretch 4.1 miles, Mayor Bernard Rychlik figured.

The festival vendors sell other Czech edibles, too: Czech sausage with sauerkraut, potato pancakes, dumplings (Czechs are famous for dumplings) with chicken, and chicken and prune soup. Also available are festival standards like shrimp on a stick and roasted corn. For those with real appetites, there's a kolache-eating contest.

More than 200 Czech dancers, musicians, and singers provide genuine Czech entertainment. There are also quilt, antique-auto, and antique-tractor shows, and arts-and-crafts and antiques vendors. Demonstrations are given of caning, weaving, wine making, lace tatting, kolache baking, and other crafts.

Czechs came to central Texas in the 1880s, many taking ships directly to Galveston, for a number of reasons. Some came because of a drought and starvation; some because they didn't want to serve in the army; some, as members of the Czech Moravian Brethren, for religious freedom. People of Czech heritage now make up about five percent of the population of Texas.

Caldwell is the Kolache Capital of Texas, as is evident by the proud smiles of these festival-going kolache bakers. (Photo by J. Griffis Smith)

Location: Central Caldwell, at the intersection of Texas 21 and 36, 75 miles northeast of Austin. **Contact:** Caldwell Chamber of Commerce, P.O. Drawer 87, Caldwell, TX 77836; Tel: (409)567-3218, Fax: (409)567-0818.

While You're There: The Czech Heritage Museum documents the lives of early Czech settlers in Texas with every-day items like clothing and dolls, works of art like crystal and hand-painted eggs. It also has the museum's authentic Czech cookbook for sale.

See Also: Nebraska Czech Festival (Wilber, NE).

Fulton

Oysterfest

First full weekend in March (Friday through Sunday)
Fulton and sister city Rockport are on a peninsula, sheltered by San Jose Island in the Gulf of Mexico. Given this auspicious location, there's a good-sized oyster industry in the area,

and when the local volunteer firefighters wanted to raise money, they thought oysters might help them.

They have. Since 1980, when the first fest was held, the department has bought a new fire truck and equipment like the "jaws of life," and enlarged the firehouse. All because of oysters, which are just called Texas oysters, but are the same species as those found on the East Coast (*Crassostrea virginica*).

About 40,000 people come to the oysterfest for oysters served fried or raw on the half shell, fried shrimp, and seafood gumbo. Away from the briny cuisine, there are dishes like turkey legs, Vietnamese egg rolls, taco salad, beef kebabs, Polish sausage, and funnel cake and ice cream.

There's a raw-oyster-eating contest, and a one-time winner slurped down 135 oysters. They still talk about it. There are also oyster-shucking and oyster-shell-decorating contests. To be entertained, look for the carnival, a parade, more than 100 arts and crafts booths, and belly dancers.

Location: Navigation Park on the waterfront, Fulton, about 30 miles north of Corpus Christi on Texas 35. ⚇ **Contact:** Oysterfest, P.O. Box 393, Fulton, TX 78358; Tel: (512)729-3248.

Gilmer

East Texas Yamboree

Third weekend in October (Thursday through Saturday)
⚇ One of the oldest festivals in Texas, attended by about 100,000, the yamboree began in 1935 in conjunction with the Texas Centennial, when counties were encouraged to promote something representative of their region during the anniversary year. A quarantine on yams, imposed because of a weevil problem, was lifted in 1935, yam growers were back in business, and thus yams as a festival theme seemed fitting.

Strictly speaking, the Yamboree is a Sweet Potato-ee. The vegetables are different but their names are often interchanged; true yams are rarely grown in the United States. But while in Gilmer, we'll call them yams.

Because it began in the midst of the Great Depression, the tribute to the yam was particularly timely. Yams grow in a wide range of conditions, are inexpensive to produce, and have high concentrations of carbohydrates and vitamin A, all important attributes when there isn't much food to go around.

Festival vendors sell baked yams, yam pies, and fried yams. To go with them are such Texas favorites as barbecued beef and chicken, catfish, sausage on a stick, turkey legs and more common festival food. There's also a farmers' market, with fruits and vegetables, including yams.

A Yam Pie Contest is held with strict rules; the pies must have little or no spice, and no extras like nuts or raisins—the pie is judged on the taste of the potato. The pies are sold after the judging, and recipes given away. There's also a contest for farmers for the best sweet potato, judged by color, size, and weight.

Entertainment is provided by bands playing for street dancing, arts and crafts shows, fiddlers' contests, a carnival, and livestock shows and judging. There are marching-band contests and two parades, and a high point is the crowning of Queen Yam, chosen for selling the most tickets.

Location: Courthouse Square, Gilmer, at the junction of U.S. 271 and Texas 155, 70 miles west of Shreveport, LA. **Contact:** Gilmer Chamber of Commerce, P.O. Box 854, Gilmer, TX 75644; Tel: (903)843-2413.

See Also: Ham & Yam Festival (Smithfield, NC).

Jacksonville

Tomato Fest

Third weekend in September In 1934, "the eyes of Texas and the eyes of the Nation" were on Jacksonville as it held its first tomato festival, observing National Tomato Week and the Centennial of the Tomato.

Tomato excitement in east Texas raged; Jacksonville, Texans claimed, was the Tomato Capital of the World and one of the oldest and largest centers of tomato culture in the United States.

Today's tomato fest celebrates history as much as the current state of affairs. Texas ranks tenth among the states in tomato production, and Jacksonville has become industrial, but the sandy soils of east Texas still produce tomatoes. Among them is what they call the World's Largest Tomato, the Delicious, an "Amazing Tomato," according to the seed packet, that will produce large one-pound to two-pound tomatoes.

The Delicious and the strange saga of the tomato is honored at the fest, which began in 1985 (the older festival died at some point) and attracts about 12,000 people. There are some far-out tomato games, a tomato-history display, and tomatoes in sandwiches, drinks, sauces, and salsas; other food is also available, including regional favorites like turkey legs and red beans and corn.

Awards of cash and ribbons are given to winners of the Tomato Hot Sauce Contest in three age categories, and there's also a chili cook-off. Among the games are the Tomato Shoot, in which participants try to shoot tomatoes with a bow and arrow; a tomato war, called the Battle of San Tomato; and for kids, tomato golf, tomato basketball, bobbing for tomatoes, and tomato pool.

What's strange about this is that there was a time when the tomato in the United States was considered not fit for the table and quite likely poisonous, even though it's a native of South America and had moved up to Mexico where the Aztecs ate the *xi-tomate*. The tomato skipped across the ocean, where the Italians named it *pomodoro*, meaning apple of gold, or possibly apple of love—there was a time it was thought to be an aphrodisiac.

Thomas Jefferson, always progressive, grew tomatoes in 1781, but most Americans were not eating them. It wasn't until the 1820s and 1830s that the tomato was commonly accepted, and then tomato mania struck.

One curious event that may have turned the tide, according to legend, was the public eating of a basket of tomatoes by one Col. Robert Gibbon Johnson. On the courthouse steps in Salem, New Jersey, the colonel devoured the tomatoes, while crowds gathered to watch, expecting him to die on the spot. He didn't, and people began eating tomatoes. Or so the story goes.

Jacksonville's celebration of the tomato's centennial in 1934 may have been a celebration of the mania of the 1830s. Accounts of the '34 festival just don't explain why it's a centennial. It's all part of the wonderfully bizarre history of the tomato.

Location: Cherokee County Exposition Center, Jacksonville, on U.S. 79, about 90 miles southeast of Dallas. **Contact:** Jacksonville Chamber of Commerce, 526 E. Commerce, Jacksonville, TX 75766; Tel: (903)586-2217, or (800)376-2217.

Luling

Texas Watermelon Thump

Last weekend in June (Thursday through Saturday) Luling, once a cattle center, was known as the toughest town in Texas, but it's a cream puff now. At least the folks are soft on children—they let kids name the watermelon festival, and they called it "Thump" for the sound a ripe watermelon makes when you tap it.

The thump was established in 1954 to pay tribute to local watermelon growers. Watermelons are raised on 500 acres in the area, which seems like a lot of watermelons, but there were even more back in '54.

Events at the thump are a melon auction for the biggest Black Diamond variety (in 1996, the biggest weighed in at 51 pounds), watermelon-eating contests, and seed-spitting contests. Luling claims the world record in seed-spitting distance—68 feet, 9⅛ inches in 1986. The spitter was Lee Wheelis. It's in the *Guiness Book of World Records.* There are also traditional activities: queen crowning, a fiddlers' contest, a carnival, arts and crafts, dancing, and a rodeo.

There's lots of food around, including to-be-expected watermelon slices, pickled watermelon rind, and watermelon popsicles, but also such Mexican foods as tacos and *gorditas,* which means little fat ones; they are tortillas fried in oil and filled with ground pork or sausage and topped with cheese and onion. The most unusual dish is probably the emu kebabs. There are emu ranches nearby.

Oil was discovered in Luling in 1922, and active pumps are all around town, on church lawns, residential backyards, and in city parks. Many of the bobbing pump jacks are decorated as animals and cartoon characters.

Location: Luling is about 50 miles east of San Antonio on U.S. 90. **Contact:** Luling Chamber of Commerce, P.O. Box 710, Luling, TX 78648; Tel: (210)875-3214, Fax: (210)875-2082.

The gloves—and shirts—come off for this down and dirty watermelon-eating contest at Luling's annual Watermelon Thump. (Photo property of Luling Watermelon Thump Association)

Mission

Texas Citrus Festival

First or second weekend in February (Thursday through Saturday) ⚬ Mission, famous for its Ruby Red Grapefruit, is also known for its citrus festival, started in 1932 and one of the oldest festivals in the state. The festival's cynosure is the Product Costume Style Show, displaying the only folk art of its kind in the world. It may have derived from a misunderstanding of the old saw that you are what you eat. Here, you *wear* what you eat.

The Friday-night style show displays people wearing costumes made of local agricultural products. Seeds, for example, become buttons, onion skins make lacy white collars, tangerine rinds are pulverized and rubber-cemented onto material in the design of blossoms, leaves become headdresses.

During the parade on Saturday, when 100,000 spectators fill the sidewalks, the costumed people ride on a special citrus-motif float, and other floats carry out the product theme with skirtings, say, of purple cabbage leaves.

Also starring in the parade are not only Queen Citriana and King Citrus, both in elaborately fruit-appliquéd costumes, but more royalty than Buckingham Palace ever sees—five princesses and a lady-in-waiting and 29 duchesses from the towns strung out along the Rio Grande, with their gowns reflecting their local products; they are Duchesses of Papaya, of Grain Sorghum, of Onion, of Seedless Grapefruit, and so on.

In case you still haven't realized that the fiesta is promoting citrus, you'll find booths with orange juice, grapefruit juice, key-lime pie, grapefruit pie, dried fruits, fruit jellies and jams, and fresh oranges, grapefruits, and tangerines.

A cook-off in the past has produced recipes for Ruby Red Turkey Salad, Fish Citriana, Texas Grapefruit Pie. Samples can be bought. Additionally, there are five stages of continuous entertainment, an arts-and-crafts show, games, and lots of food besides citrus.

Red grapefruit was born in 1929 when Texas citrus growers in the subtropical lower Rio Grande Valley discovered a grapefruit with a deep pink interior; it became the Ruby Red. Since then, through time and research, the growers have produced even redder grapefruit known as the Rio Star and the Ruby Sweet. The new Texas Red Grapefruit has been named the State Fruit of Texas, and Mission calls itself the Home of the Grapefruit.

Actually, the grapefruit is supposed to have originated in the West Indies; it was introduced to Florida in the 1800s. It wasn't commonly known in the North until after 1880, but then it began taking off.

A Catholic community of Oblate Fathers established Mission in 1824 and planted the orange groves that began the citrus industry in the southern tip of Texas.

Location: Downtown Mission, at U.S. 83 and Texas 107, about 60 miles west of Brownsville. **Contact:** Texas Citrus Festival, P.O. Box 407, Mission, TX 78572; Tel: (210)585-9724.

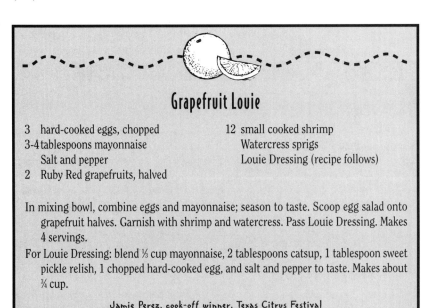

Grapefruit Louie

3   hard-cooked eggs, chopped
3-4 tablespoons mayonnaise
    Salt and pepper
2   Ruby Red grapefruits, halved

12 small cooked shrimp
    Watercress sprigs
    Louie Dressing (recipe follows)

In mixing bowl, combine eggs and mayonnaise; season to taste. Scoop egg salad onto grapefruit halves. Garnish with shrimp and watercress. Pass Louie Dressing. Makes 4 servings.

For Louie Dressing: blend ⅓ cup mayonnaise, 2 tablespoons catsup, 1 tablespoon sweet pickle relish, 1 chopped hard-cooked egg, and salt and pepper to taste. Makes about ¾ cup.

Jamie Perez, cook-off winner, Texas Citrus Festival

New Braunfels

Wurstfest

First week in November (Ten days, Friday through Wednesday) ⊛ Some of the more curious things about Texas are its German communities, the story of the German immigration to Texas, and today's Tex-Mex-German cuisine.

New Braunfels is still a predominantly German community, with German lettering on signs and many German restaurants. Its celebration of the sausage-making season is filled with polkas, lederhosen, strudel, pretzels, oompah bands, and other symbols of German culture.

People from what is now Germany began coming to Texas in the 1840s. They were encouraged to do so by the *Adelsverein*, the Association of Nobles, which was a society comprised of wealthy aristocrats who hoped to settle enough of their countrymen in the San Antonio area of Texas to start some kind of New Germany or German dependency. The *Adelsverein*, however, didn't think things through too well. They obtained a grant of nearly four million acres of land, but the land was controlled by the Comanche Indians, who had been fighting and humiliating Spanish, Mexican, and American forces for more than a century.

In 1845, Prince Carl of Solms-Braunfel, who was a cousin of Queen Victoria, led some immigrants to what became New Braunfels. The prince chose riverside land to settle on, envisioning building a castle along the lines of the Rhine castles. But the climate was a little different. Carl went home. The settlers stayed on, racked by disease and hunger, but many survived and eventually prospered on the rich soil and plentiful water. Their descendants give the town its German cast, quite apparent at Wurstfest.

There are sausages galore. There are also pretzels, potato pancakes, strudel, ham hocks with sauerkraut, sausage on a stick, and German bierocks. And then there are the dishes that make a bow to local cookery: wurst gumbo, boudin (Cajun sausage), stuffed jalapeños, pecan pralines, wurst tacos, turkey jerky.

The days are filled to overflowing with song and dance, educational displays and tours, heritage exhibits, art shows, sports events, and children's activities.

Location: Wurstfest Park along the banks of the Comal River, in New Braunfels, off I-35 about 20 miles northeast of San Antonio. ⊛ **Contact:** Wurstfest, P.O. Box 310309, New Braunfels, TX 78131; Tel: (210)625-9167, or (800)221-4369.

Poteet

Poteet Strawberry Festival

Second weekend in April (Friday through Sunday) ⊛ You have to love a town that has a seven-foot-tall, 1,600-pound concrete strawberry in front of

More than 100,000 visitors flock to the Poteet Strawberry Festival to feast on strawberries prepared in every way imaginable. (Photo by Phil Nolan, Poteet Strawberry Festival Photographer)

its volunteer fire house . . . and that founded this festival to encourage World War II veterans to stay down on the farm after they'd seen Paree.

And you also have to admire a town with a population of less than 4,000 that can
throw a party for more than 100,000, make heaps of money for scholarships and community projects, and provide all kinds of free entertainment, ranging from a hypnotist to flying
acrobats to a rodeo to tejano music to arts and crafts to racing pigs to a strawberry-eating
contest. A queen and king and their court reign over the activities.

Poteet is known as the Strawberry Capital of Texas because the sandy acidic soil of the
area produces very flavorful strawberries. There used to be more berry farms than there are
now, but the area still produces about 40 percent of the state's total. So you'll find a cornucopia of strawberry foods: strawberry shortcake, nut bread, cheesecake, parfait, ice cream,
chocolate-covered strawberries, and, of course, fresh strawberries. They also make a strawberry dessert wine, very sweet and heavy; when sold as a wine cooler with 7-Up, however,
it's eminently drinkable.

There's a cooking contest with various categories; recipes have to include at least one
cup of Poteet strawberries. Past winners have included strawberry sour cream bread and
strawberry nut loaf. There's also a strawberry jam and jelly contest. These are followed by
the Taste of Texas Food Show and Auction, in which the top entries are auctioned off. An
Italian cream cake was the best-of-show winner one year and brought in $1,100. The fresh
strawberries that are deemed the best of the crop by judges who consider color, taste, and
firmness are also auctioned and fetch as much as $24,000 for a single crate (24 pints).

If you tire of strawberries (but really, as Samuel Johnson said of London, that would mean you're tired of life), there are other regional edibles: brisket tacos, finger-rib tacos, sausage on a tortilla, beef fajitas with guacamole, pinto beans, gorditas, egg rolls, fried noodles.

By 1948, the first year of the festival, eating habits had changed; people didn't have to rely on food in season locally because of the advances made during the war in getting things to far places fast. Refrigerated railroad cars sped across the nation to meet demand, and veterans wanted to settle down and grow families and crops.

That's how Poteet got to be a strawberry capital.

Location: Poteet Strawberry Festival Grounds, 28 miles south of San Antonio on Texas 16. **Contact:** Poteet Strawberry Festival, P.O. Box 227, Poteet, TX 78065; Tel: (210)742-8144, Fax: (210)742-3608.

San Marcos

Republic of Texas Chilympiad

Third weekend in September (Friday and Saturday) The biggest part of the Chilympiad is the State Men's Championship Chili Cook-off, which is touted as the Largest Cook-off in the World. It's made for macho types: No women may compete, and there's a Harley-Davidson exhibit. (There is a state women's cook-off in Seguin in April.)

About 600 contestants try their hands at chili. Their entries are judged on taste, consistency, color, and aroma, and there's a separate category for showmanship, which can be funny or musical or whatever strikes the cooking teams. The three top winners get to compete in the big chili cook-off in Terlingua, Texas, which is in the middle of nowhere. Following the judging, festival-goers get to sample the chilis. There are standard fair foods for visitors, too—sausage on a stick, turkey legs, funnel cake.

The cooks cook on camp stoves, and have to follow specific rules. One of these is that no firearms, "concealed or otherwise," are allowed on the grounds.

Besides the chili cook-off, there's a hot-sauce contest, and besides that, there are a parade, a 5K run, live music, arts and crafts, demonstrations of sand-castle building, and a beauty contest.

San Marcos is on the edge of the Hill Country where Lyndon Johnson, a great "bowl-of-red" fan, was born. The festival here began in 1970 with 30 cooks competing. In the years since, the chefs have shown their tenacity; the 1988 cook-off was held while Hurricane Gilbert was in progress, but, of the 527 cooks entered, 422 cooks checked in.

Location: Hays County Civic Center in San Marcos, about 30 miles south of Austin on I-35. **Contact:** Republic of Texas Chilympiad, P.O. Box 188, San Marcos, TX 78667; Tel: (512)396-5400.

Sweetwater Rattlesnake Roundup

Second weekend in March (Friday through Sunday) ☼ The snakes rounded up in and around Sweetwater are western diamondback rattlesnakes, which can grow up to eight feet long and weigh as much as 12 pounds, not the sort of snake you want sitting in your backyard petunias.

In 1958, ranchers decided to thin out the snakes that were plaguing them and their livestock, so they organized a roundup. Now it's the World's Largest Rattlesnake Roundup; the harvest varies from year to year, but in a little less than four decades, more than 100 tons of snakes were captured. About 30,000 visitors attend from North and South America, Europe, and Asia, and eat more than 4,000 pounds of rattlesnake on the spot. They taste something like frogs' legs.

A parade on Thursday afternoon and the Miss Snake Charmer Pageant that evening open the roundup, and events on the following days include country music, dancing, a rattlesnake meat-eating contest, and demonstrations of snake handling and snake milking. Poisonous venom is milked from live snakes and used in medical research and as an antidote for snakebite.

Anywhere from 200 to 400 hunters (governed by state hunting laws) go out with guides to catch snakes using snake hooks or tongs, competing for prizes for the largest rattlesnake and the most pounds of snakes. Once captured, the snakes are popped into tin boxes. They are sold to dealers for their skins, and to gourmet restaurants, and, as mentioned, a couple of tons are fried in the cook shack and eaten. Those not partial to snake for supper can choose rice and beans, tacos, tamales, ribs, brisket, chili.

On Saturday, there's a cook-off to determine the best cooks in the categories of chicken, beans, pork ribs, brisket, and chili, and the World's Champion Rattlesnake Meat Cooker is crowned.

How to cook rattlers? Skin, cut into bite-size pieces, marinate in beer and vinegar, bread with cornmeal and cracker crumbs, and deep fry. Of course, there are variations, and therein lie the secrets of world champions.

The Jaycees sponsor the roundup and with the proceeds have provided Thanksgiving dinners for the homeless and contributed to Special Olympics and activities for young people and the mentally handicapped.

Location: Newman Park in Sweetwater, about 115 miles southeast of Lubbock, on I-20 near the intersection with U.S. 84. ☼ **Contact:** Sweetwater Chamber of Commerce, P.O. Box 1148, Sweetwater, TX 79556; Tel: (915)235-5466, or (800)658-6757.

Terlingua International Championship Chili Cookoff

First Saturday in November ☼ The official name of this cook-off is The Original Terlingua International Frank X. Tolbert–Wick Fowler Memorial Championship Cookoff. Since that's a mouthful, it's generally referred to as the Terlingua cook-off. Its sponsor is the Chili Appreciation Society International (CASI), which now squares off against a schismatic group, the International Chili Society.

Terlingua is a most unlikely place for a cook-off or anything else, since some crumbling adobe walls are about all that are left of a town where they once mined cinnabar for mercury. But about 5,000 chiliheads from across the nation get together in this hot spot, parking their planes at the edge of a dirt landing strip, ready for a hot and raucous time.

Terlingua is sort of the Big Bang of chili cook-offs. There had never been chili cook-offs until the first one in Terlingua in 1967, according to Jenny Kellner and Richard Rosenblatt, chilian Boswells. The beginnings are complicated and boring, but basically what happened was that Wick Fowler, a legendary chili cook, was set to compete with Dave Chasen, the Los Angeles restaurateur whose chili was so popular that Elizabeth Taylor had it flown to Puerto Vallarta when she was filming there with Richard Burton.

Chasen got sick, so humorist H. Allen Smith, who had just written a magazine article defiling Texas chili, was chosen to replace him. The two men stirred up their chili while about 300 friends watched, and the judges reached a split decision.

Terlingua cook-offs became annual events, though they resemble "an adult version of spring break," to quote Kellner and Rosenblatt in *The All-American Chili Cookbook*.

Terlingua is historically important because it led to chili cook-offs all over the country. It is important gastronomically because it's a place to get genuine Texas chili, which is basically any kind of meat cooked with spices and chile peppers. Why this matters was stated by Lyndon Johnson: "Chili concocted outside of Texas is usually a weak, apologetic imitation of the real thing. One of the first things I do when I get home to Texas is have a bowl of red. There is simply nothing better."

Location: Terlingua is in southwestern Texas on Rural Road 170 near the Rio Grande and the western edge of Big Bend National Park. Consult a map. **Contact:** Chili Appreciation Society International, 1516 Prairie Dr., El Paso, TX 79925; Tel: (915)772-2379.

See Also: La Fiesta de los Chiles (Tucson, AZ).

Weslaco

Texas Rio Grande Valley Onion Festival

A Saturday in April (date depends on onion harvest)
Weslaco is in the heart of an immense irrigated area growing citrus, vegetables, and cotton; among the vegetables is the sweet Texas onion. In recent years, sweet onions have been greatly touted and talked-about, and every state with sweet onions lays claim to the sweetest-onion title.

The onion that Weslaco celebrates is known commonly as the 1015, more officially as the Grano 1015Y. Georgia's Vidalia onion may be better known because it has had great p.r., and "Vidalia" is more melodious than 1015, sounds more juicy. Also, the 1015 has a drawback—it's difficult to transport and shouldn't touch anything after it's picked.

But it's top onion in Weslaco and figures in a number of events:

In the baking and cooking contest, recipes are judged by experts in the categories of appetizers, casseroles, main dishes, breads, and desserts. The local Chamber of Commerce publishes some of the best.

Food sheds, staffed by community groups, compete to make the best fried-onion rings. The batters are top secret. Judging is based on sweetness, texture of batter, presentation of the rings and of the booth. Festival-goers can taste samples.

Field workers compete in a clipping contest, chopping the tops and roots off onions. Competitors are judged on speed and accuracy.

An eating contest is something else again. The idea is to eat as many 1015s as possible in a specified time. But they're sweet, remember?

And then, of course, there's food for general eating, with the emphasis on 1015 onions: They come fried, grilled, or roasted, as onion blossoms (the entire onion is deep-fried), onion rings, raw, and by the bag to take home. They come in tacos and casseroles, in chili, with red beans and rice, with fajitas. There are foods that go well with onions—hamburgers, corn on the cob. If you need a taste change, vendors also have ice cream, slushes, and pumpkin and apple pie.

The festival, attended by about 15,000, features agricultural displays as well as arts and crafts. There are kids' games like onion-ring tosses, music, and other entertainment.

The grandfather of the Texas onion was called Early Barbosa, and was an onion brought from Spain in 1925. Researchers improved it and released the new version in 1931 as Early Grano. They kept working on it until they developed the Grano 1015Y, the number referring to the time of year it's planted—Oct. 15. The Grano, despite all the controversy about which state has the sweeter onion, is a hybrid closely related to Georgia's Granex. Specialists say they're all the same, the differences being in ripening times and keeping qualities.

By the way, the odd name of the town comes from the initials of the W. E. Stewart Land Company, which promoted the town site in 1919.

Location: Harlon Block Memorial Park, Seventh and Bridge Sts., Weslaco, about 40 miles northwest of Brownsville in the Rio Grande Valley, on U.S. 83. ☼ **Contact:** Weslaco Area Chamber of Commerce and Tourism Center, P.O. Box 8398, 1710 E. Pike, Weslaco, TX 78599; Tel: (210)968-2102, Fax: (210)968-6451.

See Also: Walla Walla Sweet Onion Harvest Fest (Walla Walla, WA) and Vidalia Onion Festival (Vidalia, GA).

Winnie

Texas Rice Festival

Last weekend in September through following Saturday (about seven days) ☼ Winnie is a small town, population less than 2,000. But its rice festival is a Texas giant, sprawling over more than a week, filled with entertainment—and food—of all kinds, attended by about 100,000.

It starts on Friday with barbecue and fajita cook-offs. Fajitas, marinated steak that is grilled, cut in strips, and then wrapped in tortillas, is a Texas favorite. About 50 teams compete in the cook-offs, and after the judging, samples are given away.

The festival, which continues through the next weekend, lapses at the first of the week, then starts up again in midweek and builds to its Saturday climactic events that include a blessing of the fields and crops, the introduction of the Rice Festival Queen and her court, the honoring of rice farmers, a grand parade, and finally a Saturday-night street dance.

In the course of all the doings, there are lots of Texas-rice dishes to sample. There are rice cakes (real cakes, not the dried things that you can buy packaged), rice pudding, crawfish étouffée, jambalaya, red beans and rice, boudin, rice gumbo, rice with apples, rice salad, rice casseroles, shrimp or other seafood with rice, stuffed peppers, and meatloaf with rice.

Other foods include turkey legs, fried alligator, burritos, fried and grilled shrimp, and sausages.

A rice-cooking contest is held, and there are rice-cooking demonstrations and an educational exhibit on rice. A book of rice recipes is available.

A sampling of other events: livestock judging, an ice-cream-eating contest for kids up to age 14, an old-time fiddling contest, quilt and cross-stitching exhibits, a horse show, drill-team exhibitions, a farm-equipment display, continuous music, and agricultural/historical museum tours.

The atmosphere is that of a country fair, but the reason for the festival—to pay tribute to generations of rice farmers—is always uppermost. Revenues from the festival go toward scholarship funds and agricultural projects.

Texas ranks fourth among states in rice production, following Arkansas, California, and Louisiana. The rice is all grown along the upper coast of Texas where the soil, temperature, and rainfall are in the right proportions.

Location: Winnie-Stowell Park in Winnie, which is in coastal Texas about 30 miles from the Louisiana border, off I-10. **Contact:** Winnie-Stowell Chamber County Park, P.O. Box 147, Winnie, TX; Tel: (409)296-4404.

West & Pacific

Alaska

Arizona

California

Colorado

Hawaii

Idaho

Montana

Nevada

New Mexico

Oregon

Utah

Washington

Wyoming

Alaska

Nalukataq Celebration

Mid-June or early July, from one to several days (date and duration depend on weather and number of crews that have caught whales) ⊛ Nalukataq means "blanket toss," and blanket tosses as entertainment are fairly common on the North Slope. But the Barrow Nalukataq is also a celebration of the end of the whaling season and it's a major festival, drawing 2,000 or more people. That's "quite a turnout," a Barrowite said. Barrow is geographically the world's largest municipality, covering 88,000 square miles. Its population is about 3,200, and there are only about 7,000 on the whole North Slope, so there's a fair amount of white space between homes.

The celebration is one of feasting and fun activities, blanket tossing included. The eating usually starts shortly before noon, with soups—duck, caribou, and goose. Later in the day, *quaq*—raw frozen meat, like whitefish and whale—is served. Whale is the North Slope specialty, and all parts of it are eaten: the fins, the tongue, the blubber and outer skin (called *muktuc*), and the meat. The meat, which tastes similar to beef, is often fried or baked; other parts are boiled. What's not boiled is frozen and eaten partially thawed, often dipped in seal oil.

One of the delicacies is fermented whale meat. It's made by chopping the meat and then letting it ferment for two weeks at room temperature. It's usually eaten with a whale knife, called an *ulu.*

The blanket toss began as a way of spotting whales. The blanket is made of seal skins sewn together. An individual is bounced from the seal skin into the air, as though on a trampoline, putting him high enough to see what's out there in the water. While the original purpose of the blanket toss was utilitarian, it's now a sport. Children are tossed first, and then adults. A dance is also part of the celebration.

The Inupiat Eskimos are the chief residents of the North Slope and are permitted to catch whales for subsistence; they can't export them. The Eskimo Whaling Commission sets a quota each year.

Location: Barrow is about 800 miles, as the eagle flies, north of Anchorage. It's accessible by air. ⊛ **Contact:** North Slope Borough Inupiat Historical, Language and Culture Division, Box 69, Barrow, AK 99723; Tel: (907)852-2611.

Kodiak

Kodiak Crab Festival

Memorial Day weekend (Thursday through Monday) ⊛
Kodiak's first King Crab Festival was held in 1958 as a boost to the fledgling king-crab industry. Back then, king crabs were not well known, though Kodiak, the port city on the island of Kodiak, called itself the King Crab Capital of the World. King crabs, giants that can measure up to 10 feet claw to claw and weigh as much as 15 pounds, are found in the north Pacific.

As the crabs became popular, their number dwindled, and the catch is now rigidly controlled. Thus, "king" dropped out of the name of the festival, and the name crab is retained largely for historic reasons.

However, since Kodiak is the state's largest fishing port, the home port of 770 commercial fishing vessels, you won't have much trouble finding seafood. Vendors sell halibut tacos, halibabs (grilled fish on a stick), sushi, and usually some king crab legs and claws. There are also local favorites such as bruinburgers, which are deep-fried hamburgers, turkey legs, and Chinese and Mexican food.

Sourdough pancake breakfasts are served Sunday and Monday, a reminder of the pioneer sourdough days. Russian roots are evident at the luncheon Friday at the Holy Resurrection Russian Orthodox Church, where you can savor Russian tea and *kulich,* a tall cylindrical yeast-raised cake flavored with raisins, candied fruit, and saffron.

To celebrate spring, there are lots of outdoor events—kayak races, bike races, foot races, a grand parade, and a shrimp parade for kids 10 and under. A blessing of the fleet and fleet parade take place Monday afternoon. Other events include art exhibits, basket-weaving demonstrations, dancing and music, amusement rides, and a dog show.

Kodiak is one of the oldest communities in Alaska, established in 1784 when a Russian trader came to the island looking for sea-otter pelts. The onion domes of Orthodox churches strikingly recall the times when the Russian Empire of the North Pacific was administered from Kodiak.

Location: Kodiak, south of Cook Inlet and the Kenai Peninsula, is accessible by air from Anchorage or Seattle, and by ferry from several mainland communities. ⊛ **Contact:** Kodiak Chamber of Commerce, P.O. Box 1485, Kodiak, AK 99615; Tel: (907)486-5557, Fax: (907)486-7605.

Petersburg

Little Norway Festival

Third full weekend in May (Friday through Sunday) ⊛
Petersburg, known as Little Norway, on Mitkof Island off the panhandle of Alaska, is named

for Norwegian Peter Buschmann who came here in 1897 to build a fish cannery. The cannery was completed in 1900 and packed 32,750 cases of salmon in its first year. Other Norwegians looked at the assets—abundant fish, timber for a sawmill, a natural harbor on a major shipping route—and followed Buschmann. Over the years, they celebrated "Syttende Mai" (May 17, Norwegian Independence Day) with a potluck supper.

In 1958, they decided to expand the celebration; it still honors Norway's Independence Day but also America's Armed Forces Day and the return of the local halibut fleet.

Feasting is at the core of the celebration, and fish is at the core of the feasting. A Fish-A-Rama Feast on Saturday generally showcases salmon, halibut, shrimp, black cod, crab (Dungeness or snow), but can vary depending on who's cooking and what's available. Salad and blueberry buckle (like cobbler) complete the feast. During the weekend, a Kaffe Hus serves coffee and Norwegian pastries such as *krumkaker,* crumb cake, and *spritz,* buttery cookies in fanciful shapes.

The Rotary Club puts on a Seafood Bake and Barbecue on Sunday. Chicken and prime rib are available for people who don't like seafood, though you have to wonder what a non-seafood eater would be doing on an Alaskan island.

Entertainment includes costumed Norwegian dancers, a pageant, comic performances by the Mitkof Mummers, bands of marauding Vikings in battle dress roaming the streets, Valkyries to escort dignitaries and visitors to events, tole painters and weavers, a show of rosemaling designs, a parade, a block dance, and Norwegian storytelling for children.

Location: Petersburg is about 110 miles southeast of Juneau, on Mitkof Island at the head of the Wrangell Narrows. **Contact:** Petersburg Chamber of Commerce, P.O. Box 649, Petersburg, AK 99833; Tel: (907)772-3646.

Arizona

Matsuri, Festival of Japan

Last weekend in February ⬡ Matsuri means "festival" in Japanese, and the Phoenix Matsuri is a festive display of some of the many varied facets of Japanese culture.

There are demonstrations of the ritualized tea ceremony (traditionally made with powdered green tea), of origami (paper folding), of candy sculpting, bonsai, and martial arts (jujitsu, karate, kendo, judo, aikido).

There are performances by sword dancers, Taiko Kai drummers, the Suzuki Strings, Japanese folksingers. There's also a fashion show.

There's food, and, for those who would like to try it themselves, cooking demonstrations. The food includes such well-known dishes as sushi, spring rolls, and beef teriyaki, but also *kaki kori* (shaved ice with a flavored syrup poured over it), *manju* (steamed dough stuffed with meat or chicken), *momo* (peach) muffins, *yaki soba* (pan-fried noodles), *an pan* (bread baked with red-bean curd), and more.

The matsuri originated in 1985 and is the culmination of Japan Week, which honors Phoenix's sister city in Japan, Himeji. Phoenix has an influential Japanese community of about 1,500; some in the community are relatives of those who were interned in Arizona during World War II. Of the ten Japanese internment camps, two were in Arizona, and 16,655 persons went through the Gila River Relocation Camp southeast of Phoenix.

Today the matsuri brings together about 70,000 people to celebrate—and taste—Japanese culture.

Location: The matsuri is held in Heritage Square Park, 7th Street and Monroe. Japan Week programs take place throughout the Phoenix metropolitan area. ⬡ **Contact:** Phoenix Parks, Recreation and Library Dept., Heritage Square Park, 115 N. Sixth St., Phoenix, AZ 85004; Tel: (602)262-5071; Fax: (602)534-3787.

Seventy thousand people attend the Matsuri for the sword dancers, bonsai and martial arts demonstrations, and of course, for the sushi and teriyaki. (Matsuri, A Festival of Japan, Heritage Square Park, Phoenix, Arizona)

Heard Museum Guild Indian Fair & Market

First weekend in March ☼ This fair, the most prestigious Native American cultural festival in the Southwest, is best known for its art works. And for people who want to try genuine Indian food, this is the place.

Naturally, there's fry bread. When the fair first began in 1958, there were one or two lines for this golden, fluffy bread. Now about 20,000 to 25,000 people attend the fair, and there are seven lines for fry bread. Typically, 1,300 pounds of flour and more than 800 pounds of shortening are used to make the bread. Very popular.

Piki, a Hopi staple, is a parchment-thin bread made from blue-corn meal mixed with water and the ashes of a plant called rabbit brush. The watery batter is spread on a hot stone with bare hands; it takes practice!

Other foods are less well known. Parched corn, for instance, is a popular snack for the Hopi. Corn kernels are cooked in a hot iron kettle with special sand from the Hopi reservation that keeps the kernels from sticking to the pot, because no oil is used. When the kernels pop, the cook scoops them into a loosely woven basket that sifts out the sand.

In the soup department, there's posole, acorn soup, and Hopi stew.

Tangy posole originated among the Pueblo people of New Mexico and is also popular among the Tohono O'odham people of southern Arizona. It gets its flavor from pork or beef tripe, pork rinds, hominy, and lots of red chile pods.

Visitors to the Heard Museum Guild Indian Fair & Market can enjoy such Native American staples as the piki this woman is making. (The Heard Museum, Phoenix, Arizona)

Acorn soup is an Apache dish. To make it, acorns are crushed and ground, cooked till their bitter flavor disappears, then cooked with meat (usually beef) and other ingredients.

The Hopi stew is made with hominy and mutton, beef, or rabbit, and it's more of a brothy soup than a heavy stew. The hominy is traditionally prepared by soaking it in rabbit-brush ashes, giving it a distinctive flavor and making the kernels pop.

There's Mexican and American fare, too.

Location: Heard Museum grounds, between Thomas and McDowell Rds, off Central Ave. **Contact:** Heard Museum Guild Indian Fair & Market, 22 E. Monte Vista Rd., Phoenix, AZ 85004; Tel: (602)252-8840, Fax: (602)252-9757.

Tucson

La Fiesta de los Chiles

Alternates between third and fourth weekend in October

There's chili and there's chile. Chili is the "bowl of red," as it's known in Texas, where this stew seasoned with chile supposedly originated. Chiles are chile peppers, of the genus *Capsicum*, part of the nightshade family.

But in some places, the *dish* is also spelled chile; often, both dish and fruit are spelled chili. The word comes directly from the Aztec language Nahuatl.

The Fiesta de los Chiles is held by and at the Tucson Botanical Gardens to provide a mix of fun and learning with chile-laden food, entertainment, crafts, and a look at cultures that use the chile. Among the fiesta foods you can try:

Green chile jambalaya. Jalapeño pizza. Chile beef stew, frijoles con chile, Guatemalan chile rellenos with fresh roasted chiles, and red-chile tamales. Thai chile salad and chile pasta salad with Andean garlic sauce. Sides of *nopalitos*, which are prickly pear cactus pads. Blue-corn fry bread. (Whew. A breather.) Chocolate chile ice cream. Or a specialty, "icy hot" chiltepin ice cream.

Chiltepins are round pea-sized wild chiles, among the hottest chiles in the world, that grow in the Sonoran Desert in Arizona and Mexico and also as far south as Peru, where remains of chiles about 2,000 years old have been found in ancient ruins.

The stew of events includes chile-motif crafts exhibits and demonstrations of making *ristras* (strings of chiles commonly seen in the Southwest) and of cooking: chile roasting, cleaning and cooking *nopalitos*, preparing Hopi parched corn with hot sand. For entertainment, there are Mexican, Native American, and Southwestern musicians and dance troupes.

Chiles are called peppers or chile peppers largely because Columbus was confused about where he was. He thought the chiles grown in the West Indies were related to black pepper (*Piper nigrum*), which comes from India. A major reason he made his trip, after all, was to find a route to India's spices, and especially peppers.

Columbus helped spread chiles around the world. His crew took seeds back to Europe, chiles were growing in Spain by 1500 (but were denounced by Spanish priests who said that chile "inciteth to lust"), and then chiles spread from port to port.

What makes chiles hot is an acidic oil called *capsaicin* (cap-SAY-a-sin) that exists in no other plant. There's a standardized "heat" rating for peppers that goes from zero (the bell pepper, a *Capsicum* like other chiles) to 200,000 to 300,000 for the chile called habañero. The rating for pure capsaicin is 15 million. A human can detect one drop of capsaicin in a million drops of water.

The fiesta began in 1987 and now draws close to 10,000 people. It raises funds for the Tucson Botanical Gardens, which exhibits Arizona flora and stocks about three dozen chile-plant varieties, and for Native Seeds/SEARCH, which conserves the traditional seeds and farming methods of the Southwest United States and Mexico.

Location: Tucson Botanical Gardens, on Alvernon Way between Pima St. and Grant Rd. near downtown Tucson. **Contact:** Tucson Botanical Gardens, 2150 North Alvernon Way, Tucson, AZ 85712; Tel: (602)326-9686.

Window Rock

Navajo Nation Fair

Early September (nine days) ⊙ Window Rock, the capital of the Navajo nation, the biggest of Indian reservations, hosts the World's Largest American Indian Fair; it draws 200,000 people or more. The Navajo nation spreads over 27,000 square miles that are largely in Arizona (which has the largest Native American population of any state) but also extends into New Mexico, Utah, and Colorado. The nation is larger than the entire state of West Virginia.

The fair's medley of events includes rodeos, Indian song and dance competitions, country and western music, livestock shows, a horseshoe tournament, archery competitions, a baby contest, a Miss Navajo Pageant, and displays of Navajo turquoise-and-silver jewelry, blankets, and rugs. The Saturday-morning parade is a pageant of colorful costumes, beauty queens, bands, and prancing horses.

To maintain your energy for all this, there's Navajo food aplenty: mutton stew made in a variety of ways, mutton ribs, Navajo tacos, corn baked in the ground, "kneel-down bread" made with cornmeal. There's a traditional barbecue, with meat cooked in an underground pit, steamed corn, and homemade beans. And there's a fry-bread contest that attracts up to 90 competitors of all ages. The bread can be sampled by spectators.

The fair was first held in 1938, but was suspended during war years, and the 50th-anniversary fair was held in 1996.

Location: Window Rock is 24 miles northwest of Gallup, NM, and about 25 miles north of I-40. ⊙ **Contact:** Navajo Nation Fair Office, P.O. Box 2370, Window Rock, AZ 86515; Tel: (520)871-6478.

California

Strawberry Festival

Memorial Day weekend ⚬ In 1983, the little town of Arroyo Grande decided to have a Strawberry Ice Cream Social. It went well; 750 people came.

Now close to 100,000 people flock to the social-turned-festival in what's called the Arroyo Grande Village, the picturesque center of the town, its streets lined with restored turn-of-the-century buildings, including the Hoosegow, built about 1906 to hold the bad guys. The festival features strawberry-pancake breakfasts and booths selling strawberry shortcake and other strawberry treats (strawberry cheesecake, for one), as well as ethnic food. There are strawberry-blonde and strawberry-pie-eating contests, 400 arts-and-crafts booths, and eight entertainment areas continuously entertaining.

The Arroyo Grande Valley is a rich agricultural area because of its deep fertile soil and frost-free climate.

Location: Arroyo Grande, off U.S. 101, is about 90 miles north of Santa Barbara. ⚬ **Contact:** Arroyo Grande Village Improvement Assn, 117½ E. Branch, Arroyo Grande, CA 93421; Tel: (805)473-2250, or Arroyo Grande Chamber of Commerce; Tel: (805)489-1488.

See Also: California Strawberry Festival (Oxnard, CA).

California Avocado Festival

First weekend in October (Friday through Sunday) ⚬ George Washington ate an avocado when he visited Barbados in 1751 and wrote in his journal that while "the Avagado pair is generally most admired," he preferred the pineapple.

Carpinterians don't quote George at the avocado festival, but they do mention the fact that the Aztec ruler Montezuma included avocados with the precious metals and gems he presented to Cortes.

Carpinteria is where high school cheerleaders and football players chant "Go, guac, go!" as they mash up the World's Biggest Bowl of Guacamole, a whopping 200 gallons. The kids sell it to make money for the team.

Carpinteria is where all food booths have to use avocado and therefore you'll taste it in Japanese sushi, Mexican burritos, mousse, sorbet, ice cream (tastes at first like vanilla, but "then you get a surprising blast of avocado," avows a taster), key-lime pie, salads, pizza, tri-tip sandwiches. Shrimp cocktail comes in half an avocado, brownies are made with avocado replacing the oil that would normally be used.

This is where there's an Avocado Alley, a lineup of booths that provide avocado products, including faces carved from avocado pits, and information: Avocado fruits each have about 300 calories, but no cholesterol and very little sodium, and they contain protein, eight essential vitamins, and five minerals. The oil and vitamin E in avocados are perfect as a skin moistener: mix avocado with cornmeal, rub on your skin, and you'll glow.

Here you'll also find the County Fair tent, where there are competitions for guacamole, stuffed avocado, best dessert, largest avocado, crafts (for example, quilts with avocado designs), and best-dressed avocado (people trying to look like avocados).

The festival began in 1987 and draws about 100,000 visitors. "Avo-tivities," as they call them, also include music of all sorts, a flower show, children's entertainment, a crafts fair, a four-mile run, and a poetry festival.

The avocado, although it seemed exotic to George Washington and remained so for many years, is an American fruit, native to Mexico and Central America, where it's been cul-

Fresh and Light Guacamole

2   California avocados, seeded, peeled, and mashed
1   medium tomato, seeded, chopped, and drained
1   medium onion*, finely chopped
1   tablespoon lemon juice
¼   teaspoon hot pepper sauce or to taste

Blend all ingredients together, chill if desired. (Place plastic wrap directly on surface of guacamole before refrigerating.) Serve with chips, crackers, or fresh vegetable dippers. Makes 2 cups. NOTE: For even "zestier" guacamole, add 1 small clove pressed garlic and 1/8 teaspoon ground cumin.
*May substitute 1 tablespoon instant minced onion for fresh onion.

California Avocado Commission, Santa Ana, California

Chants of "Go, quac, go!" can be heard as the World's Biggest Bowl of Guacamole (200 gallons) is prepared. (California Avocado Festival)

tivated for 7,000 years. Because of its 20-percent fat content, it's known in the tropics as the poor man's butter. It has the idiosyncrasy of not ripening on the tree as long as the skin is unbroken; it has to be cut from the tree to ripen.

In 1900, George B. Cellon, a horticulturist, started experimenting with avocados in Florida, and the industry was launched there and then spread to California, which now surpasses Florida. The valleys west of Carpinteria are rich with avocado orchards.

American acceptance of the avocado was speeded up by reverse public relations. Food historians Waverly Root and Richard de Rochemont write that when growers didn't dare advertise what they privately thought was the fruit's biggest asset, a "resourceful publicity man found the solution: he had a representative of the avocado raisers' association deny with indignation the false and malicious rumors that the avocado was aphrodisiac. Sales rose."

Location: Linden and Carpinteria Aves. in Carpinteria, off U.S. 101, 12 miles south of Santa Barbara. ⬩ **Contact:** California Avocado Festival, P.O. Box 146, Carpinteria, CA 93014; Tel: (805)684-0038.

Castroville

Castroville Artichoke Festival

Third or fourth weekend in September ⚬ The rolling hills around Castroville are lined with row after row of artichokes. If the crops don't convey the message, a sign arching over the main highway that runs through town tells you: Artichoke Center of the World.

Mediterranean countries grow more artichokes, but this is the center (locals say) because Monterey County, where Castroville is located, has the greatest *concentration* of artichokes anywhere and grows nearly 75 percent of the California crop. And the state grows virtually all the chokes consumed in the United States. Furthermore, two artichoke packing sheds and the nation's only artichoke-processing plant are located here.

Artichokes were first planted in the Salinas Valley in 1922, and the first artichoke festival was held in 1959. Now between 10,000 and 15,000 attend.

Middle East Lamb Balls in Artichoke Cups with Yogurt Sauce

8   large artichokes   Salt to taste
1   lemon

Cook trimmed artichokes in chicken broth with several cloves of garlic and drizzle of
   olive oil. Remove chokes as soon as can be handled—open artichoke and spared
   leaves to make cup.

1 pound lean ground lamb	1 teaspoon oregano
⅓ cup chopped parsley	1 teaspoon cayenne
½ cup minced onion	1 teaspoon fresh black pepper
1 teaspoon cumin	1 teaspoon salt
¾ teaspoon crushed coriander	1 teaspoon marjoram

Mix well and form bite-size meat balls. Cook for about 10 minutes. To make Yogurt
   Sauce, blend 2 cups unflavored yogurt, 3 chopped tomatoes, ½ cup chopped green
   onions, ½ medium cucumber, peeled, seeded, and chopped, and salt and pepper to
   taste.
Serve artichoke cups on warmed plates. Fill center of cup with hot meat balls and 4
   chopped hearts and stems. Top with yogurt sauce with side dish of sauce for dipping outer leaves.

Dorothy G. Hansen, 1st Place Winner, 1992 Artichoke Recipe Contest

The food booths show artichokes' versatility; specialties include artichokes battered, sautéed, or French-fried, and in soup, pizza, frittatas, cakes, pies, and muffins. Chefs give artichoke-cooking demonstrations.

This little farm town also provides a show of musical entertainment, children's activities, a 10K race, arts and crafts booths, and the crowning of a queen.

For years, there was a legend that Marilyn Monroe was the first queen. Not quite true. In 1948, when she was a starlet (and before the festivals started), she was sent on a promotional tour to the county, and Italian growers at the Kiwanis Club of nearby Salinas gave her a sash and an orchid, making her a sort of honorary queen of the artichoke fields.

The artichoke is a native of the Mediterranean area and has been known as an edible delicacy since ancient Grecian times. It's in the thistle group of the sunflower family and looks fern-like. When we eat an artichoke, we actually eat a flower bud. The bigger buds are the "terminal" ones at the end of long central stems, and smaller ones are lower on the stem. The plants, perennials, are propagated by taking root sections and replanting in new fields.

Italians have been eating artichokes for centuries, and in the mid-1500s Catherine de Medici of Florence is supposed to have introduced the artichoke to France when she married into French royalty. The story spread that they were aphrodisiacs and they caught on big with the French.

Location: Castroville is 5 miles north of Salinas, at the juncture of U.S. 101 and California 1. **Contact:** Castroville Artichoke Festival, P.O. Box 747, Castroville, CA 95012; Tel: (408)633-2465.

While You're There: Visit The Giant Artichoke, a restaurant on the edge of Castroville, for fried artichokes, and to see probably the only restaurant in the United States shaped like a 15-foot-high artichoke.

Clovis

Big Hat Festival

First full weekend in April (Second weekend if Easter falls on first) Why would a festival be called a Big Hat Festival? Presumably (nobody is quite sure) because it's a kickoff for the rodeo season, and cowboys wear big hats.

Other than that, the festival has nothing to do with big hats. It takes over the entire old Clovis, has live music, a 200-car show featuring all kinds of cars—antique to sleek sports—and 300 arts-and-crafts booths. It's the biggest two-day event in the area, drawing 140,000.

Its centerpiece is the Central California Rib Cookoff, in which 40 teams compete in cooking pork spare ribs or baby back ribs on Saturday, and 40 teams compete to cook beef back ribs on Sunday. The aroma is enough to make you drool.

Fortunately, there are food vendors at hand, and among them are sellers of tri-tip sandwiches, a delicacy unique to central California. Tri-tip is a wedge-shaped, triangular cut of sirloin tip seasoned with garlic, salt, paprika, etc. It's roasted over high heat on each side, searing it and sealing in the juices; it's then cooked over lower heat for another 10 minutes. Tri-tip originated years ago in Santa Maria when a butcher in a men's service club prepared it for his comrades. It's the second most popular piece of barbecued sandwich meat in this area, but it's unknown as such in Los Angeles or San Francisco.

Some people stuff tri-tip. At the Central California Tri-Tip Cookoff, which is part of the Clovis Fest on the last weekend in September, barbecuers get wildly innovative. One tri-tip cook uses a stuffing that combines bread crumbs, Jack cheese, shrimp, and onions.

Location: Clovis is on California 168, five miles northeast of Fresno. **Contact:** Red Dog Productions, 6271 N. Sharon Ave., Fresno, CA 93710; Tel: (209)432-6766.

Fallbrook

Fallbrook Avocado Festival

Third or fourth Sunday in April Fallbrook calls itself the Avocado Capital of the World. The town lies in San Diego County, which has 26,500 acres in avocados, producing about 60 percent of all California avocados. The state as a whole is home to

A highlight of Clovis's Big Hat Festival is the Carbecue, a 1974 Volkswagen Bug with a custom grill in place of a motor and transmission. A keg goes where the passenger seat was, with the tap poking out the gas filler door. (Red Dog Productions, Inc.)

95 percent of the nation's crop. Mexico is actually the world's largest producer, but Fallbrook chauvinists ignore that detail.

Since Fallbrook is up to its eyebrows in avocados, you can expect lots of half-pint containers of guacamole for sale as well as ripe avocados. Most of them are the Hass avocado, which has a pebbly black skin, unlike the smoother green skins of other avocados. The Hass also has a fascinating history.

The original tree was a lucky chance seedling. Rudolph Hass, a postman, bought seedlings from a Whittier grower in the late 1920s, and when they matured, his children first brought this new kind of avocado to his attention. There was some doubt at first about propagating it because it was so different from the standard Fuerte (Spanish for strong; it got the name when it survived a great freeze), which had created California's avocado industry.

But it was a better bearer than the Fuerte, and it caught on. Nobody knows what variety of seed produced the Hass. The mother tree still grows in La Habra Heights, and seedlings from it have been planted in Israel, South Africa, and other parts of the world. California grows seven varieties of avocado now, but the Hass makes up 90 percent of the harvest.

The festival, with attendance of about 65,000, was started in its present form in 1990. It's a fun affair; there are two beer gardens, live music, rides for kids, a Little Miss and Mister Avocado Festival contest (for kids 4 through 8), a best decorated avocado contest, an avocado 500 race for children, in which racers are built with avocado pits. There are contests for best tasting guacamole, most creative avocado dish, and best tasting salsa.

Location: Main St., Fallbrook, 5 miles west of I-15, about 45 miles north of San Diego. **Contact:** Fallbrook Chamber of Commerce, 233A E. Mission Rd., Fallbrook, CA 92028; Tel: (619)728-5845, Fax: (619)728-4031.

Fort Bragg

Salmon Barbecue

First Saturday in July About 2,500 pounds of chinook salmon are devoured at this barbecue, an event organized in 1971 by the Salmon Restoration Society to raise funds for the preservation of salmon.

Chinooks are the biggest of the Pacific salmon, sought after by sports fishermen and considered excellent eating. Long ago, Indians of the Northwest roasted salmon over a wood fire, and today salmon are prepared in the same way.

About 4,000 to 5,000 attend the barbecue for the salmon dinner that also includes salad, corn on the cob, and French bread. The products of local microbreweries and wineries are available, too.

The salmon situation is described by preservationists as "not good" for a variety of reasons, including droughts. Droughts dry up the tributaries where salmon spawn; if they spawn in the main river, the eggs are more likely to be swept out to sea. The chinook is not yet considered threatened, but the coho salmon, smaller than the chinook, is listed as threatened in some areas, endangered in others, and is the focus of restoration efforts. Fishing for coho is currently illegal.

Information about the salmon is displayed at the barbecue, but it's not a solemn affair—there are live bands and entertainers, games for children, and fireworks in the evening.

Fort Bragg's annual Whale Festival in mid-March features tastings of chowder and mircobrewery beer, as well as whale spottings. For information, contact (800)726-2780 or (707)961-6300.

Location: Fort Bragg is on California 101 about 100 miles north of San Francisco. **Contact:** Salmon Barbecue, P.O. Box 68, Fort Bragg, CA 95437; Tel: (707) 964-6598.

Gilroy

Gilroy Garlic Festival

Last full weekend in July (Friday through Sunday) Will Rogers cracked that Gilroy is "the only town in America where you can marinate a steak by hanging it on the clothesline." The people of Gilroy delight in the quote, and also brag about having the "smelliest party on the continent."

Southwest Bread

1 package of active dry yeast
  (2 teaspoons)
2 cups warm water
½ cup honey
¾ cup yogurt
1½ cups yellow corn meal
1½ cups whole wheat flour
¼ cup chopped garlic
1 cup cooked black beans
½ cup corn, frozen or canned
½ cup chopped red onion
¼ cup chopped fresh coriander
  (cilantro)

¼ cup chopped sun-dried tomato,
  packed in olive oil
3 tablespoons butter, melted
1 tablespoon chili powder
1 teaspoon ground cumin
1 teaspoon salt
½ teaspoon tarragon vinegar
1 mild green chili pepper, seeded;
  chopped finely
1 jalapeño pepper, seeded; chopped
  finely
4 cups bread flour
1 egg, beaten

Mix yeast, water, honey, yogurt, cornmeal, and whole wheat flour; reserve mixture
until bubbles form, about 1 hour. Stir in garlic, beans, corn, onion, coriander,
tomato, butter, chili powder, cumin, salt, vinegar, chili pepper, and jalapeño pepper.
Add bread flour until a firm dough is achieved. Knead on a lightly floured surface
until smooth and elastic, about 5 minutes.

Turn dough in a bowl that has been coated with olive oil. Cover with a tea towel; let
rise until double in volume, about 1 hour. Punch down dough; divide equally into 4
pieces. Form each piece into a ball. Arrange 2 balls of dough seam-side down on
each of two oiled baking sheets. Cover with a tea towel; let rise until nearly doubled
in volume, about 1 hour.

Brush dough with egg; slash top of each surface 3 times with a sharp knife or a razor
blade. Bake at 375 degrees until golden brown and center reaches 190 degrees,
about 25 minutes. Bread should sound hollow when tapped. Cool on wire racks.
Makes four loaves.

Jim Kelley, Washington, D.C., 1994 cook-off winner, Gilroy Garlic Festival

It is. A reeking 100,000 festival-goers chow down on whole roasted garlic heads and
garlic-enhanced snails, alligator tails, artichoke hearts, sushi, sausage, chicken wings,
Cajun catfish, you name it. More than 90 booths sell foods flavored with the "stinking
rose"—even ice cream.

Gilroy is the Garlic Capital of the World. California accounts for 90 percent of the U.S.
garlic crop, and most of that is grown within 90 miles of Gilroy or is processed in Gilroy.
The McCormick Company has the world's biggest garlic dehydrator located here, the 3,500-
acre Christopher Ranch is the country's largest producer of fresh garlic, and Gilroy compa-

Garlic: it's not just for eating anymore. At the Gilroy Garlic Festival, they wear it.
(Photo by Bill Strange, courtesy Gilroy Garlic Festival)

nies produce garlic jellies, pickles, mustard, garlic-stuffed olives, and garlic-flavored wine. As a result, there's usually a whiff of garlic in the air.

At the heart of the festival is Gourmet Alley where volunteers use more than a ton of garlic preparing pepper steak sandwiches, stuffed mushrooms, scampi, pasta con pesto, bread sopping with butter and garlic, and calamari, which provides the Alley's big show. So-called pyro chefs dump cans of calamari into oil in skillets the size of bicycle wheels, flames shoot up, and spectators shout "Whoo-ey!"

Other popular attractions are the Great Garlic Cook-Off, in which entrants' recipes must call for at least three cloves of garlic, and cooking demonstrations by celebrity chefs. The celebrities have come up with such exotica as a tomato-gin-garlic soup, which includes in its ingredients 12 ounces of gin, 20 Roma tomatoes, and 40 cloves of garlic.

Still other features are "garlic-topping" contests by field workers who chop off garlic greens with sharp knives; garlic-braiding demonstrations; arts and crafts emphasizing garlic replicas; experts with garlic information and literature; and a man dressed like a garlic strolling around with powdered garlic to sprinkle in beer.

Garlic, *Allium sativum,* a member of the lily family, is cloaked in lore. To wit:

In medieval times, people hung garlic in doorways and windows to protect against vampires. To ward off the plague, people wore pouches of garlic around their necks.

An inscription inside the Cheops Pyramid in Egypt tells of the quantity of radishes, onions, and garlic consumed by the workers building the pyramids.

Hippocrates, the father of modern medicine, used garlic to treat infections, toothaches, leprosy, and epilepsy, and recommended eating it for uterine tumors.

The ancient Romans considered garlic an aphrodisiac.

Garlic has antiseptic properties and was used by doctors on World War I battlefields to control septic poisoning and gangrene from wounds.

Today, garlic is a growth stock in the United States. Per capita consumption was 0.6 pounds in 1975, and 20 years later was 1.6 pounds. Its production is rising now at a rate of about 10 percent a year. Health benefits may be one reason. Medical researchers are concluding that garlic can reduce high blood pressure and high cholesterol levels, enhance the immune system and possibly prevent cancer and help common colds. And, they've found that dogs who eat a clove a day won't get fleas.

Location: Christmas Hill Park in Gilroy, 30 miles south of San Jose on U.S. 101. **Contact:** Gilroy Garlic Festival Assn, P.O. Box 2311, 7473 Monterey St., Gilroy, CA 95021; Tel: (408)842-1625.

Goleta

Lemon Festival

Usually third weekend in October If you're squeezing a lemon in your tea today, the chances are good it's a California lemon; California produces 85 percent of the country's lemons.

This festival, attended by about 10,000 people, started as Goleta Valley Days and then evolved into a lemon festival to honor Goleta's past fame as the lemon center of the state. In the 1930s, 2,500 acres were planted in lemons, but in the 1950s and 1960s housing tracts replaced orchards. Lemons continue to flourish on hillsides, and, while Goleta is no longer the lemon epicenter, lemons are very much in evidence at the festival.

You can pucker up and try lemon pie, lemon chicken, lemon-chicken sausage, lemon yogurt, lemon cotton candy, lemon cake, lemonade, and—did we mention tea?—iced tea with lemon. You'll also find that regional favorite, tri-tip beef sandwiches with salsa.

Lemon meringue pies are on hand for timed, no-hands pie-eating contests. A lemon cookbook is on sale. A lemon-pie-baking contest is held on Sunday.

That's about it for lemons, but other events include music and dancers, arts and crafts, rides in antique fire engines, a petting zoo, and other activities for kids.

Lemons probably originated in the district east of the Himalayas—northern Myanmar (formerly Burma) and possibly eastern India. Columbus took lemon seeds to the western hemisphere, and Franciscan priests took them to California. Today, the two great centers of lemon production are in southern Italy and Sicily, and southern California's coastal counties.

Location: The grounds of Stow House, built by Sherman Stow, a lemon rancher of the early 1900s, in Goleta, 8 miles north of Santa Barbara, off U.S. 101 at the Los Carneros Rd. exit. **Contact:** Goleta Chamber of Commerce, P. O. Box 781, Goleta, CA 93116; Tel: (800)646-5382.

A winner at the
Great Half Moon
Bay Pumpkin
Weigh-Off proudly
displays his ribbon
and winning
pumpkin. (Half Moon
Bay Art and Pumpkin
Festival)

Half Moon Bay

Half Moon Bay Art & Pumpkin Festival

Weekend after Columbus Day ☼ They carve them, weigh them, parade them, eat them. Pumpkins, that is. California is the second largest pumpkin-producing state, and pumpkins have certainly done a lot for Half Moon Bay.

In 1970, a group of residents got together for a "paint-in" to spruce up Main Street, and then decided a pumpkin-themed festival would be a good fundraiser. They were right. These days 300,000 people crowd onto Main Street for the festival, which has paid for streetlights, wooden benches, trees, flowers, and the building of two public parks.

The Great Pumpkin Weigh-Off (winners have topped 600 pounds) is held on the Monday before the festival, and the following Saturday the plumpest pumpkin has the place of honor on a Great Pumpkin Parade float.

Pumpkin lovers are in pumpkin heaven; the pumpkin foods include pie, ice cream, strudel, crepes, bread, muffins, tempura, and baked Alaska. Nonprofit organizations sell a variety of foods, including sausages, tamales, tacos, and California products such as artichokes and Brussels sprouts.

There are contests for pumpkin-pie eating and pumpkin carving, and entertainment includes all kinds of music, roving street performers, magicians, jugglers, unicycling.

Pumpkins have been grown in the Half Moon Bay area for years but originally were grown chiefly for cattle feed. Early colonists found Native Americans growing pumpkins between rows of corn and using them as a staple in their diets; they baked, boiled, fried, and dried them.

Location: Main St. in Half Moon Bay, about 20 miles south of San Francisco on California 1. **Contact:** Half Moon Bay Art & Pumpkin Festival, P.O. Box 274, Half Moon Bay, CA 94019; Tel: (415)726-9652, or (415)726-3491.

Holtville

Holtville Carrot Festival

January and early February (Sunday through Sunday)
Holtville, a small agricultural town near the Mexican border, was once the Carrot Capital of the World and shipped more carrots than any other place in the country. But most of the carrot farms have moved to the Bakersfield region or to Arizona, so Holtville has changed its title. It's now the Home of the Carrot.

The carrot celebration began in 1947, when Holtville was still a capital, not yet a home. After all that time, the festival is an unstoppable tradition, attended by about 8,000. The highlight is a Carrot Cooking Contest, attracting about 300 entrants in categories for all ages, starting with grade-school youngsters. Spectators are allowed small samples of the carrot concoctions after judging.

The concoctions are creative: carrot-pepper relish, carrot chutney, chile-honey carrots, carrot ice cream, pretzel-carrot delight, spicy hot carrot casserole, carrottini fettucini.

The festival has a Carrot Queen, a livestock show, a carnival midway, a tractor pull, and food vendors, many with carrot foods. In the parade on the final Saturday, marchers dress like carrots and bunnies, and real fresh carrots on a mound of ice are given away at the end of the parade. During the week, the town is decorated with orange-paper carrots.

Carrots are supposed to have originated in Afghanistan. It gets very, very hot and dry there, like the desert area of California, where carrots grow so well that the state now produces 55 percent of the country's carrots.

Location: Holtville is just north of I-8, about 100 miles east of San Diego. **Contact:** Holtville Chamber of Commerce, P.O. Box 185, Holtville, CA 92250; Tel: (619)356-2923, Fax: (619)356-2925.

Indio

National Date Festival

Ten days in February, including Presidents' Day ☼ Dates are strange fruits, and a good place to learn about their strangeness is at the date festival (pretty strange itself) in Indio, the Date Capital of North America.

Indio is in Arabian-like desert, so Arabia's the theme. Queen Scheherazade (who saved her neck by enthralling the king with 1,001 nights of storytelling) reigns over the festivities, and the Arabian Nights Musical Pageant is staged every night against a replica of a marketplace in "old Baghdad." Other exotic events are daily ostrich and camel races and a blessing-of-the-date-garden procession, and less exotic events include pig races and a parade.

Exhibits of varieties of dates are shown in the Taj Mahal, and you can sample the ones grown in the Indio region: Deglet Noor, Medjool, Zahidi, Khadrawy, and Halawy. You can also buy whole and pitted dates, date bread, cookies, cakes, ice cream, and milk shakes made with vanilla ice cream, milk, and date crystals. The crystals swell up and soften when they're mixed with the milk.

Frozen Date Souffle

½ cup blanched almonds, toasted and chopped
1 8 oz. package cream cheese, softened
1 tablespoon lemon juice
1 8 oz. can crushed pineapple, drained

½ cup pitted dates, finely snipped or diced
1 cup heavy cream, whipped
¼ cup honey
½ cup (1 large) banana, mashed

To toast almonds: Spread blanched almonds in single layer in skillet or shallow pan. Heat slowly, stirring occasionally on top of stove or in slow (300 degree) oven until light brown.

In mixing bowl cream cheese with honey and lemon juice. Add mashed banana. Mix well. Stir in pineapple, dates and almonds. Whip cream until it holds its shape. Fold into cheese mixture. Line 8 (2 inch) muffin cups with foil or paper baking cups. Fill with souffle. Freeze.

To serve, remove from freezer. Let stand 10 minutes, peel off foil or cups. Serve as is. Requires no extra dressing. Makes 8 servings.

(Hint: For salad, serve with finger sandwiches or as a dessert with cookies.)

Courtesy Sun Giant Dates

Vendors like Hadley Fruit Orchards hawk their date wares at the National Date Festival. (National Date Festival)

Date-recipe cooking demonstrations are presented daily, and there's a date-recipe cook-off. Among the winners have been gooseberry-date pie, barbecued spareribs with date-pineapple glaze, almond-date rice pilaf.

The festival has been held annually since 1947, as part of the Riverside County Fair, but was held off and on before that. Attendance is about 250,000.

Why dates are strange:

Dates are one of the oldest cultivated food plants; they were cultivated in Mesopotamia in 3,000 B.C., and legend mentions them long before that. The reason for cultivation is sex. Palms are male or female, but the female flower has no scent to attract bees or insects, and pollination is up to the wind. That makes fruiting a very hit-or-miss thing.

So humans intervene. Hand pollination is still most common. In California's Coachella Valley, where there are 49 female palms for every male, workers are hoisted up trees by hydraulic lift to cut male flowers and tie them in the center of the female blossoms. Sometimes a pollen duster is used.

Six to nine months after the pollination, it's harvest time, and pickers again scale trees, which can grow as high as 100 feet, to pick the dates. Generally, dates are harvested from September through December.

It's said that a date palm must live with "its feet in the water and its head in the fires of heaven." The area around Indio fits the description; the temperature often goes up to 120, and irrigation keeps feet wet. Because of this dry, hot climate, 5,000 acres of the Coachella

Valley each year produce an average 35 million pounds of dates from about 250,000 palms. The palms first came here in 1900 when the United States Department of Agriculture brought Deglet Noor offshoots from Algeria.

California grows 95 percent of all U.S. dates, and the remainder are grown in Nevada.

Other facts: A date palm's life span is about 200 years. A palm begins producing dates at about age seven. A healthy palm can produce up to 300 pounds of dates in a season. Ounce for ounce, dates have more potassium than bananas.

Location: Indio is about 120 miles southeast of Los Angeles on I-10. Exit the highway at Monroe Ave. and proceed southwest. **Contact:** National Date Festival, 46-350 Arabia St., Indio, CA 92201; Tel: (619)863-8247; Fax: (619)863-8973.

Kelseyville

Kelseyville Pear Festival

Last Saturday in September The Pear Prince and Princess at this pear festival are chosen from among fourth- and fifth-graders who have written essays on "Why Pears Are Important to Kelseyville."

There's no doubt they are important. Kelseyville is one of the areas in California that contribute to the state's standing as the number-one producer of Bartlett pears. Washington is tops in *all* pears, but California's production of Bartletts ranges from about 250,000 tons a year to well over 300,000 tons, while Washington comes through with less than 200,000.

Despite the figures on pears, Kelseyville, which has had an annual fair since the late 1980s, didn't decide to call it a pear fair until 1993. Once they decided on the name, they went all the way; Bartlett pears are available for eating in pies, breads, tarts, shakes, and shish kebabs with beef. There's a pear-pie contest, in which Bartlett pears must be used. After judging, the pies are auctioned off (with pieces missing). A pear-packing contest pits packers from packing houses in competitions to pack two boxes; the first to pack them, without bruising, wins.

A quaint old-fashioned air pervades the festival. A parade, in which the young royalty wear purple capes and ride on a float, features horses and buggies and dozens of antique tractors, and there's a show of antique tractors after the parade. Other festival features are a quilt show, clog and line dancing, a fine arts show, and children's demonstrations.

Of temperate-zone fruits, the pear is second to the apple in worldwide production. It probably originated in China or western Asia, and has been cultivated since at least 2000 B.C. There are now innumerable varieties, but the leading variety in the United States is the Bartlett: yellow, aromatic, juicy, and free of grittiness, which afflicts some pears. It was developed in England in the 1700s and introduced to America in Dorchester, Massachusetts, by Enoch Bartlett.

Location: Kelseyville is 20 miles east of U.S. 101, about 75 miles north of San Francisco, on Clear Lake. **Contact:** Lake County Marketing Program, 875 Lakeport Blvd., Lakeport, CA 95453; Tel: (800)525-3743.

Kingsburg

Kingsburg Swedish Festival

Third weekend in May (Thursday through Saturday) ☼
Kingsburg, established in 1875 by the Southern Pacific Railroad, was settled by Swedes. It's now multiethnic, but is still known as a Swedish village and boasts turn-of-the-century buildings with steep wood-shingled roofs, dormer windows, and half-timbers that are a perfect backdrop for a Swedish festival.

The festival began in 1924 as a luncheon to mark the midsummer harvest. Now about 20,000 people attend for the Parade of Trolls, dancing, arts-and-crafts booths with Swedish weavers and painters of wooden Dala horses. And food.

On Saturday morning the popular thing to do is dive into Swedish pancakes with sausage and 80 gallons of lingonberry (tart berries related to the cranberry) syrup. Because lingonberries are expensive and are shipped from Sweden, the syrup is actually a mix of lingonberries, boysenberries, and cranberries. Now you know.

You may also sample yellow split-pea soup, potato sausage, meatballs, *inlagd sill* (pickled herring), Swedish cracker bread, Swedish cucumber salad, pea salad, orange rye bread, sugar cookies . . . and more.

On the last Saturday in July, Kingsburg hosts the Kingsburg Watermelon Festival. It's a tale of former glory: The Watermelon Festival began in 1945 when Kingsburg was the Watermelon Capital of the World, shipping more watermelons than any other place in the United States. Now there are very few watermelons grown in the area, and Kingsburg has to get its festival melons from Bakersfield, California. But the celebration goes on, with attendance about 10,000, and free slices of watermelon are still given out.

Location: Kingsburg is about 25 miles south of Fresno on Rt. 99. ☼ Contact: Kingsburg Chamber of Commerce, 1401 California St., Kingsburg, CA 93631; Tel: (209)897-2925.

Monterey

The Great Monterey Squid Festival

Saturday and Sunday of Memorial Day weekend ☼ The squid is a peculiar creature when you think about it. In the mollusk family, it's considered the most highly developed, and it certainly shows more get-up-and-go than its cousin the oyster that just sits on a rock all its life. Squid, octopus, and cuttlefish are in the class of mollusks known as cephalopods, which have tentacles attached to the head, and ink sacs, with which they squirt ink to confuse enemies. Most mollusks have exterior shells, but the squid has an interior transparent shell.

You will learn this at the Monterey squid festival, which is not only an eating experience but an educational event.

Don't let it confuse you that one booth sells squid and another calamari; they're the same thing, and you have an almost inexhaustible selection to choose from: fried calamari, Cajun fried squid, squid quesadilla, calamari parmesan, key lime calamari, squid marinara, calamari flambé, calamari chowder, stuffed squid over rice, barbecued shrimp and squid.

The 45 to 50 food and beverage booths also include an assortment of non-squid foods, but they all lean heavily on seafood. There are barbecued oysters, oysters on the half shell, crab fritters, fried catfish, barbecued shrimp, shrimp tempura, garlic shrimp, pesto clams, smoked salmon, fried crawfish tails, and barbecued beef, chicken, and pork. To name only a few.

While you're walking off your meal there are other things to see or do, including 45 craft booths, three outdoor stages with music and entertainment, strolling musicians, clowns, mimes, and jugglers.

Squid-cooking demonstrations by chefs and instructions on cleaning and preparing squid for cooking are a big part of the educational side, along with displays and films on the lives of squid, and a live-creature touch tank.

The purpose of the festival, which began in 1984, is to raise funds for local charities and support the local commercial fishing industry. That industry has changed since John Steinbeck's *Cannery Row* limned the lives of the men who worked in the Monterey canneries that canned sardines. The canneries and sardines are gone, and the old Cannery Row is now a trendy section of fine hotels and restaurants, although the famously long Fisherman's Wharf remains, and the fishing industry still survives amidst all the chichi stuff.

About 30,000 attend the festival. If you're one of them, don't forget to get a squid balloon. It will have ten arms if it's a correct replica.

Location: Monterey Fairgrounds, at the intersection of California 1 and Freemont Blvd. **Contact:** Great Monterey Squid Festival, 2107 Del Monte Blvd., Monterey, CA 93940; Tel: (408) 649-6544, Fax: (408)649-4124.

Oakley

Oakley Almond Festival

Third weekend in September Almonds are a wonderful thing for California. In terms of dollars, almonds rank third in exports, and they're the state's sixth largest agricultural cash producer. Of all the almonds in the United States, California produces 99.9 percent (Texas may have a tree or two), and more almonds come from California than from the entire rest of the world.

The strange thing about this Oakley festival is not that it's an almond festival but that it's what might be called an in-memoriam almond festival. About 30,000 come to pay their respects, and to enjoy almonds in all kinds of baked and non-baked goods.

Confused? The festival began in 1990 when the last major almond orchard was bulldozed to make room for more housing in this fast-growing town, which is within commuter distance of the Bay area.

Oakley is built on sandy soil, and not too much grows on it, but in the late 1800s someone planted almond trees. They grew like clover, and soon there were orchards everywhere. But then industry began moving in, the population grew, highways made commuting easy, and the trees began disappearing in Oakley.

Fortunately for California and the rest of the world, there's still room for about 400,000 acres of almond trees in five central California counties. A ton of almonds is imported from these counties for the festival and sold in half-pound and pound boxes. There are also roasted almonds, and cinnamon-flavored, sugar-flavored, barbecue-flavored, chile-flavored, chile-lime-flavored, and even chocolate-flavored almonds.

Vendors also sell almond cookies, chicken with almond sauce, roasted almonds with a German-style cinnamon flavor, Chinese dishes with almonds. Not to mention almond-caramel popcorn and almond ice cream.

To keep people from going too nutty, there are entertainers, music, a history display, a parade, and arts and crafts.

Almonds seem to be a commonplace nut, but they have a long, interesting history. According to Charles Panati's *Extraordinary Origins of Everyday Things,* the almond is one of only two nuts mentioned in the Bible (the other is the pistachio). They were grown in Greece as early as 2500 B.C., and were a favorite dessert dish for ancient Greeks.

Location: Downtown Oakley, about 30 miles east of Oakland, on California 4.
Contact: Oakley Chamber of Commerce, P.O. Box 1314, Oakley, CA 94561; Tel: (510)779-8035.

Oxnard

California Strawberry Festival

Third weekend in May In times past, Iroquois Indians used strawberries to season meat and make soup, and they used strawberry leaves for tea. They believe the road to heaven is lined with strawberries.

An early American colonist called strawberries "the wonder of all the Fruits growing naturally in these parts. The Indians bruise them in a Morter, and mix them with meale and make strawberry bread."

Strawberries have been favorite fruits, with a touch of the divine, for a long time, and in Oxnard about 70,000 people get together to celebrate the wondrous berry. Oxnard is officially the Strawberry Capital of California, but the festival's promoters less modestly lay claim to being the Strawberry Capital of the *Galaxy.*

Their reasoning: the Oxnard area produces 148,000 tons of berries, or a quarter of all California strawberries—and California produces 75 percent of all the strawberries grown in the United States. (If the state's harvest were laid berry to berry, this strawberry rope would wrap around the world nearly 15 times.)

Culinarily interesting things are done to strawberries at the festival. You can find hot dogs with strawberry-barbecue sauce, sweet-potato pie with strawberries, strawberry pizza,

At the California Strawberry Festival, you can not only experience the build-it-yourself strawberry shortcake, but you may also spot the rare human strawberry, with or without mustache.
(California Strawberry Festival)

chocolate-dipped strawberries, strawberry funnel cakes, strawberry bread with strawberry cream cheese, and strawberry K-bobs—which are strawberries sprinkled with sugar on a stick, a favorite with kids. A favorite with gluttons of all ages is the build-it-yourself short-cake stand, where you load all the berries and whipped cream you can on a slab of cake. The days begin with strawberry-pancake breakfasts.

Festival happenings include a Berry-Off Cooking Contest, strawberry-shortcake-eating contests, strawberry-tart tosses (people throw them at each other), a man dressed like a strawberry, music, arts and crafts, Strawberryland for Children (petting zoo, train rides, clowns), and a waiter-waitress race.

All this for a berry commonly thought of as made-in-America, but actually known in Europe long ago.

Raymond Sokolov, in *Why We Eat What We Eat,* explained it this way: "In the beginning, Europeans had only wild strawberries, those little *fraises des bois* that Diderot Gallicly compared to the 'tips of wet nurses' breasts.' But enticing as this sounds, the actual berry is awfully small and often a 'little seedy on the tongue.'"

What happened was that after colonists met the big luscious American strawberry in Virginia (and named it *Fragaria virginniana*), it got taken to England and Europe, but wouldn't cross with the sweet dwarf berries. Strawberries are asexual, reproducing by sending out runners.

Then in the early 1700s a Frenchman, Amédée François Frézier, found some strawberries as big as walnuts in Chile, took them to France and England, and they somehow crossed with *F. virginniana*. Voilà! The grandchildren of those hybrid berries grow today in every state and province of the United States and Canada.

As berries go, strawberries are odd, with their seeds on the outside instead of the inside. The word itself is odd; its origin is obscure. Some sources trace the word to children stringing the fruit on straw and selling it as "straws of berries."

Location: College Park in Oxnard, 35 miles south of Santa Barbara, off U.S. 101. **Contact:** California Strawberry Festival, 1621 Pacific Ave., Ste. 127, Oxnard, CA 93033-1855; Tel: (805)385-7578, Fax: (805)486-2553.

Patterson

Patterson Apricot Fiesta

Weekend following Memorial Day The apricot has an exotic history. It's classified as *Prunus armeniaca,* because it was believed to have originated in Armenia. Actually, it began growing in China about 2200 B.C. (it still grows wild around Beijing) and eventually made its way to Armenia. Alexander the Great discovered it there and took it to Greece, and it moved around the Mediterranean. It got the Latin name *praecoqum,* meaning precocious, because of its early ripening season. The Arabs called it *alburquq,* also meaning precocious, and when it reached England in about 1620, it was abricock. A quick jump from there to apricot.

It's a healthy (lots of vitamin A and C) and delicious fruit, eaten largely dried in the United States and Canada. At least 97 percent of the apricots grown in the United States come from California, especially from the area around Patterson, the Apricot Capital of the World. The Spanish brought apricots to Mexico in the fifteenth century, to California in the early eighteenth century.

Since 1971, Patterson has been celebrating the apricot harvest slightly before the harvest because all hands are needed when the apricots are ripe. There is nonetheless a bounty of fresh and dried apricots and apricot dishes to try: jam, jelly, pies, ice-cream bars dipped in chocolate, yogurt, an apricot spread, apricot shakes. There are also numerous non-apricot food booths and a barbecue on Saturday afternoon.

A hot-air balloon launch launches the festival, which also features an arm-wrestling contest, a horseshoe tournament, a firemen's muster, a parade, and fireworks. About 20,000 attend.

Location: Downtown Patterson, about three miles east of I-5 at the Sperry Ave. exit. **Contact:** Patterson Apricot Fiesta, P.O. Box 442, Patterson, CA 95363; Tel: (209)892-3118.

Apricot Lemon Bread

½ cup solid all-vegetable shortening
⅔ cup sugar
⅓ cup honey
2   eggs
1¼ cups unsifted all-purpose flour
1   teaspoon baking powder
½ teaspoon salt

½ cup milk
2   teaspoons grated lemon peel
1   cup chopped dried California apricots
1   cup finely chopped toasted almonds
Glaze:
¼ cup sugar
¼ cup lemon juice

Cream shortening with ⅔ cup sugar and honey. Add eggs and beat mixture until light and fluffy. Sift together flour, baking powder, and salt. Add flour mixture and milk alternately to creamed mixture. Mix in lemon peel, apricots, and almonds. Pour into greased 9-inch x 5-inch loaf pan. Bake in 350 degree oven for 1 hour. Cover pan with foil (to prevent overbrowning) and bake 15 minutes longer. Remove foil and place pan on rack.

To make glaze, combine sugar with lemon juice and pour evenly over the top of loaf immediately upon removal from oven. Allow bread to remain in pan for 15 minutes, then remove from pan to cooling rack. When cool, wrap in plastic wrap or foil and keep overnight. This allows bread to mellow and slice more easily.

From "Favorite Recipes,"
published by California Apricot Growers and California Apricot Advisory Board

Riverside

Orange Blossom Festival

Third weekend in April (two days) On Orange Day in 1895, Riverside—the Town That Citrus Built—was giddy with a brass-band parade, jugglers, elephants, and clowns. It was a celebration of Riverside as the birthplace of California's citrus industry, and a commemoration of the city as the first in the United States to grow seedless navel oranges (Brazil was already growing them); the navel helped make California the premier orange producer. (Florida has since surpassed it.) The celebration was observed off and on until the 1930s, when it died out.

In 1995, the day was revived as the Sunkist Orange Blossom Festival. Floats, bands, fireworks, a circus, a magic show, and lots of orange-flavored food and drink draw 80,000 people and glorify citrus. Citrus was once so lucrative that Riverside was the wealthiest city per capita in the nation at the end of the nineteenth century. Oranges were the dominant crop from the 1870s to the 1930s, and, while Riverside is considerably more citified now, there are still 7,500 acres planted in citrus.

Riverside is the
Town That Citrus
Built, and they
celebrate in a big
way with bands,
fireworks, a
parade, and of
course, lots and
lots of citrus-
influenced food.
(Orange Blossom Festival,
Riverside, California)

Two years before the 1895 Orange Day, 60 orange growers formed a pool to sell their fruit cooperatively; this became Sunkist Growers, Inc., the nation's largest citrus cooperative, which initially sponsored the rejuvenated orange festival.

The celebration begins on Saturday morning with a parade featuring floats that all have oranges in their decoration. Then the serious food stuff starts: there's a celebrity-chef demonstration, where you can expect dishes like orange white-chocolate tiramisu and hominy-crusted chicken with orange salsa. In Gourmet Grove, vendors, who are required to use oranges in at least one dish, have come up with orange-wine burgers, an orange sauce for corn dogs and curly fries, and funnel cake with orange glaze and fresh strawberries.

Location: Twenty blocks in downtown Riverside, 6 miles south of I-10 on California 91, 60 miles east of Los Angeles. ⊛ **Contact:** Orange Blossom Festival, P.O. Box 1603, Riverside, CA 92502; Tel: (909)715-3500; Fax: (909)715-3503.

While You're There: The renovated Mission Inn, built (and added to) from 1903 to 1931 has been called a "massive architectural hallucination"; it merges Mediterranean and Asian elements, has bells hanging from arches, Tiffany stained-glass windows, balconies, courtyards, fountains, and gardens. Henry Miller, the man who built it, was also the man who put on the original Orange Days. Guided tours are offered daily.

Selma

Selma Raisin Festival

First Saturday in May ☼ Selma, the Raisin Capital of the World, started out in wheat farming. With the arrival of irrigation, wheat fields gave way to peach orchards and Selma was the Home of the Peach, even though raisins were the major crop by 1910. In 1963, Selma finally called itself the Raisin Capital because 90 percent of the world's raisin crop is cultivated within a 10-mile radius of the city.

That warrants a festival.

The raisin is celebrated with all kinds of raisin cookery. Hispanic-food vendors, for example, sell a sweet tamale with raisin filling. You will also find ice cream with raisin-rum sauce, bread puddings with raisins, homemade raisin pies, raisin bread.

A raisin-baking cook-off has categories for adults and juniors (under 16), who must use at least a half cup of raisins in their dishes—pies, cakes, quick breads, yeast breads, or cookies. The dishes are judged for taste, texture, and presentation. Cash prizes and ribbons are awarded, and a best overall prize is awarded (it went to a junior for a number of years). After the judging, what's left of the entries is sold.

The festival has a raisin queen, who wins the crown by selling the most raffle tickets. Other attractions include a parade, craft booths, children's games, displays of vehicles and agricultural equipment. The celebration originated in 1980, and is attended by 10,000.

Of the raisins produced in California, 95 percent are made from Thompson seedless grapes grown in the San Joaquin Valley, and 90 percent of those are from the Selma area. Thompson grapes are named for William Thompson, a Scottish immigrant who introduced the Lady de Coverly seedless, thin-skinned, sweet grape at a district fair in 1876. Prior to that, farmers had largely grown muscats, which have seeds, and, since consumers don't like seeds in raisins, the search was on for a seedless raisin grape.

Grapevines begin the growing cycle in spring, with heavy irrigation required. By August, the grapes are ready to become raisins, which happens by allowing them to dry naturally in the sun.

Considering that California grows almost 2½ million tons of grapes for raisins, you might think they were born there. But they've been around for centuries. Ancient Phoenicians and Armenians grew raisin grapes, and Greeks and Romans introduced raisins into their cuisine. Spanish conquistadors took viticulture to Mexico. California was next.

Location: Selma is 16 miles south of Fresno on California 99. ☼ **Contact:** Selma District Chamber of Commerce, 1710 Tucker Street, Selma, CA 93662; Tel: (209)896-3315.

Stockton

Stockton Asparagus Festival

Fourth weekend in April ☼ The Greeks and Romans used asparagus for bee stings, heart trouble, and toothache, and sometimes as an aphrodisiac. They also used it for food.

Nowadays people rarely associate asparagus with remedies for bug bites or logy libidos; it's considered more of a food delicacy. California produces about 90 percent of the fresh-market asparagus in the United States, and San Joaquin County, harvesting about 30,000 acres of asparagus, is the largest asparagus-producing county in the country. That makes Stockton, the county seat, the Asparagus Capital of the World.

Stockton's festival began in 1986, is attended by 75,000 to 80,000 people, and offers asparagus dishes you have never dreamed of. Among the many creations in Asparagus Alley are asparagus pasta, beef 'n' asparagus sandwiches, deep-fried asparagus, stir-fried asparagus, asparagus bisque, and "asparaberry" shortcake (strawberries and asparagus, which lends a nutmeg flavor to the berries).

A recipe contest has elicited recipes for asparagus enchiladas, asparagus sherry cake, and other peculiar dishes.

Filling out the festival agenda are demonstrations by celebrity chefs, a fun run where runners often wear simulated asparagus spears in their headbands, a car show, arts and crafts, strolling musicians, and music for dancing.

Asparagus is a little unusual. Most vegetables have both stamens (containing male pollen cells) and pistils (holding the egg cells) on the same flower, but about half of asparagus plants are staminate and the other half pistillate. They have to be grown near each other to pollinate the seed from which the fruits develop. It may be of interest to feminists that the pistillate plants produce fewer but bigger and better shoots than the staminate plants.

Location: Oak Grove Regional Park, at I-5 and 8 Mile Rd. ☼ **Contact:** Stockton Asparagus Festival, 1132 N. Hunter St., Stockton, CA 95202; Tel: (209)466-6674, Fax: (209)466-0431.

See Also: National Asparagus Festival (Shelby and Hart, MI).

Walnut Creek

Walnut Festival

Third weekend in September (Thursday through Sunday) ☼ There are still some black walnut trees growing in Walnut Creek, but the town, once known for its black walnut groves, is now, alas, a bedroom community, and one of the last orchards was bulldozed for a subdivision in 1996.

Sic transit *Juglans hindsii,* as the botanists call the northern California black walnut. Juglans is the shortened form of *Jovis glans,* the acorn of Jupiter; Hinds was the man the tree is named for.

The festival, started in 1938, nonetheless goes on, and it still features walnuts, but not black walnuts. About 40,000 people come to enjoy the entertainment—arts and crafts, amusement rides, children's activities—and eat nutty foods. The nuts are English walnuts, blander than the native black walnut. The more mild-tasting English walnut has been grafted onto black walnut trees, especially in the nearby Stockton area, and they help account for California's standing as the number-one nut state. China and the United States are the world's top producers of walnuts, and California produces virtually all of America's walnuts.

Some of the walnut products you may find at the festival are oil, candy, and roasted and chopped nuts.

Local nonprofit booths sell walnut-laced cookies, brownies, and even hamburgers with chopped nuts in them; other festival food is also available.

A Great Chefs Competition is open to cooks in three categories: firehouse chefs, college students, and professional restaurant chefs. They do wizardry with walnuts; a recent firehouse chef winner came up with three-pepper chicken with walnuts.

Location: Heather Farm Park, Walnut Creek, about 15 miles east of San Francisco, at I-680 and California 24. ❀ **Contact:** Walnut Festival, P.O. Box 3408, Walnut Creek, CA 94598; Tel: (510)935-6766.

See Also: Black Walnut Festival (Stockton, MO).

Yuba City

California Prune Festival

Second or third weekend in September ❀ Twelve U.S. crops are grown exclusively (meaning 99 percent or more of U.S. production) in California and prunes are one of them. Prunes can mean either dried plums or the trees that bear the plums. In California, farmers generally speak of growing prunes, referring to the sweet plum that makes the best prunes.

Yuba City is centrally located in the prune-growing area of California, and all the major companies that package prunes—Sunsweet Growers, Del Monte, Dole Food, Valley View Packing, and others—have plants in the region, and there are a number of smaller dehydrators, dryers, and processors.

The festival celebrates the prune with dishes not usually associated with prunes: prune couscous, ice cream, cookies, chili, salsa, burgers (meat plus prunes). Celebrity chefs demonstrate elaborate dishes using prunes, give out recipes, and offer samples. The food vendors get into the prune mania, too, with unusual, often ethnically influenced prune dishes.

In the children's area, kids make prune pops, which are prunes frozen on a stick and dipped in sugar, and other odd prune-shaped edibles.

Festivities include a parade, a photography contest, a farmers' market, music, and other events. About 30,000 attend the festival, which began in 1984. Prunes came to California long before. According to Betty Fussell in *I Hear America Cooking*, cuttings from a

French prune arrived in San Jose in 1856, and were grafted to the root stock of a native wild plum. In the 1920s, Fussell reports, a prune yeast bread was one of the commonest uses of prunes.

The practice of drying prunes supposedly originated in the Middle East. When the Romans took over the Middle East, they had pickled plums, but not prunes.

Location: Yuba City is about 40 miles north of Sacramento on California 99. **Contact:** California Prune Festival, P.O. Box 3006, Yuba City, CA 95992; Tel: (916)671-3100.

While You're There: Many of the food processing plants in the area give tours. Call first to make arrangements.

Colorado

Harvest Festival

Usually second weekend in October (Thursday through Sunday) If you think all western potatoes grow in Idaho, come to Colorado. The state is the number-one producer of summer potatoes, and a close second to Idaho in total potatoes harvested for fresh use. Colorado's not in the running for most potatoes processed into chips and dehydrated potatoes; it sticks to the spuds sold to grocery stores.

Some 90 percent of Colorado's potatoes, as well as carrots, spinach, and lettuce, are grown in the San Luis Valley, 90 miles long and 60 miles wide, running down to the New Mexico border. The valley is from 7,500 to 8,500 feet above sea level, surrounded by peaks of 14,000 feet, which protect it from severe winter conditions. It's the highest alpine valley in the nation, and has 78,000 acres growing potatoes, making it the *world's* largest alpine area producing major vegetable crops.

The festival has been going on since 1980, draws a few thousand people, and mixes art and potatoes. On Thursday and Friday evenings, concerts of classical music are presented, preceded by harvest suppers of Colorado products, including a potato dish, breads made from natural stone-ground flour (a mill is nearby), fruits of the state, and an apple dessert. Vendors sell things like roasted corn and Wisconsin cheese curds, and businessmen sell 10-pound bags of potatoes for 75 cents to help promote the potato industry.

A potato-recipe contest is held, and, after the tasting and judging, visitors can sample the entries, which often include potato brownies and spudnuts (potato doughnuts). Memorable dishes have included potato lasagna and a potato casserole made with chorizo (a spicy sausage), sliced potatoes, green chiles, and melted cheese.

Other events are 5K and 10K Tater Trots, a pancake breakfast on Saturday, and contests for big and ugly potatoes, for guessing the weight of a potato, and for potato-decorating. The latter is for youngsters up to the fifth grade. Their creations are an eyeful.

Location: Monte Vista is on U.S. 285, about 100 miles southwest of Pueblo. **Contact:** Monte Vista Chamber of Commerce, 1035 Park Ave., Monte Vista, CO 81144; Tel: (719)852-2731.

Rocky Ford

Watermelon Day

Saturday of third week in August ☼ Not too many places can boast a Watermelon Day that began in 1878 and was started by a man named Swink. But Rocky Ford can.

Watermelon Day is part of the Arkansas Valley Fair, a fair you have to have warm feelings about because it is "still too small to provide great ostentation," the promoters say. Less modest about watermelons, they say Otero County is the Watermelon Capital of the Nation.

State Senator George W. Swink started it all. He was a trading-post owner, timber farmer, and watermelon grower, not yet a senator, when he decided to share his watermelon harvest in 1878 (the date considered the start of the fair). About 25 people came to the Rocky Ford train depot in a Santa Fe caboose, and Swink gave them whole watermelons and slices. He continued the practice each summer, and the number of visitors kept increasing, and Swink kept bringing in more wagonloads of watermelons, and then he also gave away plums, grapes, and apples, and by 1884, the Rocky Ford women were even preparing a dinner.

One thing leads to another. Now the Arkansas Valley Fair takes place the third week in August, from Wednesday through Sunday, and everybody still gets a free watermelon on Watermelon Day; about 50,000 pounds are eaten or taken away. Rocky Ford melons tend to be small and round and very sweet. There are also watermelon jams, jellies, relishes, pickles, and breads for sale, and there's a barbecue.

Events of the day include a seed-spitting contest, a rolling-the-watermelon contest for kids, and a cantaloupe-throwing contest. (More acres are in cantaloupes than watermelons now.) During the fair, there are rodeos, horse shows, music, a flower show, and a parade on Friday.

Location: Rocky Ford is about 55 miles east of Pueblo on U.S. 50. ☼ **Contact:** Rocky Ford Chamber of Commerce, 105 N. Main St., Rocky Ford, CO 81067; Tel: (719)254-7483.

Silverton

International Rhubarb Festival

Fourth of July ☼ About all they can grow in Silverton are dandelions, horseradish, and rhubarb, because this town of 500 is 9,318 feet high and surrounded by mountains. There's not a single agricultural acre in the county. In 1906, the town was a mining camp, and about a third of the heads-of-households are still employed in mining.

In the early 1980s, a local rhubarb historian counted 390 rhubarb plants in town, and figured out that an Italian family immigrating to Silverton brought along rhubarb (which the wife called rabarbara in letters) because it was useful for treating diarrhea and was good to eat. As time went on, the woman split the rhubarb root and gave it to friends, and it proliferated.

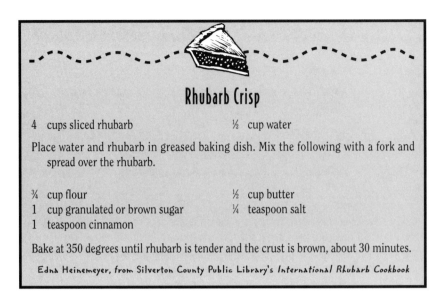

Rhubarb Crisp

4   cups sliced rhubarb   ½   cup water

Place water and rhubarb in greased baking dish. Mix the following with a fork and spread over the rhubarb.

¾   cup flour   ½   cup butter
1   cup granulated or brown sugar   ¼   teaspoon salt
1   teaspoon cinnamon

Bake at 350 degrees until rhubarb is tender and the crust is brown, about 30 minutes.

Edna Heinemeyer, from Silverton County Public Library's *International Rhubarb Cookbook*

The Silverton Public Library has sponsored the festival since 1982. Dozens of rhubarb pies are sold by the piece, and there are also rhubarb cakes, strudels, cookies, barbecued ribs with rhubarb sauce, punch, and ice cream.

For entertainment, a theater group puts on a matinee performance, there's a rhubarb-pie-eating contest, and, this being the Fourth of July, there are fireworks.

The main event, though, is the recipe contest. The library has published the *International Rhubarb Cookbook and Other Little Gems,* a combination history/ecology/recipe/odd facts book. It illustrates the ingenuity of Silverton cooks with contest-winning recipes for rhubarb brown betties, crisps, cobblers, cakes, pies, puddings, and mousses, as well as cordials, punches, coolers, and daiquiris. And rhubarb toothpaste.

Location: Between Montrose and Durango, on U.S. 550. ☼ **Contact:** Silverton Public Library, P.O. Box 68, Silverton, CO 81433; Tel: (970)387-5770.

While You're There: Buy a buffalo burger at Handlebars Food & Saloon and eat it on the Durango & Silverton Narrow Gauge Railroad, a coal-burning passenger train built in 1882.

See Also: Rhubarb Fest (Intercourse, PA).

Hawaii

East Maui Taro Festival

Last weekend in March (Friday through Sunday) When the Polynesians came to the Hawaiian Islands sometime around A.D. 400, they brought taro with them, and from the earliest days the staple of Hawaii has been poi, made from taro roots. In ancient days, Hawaiians grew more than 300 varieties of taro, but just eight edible varieties are grown on the islands now. Poi, a sticky mash, is eaten with the fingers and is made in three grades: one-finger, two-finger, and three-finger. The more watery it is, the more fingers you need to scoop it up; thus, one-finger poi is the thickest.

The festival was started in 1993, and a few thousand attend, far more than Hana's population of about 700. Because the purpose of the festival is to promote taro and the Hawaiian culture, there's poi to eat—as an accompaniment to meat, possibly pig steamed in an underground oven, or fish or chicken. You can also try taro in other ways—cooked like a potato in stews, converted to flour and used in Portuguese *malasadas* (deep-fried holeless doughnuts), pancakes, or chips.

You'll find explanations of the taro and its nutritional qualities and cooking presentations. You'll learn how to make poi: boil the taro corms or tubers, then mash them with a pestle in a mortar, mixing with water. The mash can be eaten fresh or allowed to sit a few days to ferment, giving it an acidic taste.

The festival also offers plenty of other Hawaiian foods, farmers' markets (Maui onions and all kinds of fruit), hula dance troupes, Hawaiian music and chants, and an art exhibit.

Hana is on the "other side" of Maui, meaning the east side. It takes about 2½ hours to drive the 52-mile road around the base of Haleakala Crater to Hana, maneuvering 617 hairpin turns and 54 one-lane bridges. But the scenery is breathtaking: waterfalls, mango, guava, and banana trees, and then the pastures of the Hana Ranch rolling right up to the main street.

Location: Most events are at Hana Ball Park. To get to Hana, drive the Hana road, or fly to the town's airstrip on a local carrier. **Contact:** East Maui Taro Festival, Box 111, Hana, Maui, HI 96713; Tel: (808)248-8972.

Hilo (Hawaii)

Hilo Macadamia Nut Festival

Last Saturday in October ❀ Macadamia nuts, native to Australia, got their name because the botanist who first described the nut named it in honor of his friend, Dr. John Macadam, who was an early promoter of the nut as something good to eat.

In Australia, they were primarily grown as ornamentals, but in 1921 Ernest Shelton van Tassel, a Massachusetts man, imported some to Hawaii to grow them commercially. They didn't do too well, leading to 20 years of research by the University of Hawaii. It wasn't until some large firms entered the macadamia industry that production was in significant amounts. That was the 1950s, and the nuts started being marketed under the Mauna Loa Macadamia Nut brand in 1976.

So it's a fairly young industry, but now about 18,500 acres are harvested in all of Hawaii, with most of the acres on the Big Island, Hawaii, and smaller orchards on Maui, Oahu, and Kauai. Roasted, lightly salted nuts are shipped all over the world.

At the festival, about 7,000 to 9,000 people honor the nut with Hawaiian music, hula dancing, a Nut Orchard Fun Run, a parade, crafts exhibits, chefs' demonstrations (of dishes like Pan-Fried Macadamia Nut Sweetbread Pudding with Guava Butter and Whipped Cream), and food booths. Food vendors all have to use macadamia nuts in something they're serving, and so the nuts are in desserts, Chinese foods, and in the popular *malasadas,* Portuguese holeless doughnuts, deep-fried and rolled in sugar and finely chopped macadamias.

Macadamia nuts are supposed to be the toughest nut to crack. Old-timers put nuts under boards and drove their cars over them to crack the shells, but now the nuts are passed between rotating steel rollers.

Hawaii is good for macadamias because of the abundant rainfall, good drainage in the volcanic soil, and a long growing season. A number of other countries also grow them, with Australia, Guatemala, the Republic of South Africa, and Costa Rica among the largest producers. Their rising popularity is attributed to an unusual creamy flavor and a crisp-light texture.

Location: Nani Mau Gardens, about three miles south of the Hilo International Airport. ❀ **Contact:** Mauna Loa Macadamia Nut Corp., H.C. 01 Box 3, Hilo, HI 96720; Tel: (808)966-9301, Fax: (808)966-8410.

While You're There: At the Mauna Loa Macadamia Nut Visitor Center, see the roasting process, watch nut chocolates made, and taste free samples.

Kaanapali (Maui)

Maui Onion Festival

First weekend in August ❀ The sweet onion that grows in Maui has been described as so sweet that it seems as though it's been soaked in sugar water.

It's an onion of the Granex variety, the same variety as the Vidalia onion of Georgia and a close cousin of Texas sweet onions. Champions of each onion say their onion is the sweetest, and in Maui they chalk the sweetness up to the volcanic soil on the slopes of Haleakala, where the onion grows.

You can decide for yourself how sweet it is at the Maui festival, which has onion rings available in all sorts of variations, Maui onion pizza, and sandwiches of sausage, pepper, and Maui onion.

Resort chefs create onion dishes, demonstrate how to prepare them (with the help of overhead mirrors and microphones), and allow spectators to sample their creations. You will see how to make such dishes as gumbo, salad dressing, braided bread, spring rolls, tomato salad with goat cheese, egg rolls, sushi, and chicken barbecue, all, of course, containing Maui onions.

There's also a recipe contest, with elaborate presentations judged on taste and presentation in categories of appetizers and entrees.

A contest of a different ilk is the Maui-onion-eating contest for juniors (under age 16) and seniors. The first 10 to sign up at the event participate. Each entrant gets a bowl with three-quarters of a pound of onion, which is usually a whole onion and some bits to make up the weight. The contestants have 45 seconds to eat as much as possible. Sweet though they may be, no one has ever eaten all the onion. The first prize is $100.

The festival is presented in part to benefit the local humane society, and a parade of pets, including ones available for adoption, is one of the favorite events. There are also displays of crafts and a market of Maui produce. The event began in 1990 and attracts about 5,000 visitors.

Location: Whalers Village, Kaanapali, west shore of Maui. ✸ **Contact:** SANTOS!PR, Barbara Santos, P.O. Box 537, Puunene, HI 97684; Tel: (808)875-0457.

See Also: Vidalia Onion Festival (Vidalia, GA) and Walla Walla Sweet Onion Harvest Festival (Walla Walla, WA).

Kailua-Kona (Hawaii)

Kona Coffee Cultural Festival

Usually first two weeks of November, about 10 days ✸
Hawaii's oldest festival honors one of its oldest commercial crops, Kona coffee, known for its strong, rich character. The Kona coffee belt is a 20-mile strip that runs along the western slopes of Hawaii's two great mountains, Mauna Loa and Mauna Kea, and the festival events, centered in Kailua-Kona, take place throughout this Big Island region.

Experts say there are three factors that make Kona coffee (which is the arabica variety) so good: prime growing conditions, sun in the morning and clouds in the afternoon; fertile volcanic soil, giving a sweetness to the coffee; and hand picking, which means only the ripest coffee cherries are picked.

Hand-picked Kona coffee beans are celebrated at Hawaii's oldest festival, the Kona Coffee Cultural Festival. (Current Events)

The festival began in 1971 and organizers have brewed up dozens of events: a grand parade and an evening lantern parade; tours of coffee farms and mills; a coffee-farm fair, featuring cooking demonstrations, coffee displays, food vendors, and orchid exhibits; and dancing, eating, and art exhibits.

The Kona Coffee Cupping Competition is the growers' big event. It's like a wine-tasting, with judges swirling and grading brewed coffee and sniffing green and roasted beans. The public may taste private-label Kona coffees while the competition is under way, and one of the judges gives a seminar on coffee tasting.

A Kona Coffee Recipe Contest has divisions for amateur and professional cooks; each recipe must contain half a cup or more of 100 percent Kona coffee. There's a special prize for the best entry using both Kona coffee and macadamia nuts.

Past winners have included a simple-sounding Kailua boiled dinner that turns out to be roasted pork loin with a coffee and brandy ("generous portion" specified) sauce, and Kona coffee cappuccino cheesecake.

There are also coffee-picking and coffee-lei contests. And there's a steak fry, a brunch featuring local products, and luau food at the coffee queen's luncheon.

Kailua Boiled Dinner

Sear outer portion of smoked pork loin in a roasting pan, add:

5 potatoes (cubed)	2 round onions (oblique cut)
3 carrots (oblique cut)	1 tablespoon cracked black pepper

Stir until all vegetables are coated with fat from pork loin, deglaze with Brandy (generous portion), add:

½ cup Kona coffee, dry roasted	3 quarts demi glaze

Stir all together. Place in roasting pan in oven and continue to cook as you would a New England Boiled Dinner for approximately 2 hours. Remove from oven and bring to a boil on stove top.

Steam 10 potatoes, peeled, until tender. Gently whip as you would regular potatoes. Add 1 part cream, 1 part Baileys Irish Cream to desired stiffness, add 2 egg yolks and salt and pepper to taste.

Matthew Pike, King Kamahameha's Kona Beach Hotel; 1995 recipe contest winner, professional division—entrée

Coffee first came to the islands in 1813 as ornamental trees brought to Honolulu by King Kamehameha's Spanish doctor. Cuttings from these were planted by a missionary in Kona in 1828 or 1829. Originally coffee was grown on big plantations owned by white settlers, but when the coffee market crashed in 1899, the growing shifted to small Japanese-owned farms. Today there are about 200 small independent farmers making up the Kona coffee industry. Hawaii is the only state in the United States where coffee is grown commercially.

Coffee blooms in the spring, and the white blossoms are called Kona snow; harvesting of the ripe red cherries is from July through January. About 95 percent of the cherries have two seeds. The outer red skin is removed by pulping, and then the drying process removes parchment-like skins, and then the beans are roasted.

Location: Throughout Kona region on Big Island. **Contact:** Kona Coffee Cultural Festival, P.O. Box 1112, Kailua-Kona, HI 96745; Tel: (808)326-7820, Fax: (808)326-5634.

Idaho

Cherry Festival

Second weekend in June ❁ A network of canals irrigating western Idaho has transformed an arid valley into a land of orchards growing cherries, plums, peaches, grapes, and apples, and row crops including sugar beets, onions, and beans—70 cash crops in all. Idaho ranks eighth among states in the production of sweet cherries, and 16,000 people get together at the festival to celebrate this juicy statistic.

To keep them smiling, there are cherry cobblers, ice cream, cookies, cakes, pies, and plenty of fresh cherries. Other foods include regional specialties like Basque sausage, and the more standard hamburgers and barbecued beef ribs. When it's time to sit around and think about food, there's a beer garden.

After thinking, there are things to do: There are a cherry-pie-eating contest and a cherry-pit-spitting contest. There are hot-air balloon races, children's games, live music, a parade, and an art show.

The festival began way back in 1934, by which time it was safe for people to get together in Emmett. Pickett's Corral in the foothills east of Emmett had been a notorious "robbers' roost," home base for a band of road agents and horse thieves. A vigilante group wiped out the nest of ruffians in the late 1800s.

Location: Emmett City Park. Emmett is about 25 miles west of Boise on Idaho 52. ❁ **Contact:** Emmett Chamber of Commerce, P.O. Box 592, Emmett, ID 83617; Tel: (208)436-4793.

Idaho Spud Day

Third Saturday in September ❁ Today Idaho is the Potato Capital of the World, and it seems as though it's always been that way. But it was a long, winding road to Idaho's potato capitalism—from the Andes to Europe to Maine and finally to Idaho.

Spanish conquistadors discovered potatoes in the South American Andes in 1537 and took them to Europe. They weren't an immediate hit. Scots wouldn't eat them because they weren't mentioned in the Bible. Others were wary of a vegetable related to the poisonous nightshade. The French considered them flowers and Marie-Antoinette wore the blossoms in her hair. Then scientist Antoine-Auguste Parmentier started growing them and experimenting with potato dishes, and soon potatoes were everywhere—and today the word *parmentier* means a food garnished or made with potatoes.

Partly because of Parmentier, Idaho now celebrates its number-one rating in potato production in the United States with Spud Day, which dates back to 1928 and attracts 7,000 to 10,000 people. The celebrating takes strange turns: wrestling in big mounds of mashed potatoes and team competitions to peel the most potatoes in 45 minutes—1,064 pounds and six ounces was a long-standing record. Others compete in potato picking and dutch-oven potato cooking.

The festival trademarks are a big parade and 5,000 baked potatoes given away. There are also spuds fried, scalloped, and mashed, and standard festival dishes.

Potatoes came to North America in the mid-1700s via Scotch-Irish immigrants. Thomas Jefferson served French fries in the White House. Maine started growing potatoes in the early 1800s and became the nation's major producer until Idaho and Washington outspudded it in 1958.

Potatoes are easily grown, and after they first caught on in Europe, they became an inexpensive staple. The Irish grew them almost exclusively, and when the fungus *Phytophthora infestans* killed the plants in 1845, the result was the Great Potato Famine of Ireland. At least a million people died, and more than a million sought refuge in North America in the famine years 1845–1851.

One of the great accomplishments of Luther Burbank, the horticulturist, was his development in 1872 of the blight-resistant Russet Burbank potato—a long, white potato with a russet skin now known as the Idaho potato.

It was unthinkable in Burbank's time to envision Idaho as a major grower of anything, since the state was mostly mountains and volcanic desert. But it had the Snake River. Irrigation was introduced in 1894, giving Idaho a lot of arable acres, and by the 1950s, agriculture was the state's main source of income. Today Idaho growers produce about 100 million 100-pound bags of potatoes annually, a quarter of the nation's crop.

P.S. There are thousands of varieties of potato, but the sweet potato is not one of them.

Location: Shelley City Park, seven miles south of Idaho Falls. **Contact:** Shelley Chamber of Commerce, Box 301, Shelley, ID 83274; Tel: (208)357-7661; Fax: (208)357-3435.

See Also: Maine Potato Blossom Festival (Fort Fairfield, ME).

Montana

Rocky Mountain Oyster Feed

Third weekend in September (Thursday through Sunday) In cowboy country, some cuts of beef are considered gourmet delicacies, and Rocky Mountain oysters, another name for testicles, are so considered. The feed has been going on since 1982, when a few hundred people came; now about 9,000 come and eat more than 4,500 pounds of the Montana tendergroin (as they also call the "oysters"). The oysters are marinated, breaded, and cooked in deep fat, then served with Texas toast (grilled bread) and beans. For non-gourmets, chicken strips are available.

Besides food, the festival offers nonstop country music, and it's held at the Rock Creek Lodge, where there is a bar, casino, and gift shop selling items such as postcards and posters of a life-size sculpture of Ol' Testy, a bull.

Location: Clinton is 22 miles east of Missoula on I-90 at exit 126. **Contact:** Rock Creek Lodge Testicle Festival, Box 825, Clinton, MT 59825; Tel: (406)825-4968; Fax: (406)825-4062.

See Also: Calf Fry Festival (Vinita, OK).

Montana State Chokecherry Festival

Saturday after Labor Day The chokecherry, a North American native that's a variety of wild cherry, grows along the creeks of Lewistown, and people start picking them in August to beat the birds to them. The cherries grow in clusters, almost like grapes, and when ripe, they're deep purple-black, about the size of peas, and bitter tasting. But they make good pies, cakes, jams, jellies, syrup, and even wine, so that's the reason they celebrate them.

The festival features a chokecherry-pie cook-off, and some recipes are quite gourmetish; one year's winner was a chokecherry cordial pie. There's a pit-spitting contest too, and the cherry's bitter taste, they say, makes for the "pucker power" that sends pits into orbit.

A pet show, parade, 100 arts-and-crafts booths, a rubber-duck race, a farmers' market, and a taste of Lewistown, providing samples of food (including dishes using chokecherries) from local restaurants, round out the festival, which began in 1990.

Lewistown was established as a trading post in 1876, and is still a trading center for the cattle ranchers and wheat farmers of the area. A few thousand come here on chokecherry day.

Location: Lewistown is about 100 miles north of Billings on I-94. **Contact:** Lewistown Area Chamber of Commerce, 408 N.E. Main St., Box 818, Lewistown, MT 59457; Tel: (406)538-5436.

Libby

Nordicfest

First weekend after Labor Day Hundreds of Norwegians who had been living in Minnesota came to this northwest corner of Montana in the late 1880s to work at lumber mills. Earlier, Libby had been a mining town, named for the daughter of one of the men who found gold in a nearby creek. In the 1900s, mines were closed, and timber harvesting was in decline. Late in the century, it began to seem that tourism was the means to survival.

That's why Nordicfest began in 1985. There were a few people and one Fjord horse at the first fest; now about 12,000 people and up to 100 Fjord horses gather to celebrate Nordic culture and food. Food booths provide sustenance during the day, and on Friday and Saturday nights Nordic dinners feature *arta suppa,* yellow-pea soup; ham loaf with cabbage; Swedish meatballs; lutefisk; ham loaf with cherry sauce; Danish pickled cucumbers; *lefse,* a sweet crepe; rhubarb dessert; and assorted accompaniments. Breakfasts on Saturday and Sunday fill you up with Scandinavian pastries and Swedish pancakes.

There's a full schedule of entertainment (quilt and antique shows, a juried craft show, fiddlers), but the highlight is the International Fjord Horse Show. Fjords are draft horses, a breed dating back to when Norse soldiers wore armor and carried heavy spears. They were first introduced to the United States in about 1888. They are small for draft horses, standing about 14 hands high, compared to Clydesdales, which average 18 hands, and are so gentle they've been called the "cocker spaniels of the horse world."

The Fjord's most distinguishing feature is its mane. When trimmed, it stands as stiff as brush bristles, with a streak of black hair splitting the blond hair on either side.

Location: Libby is about 60 miles west of Kalispell on U.S. 2. **Contact:** Libby Nordicfest, P.O. Box 791, Libby, MT 59923; Tel: (406)293-7747.

While You're There: The Heritage Museum displays artifacts of American Indians, trappers, miners, and lumbermen. Agricultural exhibits are also displayed.

Nevada

National Basque Festival

Fourth of July weekend or first weekend after July 4 (Friday through Sunday) ☼ The Basques were sheepherders and fishermen at home in the Pyrenees of France and Spain, and when they trickled into the United States throughout the 1900s, many went west to where the sheep were. They led lonely shepherding lives, but at the same time developed a distinctive outdoor-cooking cuisine and the custom of summertime celebrations.

The number of sheep ranches has declined, the remaining sheepherders are not all Basques, and not all Basques are sheepherders. Paul Laxalt, a sheepherder's son, was governor of Nevada.

But celebrations continue. The Elko festival began in the early 1960s and is the largest of several Basque festivals held in Nevada and Idaho, with attendance between 5,000 and 6,000. The food is hearty.

The most popular item is *chorizo,* a garlicky pork sausage served plain with no condiments, the way it's eaten on the range. People also put away vast amounts of Basque beans (pinto beans with pork or lamb), roasted onions and garlic, and, on Sunday, lamb (cooked on a spit) and beef dinners, followed by wine cake. There's also brandy-spiked coffee and red wine that was traditionally drunk from a goatskin *bota.*

A bake-off is held for the best sheepherders' bread, which is baked in a covered Dutch oven over hot bricks placed in a pit.

Festivities include folk dancing with dancers in Basque costume, a parade to celebrate both the Basque heritage and the Fourth of July, sheepdog demonstrations, and contests of strength—log chopping, tug-of-war, and weight-lifting, in which men lift 300-pound steel cylinders shoulder high. One of the more memorable events is the *Irrintzi* (Basque war cry) contest. Competitors try for the longest and loudest yell.

The origin of the Basque language is unknown; it's unlike any other European language. A sample: "Osagarria" is a toast meaning "The good life."

Location: Elko is in northern Nevada on I-80. ⊛ **Contact:** Basque Club, P.O. Box 1321, Elko, NV 89803; Tel: (702)738-7991.

Genoa

Genoa Candy Dance

Last full weekend in September ⊛ This is called a dance, and once that's all it was, but it has evolved into a full-fledged festival, with about 30,000 visitors.

On the night of the dance, you can get a substantial buffet dinner, and sandwiches and hamburgers are available during the days. But the point of this festival is candy—3,000 pounds of candy, all made by the ladies of Genoa, which has a population of about 200.

The ladies, whose mothers or grandmothers or great-grandmothers started making candy for the first dance in 1919 to raise money to buy streetlights, are famous for their nut fudge, plain fudge, turtles, almond roca, brittle, dipped chocolates, divinity, and mints, to name a few. And homemade cookies.

These candies are the sweet heart of what is now a two-day affair that raises money for snow removal, maintenance of public buildings and streets, insurance, the Genoa Town Park, etc. Residents' property taxes are about nil.

Lillian Virgin Finnegan had the idea for the first Candy Dance, a midnight supper and dance at the Raycraft Dance Hall. Homemade candies, an afterthought, were the hit of the evening. So the Candy Dance has continued, still Saturday night, still at the same hall, which is now the Town Hall. Other events include an arts and crafts fair, an egg toss, a "revue/melodramer," candy-cookbook sales, and, of course, candy sales, all day both days, or until they're gone.

Location: Genoa is 12 miles south of Carson City, off U.S. 395. ⊛ **Contact:** Candy Dance Committee, P.O. Box 155, Genoa, NV 889411; Tel: (800)727-7677.

Sparks

Cinqo de Mayo Fiesta Nevada Celebration

First weekend in May (Friday through Sunday) ⊛ They're a bit casual about specific dates in Sparks. The Mexican holiday, Cinqo de Mayo, is sometimes celebrated before or after the fifth of May. Furthermore, it lasts three days. But why quibble? This is a popular fiesta, with attendance at about 40,000. Sparks has a large Mexican-American community; many originally came for jobs in railroading when the Southern Pacific created this twin city to Reno by establishing a rail center here in 1904.

The fiesta showcases not only Mexican culture but the heritage of other Latin and South American countries with music, a Latin marketplace, costumed entertainment, and folkloric dancing.

And the food is as Cinqo de Mayo as you could wish: all kinds of tacos, several kinds of chilis, beef and chicken fajitas, chicken enchiladas, burritos, ribs with Mexican lime sauce. Hot stuff, like jalapeño poppers; mild stuff, like empanadas; sweet stuff, like fresh fruit and chocolate-dipped fruit. You have your choice on the second, third, fourth, cinqo or whatever of May in Sparks.

Location: Victorian Square, Sparks, off I-80. **Contact:** Redevelopment Agency, P.O. Box 857, Sparks, NV 89432; Tel: (702)353-2291.

New Mexico

Inter-Tribal Indian Ceremonial

Usually second Tuesday in August (through Sunday) ☼ The Gallup ceremonial, the oldest celebration of American Indian heritage, began in 1922 as an "Indian Pageant and Exposition." Now it's a gathering of about 75,000 who come to see some 20 North American tribes stage dance performances, rodeos, and displays of traditional jewelry, rugs, kachina dolls, basketry, beadwork, pottery, painting, and sculpture.

This is the grandfather of all inter-tribal Indian powwows, and one of America's oldest ethnic dance festivals. The dances range from Pima coming-out or puberty dances to the Navajo Ribbon Dance. Since most dances have religious meaning, and weren't originally meant to be public performances, the ones presented are altered somewhat or are those that the tribes have decided are not so sensitive they would violate tribal mores.

On the food side, there's a grand barbecue, meals in the cafeteria, fair-style food in concessions booths, and authentic Indian food in the Native American booths. Among the latter are corn roasted in the husk, fry bread, roast mutton wrapped in fry bread, Pueblo green chile stew (sometimes with mutton), tamales made with a corn husk, and Navajo tacos, which are fry bread topped with chili, beans, meat, cheese, lettuce, and tomato. *Hornos*, adobe ovens that are a legacy of the Spanish, are set up by the Zunis, and big round loaves of soda bread come from them. People wait in lines for up to 20 minutes to get bread from their favorite cook.

The highlight of the ceremonial is the grand nonmechanized parade (although sometimes there's a vehicle for the grand marshal), a one-hour circuit through town, filled with the sounds of rattles and drums, colorful with dancers and paraders in costume.

Location: Red Rock State Park, six miles east of downtown Gallup on I-40. ☼ **Contact:** Gallup Convention and Visitors Bureau, P.O. Box 600, Gallup, NM 87301; Tel: (505)863-3841, or (800)242-4282.

While You're There: Red Rock Museum, in the park, has exhibits on the prehistoric Anasazi up through present-day Native American tribes. In the summer, wildflower gardens and Pueblo "waffle gardens" of corn, beans, and squash are grown.

Hatch

Hatch Chile Festival

Labor Day weekend (Saturday and Sunday) ✦ Chiles are the state's top cash-producing food crop, and Dona Ana County, where Hatch is, seems to be covered with chiles. Those facts have a direct relationship to what happens to the Hatch airport in late summer; a hangar turns into a big tangy market of chiles and chile dishes, and people strolling around in cowboy hats eating and talking about the best way to make chile. (In New Mexico, both plant and stew are called chile.)

There's an official answer to this with the cooking contest, in which recipes have to be totally original. Some of the winners have been red-chile bread and chile noodles. Needless to say, Hispanic dishes—tamales, enchiladas, empanadas—make up most of the entries.

There's also a contest for growers competing to produce the best quality chiles; what's called the long mild is the most widely raised chile, and the jalapeño is in second place, accounting for about a quarter of all chiles grown in the state.

Chile meals are served both days. Chile con carne simmers at the back of the hangar and is served with tortillas and beans and chile enchiladas and chile tamales.

Other events include carnival rides, a Saturday night dance, an art show that features paintings of chiles, and the crowning of a chile queen.

Location: Hatch is about 70 miles north of El Paso, TX, off I-25. ✦ **Contact:** Hatch Chamber of Commerce, P.O. Box 38, Hatch, NM 87937; Tel: (505)2667-5050.

See Also: La Fiesta de los Chiles (Tucson, AZ).

Las Cruces

New Mexico Wine & Chile War Festival

Memorial Day weekend (Saturday through Monday) ✦ Four centuries ago, European settlers brought grapes to the Rio Grande valley, and by the nineteenth century vineyards and wineries were flourishing from Bernalillo, near Santa Fe, to the Mexican border.

Chiles have been growing in the Southwest approximately forever, and Las Cruces is the county seat of Dona Ana County, where up to 30 percent of the state's chiles are grown.

In 1989, the New Mexico Wine Festival began, bringing together 15 state wineries that present more than 50 wines. The entrance ticket allows visitors to taste all the wines.

In 1993, war was added to the wine festival. That year, the New Mexico legislature declared war on Texas and called for a competition to see which state has the best chile (meaning the dish). Amateur and professional chefs compete separately in five categories: red, green, unique, salsa, and Texas chile. There's also a best-chile-salsa competition for home cooks, with audience judging.

Furthermore, the long weekend begins with a chile cook-off sponsored by the Chili Appreciation Society International, and conducted according to CASI rules.

To keep the chile warriors happy, there are entertainers and an art show, and lots of wine and food. The food is largely chile dishes—green chile egg rolls, green chile stew— along with southwestern favorites such as fajitas, sopapillas, cornmeal tortillas stuffed with fried meat, lettuce, and tomatoes, and lots of chips and salsa.

National sales of salsa, by the way, overtook catsup in 1991.

Location: Southern New Mexico State Fairgrounds, off I-10. Las Cruces is about 175 miles south of Albuquerque, near the Mexican border. **Contact:** Las Cruces Convention Bureau, 211 N. Water St., Las Cruces, NM 88001; Tel: (800)FIESTAS.

See Also: La Fiesta de los Chiles (Tucson, AZ).

Whole Enchilada Fiesta

First weekend in October (Friday through Sunday) Las Cruces loves festivals and has lots of them, but the Whole Enchilada Fiesta is what puts the town on the map. A ten-foot-long enchilada, supposedly the World's Biggest Enchilada, is created as the climactic event Sunday when giant tortillas, made with 185 pounds of masa (corn flour), are lifted from 75 gallons of bubbling oil and smothered in 60 gallons of red chile sauce and 175 pounds of cheese. The 100,000 fiesta-goers scramble to get a bite and pretty soon it's adios enchilada.

Enchiladas are tortillas layered with cheese and sometimes chicken or meat and bathed in chile sauce. The Las Cruces enchilada is basic enchilada.

There's more food to be had at the fiesta, though. The Farmers' Market has a kind of mishmash of German pretzels, Mexican chile sauce, pecan pies, chile jelly, chile cakes and cookies, chile with eggs or a hamburger, enchiladas. And burritos, which are flour tortillas rolled around all kinds of fillings (chopped meat, refried beans, grated cheese, etc.) with chile on top. And chiles rellenos, meaning stuffed peppers; these are cheese-stuffed mild green chiles, dipped in a batter and fried. Locally grown pecan, piñon, and macadamia nuts are also for sale.

The weekend activities include street dances, arts and crafts, a rodeo, horseshoe contests, mariachi and country music, and a children's playground.

The fiesta began in 1985 to spotlight chiles, the area's major crop. Las Cruces claims to have 350 sunny days a year, conducive to growing fine chiles.

Location: Downtown Mall of Las Cruces. **Contact:** Las Cruces Chamber of Commerce, 201 N. Church St., Ste. 308, Las Cruces, NM 88001; Tel: (505)523-8808.

While You're There: The nearby Stahmann Farms, one of the world's largest pecan growers, can be visited. On New Mexico 28, 7 miles south of Las Cruces.

Santa Fe

Santa Fe Wine & Chile Fiesta

Last weekend in September (Thursday through Sunday) This is an Occasion—a classy, expensive, and fascinating eat-drink-and-learn long weekend.

The fiesta's big event is the Grand Food & Wine Tasting; it features more than 180 different vintages of wine from more than 60 world-class wineries alongside food pairings from 60 of Santa Fe's restaurants. Among the dishes at a recent tasting were chipolte-stuffed chicken (chipoltes are smoked jalapeño chiles), grilled antelope with polenta, and fillet of beef with chile sauces.

A sample of other highlights is the trip to a farm in Abiquiu to see the heritage beans and chiles grown there, enjoy a garden luncheon, and then tour painter Georgia O'Keeffe's cliffside home. There are wine and food seminars, cooking demonstrations by nationally known chefs, and horseback rides. On Friday and Saturday, the rides end with mesa-top campfire breakfasts; the Sunday ride is followed by a champagne brunch.

Not for Joe Six-Pack.

Location: Throughout Santa Fe. **Contact:** Santa Fe Wine & Chile Fiesta, 115 E. Water St., Santa Fe, NM 87501; Tel: (505)982-8686, Fax: (505)982-9168.

Oregon

Astoria-Warrenton Crab and Seafood Festival

Last full weekend in April (Friday through Sunday) ☼ The 30 food vendors and 30 wineries at the crab festival give an ample sample of what's good to eat and drink in Oregon. Among the drinks are not only Oregon grape wines but a number of fruit wines—blackberry, peach, currant, and cranberry. The seafood menu includes all kinds of shellfish as well as salmon and tuna; the dessert menu features hazelnut brittle because Oregon is big in nuts, especially hazelnuts.

The festival tantalizes. Where to begin? With the dinner of Dungeness crab accompanied by baked beans, salad, and garlic bread? Or with the barbecued oysters on the half shell with a special seasoning and Parmesan? Or should it be the teriyaki barbecued tuna, or the salmon chowder, or the shrimp cocktail?

Other choices are grilled Willapa Bay oysters, which some call "the sweetest oysters you can find in the world"; cold smoked oysters on a skewer; shrimp or crab melt on French bread with a top-secret buttery sauce; rounds of French garlic bread with crab and a Brie dip. Non-seafood is available, too.

For entertainment, there are three or four bands that play everything from country to rock; helicopter and boat rides; a carnival; and about 120 crafts vendors.

Astoria, the first permanent settlement west of the Mississippi, dates from the winter of 1805–1806, when Lewis and Clark camped here at the mouth of the Columbia River, which was chock-full of salmon then. Fort Astoria was built in 1811 by the fur-trading company that made John Jacob Astor rich, and in the coming decades Astoria was a city that rivaled San Francisco in splendor; the Victorian homes attest to that. Warrenton was built in 1891 on tidal flats; dikes keep the town dry.

The festival, held since 1983, is attended by about 12,000.

A newer festival, started in 1996, is the OktoberFisht, held in October and featuring beer from state microbreweries, salmon and tuna, and a newly created dish: salmonwurst.

Location: The Crab and Seafood Festival is held at the Hammond Mooring Basin in Warrenton, just off U.S. 101 in the northernmost corner of the state. OktoberFisht is held at the Clatsop County Fairgrounds in Astoria on Oregon 202. ⬚ **Contact:** For either festival, contact the Astoria-Warrenton Chamber of Commerce, P.O. Box 176, Astoria, OR 97103; Tel: (503)325-6311, Fax: (503)325-9767.

Bandon

Bandon Cranberry Festival

Usually last weekend in September (Friday through Sunday) ⬚ A Massachusetts man named Charles Dexter McFarlin went west to pan for gold in California, but he didn't find any, so he had his brother send him some cranberries from his home state's Cape Cod. In 1885, McFarlin planted his first bog (which is still producing), said he was "mining for red gold," and now that's what people in Oregon call cranberrying.

The harvest of red gold has been celebrated every fall since 1947. Several thousand people come for a parade, dances, an art show, wood-carving demonstrations, bog tours, a talk and video on cranberries, and homemade cranberry foods for sale. There's a cranberry cooking contest, where entrants invent all kinds of muffins, jellies, barbecue sauces, and molds, and the winner is called Queen of the Kitchen. The Lions also put on a beef barbecue.

Cranberries were growing wild on Oregon's Clatsop Plain south of the Columbia River well before McFarlin came along. They were an important part of the diets of the Quinault and Queet Indians, and Lewis and Clark are known to have bought berries from the natives of the region. Later, bogs were built by Chinese laborers, and cranberries helped prevent scurvy in logging camps and mining communities.

Today Oregon growers produce about 100,000 tons of cranberries a year on about 750 acres, and account for about four percent of all the cranberries grown in the United States.

Most of the world's cranberries are cultivated in five states, Massachusetts, Wisconsin, New Jersey, Oregon, and Washington, with another 4,000 acres in British Columbia and other parts of Canada. Oregon may not have a giant share of cranberries, but Oregonians say they're redder than East Coast berries.

Location: Bandon is on U.S. 101 on the Pacific coast, about 70 miles from the Canada border. ⬚ **Contact:** Bandon Chamber of Commerce, P.O. Box 1515, Bandon, OR 97411; Tel: (541)347-7006.

See Also: Massachusetts Cranberry Harvest Festival (South Carver, MA).

Charleston

Charleston Seafood Festival

Third weekend in August (Friday through Sunday) ⬚ This homage to seafood began in 1989 to promote the fishing industry, which is *the* way of life in Charleston. The village is on the tip of the "thumb" area of Oregon that has the Pacific on the west and Coos Bay on the east, where halibut, salmon, snapper, tuna, and oysters abound. Crabbing and clamming are major pastimes for non-commercial seafood-loving dilettantes.

The festival features four bands, crafts booths, harbor tours, and the Sea Woman, an exotically garbed figure who tells stories of the sea to children (adults can listen in).

But the focus is food. Local groups prepare and sell Chinook salmon, Dungeness crab, tuna, shrimp, and lingcod, an ugly Pacific-coast fish with a huge mouth and sharp teeth but a mildly sweet flavor.

About 10,000 attend the festival.

Location: Charleston is about eight miles southwest of the North Bend exit from U.S. 101. **Contact:** Charleston Bay Chamber of Commerce, P.O. Box 5883, Charleston, OR 97420; Tel: (800)824-8486.

Mt. Angel

Mt. Angel Oktoberfest

Weekend after Labor Day (Thursday through Sunday)
This little Willamette Valley town with less than 3,000 souls is jammed with 350,000 people during Oktoberfest, the biggest folk festival in the Northwest. The town was founded in the 1850s by Swiss and German immigrants who came over the Oregon Trail to the fertile valley beneath Mt. Hood. It seemed like home, and they stayed, and the town retains its German character, celebrating Bach in late July, the harvest at Oktoberfest.

In the food category, the festival features schnitzel—even has a Schnitzelgarten. Schnitzel, which means cutlet, is made by pounding the meat flat and thin, and breading and frying it. Wienerschnitzel is veal, and schweineschnitzel is pork.

The Schnitzelgarten sells its schnitzel in a sandwich, with cold German potato salad and a garlic-dill pickle. The schnitzel sandwich was almost unknown in Germany until American soldiers on maneuver, not having time to sit and eat, would go to gasthauses and ask for schnitzel between bread. Now schnitzel sandwiches are a permanent fixture in Germany.

Other foods with a history include all kinds of sausages, many made in a local food plant; Swiss cheese fondue for dipping locally grown vegetables; *Brathendl,* a barbecued half-chicken; *koenigsklopes,* sweet-and-sour meatballs; sauerbraten; stuffed cabbage rolls; soft Bavarian pretzels. The Benedictine sisters from the Mt. Angel Abbey and Queen of Angels Monastery prepare breads and coffee cakes, homemade pies, and strudels.

Foods are sold from more than 60 booths designed to look like Bavarian chalets. All are operated by nonprofit groups, and through the years, Oktoberfest has enabled them to donate more than $1.25 million to worthwhile causes. In addition, there are a Biergarten, a Weingarten, a Microgarten, all offering food, wine, beer, and music.

The Kindergarten has entertainment for kids—magic shows, clowns, puppets, rides— and the Cabaret Magnifique is a troupe of singers and dancers who perform show tunes during 19 performances.

The Mt. Angel Oktoberfest is the biggest folk festival in the Northwest, attracting crowds of 350,000. (Oktoberfest, Mt. Angel, Oregon)

The festival kicks off on Thursday with a traditional German Webantanz (May-pole dance) performed by Mt. Angel schoolchildren. And then it's band music, dance, yodeling, accordion playing, folk singing, a car show, sports, and a 10K volkswalk that starts each morning at 8 a.m. near the Okotober Fruchtsaeule. You can't miss the Fruchtsaeule. It's a traditional harvest monument constructed of seeds, fresh fruits, nuts, and vegetables, located in the center of the festival area.

Location: Mt. Angel is about 40 miles south of Portland on U.S. 214. **Contact:** Oktoberfest, P.O. Box 437, Mount Angel, OR 97362; Tel: (503)845-9440, Fax: (503)845-6190.

While You're There: Free bus tours leave the village bandstand every half hour on Saturday and Sunday to take visitors to Mt. Angel Abbey and the Benedictine Sisters' historic monastery, where the sisters give tours.

Verboort

Verboort Sausage Festival

First Saturday of November Verboort is just a little place, about 130 families, a part of the incorporated town of Forest Grove, but it likes to assert its Dutch identity and heritage—there are lots of surnames starting with "van" here—and show off its sausage-making skills. Since 1935, the Visitation Catholic Church of Verboort has been putting on a day-long dinner of sausage, made by parish members, and sauerkraut, homemade from locally grown cabbage. People stream into town for the sausage, which they can also buy to take home if they arrive soon enough; the packaged sausage is generally gone before noon.

The dinner is served from 11 a.m. until people stop eating some time after 8 p.m. when the last tickets are sold. A beer garden is set up near the church hall where the dinner is served, and there are booths where baked goods, sausage on a stick, and homemade candy are sold.

The theme is Dutch. The dining tables are decorated with wooden shoes holding flowers, the servers wear Dutch hats and aprons. There are displays of crafts, a quilt raffle, a country store, bingo, and children's activities. Music is piped over the church loudspeaker, and sometimes there are dancers.

About 8,000 attend the festival; proceeds help support the church school.

Location: Verboort is on Oregon 8, about six miles south of Portland and U.S. 26. **Contact:** Visitation Church, 4285 N.W. Visitation Rd., Forest Grove, OR 97116; Tel: (503)357-3860.

Utah

Peach Days

Weekend after Labor Day (Friday through Sunday) ☼ Utah's oldest festival was first held in 1904, and it's a wonder it's still held because the first was not too auspicious: the most spectacular event was supposed to be a gas balloon ascending with a human passenger, but the balloon caught fire and was destroyed.

But still, a lot of peaches were given away, and they still are. Brigham City is in a 10- to 25-mile-wide valley at the foot of the Wasatch Mountains; most of the cities and agricultural land are in the valley. Peaches and apples are major crops in the Brigham City area, even though peach production is way down from what it was from 1915 through the 1950s.

Peach cobblers, pie, and ice cream are sold, and other peach events are a peach-pie-eating contest and the crowning of a Miss Peach Queen. There are also children's activities, horse and old-car shows, arts and crafts, parades, music, and a carnival. About 40,000 attend.

The city was first called Box Elder because there were so many of them. Its name was changed in 1856 to honor Mormon leader Brigham Young. He gave his last public address in the town in 1877.

Location: Downtown streets of the city, just off I-15. ☼ **Contact:** Brigham City Area Chamber of Commerce, P.O. Box 458, Brigham City, UT 84302; Tel: (801)723-6769.

While You're There: Near the top of Willard Peak, you can see the valley orchards, get a glimpse of Idaho, and, on a clear day, you can see Nevada, too.

Swiss Days

Weekend before Labor Day (Friday and Saturday) ☼ The Swiss came to the fertile valley of the Wasatch Mountains to create a thriving dairy industry. The area was appealing because the mountains looked like home, and many Swiss immigrants were converts to the Church of Jesus Christ of Latter-day Saints, which has its mother church in Utah.

The festival might make you think you're back in the Alps. You'll hear a Swiss alpenhorn, a long wooden horn used by herdsmen of the Alps; Swiss handbell ringers; Swiss adult and children's choruses; a yodeler. The legend of William Tell is performed by school children. The Swiss Market has one of the state's biggest displays of arts and crafts. Other activities include a parade and the presentation of Swiss Miss Royalty and her court—girls under 12, wearing full-skirted Swiss dirndl costumes.

The food emphasizes Swiss but shows melting-pot influences. Swiss braided bread, made with more eggs and butter than run-of-the-mill bread, is especially popular. A really big favorite is what's called the Swiss Navajo Scone—Indian fry bread stuffed with chili, tomato, lettuce, cheese, and onion. Other foods include knockwurst with sauerkraut, hamburgers, and Swiss cookies, washed down with lemonade; Mormons don't permit alcohol. In addition there are chuckwagon breakfasts and barbecue dinners.

The Mormons display a living legacy exhibit, and answer genealogical questions.

Back in the 1920s, Swiss families and friends gathered for a Harvest Celebration, but later the descendants of the pioneers decided to honor their heritage by calling the celebration Swiss Days. About 75,000 attend.

Location: Midway is about 45 miles east of Salt Lake City, on U.S. 40. **Contact:** Heber Valley Chamber of Commerce, P.O. Box 427, Heber City, UT 84032; Tel: (801)654-3666.

While You're There: Unusual mineral springs in craters, called hot pots, are located near Midway.

Washington

Berry Dairy Days

Week after Father's Day (Thursday through Sunday)

This is an old festival that has changed with the years. The volunteer fire department started it in the 1930s as a fall harvest festival, and then moved it to June in 1938 to become a strawberry festival. With the growth of the dairy industry, Berry Dairy Days was born.

And at some point, a silent partner was added—salmon. Salmon doesn't rhyme with berry and dairy, but like them it's a major product here, and it's a smash at the salmon barbecue held all afternoon Saturday.

The highlight of the festival, attended by about 10,000, is something unusual done with strawberries. It's usually big; in 1996, 72 sheet cakes were baked and blanketed with mounds of strawberries and whipped cream. That was enough to take care of the dairy and berry part of the festival.

A strawberry shortcake booth is open Thursday through Saturday, and vendors sell usual festival food, too.

Washington ranks in the top 10 states in both strawberry and milk production, and milk is the number-two agricultural commodity in the state (apples are first). The festival recognizes this with tours of berry and dairy farms and a food-processing plant.

Other festival events include a parade, arts and crafts, bluegrass bands, 10K and 2-mile runs, a carnival, and children's activities.

Location: Maiben Park, S. Skagit St., in Burlington, off I-5 at Washington 20, about 65 miles north of Seattle. Contact: Burlington Chamber of Commerce, P.O. Box 522, Burlington, WA 98233; Tel: (360)755-9382.

Apple Days

First weekend in October ❂ There's an apple-juice factory in Cashmere, so when you arrive here in the harvest season, the whole town smells of apples. By the time you leave the festival, you'll be imbued with apples—the smell, the taste, the sight.

Washington is the top apple-producing state; it grows more than half of all apples for fresh eating in the United States, and more than 40 percent of the nation's apples for both fresh and processed use. The little town of Cashmere is in the foothills of the Cascade Range, one of the state's biggest apple-growing areas. This is the place to be at apple-harvest time.

Apple Days is sponsored by a historical museum, so you'll find townspeople dressed in pioneer garb and activities with a pioneer theme: demonstrations of pioneer crafts, a historic fashion show, country dancing, and a procession of horses and vintage cars, led by the mayor and first lady.

You will also find a variety of apple dishes: there's apple pie, of course, apple cider, apple juice, apple dumplings, and various apple baked goods—muffins, cakes, buns. At the Cashmere Coffee Company, you can indulge yourself with caramel apple sundaes—vanilla ice cream topped with chunks of apple, caramel sauce, whipped cream, and nuts.

Liberty Orchards, which makes fruit and nut confections called Aplets and Cotlets, gives free samples of its candies and tours of the factory and kitchen with antique copper kettles. Aplets and Cotlets are candies of the West that were created in Cashmere in the 1920s by two Armenian immigrants, Armen Tertsagian and Mark Balaban. After naming their orchard Liberty, they recalled a Middle East sweet, and adapted the recipe, boiling down apple juice for Aplets and apricot juice for Cotlets. These are popular health-food candies today.

Bob's Apple Barrel has bins of fresh fruits, and apple butter, cider, and apple milk shakes. Other dishes available in town include barbecued chicken and dumplings, sausages, and hot dogs.

An apple-pie contest is a favorite feature; so is the apple-pie auction.

Most of the apples grown in the Cashmere area are Red and Golden Delicious. The Red Delicious, the world's leading apple, wasn't planted in the state until the 1920s, but it now accounts for about 60 percent of the state's total crop. Among other apples grown in Washington are the Granny Smith, Rome Beauty, Winesap, and the relatively new specialty apples, Fuji and Gala.

The foothills of the Cascades became known to pioneers in the early 1800s, and settlers discovered that the rich lava-ash soil and plentiful sunshine were perfect for growing apples. They first planted trees along stream banks, and then developed irrigation systems. In Wenatchee, a few miles east of Cashmere, the first apple trees were planted in 1872, and by 1889 commercial orchards were established.

Cashmere was named for the Vale of Kashmir in northwestern India. Records don't seem to indicate how the spelling got changed.

Location: Throughout Cashmere and at the Chelan County Historical Society Museum and Pioneer Village. ⛬ **Contact:** The Museum, P.O. Box 22, Cashmere, WA 98815; Tel: (509)782-3230.

George

George Washington's Fourth of July

Fourth of July ⛬ A man named Charlie Brown founded this little town just to have a town named George, Washington. A celebration of the first president on the birthday of the nation seemed natural, and it was also expected to be a community money-raiser; in fact, it loses money. It began some time in the 1960s, and about 5,000 people come, not bad for a town of 350. Admission and pie are free.

A cherry pie is the big thing here, because of that story about George Washington not being able to tell a lie and, yes, he cut down the cherry tree. So an 8-by-11-foot pie, using half a ton of cherries, is baked in a special pan that the fire department steam-cleans. Each year the top crust has a new design of flags (sometimes a foot in size), hatchets, colonial-style hats, or letters spelling out Happy Fourth.

The pie-making preparations begin about 5 a.m. When it's ready, the pie is displayed under a tent for gawking and picture-taking. It's cut about 2 p.m., pieces are given away, and soon it's all gone. The first pies were made exclusively from cherries from a local orchard, but today it's sometimes necessary to import some cherries.

Other cherry events are a cherry-pit-spitting contest and a cherry-pie-eating contest. Eating contestants are given a whole pie (of normal size) and more whole pies if necessary, and the winner is the one who eats the most in a set time.

There are also games, a parade, pet-judging, a dunking tank, a rodeo, a 5K run, a bluegrass band, cloggers, and other food, too.

There's another reason besides the George Washington cherry legend for all the cherry eating. Washington (the state) is the number one producer of sweet cherries in the United States, growing about 70,000 tons, or more than 45 percent of the nation's total.

If you miss the Fourth, take heart: On Presidents' Day, the town bakes a big birthday cake for George Washington. The cake plate is a door, and 40 cake mixes are used. The cake decorations are wonderfully elaborate: once there was an open book containing George's sayings; another time George knelt in prayer with his horse. Lunch is served, then the cake and coffee are given away. About 400 attend.

Location: George is on I-90 halfway between Seattle and Spokane. ⛬ **Contact:** George Washington Visitor Information Center, P.O. Box 5205, George, WA 98824; Tel: (509)785-6955.

Ilwaco Cranberrian Fair

Second weekend in October (Friday through Sunday) ☼
Ilwaco has just 800 full-time residents, and a good many of them tend the 450 acres of cranberry bogs in the area. Washington is one of only five states that produce enough cranberries to be counted statistically, and in Ilwaco they express their cranberry pride with a festival that brings in about 5,000 visitors.

They're treated to cranberry elephant ears, chicken breasts with cranberry sauce, and condiments like cranberry catsup, cranberry chutney, and cranberry mustard. For a sweeter taste, there are cranberry pies, cranberry fudge, and cranberry saltwater taffy. And to accompany all this, a beer garden offers cranberry beer and cranberry wine.

The festival's main event is the cranberry cook-off, featuring a People's Choice award. One winning entry was a 14-inch dessert tart filled with custard and topped with a sauce made from cranberries, blueberries, and mandarin oranges. Visitors are able to taste the cranberry cook-off entries as long as they last.

Other festival attractions include tours of cranberry bogs (reservations a must), a petting zoo, and a crafts display.

The first of these festivals was held in 1920, and the word used for it was "cranberrian"—the old word for such affairs. It was updated to cranberry festival, but in the 1980s, reverted to "cranberrian." Sounded more appealing.

Local lore says Lewis and Clark made their "seafall" on the Pacific Ocean here after paddling down the Columbia River. The explorers brought their boats ashore first in Ilwaco, but later that day crossed the Columbia and spent the night in what is now Astoria, Oregon. The Astorians, of course, claim that Lewis and Clark first saw the Pacific from the banks of Astoria. Cranberries grow on both sides of the river—that's not in dispute.

Location: The Ilwaco Heritage Museum in Ilwaco, which lies on U.S. 101 just above Cape Disappointment at the mouth of the Columbia River, on a peninsula that runs parallel to the Washington coast. ☼ **Contact:** Ilwaco Heritage Museum, P.O. Box 153, Ilwaco, WA 98624; Tel: (360)642-3446.

See Also: Bandon Cranberry Festival (Bandon, OR) and Massachusetts Cranberry Harvest Festival (South Carver, MA).

Fiery Food Festival

First weekend after Labor Day ☼ The logo for Pasco's Fiery Food Festival is a green dragon spitting fire—the fire of 105 varieties of chile grown in the Pasco-Richland-Kennewick Tri-Cities area. The cities are at the confluence of the Columbia, Snake, and Yakima Rivers, and Pasco is the largest city in the million-acre Columbia Basin irrigation project. This land that was once a carpet of sagebrush has been converted, through irrigation that began in the late 1800s, into what's now called the Heart of Washington Wine Country and one of the richest agricultural areas in the world.

The boast at the Pasco festival is "We've Got ALotta Hotta." The festival "hotta" includes tacos with hot spicy salsa, Mexican and Italian tacos, a hot-sauce barbecue, hot fajitas. There are also less fiery foods of the region—corn on the cob, plums, watermelon. To wash it all down, there are local ales, lagers, and wines in the Microbrew and Wine Garden.

About 40,000 people come to the fair, which began in 1987. It includes pottery-making demonstrations and displays, winery tours, a kids' corner, the state's largest farmers' market, and live entertainment.

Location: Downtown Pasco, off I-82, 47 miles northwest of Walla Walla. **Contact:** Pasco Downtown Development Assn., P.O. Box 842, Pasco, WA 99301; Tel: (509)545-0738.

See Also: La Fiesta de los Chiles (Tucson, AZ).

Pullman

National Lentil Festival

Fourth Saturday in August Lentils have been found in Egyptian tombs dating back 5,000 or so years, and they probably originated in that area. But today

Meatless Lentil Chili

2½ cups (1 pound) USA lentils, rinsed
5 cups water
1 packet (1 ounce) dry onion soup mix

1 can (16 ounces) tomatoes or tomato sauce
1½ teaspoons chili powder
½ teaspoon cumin

In a large saucepan, bring lentils and water to a boil. Add dry onion soup mix and simmer for 30 minutes. Add the rest of the ingredients and simmer 30 minutes longer. Serve over spaghetti.

Serves 6–8. Each serving provides 209.6 calories, 14.37 grams protein, 333 mg. cholesterol, 40.07 grams carbohydrate, .674 grams fat, 1129 milligrams sodium, 9.426 grams dietary fiber.

USA Dry Pea and Lentil Council

they have a happy home in the 75-mile-by-75-mile Palouse area of eastern Washington and northern Idaho. Almost all—about 98 percent, or some 135 million pounds—of the lentils grown annually in the United States are grown there.

Farmers started growing lentils on an experimental basis in the Northwest shortly before World War II. The soil and the weather pattern (wet springs and adequate rainfall) proved just right for them, and lentils became a major crop. Lentils are not beans, although they're in the same family; they have tiny disk- or lens-shaped seeds, are a good protein source, and are high in fiber. The lentils grown in the Palouse are Red Chiefs, which have a red-orange seed, and Brewer browns.

What with this profitable and nutritious crop growing all around it, Pullman began a festival to honor it in 1989. Local restaurants offer their best lentil dishes in the Lentil Lane Food Court, where you'll find lentil pizza, vegetarian submarines with lentils, lentil chili, barbecued baked lentils, lentil muffins, salad, and burgers, and sometimes more unusual dishes like lentil and fish tacos (a Guatemalan dish).

Desserts? Of course. There are lentil cookies, lentil chocolate cake, and lentil ice cream. And there's a lentil cook-off, with six categories of dishes.

The festival also provides a lentil-pancake breakfast to start things off right, and then the day is packed with an arts-and-crafts fair, kids' activities, a Little Lentil Sprout Parade and a Grand Parade, folk-art demonstrations, music, and microbrewery tasting.

Pullman was named for George Pullman, the railroad sleeping-car inventor. The city was founded in 1890, and the founders thought Pullman might feel honored and help them financially. He didn't.

Location: Pullman is in the southeast of Washington, off U.S. 195, about 5 miles from the Idaho border. **Contact:** Pullman Chamber of Commerce, 415 N. Grand Ave., Pullman, WA 99163; Tel: (800)365-6948, or (509)334-3565, Fax: (509)332-3232.

Seattle

Millstone Coffee Bite of Seattle

Third weekend in July (Friday through Sunday) Considering that Seattle has gotten to be almost synonymous with coffee bars, it would be hard to ignore this coffee-sponsored eat-in that gets 350,000 people out to indulge.

The Bite is a showcase for dozens of restaurants and food-product companies, among them the sponsoring Millstone coffee, which pours out about 12,000 free cups of java during the weekend. Visitors also toss down about 300 kegs of beer, 18,000 gallons of Pepsi Cola, and 480 gallons of milk mixed with 600 gallons of ice cream that make up the Millstone Java Shake. Folks also manage to go through about 4,000 pounds each of mussels and salmon and 6,000 oysters.

The point of the Bite is to acquaint people with local restaurants, which set up food booths and are judged on entrees, barbecues, desserts, and booth design. Three entertainment stages, four beer gardens, a comedy club, and a dance palace help people while away the time when they're not snacking or sipping.

Location: Seattle Center, a 75-acre park just north of downtown Seattle. ☼
Contact: Festivals, Inc., P.O. Box 1158, Mercer Island, WA 98040; Tel: (206)232-2982, Fax: (206)236-5241.

Shelton

Oysterfest and Shucking Contest

First weekend in October ☼ Shelton, a small town on South Puget Sound, is known for oysters. You'll find this out at the fest, a tradition since 1982, attended by about 25,000 oyster fans.

What you eat here are Pacific oysters, *Crassostrea gigas,* a different species from East Coast oysters, *Crassostrea virginica.* They go by such names as Malaspina and Willapa Bay, after the bays where they live. While they're all the same species, varieties taste and look different and have different spawning seasons and growing periods.

Festival vendors sell them on the half shell, bacon-wrapped and broiled, as fritters, in stew, in oyster loaf, and as Cajun sandwiches. You can also try other kinds of seafood and non-seafood dishes.

Three oyster-cooking contests are held: for amateurs, culinary students, and professional chefs. After the judging, spectators can get mini-samples of the entries.

Sunday's oyster-shucking contest determines the West Coast Champion who goes to the national shucking contest in Maryland. The winner of that goes to Ireland. Contestants have to shuck a specified amount of oysters, and the first to shuck them all, without losing points for nicks or broken shells, wins.

Taylor United, Inc., of Shelton, the largest shellfish producer on the West Coast, donates the oysters for the shucking contest and also is the supplier for vendors. All told, Taylor dispenses about 1,000 dozen live oysters and 150 gallons of shucked meats for the festival. These are farmed oysters (in Chesapeake Bay on the East Coast, oystermen harvest oysters wild), because Pacific oysters were introduced from their native Japan to the American Northwest, and they reproduce better in farm conditions than in the wild in this part of the Pacific.

The fest is much more than food. It's entertainment, which can include American Indian tribal dancing, folk singing, clog dancing, and barbershop harmony. It's learning: There are demonstrations of shellfish and fish cookery. A touch-tank aquarium is arranged by tidal zone, and holds a starfish, an oyster, a sea cucumber, and a hermit crab. Exhibits show clam harvesting, shellfish-opening techniques, and geoduck and seaweed aquaculture.

Geoducks (pronounced gooeyducks), you will learn, are odd ducks—the largest burrowing clams in the world and the largest clam of any sort in the northern hemisphere. The neck or siphon can be three or four feet long, and the clams can weigh as much as 15 pounds, although the average is about 2 or 3 pounds. The shell is seven or eight inches, so obviously the meat—the "body"—and siphon can't all fit into the shell, so geoducks look a little like hamburgers too big for their buns with a long neck sticking out. At the festival, you can get geoduck stew and fritters (the neck, cut in strips, is used).

What you may *not* see at the festival is the famous Olympia oyster, *Ostrea lurida,* a different species from the Pacific. Olympias are tiny, about the size of a dime, native to the Pacific coast of the United States, but have become very rare. However, in nearby Olympia, you will be quite sure (this is not a guarantee) to find Olympias at the Olympia House Restaurant. Speaking of Olympias: they're different. The female holds her eggs instead of spraying them about and ingests the sperm of the male so the eggs are fertilized internally. Eastern and Pacific oysters spray eggs and sperm into the waters and hope they'll meet.

Location: Mason County Fairgrounds, Shelton, on U.S. 101. **Contact:** Mason County Chamber of Commerce, P.O. Box 2389, Shelton, WA 98584; Tel: (360)426-2021.

See Also: St. Mary's County Oyster Festival (Leonardtown, MD).

Steilacoom

Apple Squeeze

Third Sunday in October Apple Squeeze is the perfect name for a festival where people come to squeeze apples.

Each year, press owners bring in about 26 presses, ranging from antique to modern hydraulic ones, and cider is pressed all day, on a do-it-yourself basis. The press owners are there to help out with instructions on pressing, and there are also apple experts to identify varieties of apples. Several thousand attend the festival, many with apples in wagons, baskets, and boxes, and their own jugs. Others may purchase fruit and jugs from the Boy Scouts.

The squeeze began in 1973 as a community activity when people with old cider presses wanted to show children how they worked. Those who donate a press for the day get a small brass plaque, which they proudly mount on the press.

Anybody who doesn't feel like pressing can buy cider hot, cold, spiced, by the jug, or by the glass. Generally, about 1,000 gallons are sold. Other foods available are hot apple butter on bread, candied apples, apple fritters, and apple pie with hot caramel sauce, sold by the slice.

Apple-related arts and crafts are displayed and sold; and children's activities include painting pumpkins, stringing Cheerios, and making designs with apples carved into stamp pads. Jugglers and street musicians add to the festive air.

Steilacoom is on an estuary of the Puget Sound, where there are fish ladders for the salmon to migrate upstream. Not surprisingly, then, the city has had a Salmon Bake since 1972, held on the last Sunday in July. They serve salmon, clams on the half shell, clam nectar (a broth made by boiling clam shells, reputed to be an aphrodisiac), corn on the cob, and homemade pies.

Location: Steilacoom is about 35 miles south of Seattle. Take exit 119 off I-5, go north about 6 miles. ☼ **Contact:** Steilacoom Historical Museum Assn., P.O. Box 88016, Steilacoom, WA 98388; Tel: (206)584-4133.

While You're There: Have a drink of sarsaparilla, a favorite drink in Victorian days, made of the roots of tropical plants. It's dispensed from a 1906 soda fountain at the Bair Drug and Hardware Store, a working museum at Wilkes and Lafayette Streets. Steilacoom, founded in 1854, built the state's first library, courthouse, and jail.

Walla Walla

Walla Walla Sweet Onion Harvest Fest

Second Saturday in July ☼ In the war of the sweet onions, Walla Walla is in a regiment of its own because sweet onions grown in milder climes—especially Georgia, Texas, and Hawaii—are a different variety from the Walla Wallas. But more about these onions later.

The highlight of the onion fest, sponsored by 25 growers, is the Onion Recipe Competition. Contest winners in the past have created chocolate cake, soups, vinegar, casseroles, liquor, and jelly. No end to the possibilities. The only rule is that each dish must contain Walla Walla sweet onions. Judges look for eye appeal, texture, flavor, originality, and sweet-onion taste.

While the cooks present their creations, children play at raw-onion-ring toss and onion-sack races. In addition, there are onion-eating contests, an onion-slicing contest, an onion shot put. And onions to eat are everywhere—with hamburgers, on pizza, in quiches, as blooming onions, on hot dogs, with fajitas. Plain old fried onion rings are the most popular.

The origin of Walla Walla sweet onions is a bit vague. Most of the warm-climate onions are a type called Granex or Grano onions but not the Washington sweets. Commonly called Walla Wallas (as certain Granex in Georgia are called Vidalias), they come in two varieties. One is the Arbini, named for its developer John Arbini; the other is called "the French" because Peter Pieri, who had been stationed in Corsica with the French Army, brought the seed to Washington in the early 1900s. Corsica and Washington are both about the same degree of latitude, with days of the same length.

Less sulfur is what makes all these onions, northern and southern, sweet, so sweet you can eat them like an apple, if that's your inclination. Genes, heat, hours of sunlight, moisture, and soil all have an effect on the amount of sulfur; the more sulfur, the more pungency, which makes you cry when you slice them.

The harvesting times for the sweet onions from different regions varies, and this affects the taste-offs held now and then. The Vidalia Granex has won by a slight edge over the Walla Walla onion, but the problem is that onions are best when they're fresh, and the different harvest times make it impossible to test *fresh* Georgia and Washington onions side by side.

Location: Fort Walla Walla Park, on the south end of town off Washington 125. Walla Walla is in eastern Washington, on U.S. 12, about 5 miles from the Oregon border.

Contact: Walla Walla Chamber of Commerce, P.O. Box 644, Walla Walla, WA 99362; Tel: (509)525-0850.

See Also: Vidalia Onion Festival (Vidalia, GA) and Maui Onion Festival (Kaanapali, HI).

Westport

Crab Races and Feed

Third Saturday in April ⊛ Westport is the home of the largest commercial fishing fleet in Washington, as well as the home of quite a few Dungeness crabs, which have the scientific name *Cancer magister,* meaning chief crab. They get their more common name from a promontory on the Olympic Peninsula off the Juan de Fuca Strait, where Washington's first commercial fishery was spawned.

Westport and Garibaldi, Oregon, which also has a lot of crabs, have had a standing crab-racing competition since 1988, alternating race sites. Attendance is something over 1,000.

The event was started to promote commercial fishing and the joys of fresh seafood, so the races are followed by crab dinners with garlic bread and salad.

The crabs race in six separated lanes on a board that's angled so the crabs can slide. People may beat on the board to encourage their crab, but Dungeness crabs have nasty dispositions, putting up their claws at anyone urging them too energetically. There are about 150 entries, horse-race music (live) is played, and the races are announced in horse-race style. Excitement builds.

The difference between a horse race and a crab race is that if a crab dies during the race, it is immediately cooked.

Location: Westport, about 110 miles southwest of Seattle, is 18 miles west of Aberdeen on Washington 105. ⊛ Contact: Westport-Grayland Chamber of Commerce, P.O. Box 306, Westport, WA 98595; Tel: (800)345-6223 or (360)268-8422.

While You're There: Westport has three canneries, and tours can be arranged. The town also has an 18-mile-long beach for surf fishing, clam digging, crabbing, or wading.

Wyoming

Chugwater Chili Cook-off

Usually the third Saturday in June ☼ Chugwater gets a lot of snow in the course of a year; maybe that's why it likes a real hot festival in June. Up to 5,000 people come for the cook-off, and there are as many as 60 or 70 contestants from several states. Not bad for a town, at last count, of 192. It's the largest one-day event in Wyoming.

The festival was started in 1986 by Chugwater Chili, a small company that packages chili mixes. The company, owned by five families, was founded in that same year to add vitality to the economy of this rural agricultural area.

Now the festival is a community project, raising money for non-profit groups. The cook-off is officially sanctioned by the Chili Appreciation Society International, meaning the winner gets to compete in the CASI Terlingua, Texas, international cook-off.

The one rule for the chilis is that no beans are allowed; all kinds of meats might appear, including buffalo and game. Chilis are judged by "referees" in several categories including showmanship, based on the decor of their cooking booths. Visitors buy a ticket allowing them to taste the chilis and vote; the people's choice also gets an award.

The festival is held at a working cattle ranch, formerly a polo-pony farm. There are dances both Friday and Saturday nights, and during the day a fiddle contest, trail rides, hay rides, fishing, bluegrass music, and swimming, topped off with the awarding of trophies and a barbecue. Vendors sell a variety of things, and Chugwater Chili, which started all this, is on hand with red-pepper jellies, their special mixes for chilis and dips, and Chugwater Chili Nuts, which are Spanish peanuts baked with chile and seasonings.

The little town of Chugwater is not facetiously named. Legend says an Indian chief's son thought up the idea of diverting stampeding buffalo to the nearby chalk cliffs that break abruptly away. Because of the sound of the buffalo falling on the rocks below, the area became known as "water at the place where the buffalo chug," and white settlers shortened the name to Chugwater.

Location: Diamond Guest Ranch, 14 miles west of Chugwater, which is on I-25, 45 miles north of Cheyenne. ❁ **Contact:** Chugwater Chili, P.O. Box 92, Chugwater, WY 82210; Tel: (307)422-3345, or (800)972-4454.

See Also: Terlingua International Championship Chili Cookoff (Terlingua, TX).

Glossary

Aebelskiver: A round fluffy Danish pastry, eaten with jam or sprinkled with sugar. See Rutabaga Festival, Askov, MN.

Andouille: A spicy Cajun sausage, made of pork chitlins and tripe, usually used as an accent in other dishes. See Saint John the Baptist Parish Andouille Festival, LaPlace, LA.

Beef on Weck (pronounced wick): Heaps of thinly sliced roast beef with horseradish on a kummelweck (caraway seed) roll. See Peach Festival, Lewiston, NY.

Blooming Onions: Onions cut to look like chrysanthemums and then deep-fried, served with dressing. See North Carolina Watermelon Festival, Murfreesboro, NC.

Boiled Peanuts: Peanuts boiled unshelled in salted water. A southern specialty. See National Peanut Festival, Dothan, AL.

Booya: A long-simmered stew of ox tails, other meats, vegetables, and spices, preferably cooked over an open fire. Indigenous to the Minneapolis–St. Paul region. See World's Championship Booya Competition & On the Road Again Festival, South St. Paul, MN.

Boudin: A Cajun sausage of pork, rice, and onions. See Festivals Acadiens, Lafayette, LA.

Bratwurst: Commonly called brats (rhymes with hots). A German sausage made of pork and veal or beef, seasoned with various spices, widely eaten in Wisconsin and the Midwest. See Bratwurst Days, Sheboygan, WI.

Brunswick Stew: A hearty stew that originated in Georgia or Virginia, originally made with squirrel and onions, now a medley of vegetables, often okra, lima beans, tomatoes, and corn, and chicken, rabbit, ham, or beef. See Blue Ridge Folklife Festival, Ferrum, VA.

Buffalo Chicken Wings: Chicken wings deep fried, tossed in a hot sauce, served with blue cheese and celery. See Italian Heritage & Food Festival, Buffalo, NY.

Burgoo: A thick stew of meats and vegetables that may or may not have originated in the Civil War, best known in Kentucky, Illinois, and Indiana. See International Bar-B-Q Festival, Owensboro, KY.

Burrito: A tortilla with various fillings (chopped meat, refried beans, cheese) and topped with chile sauce. See Whole Enchilada Fiesta, Las Cruces, NM.

Cheese Curds, Fried: The semi-solid curds of coagulated milk, deep-fried. A festival standard in Midwest dairy states. See Great Wisconsin Cheese Festival, Little Chute, WI.

Chiles Rellenos: Cheese-stuffed mild green chiles, coated in batter and fried. See Whole Enchilada Fiesta, Las Cruces, NM.

Chitlins: Short for chitterlings. The small intestines of pigs, usually batter-fried. See Chitlin Strut, Salley, SC.

Chorizo: A Spanish pork sausage, spiced with garlic, generally associated with Basques. See National Basque Festival, Elko, NV.

Crawfish: A small fresh-water crustacean, especially popular boiled or in gumbo in Louisiana and other southern states. See Crawfish Festival, Breaux Bridge, LA.

Dirty Rice: A Cajun dish of rice cooked with ground-up chicken liver, gizzards, and spices. See Cochon de Lait Festival, Mansura, LA.

Enchiladas: Tortillas with a filling of cheese or meat, covered in chile sauce. See Whole Enchilada Fiesta, Las Cruces, NM.

Étouffée: A Cajun stew usually with crawfish or shrimp, thickened with roux, served over rice. See World's Championship Crawfish Étouffée Cook-Off, Eunice, LA.

Fajitas: Marinated steak, grilled, cut in strips, and wrapped in tortillas. See Texas Rice Festival, Winnie, TX.

Fried Pie: Usually dried apples stewed and sweetened, wrapped in pie dough, and deep-fried. A specialty of the mountain regions of the Southeast. See Blue Ridge Folklife Festival in Ferrum, VA.

Fry Bread: A wheat-flour bread, round and flat but puffy, fried in hot fat, often served with honey. A favorite Native American dish. See Heard Museum Guild Indian Fair & Market, Phoenix, AZ.

Funnel Cake: A Pennsylvania Dutch treat now ubiquitous at fairs and festivals, made by pouring batter in spirals through a funnel into hot fat. See Kutztown Pennsylvania German Festival, Kutztown, PA.

Geoduck (pronounced gooey-duck): The largest burrowing clam in the world, found off the West Coast, eaten chiefly in stew and fritters. See Oysterfest and Shucking Contest, Shelton, WA.

Gordita: A fried tortilla, filled with ground pork or sausage, usually topped with shredded lettuce, onion, and cheese. See Texas Watermelon Thump, Luling, TX.

Grits: Coarsely ground grain, commonly the grain called hominy, which is dried corn from which the hull and germ have been removed. A staple in the South. See World Grits Festival, St. George, SC.

Gumbo: A thick soup-like dish of seafood or meat or sausage, served over rice. The Cajun gumbo uses dark roux and okra as thickener, the Creole gumbo uses file powder. See Gumbo Festival, Bridge City, LA.

Gyros: A Greek dish of minced lamb, spit-roasted and served in pita topped with onions, peppers, and yogurt. See Greek Orthodox Epiphany Celebration, Tarpon Springs, FL.

Hush Puppies: Crisp balls of cornbread fried in deep fat, almost always an accompaniment for fried fish in the South. The story behind the name is that dogs nosing around a fish fry were tossed fried bits of fish batter and told, "Hush, puppy."

Indian Tacos: Also called Navajo tacos. Fry bread topped with green chile, beans, shredded lettuce, diced tomatoes, onions, grated cheddar cheese. See Inter-Tribal Indian Ceremonial, Gallup, NM.

Jambalaya: A mixture of cut-up seafood, ham, or poultry with vegetables and rice, slow-cooked in a pot. See Jambalaya Festival, Gonzales LA.

Jerk Chicken: Chicken cooked with a crust of "jerk" seasoning, generally combining chiles, garlic, onions, and other spices. A Caribbean specialty that originated in Jamaica. See Caribbean Carnival, Boston, MA.

Kielbasa: A garlic-flavored Polish sausage, usually made with pork. See Polish Town Street Fair and Polka Festival, Riverhead, NY.

Kolache: A Czech favorite, sweet buns filled with fruits, sausage, cheese, or ham. See Kolache Festival, Caldwell, TX.

Lefse: A Norwegian potato and flour crepe or pancake, served with sugar or rolled around fillings. See Barnesville Potato Days, Barnesville, MN.

Linguiça: A Portuguese pork sausage flavored with garlic. See Feast of the Blessed Sacrament, New Bedford, MA.

Lutefisk: Dried cod, soaked in lye and then in water, and cooked with a cream sauce. A Swedish specialty, traditionally a Christmas food. See Norsk Hostfest, Minot, ND.

Mayhaw: A southern tree with red, tart fruit used largely in jellies and wines. See National Mayhaw Festival, Colquitt, GA.

Pemmican: A Native American food made of dried meat, shredded and mixed with fat and wild berries, and formed into loaves. It was nutritionally balanced and kept well without spoiling.

Pierogi: A dough pocket with fillings of cheese, fruit, meat, sauerkraut, or mushrooms. A Polish treat. See Polish Town Street Fair and Polka Festival, Riverhead, NY.

Po' Boy: A submarine-like sandwich, using meats or shellfish with cheese on French bread. This Louisiana specialty is related to the grinder, hero, and Philadelphia hoagie. See Festivals Acadiens, Lafayette, LA.

Quahog: A hard-shelled clam usually eaten ground up in chowder or as stuffed clams. Also called a round clam. See Warren Barrington Rotary Quahog Festival, Warren, RI.

Ramp: A bulb vegetable that grows wild in Appalachia and is related to the onion but has a more pungent taste and smell. See Ramp Convention, Waynesville, NC.

Red-eye Gravy: The drippings from fried country ham mixed with water and coffee, which creates the "red eyes." See Virginia Pork Festival, VA.

Rocky Mountain Oysters: Usually calf but sometimes lamb testicles, cooked by marinating and deep frying. See Calf Fry Festival, Vinita, OK.

Rotis: Crepes filled with chicken, beef, goat, or conch, usually cooked with curry; a popular Caribbean dish. See West Indian-American Carnival, New York, NY.

Sauce Piquante: A Cajun sauce of tomatoes, peppers, and spicy seasonings.

Snitz: Pennsylvania Dutch for cut and dried apples. See Snitz Fest, Willow Street, PA.

Sonker: A deep-dish pie with fruit or sweet-potato filling, sometimes served with a sauce of milk, sugar, and vanilla. See Sonker Festival, Mount Airy, NC.

Spiedie: Originally spit-cooked chunks of marinated lamb, now can be made with any meat. A regional food of northern New York State. See Spiedie Fest and Balloon Rally, Endicott, NY.

Steamers: Soft-shell clams with rubbery necks (siphons) that burrow into tidal flats. Most frequently eaten steamed, fried, or in fritters, best known on the East Coast. See Essex ClamFest, Essex, MA.

Sugar on Snow: A taffy-like confection made by pouring maple syrup onto snow after the sap has been boiled past the syrup stage. A standard at "sugaring" festivals when maples are tapped. See Vermont Maple Festival, St. Albans, VT.

Tri-Tip Sandwich: A triangular cut of sirloin tip, seasoned and roasted over high heat, eaten as a sandwich. Popular festival fare in central California. See Big Hat Festival, Clovis, CA.

Selected Bibliography

It would be impossible to name all the publications, including federal and state documents, that have been consulted. Listed here are those most often used.

Of the numerous periodicals, including magazines and newspapers, gleaned for information, these were especially helpful: *American Bus Association's Top 100 Events in North America,* American Automobile Association's Tour Books, *Country Living* publications, *Fine Cooking, Food & Wine, Gourmet, National Geographic, National Geographic Traveler, Organic Gardening, Saveur, Smithsonian, Travel America, U.S. News & World Report Great Vacation Drives* (1994), and *Yankee.*

Allen, Terese. *Wisconsin Food Festivals.* Amherst, Wis.: Amherst Press, 1995.

American Cooking. Series of regional food books. New York: Time-Life Books, 1968–1971.

Camp, Wendell H., Victor R. Boswell, and John R. Magness. *The World in Your Garden.* Washington, D.C.: National Geographic Society, 1957.

Cantor, George. *Historic Festivals.* Detroit: Gale Research Inc., 1995. Visible Ink Press, 1996.

Chase's 1996 Calendar of Events. Chicago: Contemporary Books, 1995.

Coyle, L. Patrick Jr. *The World Encyclopedia of Food.* New York: Facts on File Inc., 1982.

DiVecchio, Jerry Anne, ed. *Italian Cookbook.* Menlo Park, Calif.: Lane Publishing Co., 1981.

Elkort, Martin. *The Secret Life of Food.* Los Angeles: Jeremy P. Tarcher, 1991.

Fussell, Betty. *I Hear America Cooking.* New York: Viking, 1986.

Geffen, Alice M. and Carole Berglie. *Food Festival.* Woodstock, Vt.: The Countryman Press, 1994.

Gibbons, Euell. *Stalking the Blue-Eyed Scallop.* New York: David McKay Co., 1964.

Harris, Lloyd J. *The Book of Garlic.* New York: Addison-Wesley, 1993.

Heberle, Marianna Olszewska. *Polish Cooking.* Tucson: HP Books Inc., 1985.

Herbst, Sharon Tyler. *Food Lover's Companion.* Hauppauge, N.Y.: Barron's, 1995.

Jones, Evan. *American Food.* Woodstock, N.Y.: The Overlook Press, 1990.

Lambert, Marjie. *Cajun Cooking.* New York: Crescent Books, 1991.

Lee, Hilde Gabriel. *Taste of the States.* Charlottesville, Va.: Howell Press, 1992.

McGee, Harold. *On Food and Cooking: The Science and Lore of the Kitchen*. New York: Charles Scribner's Sons, 1984.

O'Neill, Molly. *New York Cookbook*. New York: Workman Publishing, 1992.

Root, Waverly and Richard de Rochemont. *Eating in America*. Hopewell, N.J.: The Ecco Press, 1981.

Schulz, Phillip Stephen. *Celebrating America*. New York: Simon & Shuster, 1994.

Shosteck, Patti. *A Lexicon of Jewish Cooking*. Chicago: Contemporary Books Inc., 1979.

Simmons, Amelia. *American Cookery*. Hartford: Hudson & Goodwin, 1796. Rpt. Oxford University Press.

Sokolov, Raymond. *Fading Feast*. New York: Farrar Strauss Giroux, 1981.

———. *Why We Eat What We Eat*. New York: Simon & Schuster, 1991.

Spivack, Carol and Richard A. Weinstock. *Gourmet Food & Wine Festivals of North America*. Ventura, Calif.: Printwheel Press, 1986.

———. *Best Festivals of North America*. Ventura, Calif.: Printwheel Press, 1989.

Stern, Jane and Michael Stern. *Goodfood: The Adventurous Eaters Guide to Restaurants Serving America's Best Regional Specialties*. New York: Alfred A. Knopf, 1983.

Thompson, Sue Ellen and Barbara W. Carlson. *Holidays, Festivals, and Celebrations of the World Dictionary*. Detroit: Omnigraphics Inc., 1994.

Trillin, Calvin. *Alice, Let's Eat*. New York: Random House, 1978.

———. *Third Helpings*. New York: Ticknor & Fields, 1983.

United States. Department of Agriculture. *Agricultural Statistics 1995–1996*. Washington, D.C.: Government Printing Office, 1996.

———. Department of Agriculture. *1996 Agriculture Fact Book*. Washington, D.C.: Government Printing Office, 1996.

Cook-offs and Recipe Contests Index

Date Index

January

February

March

April

May

June

July

August

September

October

November

December

Date Index

Food Type Index

Food Type Index

Food Type Index

Food Type Index

Food Type Index

General Index